Christian Spirituality

*Two thousand years,
from East to West*

THE STORY OF
Christian
Spirituality

*Two thousand years,
from East to West*

General Editor
Gordon Mursell

A LION BOOK

Copyright © 2001 Lion Publishing plc
This edition copyright © 2001 Lion Publishing
Individual chapters are copyright of individual authors

The authors assert the moral right
to be identified as the authors of this work

Published by
Lion Publishing plc
Sandy Lane West, Oxford, England
www.lion-publishing.co.uk
ISBN 0 7459 3641 5

First edition 2001
10 9 8 7 6 5 4 3 2 1 0

A catalogue record for this book is available
from the British Library

Typeset in 9.5/13 Caslon 224
Printed and bound in Singapore

CONTENTS

ACKNOWLEDGMENTS

Abbey of Gethsemani: p. 341. Used by permission of the Abbey of Gethsemani, KY, USA.

AKG London: pp. 27 (Erich Lessing), 37 (Erich Lessing), 42, 81, 82 (bottom, British Library), 84 (British Library), 91, 101 (Erich Lessing), 113 (S. Domingie), 114, 119, 131, 136, 151 (Russian icon of Boris and Gleb from the second half of the 14th century; Tretiakov Gallery, Moscow), 152 (Erich Lessing), 155, 161 and 163.

Andes Press Agency / Carlos Reyes Mazo: pp. 311, 314, 321, 322, 325 and 326.

Sant'Anselmo, Rome: p. 92. Courtesy of the Pontifical Athenaeum of St Anselm, Rome, Italy.

The Art Archive: pp. 20, 24, 31 (6th-century mosaic of vines and grapes; San Prisca Chapel), 33, 35, 83, 99, 121, 167, 170 and 247.

Ashmolean Museum: p. 86. By courtesy of the Visitors of the Ashmolean Museum, Oxford, UK.

The Bodleian Library, University of Oxford: p. 88 (roll 135A, frame 16).

Bridgeman Art Library, London: title page and cover (Angels [1459], detail of a fresco by Benozzo di Lese di Sandro Gozzoli [1420–97]; Palazzo Medici-Riccardi, Florence, Italy), pp. 11 (1st-century BC mosaic of a fish from a Roman amphitheatre; Extremadura, Merida, Badajoz, Spain), 26, 38, 41 (Biblioteca Nazionale, Turin, Italy), 49, 52, 54, 60 (Louvre, Paris, France), 66 (Bibliothèque Nationale, Paris, France), 69 (Biblioteca Medicea-Laurenziana, Florence, Italy), 71 (Abbey of Montecassino, Cassino, Italy / Roger-Viollet, Paris, France), 75 (Huntington Library and Art Gallery, San Marino, CA, USA), 89 (historiated initial C depicting the Eucharist, from Missal D, by a Tuscan illuminator, from San Marco e Cenacoli, by the 14th-century Italian school; Museo di San Marco dell'Angelico, Florence, Italy), 95 (Bibliothèque Nationale, Paris, France), 97 (Bibliothèque Nationale, Paris, France), 103 (Museo della Pittura Murale, Prato, Italy), 105, 106 (top), 106 (bottom, Corpus Christi College, Oxford, UK), 115 (Museo di San Marco dell'Angelico, Florence, Italy), 123 (Musée de Blois, Blois, France), 127 (Richardson and Kailas Icons, London, UK), 145 (Museum of Art, Novgorod, Russia), 146–47, 149 (Richardson and Kailas Icons, London, UK), 156 (Private Collection), 157 (Tretiakov Gallery, Moscow, Russia), 159 (Private Collection), 165 (19th-century lithograph of Christian under Mt Sinai, illustration to *The Pilgrim's Progress* by John Bunyan, pub. by Adam & Son; Private Collection), 169 (Private Collection / Johnny Van Haeften Ltd, London, UK), 173 (Bibliothèque de Protestantisme, Paris, France), 175 (National Gallery of Scotland, Edinburgh, Scotland), 177 (British Library, London, UK), 178 (Private Collection), 179 (British Library, London, UK), 184 (Private Collection), 189 (Louvre [Cabinet de dessins], Paris, France), 191 (British Museum, London, UK), 192 (Central Saint Martin's College of Art and Design, London, UK), 194 (Anonymous Collection, New York, USA © All Rights Reserved), 201 (*The Agony in the Garden*, by El Greco [1541–1614], Museum of Fine Arts, Budapest, Hungary), 203 (Musée de Sibiu, Romania), 207 (Convent of Saint Teresa, Avila, Spain), 209 (Metropolitan Museum of Art, New York, USA), 213 (Palazzo Pitti, Florence, Italy), 215 (Private Collection), 220 (Private Collection), 222 (Central Saint Martin's College of Art and Design, London, UK), 225 (Private Collection), 229 (Musée de l'Assistance Publique, Hopitaux de Paris, France), 234 (Index, Barcelona, Spain), 238 (Chateau de Maintenon, Maintenon, France / Roger-Viollet, Paris, France), 245 (frontispiece of Queen Elizabeth's Prayer Book [1569] showing Queen Elizabeth I at prayer; Lambeth Palace Library, London, UK), 249 (National Portrait Gallery, London, UK), 250 (Private Collection), 253 (Private Collection), 254 (Private Collection), 257 (Lambeth Palace Library, London, UK), 258 (Guildhall Art Gallery, Corporation of London, UK), 264 (Private Collection / Philip Mould, Historical Portraits Ltd, London, UK), 267 (Birmingham Museums and Art Gallery, UK), 271 (Coram Foundation, London, UK), 273 (Private Collection / Stapleton Collection, UK), 275 (*Penn's Treaty with the Indians* [c. 1830–40], by Edward Hicks [1780–1849]; Gift of Alice C. Simkins in memory of A. Nicholson Hanszen, Museum of Fine Arts, Houston, Texas, USA), 295 (Stapleton Collection, UK), 309 (Chapelle du Rosaire, Vence, France), 348 (Victoria & Albert Museum, London, UK) and 363 (Christie's Images, London, UK).

The British Library: pp. 108 (Y.T. 36, fol. 184) and 110 (Arundel 83, fol. 127). By permission of the British Library.

The British Museum: p. 74. © The British Museum, London.

Chester Beatty Library: p. 206 (Akbar Narna fol. 263v). Reproduced by kind permission of the Trustees of the Chester Beatty Library, Dublin, Ireland.

Corbis: pp. 279 (Bettmann), 303, 332 (Bettmann), 335 (Bettmann), 343 (Bettmann), 344 (Bettmann), 347 (Reuters Newmedia Inc.), 353 (Bettmann) and 357 (Bettmann).

Corpus Christi College: p. 77 (ms 286, fol. 129v.). With the permission of the Master and Fellows of Corpus Christi College, Cambridge, UK.

Dover Publications, UK: p. 281.

Durham Cathedral, UK: p. 82 (top).

Flower Pentecostal Heritage Centre, Springfield, MO, USA: p. 312.

Haverford College Library, Haverford, USA: p. 300.

Jon Arnold: 15, 17 and 18.

Eileen McGuckin, The Icon Studio, New York, USA: p. 51.

Marion E. Wade Center: p. 361. Used by permission of the Marion E. Wade Center, Wheaton College, Wheaton, IL, USA.

Mary Evans Picture Library: pp. 45, 47, 55, 180, 182, 185, 186, 195, 196, 198, 219, 226, 230, 232 (both), 236, 240, 243, 261, 262, 266, 268, 272, 283, 286, 289, 291, 292, 296 and 298.

Mick Sharp Photography: pp. 73 (St John's Cross and St Columba's Shrine, Iona Abbey, Strathclyde, Scotland; replica of original 8th-century cross), 76 and 80 (Jean Williamson).

National Gallery: pp. 22 (NG1077) and 29 (NG13). © National Gallery, London, UK.

Jeff Saward: p. 338.

Scala, Florence: pp. 36, 39, 58, 62, 132, 139, 153 and 277.

SCM Press, London, UK: p. 329.

Sonia Halliday Photographs: pp. 61 (Bibliothèque Nationale, Paris, France), 65 (Andre Held), 128, 143 and 307 (Bibliothèque Nationale, Paris, France).

Teilhard Association: p. 330 (John Anderson).

Trinity College Library, Dublin, Ireland: p. 79 (ms 58, fol. 32v).

Trip: pp. 305 (icons for sale at Fatima, Portugal, pilgrimage destination; A. Tjagny-Rjadno), 316 (D. Butcher), 318 (S. Harris), 336 (A. Tjagny-Rjadno) and 359 (B. Turner).

Werner Forman Archive: pp. 21 (British Museum, London), 59 (Coptic Museum, Cairo), 125 (Byzantine mosaic of the enthroned Christ [the Deesis]; South Gallery of the Hagia Sophia, Istanbul), 142 (National Library, Athens) and 148 (Treasury of the Basilica of Our Lady, Maastricht).

Zev Radovan, Jerusalem, Israel: pp. 13 and 14.

CONTRIBUTORS

General Editor

The Very Rev. GORDON MURSELL

Dean of Birmingham Cathedral, UK
Formerly Senior Lecturer in Pastoral Studies,
Salisbury and Wells Theological College, UK

Author of *The Theology of the Carthusian Life* (Salzburg,
1988), *Out of the Deep* (Darton, Longman and Todd,
1989), *English Spirituality* (2 vols, SPCK, forthcoming),
and compiler of *The Wisdom of the Anglo-Saxons*
(Lion, 1998)

Rev. Dr RICHARD A. BURRIDGE

Dean of King's College, London, UK,
and Honorary Lecturer in New Testament

Author of *What are the Gospels? A Comparison
with Graeco-Roman Biography* (Cambridge
University Press, 1992), *Four Gospels, One
Jesus? A Symbolic Reading* (Eerdmans/SPCK,
1994) and *John: The People's Bible Commentary*
(Bible Reading Fellowship, 1998)

Rev. Dr LIZ CARMICHAEL

Chaplain and Tutor in Theology
St John's College, Oxford, UK
Formerly adviser in spirituality, Diocese
of Johannesburg, South Africa

Rev. DOUGLAS J. DALES

Chaplain and Head of Religious Studies
Marlborough College
Marlborough, Wiltshire, UK

Author of *Dunstan: Saint and Statesman*
(Lutterworth Press, 1988), *Living Through
Dying* (1994), *Light to the Isles* (Lutterworth
Press, 1997) and *Called to Be Angels*
(Canterbury Press, 1998)

DAVID H. FARMER

Former Reader in History
Reading University,
Reading, Berkshire, UK

Author of *The Oxford Dictionary of Saints*
(Oxford University Press, 4th ed. 1997),
St Hugh of Lincoln (1985), and editor of *Bede's
Ecclesiastical History, Magna Vita Sancta
Hugonis* (2nd ed. 1986), *The Age of Bede*
(Penguin Classics) and *Benedict's Disciples*
(1980 and 1995)

Dr STEPHEN R. GRAHAM

Dean of Faculty and Professor
of American Church History
North Park Theological Seminary
Chicago, Illinois, USA

Author of 'Cosmos in the Chaos': Philip Schaff's
Interpretation of Nineteenth-Century American
Religion (Eerdmans, 1995)

Rev. Dr SERGEI HACKEL

Former Reader in Russian Studies
University of Sussex
Brighton, Sussex, UK

Author of The Pearl of Great Price: The Life of
Mother Maria Skobtsova (1891–1945) (1965),
The Poet and the Revolution: Aleksandr Blok's
The Twelve (Oxford, 1975) and The Orthodox
Church (1971; rev ed. 1990)

Rev. Dr BRADLEY HOLT

Professor of Religion
Augsburg College, Minneapolis, USA

Author of Thirsty for God: A Brief History of
Christian Spirituality (Augsburg Fortress, 1993;
revised as A Brief History of Christian Spirituality,
Lion, 1997), and compiler of The Wisdom of
the Cloud of Unknowing (Lion, 1999)

Rev. Dr JOHN A. MCGUCKIN

Professor of Early Church History
Union Theological Seminary
New York, USA

Author of Symeon the New Theologian: Chapters
and Discourses (Cistercian Publications, 1982),
St Gregory Nazianzen: Selected Poems (SLG
Press, 1986), The Transfiguration of Christ in
Scripture and Tradition (Mellen Press, 1987),
St Cyril of Alexandria and the Christological
Controversy (Brill, 1994), At the Lighting of
the Lamps: Hymns from the Ancient Church
(SLG Press, 1995), St Cyril of Alexandria:
On the Unity of Christ (SVS Press, 1995) and
St Gregory of Nazianzus: An Intellectual
Biography (SVS Press, 2000)

Rev. Dr HERMAN J. SELDERHUIS

Professor of Church History
Theological University,
Apeldoorn, The Netherlands

Author of Marriage and Divorce in the
Thought of Martin Bucer (Kirksville, 1999) and
John Calvin's Theology of the Psalms
(forthcoming)

PROLOGUE

Christian Spirituality

What is 'spirituality'? The word 'spirit' comes from the Latin *spiritus*, whose primary meaning is 'breath'. In this sense it is something physical but invisible: the air we breathe, the odours we smell. But *spiritus* had an important secondary meaning even in classical times: 'inspiration' (a word that literally means 'breathing in'), perhaps of a poet or a god. So Cicero could speak of people with a 'Sicilian spirit', and Livy of being 'touched by the divine spirit' (*spiritu divino tactus*). The word 'spirit', then, came to denote those invisible but real qualities which shape the life of a person or community – such as love, courage, peace or truth – and a person's or community's own 'spirit' is their inner identity, or soul, the sum of those invisible but real forces which make them who they are.

The link between 'breath' and 'spirit', between the physical and the incorporeal, is crucial for understanding one of the two great traditions which helped to shape Christian 'spirituality'. This is the Hebrew tradition, supremely manifested in the Bible. The Hebrew word *ruach*, like the Latin *spiritus*, means both 'breath' and 'spirit'. So when, in the opening verses of scripture, the writer of Genesis speaks of 'a wind from God' that 'swept over the face of the waters', the word translated 'wind' could as easily be translated 'spirit'. And that is precisely the point. Hebrew knows no

absolute distinction between the physical, material world, and a wholly separate 'spiritual' world. The two are inextricably linked. The wind, or spirit, of God works together with the 'word' of God: God speaks ('Let there be light'), and what God says comes to be, is given breath, comes alive. So 'spirituality', in the Hebrew tradition of scripture, is that process by which God seeks continually to work upon, or address, the raw unstable chaos of our lives and experience, and of our world, drawing forth meaning, identity, order and purpose.

This fundamental notion of what is spiritual is further developed in the New Testament, and especially in the letters of the apostle Paul. His famous distinction between 'flesh' and 'spirit' can easily be misunderstood as implying an absolute separation of the physical from the spiritual. But Paul is a Jew; and his thought is rooted in Jewish ideas. By 'flesh' he does not mean what is physical: he means all of life (including religion) seen in a narrowly materialist, this-worldly, me-centred perspective. And by 'spirit' he again means all of life (including physical life) seen in the perspective of our relationship with God through Jesus Christ. So 'spirituality' comes to mean something more than simply God's continuing work of creation, though it certainly includes that: it denotes all that is involved in living 'according to the spirit' – a free dependence on grace, a longing for what

Paul calls the 'fruits of the spirit' (love, joy, peace and others – see Galatians 5:22), and above all the experience of God the Holy Spirit at work within us, turning our groans and longings into prayer (Romans 8:26), and slowly transforming us into the unique people God created us to be. This is how Paul puts it:

> Now the Lord is the spirit, and where the Spirit of the Lord is, there is freedom. And all of us, with unveiled faces, seeing the glory of the Lord, as though reflected in a mirror, are being transformed into the same image from one degree of glory to another; for this comes from the Lord, the Spirit (2 Corinthians 3:17–18).

'All of us', notice – not just our religious or 'spiritual' parts. Paul believed the body too was to be raised at the resurrection and would live for ever in heaven. And he even goes so far as to say that 'the creation itself will be set free from its bondage to decay and will obtain the freedom of the glory of the children of God' (Romans 8:21), in the final consummation of what was begun by the wind or spirit of God sweeping over the waters of chaos.

This is the bedrock of Christian spirituality. But there is another ancient tradition which also exerted a profound influence on how that spirituality developed: the Greek tradition, which found supreme expression in the thought of Plato. Where the Hebrew tradition sought to hold the physical and the spiritual together, Plato wanted to separate them. For him, broadly speaking, what is good is 'spiritual' (invisible, incorporeal, immortal), while what is bad is 'physical', not only because it does not last but also because it draws us downwards, so to speak, and makes us earthbound. For him, each human person consisted of a physical body and an invisible soul: the body is transient and ultimately worthless, while the soul is immortal – it came from an invisible spiritual world and will return to it when we die.

The influence of Platonism on Christianity was enormous, and not only in the early centuries of the church's life. It encouraged many Christians to regard 'spirituality' as essentially world-denying, the practice (often called asceticism) of disciplines designed to repress or redirect physical drives and longings and to experience, as far as was possible in this world, the life of the Spirit. But there was a positive aspect to Platonism too: his emphasis on the beauty, the sheer attractiveness, of the divine or spiritual world encouraged Christians (such as Augustine of Hippo) to see that world as the fulfilment of all our deepest desires, and thus to give Christian spirituality a dynamism and energy that it might otherwise have lost.

Broadly speaking, then, the Hebrew tradition gave spirituality its stress on *integration*: read Leviticus 19, and you will find a luminous and comprehensive vision of holiness as embracing every aspect of individual and corporate life, from the breeding of cattle to the worship of God. The Greek tradition gave spirituality its stress on *desire*, an insistent longing not only, or even primarily, to leave this world for the next one, but to experience and manifest the next one in the midst of this one, until the whole of creation is transformed and made new. The two together gave, and still give, the Christian spiritual tradition an astonishing vitality and inventiveness, enabling those who make it their own to see life not as a pre-determined routine, or even simply as a journey, but as something at once attractive and challenging: an *adventure*.

Gordon Mursell

Jesus and the Origins of Christian Spirituality

Richard Burridge

Timeline

1000 BC	?18th c.	**Abraham and the early patriarchs**
	?1300–1250	**Moses and the exodus**
	1000	**David conquers Jerusalem**
	c. ?960	**Solomon builds the temple**
	933	**The nation divides into the kingdoms of Israel and Judah**
	722	**The fall of Samaria**
	621	**Reforms of King Josiah**
	612	**Assyrian empire defeated by the Babylonians**
	587	**Nebuchadnezzar captures Jerusalem and destroys the temple; the people are exiled to Babylon**
	538	**The fall of Babylon; many Jews return to Jerusalem**
500 BC	520–515	**Rebuilding of the temple**
	c. 500	**Establishment of the Roman Republic**
	332	**Alexander the Great conquers Jerusalem**
	167–164	**Desecration of the temple, Maccabean revolt and rededication of the temple**
100 BC	63	**Pompey conquers Jerusalem**
	37–4	**Herod the Great rules**
	21	**Herod begins rebuilding temple**
0	?6/4	**Jesus of Nazareth born**
	?30	**Jesus of Nazareth crucified**
	46–60	**Paul's journeys**
	66–70	**Jewish War**
AD 100	70	**Destruction of the temple**
	130	**Hadrian rebuilds Jerusalem as a Gentile city**
	132–35	**Simon bar Kochba's revolt defeated; Jews leave Jerusalem**

The story of Christian spirituality must begin with the story of Jesus Christ, his life and teaching, death and resurrection – and the impact this had on his first followers. From these beginnings, the rich tapestry of Christian spirituality, prayer and worship develops. As the rest of this book will show, various key elements recur: one is the relationship between corporate worship centred around religious buildings and the individual's personal spiritual life; another ranges from a spirituality centred upon religious activity and ritual acts, sacraments and services, to a more word-based attention to preaching, teaching and scripture; and behind them all the constant tension between a quiet retreat into communion with God and being driven out again to earth spirituality in social action and the politics of the world. These polarities are not alternatives; all of them are needed in Christian spirituality, and all of them can be found in the story of Jesus himself and from his own background and context. For even Jesus does not come to us out of a vacuum, but from hundreds and thousands of years of Jewish spirituality and devotion to God.

The Jewish background
The story of God's people

The story begins with God's call to Abraham (Genesis 12) and the subsequent wanderings of patriarchs such as Isaac, Esau and Jacob. At this time God ('El' in Hebrew) has various names, such as El Elyon (Genesis 14:18), El Shaddai (17:1), El Olam (21:33) or El Bethel (31:13), and he could be worshipped anywhere where they could offer sacrifice or set up a stone (Genesis 28:18). During the exodus from Egypt under Moses the Israelites' experience of God as 'YHWH' (usually translated as 'the LORD' in English versions of the Old Testament, but widely known as 'Yahweh') at Mount Sinai becomes central, with the giving of the law and covenant, establishing the system of priests and sacrifices and taking the tablets in the ark with them on their journey (Exodus 19–27). The conquest of Canaan under Joshua and the judges brought the Israelites into contact with the local religion and gods in the urban environment of the small towns. This period reaches its climax with the establishment of the monarchy under David, who takes Jerusalem as his capital, and the construction of the temple for the ark of the covenant by his son, Solomon (2 Samuel 5–6; 1 Kings 5–8). For the next thousand years, the temple and its sacrificial system were the centre of Jewish spirituality, as is seen in many psalms, despite the split into two kingdoms: the North (Israel) and the South (Judah).

The relationship of political power, especially under a monarchy, with worship and spirituality is never easy. The next few centuries were marked by clashes between kings like Ahab and prophets like Elijah and Elisha, over the worship of other gods such as Baal (1 Kings 18–19). Other prophets protested about the oppression of the poor, denouncing the temple and its sacrifices (Amos 5:21–25; 8:1 – 9:8) and pleading for a spirituality based on God's infinite love for his people (Hosea 11). The fall of Samaria and the northern kingdom in 722 BC was seen as the judgment of God (2 Kings 17). The mixture of peoples which resulted became the Samaritans. Meanwhile, in the southern kingdom of Judah, the discovery of the book of the law (perhaps the book of Deuteronomy) in the temple in 621 BC prompted major reforms under King Josiah

(2 Kings 22–23). However, not many years later, in 587 BC, Jerusalem was also captured, the temple destroyed and the people taken into exile in Babylon (2 Kings 24–25).

Being in a foreign land 'by the waters of Babylon' (Psalm 137), away from Jerusalem with the temple system abolished, necessitated changes in Jewish spirituality as prophets like Jeremiah, Ezekiel and the author of the second half of Isaiah sought to understand what God was doing and promised a return from exile. Those who returned after the fall of Babylon in 538 BC had the task of rebuilding not just the temple and the walls, but also re-establishing the law at the centre of Jewish spirituality in the midst of hostile cultures and eastern empires (Ezra, Nehemiah).

After the conquest of Jerusalem by Alexander the Great in 332 BC, the Jews had to cope with the impact of Greek culture and, later, the Romans as the Mediterranean powers became dominant. The period of the desecration of the temple by the Seleucids and the Maccabean revolt (167–164 BC)

◆ **Abraham receiving God's promise of the covenant; wall-painting from Dura Europos, Iraq, from c. 245 BC.**

Jewish groups at the time of Jesus

- The Sadducees were mostly aristocrats in Jerusalem, cooperating with the Romans. They were linked to the chief priests and active in the temple with its sacrifices and cult. Their spirituality was centred on the Pentateuch (the first five books of the scriptures) and they did not believe in the resurrection after death.

- The Pharisees were a mostly non-priestly renewal movement, trying to interpret all the scriptures, as well as the oral traditions; they believed in the resurrection and the importance of purity laws. They would be found in synagogues and communities across the country.

- The Essenes included both priests and lay people, with particularly strict views about the temple and purity. As exclusivists, many withdrew into desert communities such as Qumran, where the Dead Sea Scrolls were produced.

- For others, their 'zeal' for Jewish law and belief led not to withdrawal but to active armed resistance against the Romans. Some of these were called Zealots, while others were *sicarii*, dagger carriers, or what we might term 'freedom fighters'.

In some ways these four main groupings may embody the tensions between a church- and ritual-based spirituality and a more scripture-centred approach, or between pietistic withdrawal and social or political action. Only the Pharisees really survived the war and the destruction of Jerusalem, becoming the dominant force in the reconstruction of rabbinical Judaism.

◆ **The 'Temple Scroll' found at Qumran, one of the Dead Sea Scrolls.**

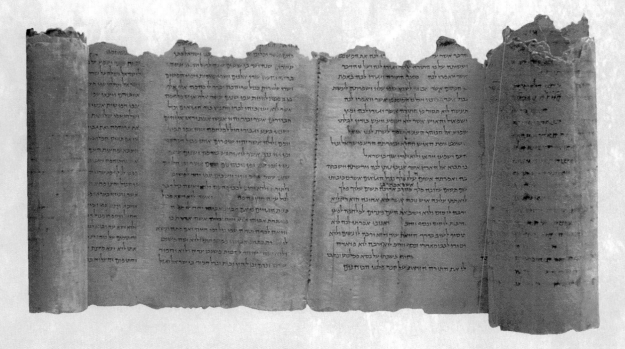

also inspired the development of apocalyptic spirituality which looked beyond the politics of this world to the heavenly rule of God (seen in books such as Daniel), while others began to withdraw into monastic groups in the desert, as at Qumran. In their different ways, the Maccabean freedom fighters, the apocalyptic writers and the ascetic communities were all seeking the renewal of Jewish spirituality and faith in God.

The conquest of Judea by Pompey in 63 BC brought a mixture of direct Roman rule and client kings such as Herod the Great, who ruled from 37 to 4 BC and started the massive rebuilding of the temple. However, this all came to an end with the Jewish revolt of AD 66, which led to the destruction of Jerusalem and the newly completed temple by the Romans in AD 70. After the final defeat of another revolt under Simon bar Kochba in AD 132–35, Jews were forbidden even to enter Jerusalem, which had been rebuilt as a Gentile city, Aelia Capitolina, in AD 130 by the Roman Emperor Hadrian. Jewish faith

◆ **The treasures from the temple after the capture of Jerusalem in 70 AD depicted on the arch of Titus in Rome.**

and spirituality had to be completely reformed by the rabbis for a life dispersed out among the nations until the latter part of the twentieth century. With the temple and the sacrificial system gone for ever, Jewish spirituality becomes centred around the synagogue and the interpretation of the scriptures and traditions.

Jewish prayer and worship

Before the destruction of Jerusalem and the temple by the Romans in AD 70, Judaism was very varied in its groups, beliefs and customs (see box, p. 14). E.P. Sanders, the most prolific expert on Jewish belief and practice at the time of Jesus, has described it as 'dynamic and diverse'. After the wars, early Jewish liturgy and worship were reorganized by rabbis such as Gamaliel II who had to deal with the impact of the loss of the temple. Most surviving rabbinic texts about prayer and worship date from after this period of consolidation.

The temple and festivals

For a thousand years before its destruction, the temple was the pre-eminent centre of all Jewish life and worship. The original temple was built by Solomon around 960 BC and destroyed by Nebuchadnezzar in 587. It was rebuilt by those who returned from exile in 520–515, and reassumed its central place. Its profanation by the Seleucid king, Antiochus IV Epiphanes in 167 BC sparked the Maccabean revolt, resulting in its rededication in 164. The temple was completely rebuilt by Herod the Great, who started work around 21 BC, although it was not completely finished until just before the revolt of AD 63.

The temple was a large building, surrounded by a whole series of courts to accommodate the huge crowds; by Herod's time the complex was 400 metres long. The outer courts were open to Gentiles, and Jewish women were allowed as far as the inner courts; there were special courts for men in front of the sanctuary itself. This was comprised of an imposing entrance, the first chamber for burning incense, and then the holy of holies, entered only by the high priest once a year on the Day of Atonement.

At the centre of the temple's life were the different sacrifices of meal or flour, oil and wine, animals and birds, each for different types of offerings. Sacrifices could be made by individuals, or on behalf of the whole community. The instructions for all these offerings and sacrifices are described in the book of Leviticus. It was an enormous, and costly, operation. People contributed tithes for the priests who would also eat from the sacrifices (Deuteronomy 18:1–8). The census tax from the period of the exodus was devoted to the temple for its overheads and

A psalm for temple worship

How lovely is your dwelling-place,
*   O Lord of hosts!*
My soul longs, indeed it faints
*   for the courts of the Lord;*
my heart and my flesh sing for joy
*   to the living God.*

Even the sparrow finds a home,
*   and the swallow a nest for herself,*
*   where she may lay her young,*
at your altars, O Lord of hosts,
*   my King and my God.*
Happy are those who live in your house,
*   ever singing your praise…*

For a day in your courts is better
*   than a thousand elsewhere.*
I would rather be a doorkeeper
*   in the house of my God*
*   than live in the tents of wickedness.*
For the Lord God is a sun and shield;
*   he bestows favour and honour.*
No good thing does the Lord withhold
*   from those who walk uprightly.*
O Lord of hosts,
*   happy is everyone who trusts in you.*
(Psalm 84:1–4, 10–12)

upkeep down through Jewish history and on into New Testament times (Exodus 30:13–16; Nehemiah 10:32–33; Matthew 17:24).

Pilgrimage to the temple was important for the three main festivals (Deuteronomy 16). Passover celebrated the exodus from Egypt (Exodus 12; 2 Kings 23:21–23). Seven weeks later the beginning of the harvest and offering of new grain were celebrated at the festival of Weeks or Pentecost (Greek for 'fifty days'), and the end of harvest or the ingathering at Tabernacles. In addition, there was the Day of Atonement, Yom Kippur (Leviticus 23:26–32). Psalms were sung on the journey or 'ascent' to Jerusalem (Psalms 120–134) and in the worship of the temple itself (Psalm 84; see box, p. 16). While Josephus's claim that millions were in Jerusalem for Passover during the years before the Jewish revolt may be an exaggeration, large numbers in the tens and hundreds of thousands would have been accommodated.

Synagogues, prayer and scripture reading

The origins of the synagogue are unclear. The word means 'gathering together' in Greek and it was a place for reading of scripture, discussion and prayer, particularly on the sabbath. This suggests that it began among those who were a long way away from the temple, probably among the exiles.

The custom of praying at the same time as the temple services is seen in the practice of Ezra (9:5) and Daniel, who prays towards Jerusalem three times a day (Daniel 6:10). Psalm 55:17 suggests prayer at morning, noon and evening, and this became the pattern.

The *Shema*, the opening word of 'Hear, O Israel' (Deuteronomy 6:4–9) was recited twice daily together with Deuteronomy 11:13–21 and Numbers 15:37–41. Later, prayers (the *tefillah*) were to be said three times a day which may have concluded with the priestly blessing of Numbers 6:24–26 (see box, this page). Such prayer patterns were based around blessing God ('blessed be the Lord', Psalms 89:52; 119:12; Exodus 18:10) or thanking God (Psalm 30:4, 12). Such praise and thanksgiving would often lead into petition (e.g. 1 Kings 8:15–21, 56–61). Prayers and blessings were particularly important before and after meals.

Studying and interpreting the scriptures was at the centre of much synagogue activity, as is seen in the synagogue at Beroea (Acts 17:10–11). There were readings from the Law (see box,

◆ **Remains of the 4th-century AD synagogue at Capernaum, Galilee.**

p. 18) on the sabbath and other days, such as Mondays and Thursdays, which were market days when people would be in town. There also developed the custom of reading from the

The priestly blessing

The Lord bless you and keep you;
the Lord make his face to shine upon you,
    and be gracious to you;
the Lord lift up his countenance upon you,
    and give you peace.
(Numbers 6:24–26)

The Hebrew scriptures

There are three sections of the Hebrew scriptures, collectively referred to as the Tanakh, or T-N-K for Torah (Law), Neviim (Prophets) and Ketuvim (Writings).

■ The Torah, or law, refers to the five books of Moses – Genesis, Exodus, Leviticus, Numbers and Deuteronomy – known together as the Pentateuch (*pent* being Greek for 'five'). Devotion to the law is the centre of Hebrew spirituality (see Psalm 119). The law was kept not out of a sense of duty or legalism, but as a response to God's love in making his covenant with Israel. The books of the law also include all the instructions for the ritual and sacrificial system, the tabernacle and the later temple.

■ The prophets are in two groups: the former prophets (Joshua, Judges, 1 and 2 Samuel, and 1 and 2 Kings) and the latter prophets (Isaiah, Jeremiah, Ezekiel, and the twelve minor prophets from Hosea to Malachi). While the Christian arrangement within the Old Testament suggests that the first group are narrative history books, the Jewish description of them reminds us that they are primarily prophetic – an account of how God was dealing with his people.

■ The writings include other books considered divinely inspired. At their heart are the Psalms, the hymn and prayer book of the Jews, used in both communal worship and individual devotion, including laments, thanksgivings, prayers and praises, royal and enthronement songs, pilgrimage songs, etc. Other books take the form of wisdom literature, such as Job, Ecclesiastes and Proverbs, in which the writers reflect on some of the great questions of life and on the wisdom of God. The writings also include the narratives of Ruth, Esther, Daniel, Ezra, Nehemiah and 1 and 2 Chronicles.

Other books written by Jews during the centuries after the return from exile did not become part of the accepted list, or canon, of scripture. These deutero-canonical books, or Apocrypha, are fifteen books, including the Wisdom of Solomon, Ecclesiasticus or Sirach, Tobit, Judith, 1 and 2 Maccabees and 1 and 2 Esdras. These books were accepted by Catholic and Orthodox churches, but not generally by Protestants. Yet another group is known as the Pseudepigrapha, including the Psalms of Solomon, Jubilees and Enoch. Despite not being included in the canon of the Old Testament, such books continued to influence the development of Christian spirituality.

◆ **Jews studying Torah scrolls at the Western Wall of the temple in Jerusalem.**

prophets, as well as the law; such readings could be followed by an interpretation as is seen when Jesus reads from Isaiah in Nazareth synagogue (Luke 4:16–30; see also Acts 13:15). Although lectionaries of passages from the scriptures to be read regularly developed later, it is unclear how systematic this was at the time of Jesus.

Jesus
Reading the gospels

How can we know about Jesus' life of prayer and spirituality? Unlike most of the people who will feature throughout the rest of this book, he wrote nothing himself which we can study and analyse today. Even the gospels, which are the main sources through which we know about Jesus, are not primarily designed to tell us about his spiritual life. Instead they contain many different stories about the kinds of things he went around doing and saying. Luke makes this explicit when he says that in his 'first book', that is, in his gospel, 'I wrote about all that Jesus did and taught from the beginning' (Acts 1:1). John tells us that they had far too much material about Jesus which they could not include, so he made a selection in writing his gospel (see John 20:30–31 and 21:25).

This is typical of ancient biographical writings about people. Modern biographies try to cover the whole of a person's life, analysing their upbringing, personality and activities in great detail. Greco-Roman 'Lives' were much shorter – about 10,000 to 20,000 words. This is all you can get onto a single ancient scroll, which would take an hour or two to read aloud or even 'perform'. Such accounts attempted to provide an understanding of the person, their deeds and words, and how these revealed their character, leading up to the climax of describing how the way in which they died provided a fitting conclusion to their life.

The same is true of the gospels. In their different ways, they too provide accounts of Jesus' deeds and words, leading up to his eventual death on the cross and his resurrection. Thus Matthew depicts Jesus as the teacher of Israel, arranging his gospel around five great sermons or discourses (Matthew 5–7, 10, 13, 18, 23–25), interspersed with stories about Jesus' healings and other activities. Mark concentrates more on Jesus' actions, especially in healing and delivering people from the powers of evil, as he heads inexorably towards his own suffering on the cross. Luke structures his gospel more geographically, as Jesus conducts his ministry first in Galilee (Luke 4:1 – 9:50) and then journeys south down the Jordan valley (9:51 – 19:27) to the climax of his last week in Jerusalem (19:28 – 24:53); along the way, his teaching is delivered in conversations and debates with people he encounters, caring especially for the poor and the marginalized. John skilfully weaves together Jesus' miraculous 'signs' with extended discourses about their significance: thus the multiplication of the loaves and fishes leads into the debate about Jesus being 'the bread of life' (John 6:1–14, 25–58), while the one who is 'the light of the world' (8:12; 9:5) brings sight to a blind man (9:1–41). Through it all, Jesus is supremely in control, the one who was with God 'in the beginning', but who 'dwelt among us' (1:1–14), who is glorified in his suffering on the cross where everything is 'accomplished' (12:23; 19:30) so that he can rise again to be worshipped as 'my Lord and my God' (20:28).

Thus the gospels are not designed specifically to tell us about Jesus' life of prayer, worship and spirituality. Instead, we have to use their biographical nature to look at his deeds and words, to consider the whole story of his ministry, death and resurrection, his example of prayer and his teachings on the subject. When we do so, we discover an enormously rich spiritual source which changed for ever the way human beings worship God and which has continued to inspire millions of men and women down through the ages and across the world.

The story of Jesus – his deeds

It is Luke who sets his account of Jesus fairly and squarely within a context of prayer, praise and worship. The opening scenes of his gospel are very reminiscent of Old Testament stories. Thus he starts with a priest, Zechariah, serving before God in the temple, where he receives the good news from an angel that he and his wife Elizabeth will have a son, who will prepare the way for Jesus (Luke 1:8–23). We return to the temple again after Jesus' birth for Mary and Joseph to present him to the Lord, where the elderly Simeon and Anna recognize who Jesus is (2:22–38). Luke's whole opening section is full of praise to God, from the meeting of Mary and Elizabeth (1:39–56) and Zechariah's outburst at the birth of John the Baptist (1:57–80), to the song of angels and the shepherds' joy at Jesus' birth (2:8–20), ending with Simeon and Anna's prophecies (2:25–38). This has given the church three great hymns which have been central in many services and liturgies: the Magnificat (1:46–55), the Benedictus (1:68–79) and the Nunc Dimittis (2:29–32). Yet this theme is also there in Matthew's account of the wise men coming to worship the baby Jesus 'with great joy' (Matthew 2:10–11), while John uses Jewish worship in the tabernacle to explain that 'the Word became flesh and dwelt [tabernacled] among us' (John 1:14).

It was common in ancient biographies not to include the 'hidden years' of a person's life before their public debut, except for an occasional little story from their childhood which anticipates what they will become in adult life. Thus Luke tells us about the twelve-year-old Jesus staying in the temple, leading up to his declaration that 'I must be in my Father's house' or 'about my Father's business' (Luke 2:41–51).

All the gospels then jump forward many years to the arrival of John the Baptist. He immediately reminds us of the prophets, both in his general appearance and in his preaching. John calls for Israel's repentance, for the renewal of God's people, and offers them baptism for the forgiveness of sins. Jesus is also baptized by John to identify himself with human beings. Yet it is also a moment of revelation for him – 'you are my beloved son' (Mark 1:11). This leads, as so often after such a special spiritual experience, to temptation about what has been revealed: 'if you are the Son of God…' (Matthew 4:1–11; Luke 4:1–13). The same revelation of being the 'beloved' son of God is repeated again when Jesus is transfigured (Mark 9:2–8).

All four gospels depict much of Jesus' ministry happening in the context of worship, as Jesus went around 'teaching in the synagogues and proclaiming the good news of the kingdom' (Matthew 4:23). Similarly, many of his miracles also take place here, such as the man with an unclean spirit (Mark 1:23), the man with a withered hand (Mark 3:1) or the woman with a bent back (Luke 13:10–17). To be effective, such healings and exorcisms require prayer (Mark 9:29).

◆ Baptism of Jesus by John the Baptist; mosaic from the Orthodox baptistry in Ravenna, Italy, dating from c. 440–50.

At the heart of all Jesus' teaching and activity was that 'the kingdom of God is at hand' (Mark 1:15). The dominant idea behind Jesus' spirituality was the Jewish belief that everything belongs to God 'the King of glory' (Psalm 24:7–10) so that we must proclaim, 'Your God reigns' (Isaiah 52:7), until his sovereignty is recognized 'over all the earth' (Zechariah 14:9). Proclaiming the kingdom of God is central to Jesus' preaching, and much of his teaching takes the form of parables about the kingdom (Matthew 13; Mark 4). Even his exorcisms are a sign that 'the kingdom of God has come upon you' (Luke 11:20), which is why Jesus calls for repentance (Matthew 11:20–24). This will mean keeping the commandments (Matthew 19:17), but Jesus puts justice and mercy before the demands of religion. Thus he is willing to pluck grain and to heal people on the sabbath (Mark 2:23 – 3:6). Jesus is not afraid to criticize religious traditions if they cause people suffering (Mark 7:1–13). The two great commandments – to love God and to love our neighbour – are more important than anything else, even the ritual and sacrificial system (Mark 12:28–34). Not only is this Jesus' mission, but he sends out his disciples to teach, preach and do the same (Matthew 10).

At the end of his ministry, he comes to Jerusalem for his last week. It begins with his protest in the temple that it should be a 'house of prayer for all the nations' not a 'den of robbers' (Mark 11:17). He continues teaching in the temple through the week, with parables such as the Tenants of the Vineyard (Mark 12:1–12) and more debates about the worship of God ('Render to Caesar the things that are Caesar's, and to God the things that are God's', Mark 12:17) and the commandments (Mark 12:28–34). Thus it is not surprising that in John's account of his trial, Jesus says, 'I have always taught in synagogues and in the temple, where all Jews come together' (18:20).

It was common in ancient biographies to note how the manner of a person's death reflected how they lived. So, even at the crucifixion, Luke shows Jesus still at prayer, asking for forgiveness for the soldiers and the penitent thief (Luke 23:34, 43).

◆ **Byzantine ivory triptych, dating from the 10th century, showing the crucifixion. Jesus is flanked by his mother Mary and the apostle John.**

He dies as he lived, with a simple prayer of commitment, 'Father, into your hands I commit my spirit' (Luke 23:46) which is taken from a psalm often used in Jewish night prayer (Psalm 31:5). This aspect of prayer and worship continues through into his resurrection as Jesus is worshipped on the mountain (Matthew 28:17) and by Thomas (John 20:28). Luke ends his gospel as he began, back in the temple with the disciples praising God (Luke 24:53).

Jesus' example of prayer

Luke may begin his gospel in the spiritual atmosphere of the temple, but Mark starts his with a whirlwind of activity. After a few verses of introduction, we quickly cover John the Baptist and Jesus' baptism and temptation. Then, in a frantic burst of ministry, Jesus calls the first disciples, teaches in the synagogue, casts out an unclean spirit, heals Peter's mother-in-law, and cures all the sick and possessed in the area! There follows a very important little verse: 'In the

Some of Jesus' prayers

I thank you, Father, Lord of heaven and earth, because you have hidden these things from the wise and the intelligent and have revealed them to infants; yes, Father, for such was your gracious will. All things have been handed over to me by my Father; and no one knows the Son except the Father, and no one knows the Father except the Son and anyone to whom the Son chooses to reveal him.'

(Matthew 11:25–27)

'So they took away the stone. And Jesus looked upward and said, "Father, I thank you for having heard me. I knew that you always hear me, but I have said this for the sake of the crowd standing here, so that they may believe that you sent me." When he had said this, he cried with a loud voice, "Lazarus, come out!"'

(John 11:41–43)

'Father, glorify your name.'

(John 12:28)

'Simon, Simon!… I have prayed for you that your own faith may not fail; and you, when once you have turned back, strengthen your brothers.'

(Luke 22:31–32)

'Father, the hour has come; glorify your Son so that the Son may glorify you… Father, protect them in your name… so that they may be one, as we are one… Father, I desire that those also, whom you have given me, may be with me where I am.'

(John 17:1, 11, 24 – from Jesus' 'High Priestly' prayer)

'Abba, Father, all things are possible for you; remove this cup from me; yet, not what I want, but what you want.'

(Mark 14:36)

'Father, forgive them; for they do not know what they are doing.'

(Luke 23:34)

'My God, my God, why have you forsaken me?'

(Mark 15:34; Psalm 22:1)

'Then Jesus, crying with a loud voice, said, "Father, into your hands I commend my spirit." Having said this, he breathed his last.'

(Luke 23:46)

◆ **Jesus praying in the Garden of Gethsemane:** *The Agony in the Garden*, **by Ambrogio Bergognone (c. 1501).**

morning, while it was still very dark, he got up and went out to a deserted place, and there he prayed' (Mark 1:35). This gives us a clue to Jesus' own rhythm of prayer and activity. Ministering to people is very draining; when a bleeding woman touches Jesus, it 'takes it out' of him: 'Immediately aware that power had gone forth from him, Jesus turned about in the crowd and said, "Who touched my clothes?"' (Mark 5:30). Jesus needed a regular pattern of withdrawal into solitude to pray before going out to teach, preach and heal. Similarly, after events such as the feeding of the 5,000, 'he dismissed the crowds and went up the mountain by himself to pray. When evening came, he was there alone' (Matthew 14:23). He taught the same habit to his disciples, when they returned from their own mission practice, full of 'all that they had done and taught. He said to them, "Come away to a deserted place all by yourselves and rest a while." For many were coming and going, and they had no leisure even to eat' (Mark 6:31).

Luke shows this pattern of prayer most clearly at every significant event of Jesus' ministry. Things happen when he prays!

Now when all the people were baptized, and when Jesus also had been baptized and was praying, the heaven was opened (Luke 3:21).

Great crowds gathered to listen and to be healed. But he would withdraw to deserted places and pray (Luke 5:15–16).

He went out to the mountain to pray; and he spent the night in prayer to God. And when day came, he called his disciples and chose twelve of them (Luke 6:12–13).

Once when Jesus was praying alone, with only the disciples near him, he asked them, 'Who do the crowds say that I am?' (Luke 9:18).

Jesus took with him Peter and John and James, and went up on the mountain to pray. And while he was praying, the appearance of his face

changed, and his clothes became dazzling white (Luke 9:28–29).

No wonder that his example inspired others: 'Jesus was praying in a certain place, and after he had finished, one of his disciples said to him, "Lord, teach us to pray"' (Luke 11:1).

The teaching of Jesus – his words

Luke depicts Jesus at the age of twelve as already 'about my Father's business' in the temple, 'my Father's house' (Luke 2:49). Jesus' characteristic address to God was as Abba, 'Father'. It is, therefore, no surprise that Jesus' teaching on prayer is encapsulated not in a lecture, but actually in prayer to 'Our Father'. Matthew introduces it with the instruction, 'Pray then in this way,' at the start of the Sermon on the Mount, while Luke shows Jesus teaching the disciples this prayer in response to their request after observing him at prayer himself (Matthew 6:9–13; Luke 11:1–4).

Our Father in heaven,
hallowed be your name.
Your kingdom come.
Your will be done,
on earth as it is in heaven.
Give us this day our daily bread.
And forgive us our debts,
as we also have forgiven our debtors.
And lead us not into temptation,
but deliver us from the evil one.
(Matthew 6:9–13)

Like all of Jesus' teaching, the 'Lord's prayer' depends on the fatherhood of God. In both Matthew and Luke's gospels, the prayer is followed quite soon by a section of Jesus' teaching about the goodness of God who delights to answer our prayers. Even sinful human beings will give their children good things like fish, bread and eggs, not evil things like snakes, stones and scorpions. Therefore, we can be sure that our heavenly Father will give us good things and his own Holy Spirit when we pray. Therefore we must 'ask, seek and knock' in prayer to the Father (Matthew 7:7–11; Luke 11:9–13).

After addressing God as Father, the next three petitions are concerned with God – that his name is kept holy, his kingdom may come and his will be done. These themes lie close to the heart of the rest of Jesus' teaching and are a reminder that in prayer, as in everything else, we are first to seek God and his kingdom (Matthew 6:33). Only after this concentration upon God, and trusting him as Father, can we pray the second group of three petitions for our own daily needs – for bread, forgiveness and protection.

■ The word *epiousios*, usually translated as 'daily', has the same mixture of the future and the present as the rest of Jesus' teaching; it is asking for the bread of the future reign of God to be given to us here and now, day by day – a practical concern in a hungry world.

■ The prayer for forgiveness for our own sins is linked to our forgiving others. Jesus' entire ministry was one of forgiving and accepting 'sinners' – and his followers must do the same. The Sermon on the Mount links God's forgiveness of our sins to our attitude to the sins of others, and warns us of the dire consequences of being unforgiving (Matthew 6:14–15). The same point is later reinforced by the parable of the unforgiving servant (Matthew 18:21–35) and by Jesus' direct teaching on prayer and forgiveness in Mark 11:25. Indeed, this attitude must even extend to praying for our enemies: 'Love your enemies and pray for those who persecute you' (Matthew 5:44; Luke 6:27–28).

■ Finally, we pray that we may not suffer the *peirasmos*, the period of 'testing'. Here again we have the mix of the future and the present: at one level, it can mean temptation in general (the traditional translation), while it is also used for the 'time of trial' immediately before the cataclysmic end of all things. Elsewhere, Jesus tells his followers to pray for courage at the 'end', that it might not find us unprepared (Luke 21:36) or come 'in winter or on a sabbath' (Matthew 24:20).

The Sermon on the Mount also contains some general teaching on prayer, that we should pray to our Father 'in secret'. Like almsgiving, prayer is not something to be paraded or boasted about, nor does it require long repetitions and 'many words' (Matthew 6:1–7; see also Mark 12:40). Once again, we must rely not on our words but on the Father's love, 'for your Father knows what you need before you ask him'.

Luke's particular stress on prayer is also seen in three parables about prayer which only his gospel records. The first, often called the 'Friend at Midnight' comes immediately after the Lord's prayer. It describes someone banging on a neighbour's door asking for bread; despite initial rebuffs, eventually, 'even though he will not get up and give him anything because he is his friend, at least because of his persistence he will get up and give him whatever he needs' (Luke 11:5–8). A similar point is made about 'a judge who neither feared God nor had respect for people' but who eventually gave in to a 'widow who kept coming to him and saying, "Grant me justice against my opponent."' The judge grants her request grudgingly – so how much more will God hear the cry of his people when they pray (Luke 18:1–8). Finally, the parable of the Pharisee and the tax collector praying in the temple restates the topsy-turvy values of the kingdom of God where 'all who exalt themselves will be humbled, but all who

humble themselves will be exalted'. The good religious person may try to rely on prayers, fasting and giving, but our loving Father answers the simple prayer, 'God, be merciful to me, a sinner!' (Luke 18:9–14).

The 'Jesus prayer' – 'Lord Jesus Christ, Son of the Living God, have mercy on me, a sinner' – is based upon various pleas to Jesus made by blind men (Matthew 9:27; 20:30; Mark 10:47; Luke 18:38), the Canaanite woman (Matthew 15:22) and some lepers (Luke 17:13). It is also linked to the prayer of the tax collector in the parable (Luke 18:13). It has been important in Orthodox spirituality through the centuries, but is now commonly used across many traditions (see chapter 4, pp. 135, 137, 148).

All of Jesus' teaching on prayer must be placed in the context of his stress on God as Father. He calls for faith and confidence in prayer, enough even to move mountains (Mark 11:23–24; Matthew 21:21–22). But prayer is not some kind of cosmic slot-machine whereby if only we can insert enough faith, we can wrest something out of a grudging God. Instead, such is the love of God that 'your Father knows what you need before you ask him' (Matthew 6:8). He delights to hear his children's prayers. 'Ask, and you will receive, that your joy may be full' (John 16:24).

The New Testament church

It is difficult to be certain about the habits of worship, prayer and spiritual practices of the Jews at the time of Jesus, and the same is true for the early Christians. In both cases, there is the danger of 'reading back' the practices and spirituality of later years into the first century. Nonetheless, the early Christians will have been greatly influenced both by their Jewish heritage and by Jesus' own spirituality as they tried to respond to what God had done in Jesus.

◆ **Opposite: The parable of the Pharisee and the tax collector in the temple; a 6th-century mosaic, San Apollinare Nuovo, Ravenna, Italy.**

The book of Acts shows them constantly at prayer – all together 'of one accord' (1:14), praying by day and night in places as diverse as prison or a beach (16:25; 21:5). Peter and John go to the temple at the hour of afternoon prayer, which is also when Cornelius prays (3:1; 10:3, 30). Paul is also shown going to the temple, and even paying for people's vows and offerings (21:23–27; 22:17). At the same time, other Christians such as Stephen stood in the prophetic tradition of protest about the temple, recalling Jesus' own warnings about its coming destruction (Mark 13; Acts 7:47–49).

Acts also shows Paul going straight to the synagogues around the Mediterranean to join in the discussion of the scriptures there, seeking to interpret them about Jesus (Acts 9:20; 13:5,

◆ **A 3rd-century fresco from the catacombs of St Calixto, Rome, Italy, showing an early Christian representation of a eucharistic banquet.**

Heavenly worship

'Worthy is the Lamb who was slain to receive power and wealth and wisdom and might and honour and glory and blessing!'

And I heard every creature in heaven and on earth and under the earth and in the sea, and all therein, saying,

'To him who sits upon the throne and to the Lamb be blessing and honour and glory and might for ever and ever!'
(Revelation 5:12–13)

Paul prays for the Ephesians

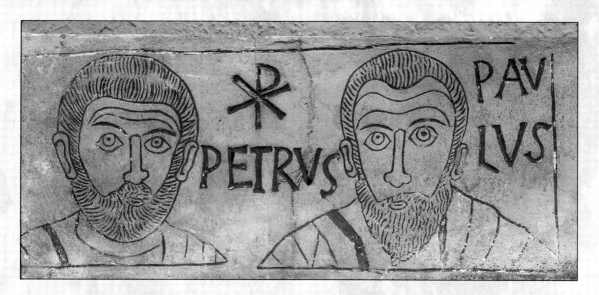

I have heard of your faith in the Lord Jesus and your love towards all the saints, and for this reason I do not cease to give thanks for you as I remember you in my prayers. I pray that the God of our Lord Jesus Christ, the Father of glory, may give you a spirit of wisdom and revelation as you come to know him, so that, with the eyes of your heart enlightened, you may know what is the hope to which he has called you, what are the riches of his glorious inheritance among the saints, and what is the immeasurable greatness of his power for us who believe, according to the working of his great power. God put this power to work in Christ when he raised him from the dead and seated him at his right hand in the heavenly places, far above all rule and authority and power and dominion, and above every name that is named, not only in this age but also in the age to come. And he has put all things under his feet and has made him the head over all things for the church, which is his body, the fullness of him who fills all in all.'

(Ephesians 1:15–23)

'For this reason I bow my knees before the Father, from whom every family in heaven and on earth takes its name. I pray that, according to the riches of his glory, he may grant that you may be strengthened in your inner being with power through his Spirit, and that Christ may dwell in your hearts through faith, as you are being rooted and grounded in love. I pray that you may have the power to comprehend, with all the saints, what is the breadth and length and height and depth, and to know the love of Christ that surpasses knowledge, so that you may be filled with all the fullness of God. Now to him who by the power at work within us is able to accomplish abundantly far more than all we can ask or imagine, to him be glory in the church and in Christ Jesus to all generations, for ever and ever. Amen.'

(Ephesians 3:14–21)

◆ **Above: The apostles Peter and Paul; stone slab from the sepulchre of a child, Rome, c. 313.**

14–43; 17:1–3; 18:4). The pattern of synagogue prayers and scripture readings would have contributed much to early church meetings. Equally, meals and social gatherings in both Jewish and Graeco-Roman culture included prayers and blessings, and were often followed by public readings – and this would also have influenced the first Christian meetings. Luke suggests that there were four elements to these: the apostles' teaching, fellowship, the breaking of bread, and prayers (Acts 2:42). Paul also describes them gathering together for 'the Lord's supper' (1 Corinthians 11:20), and tells them to give their financial offerings 'on the first day of every week' (16:2). John says that he received the revelation of the worship around God's throne in heaven when he was 'in the Spirit on the Lord's day' (Revelation 1:9–10; and see box, p. 29). Other writers urge their readers to gather together for worship and 'spiritual sacrifices' (Hebrews 10:25; 13:15; 1 Peter 2:5). They are told to use 'psalms and hymns and spiritual songs' (Ephesians 5:19) and some of these may be quoted in the epistles (for example, Philippians 2:6–11; Colossians 1:15–20; Hebrews 1:3; 1 Timothy 3:16; 1 Peter 3:18–22).

The letters also contain instructions for meetings and worship. The largest treatment comes in 1 Corinthians 10–14. First, Paul warns the Corinthians against the worship of idols, referring to both baptism and communion. He gives them instructions about head coverings when praying or prophesying, and about the proper way to celebrate the communion. This is followed by a detailed discussion of spiritual gifts, interspersed by his great hymn about love, since love for one another should characterize Christian behaviour in worship as in everything else. Such early church gatherings were clearly highly participative, as different people brought different elements, such as a reading, hymn or a spiritual gift – so Paul is seeking some order, since 'God is not a God of confusion but of peace' (1 Corinthians 14:33). Spiritual gifts are *charismata*, gifts of God's grace (*charis*), and the various lists of them include supernatural offerings like miracles and tongues, practical gifts like service, administration and

giving, as well as the various forms of church leadership (1 Corinthians 12:4–11, 27–31; Romans 12:4–8; Ephesians 4:1–15).

At the heart of these instructions is a spirituality centred on being the body of Christ, where everyone is a member united under Jesus as the head. Entry into the body is through baptism in water, which includes the forgiveness of sins, receiving the Holy Spirit and participation in Christ's death and resurrection (see Acts 2:38; 10:44–48; Romans 6:2–11). While baptism could only happen once, participation was continued through the 'breaking of bread', recalling Jesus' last supper with his disciples and drawing upon both Jewish Passover traditions and ancient Mediterranean fellowship meals to form a veritable 'communion' (Mark 14:22–25; Acts 20:7; 27:35; 1 Corinthians 11:17–26). Thus, the early Christian spirituality was rooted in fellowship – a 'community' or 'sharing together' in the life of God through the Holy Spirit (2 Corinthians 13:14).

This is all undergirded by a stress on prayer. Paul constantly exhorts his reader to 'pray without ceasing' and 'in everything' (1 Thessalonians 5:17; Philippians 4:6). At the start of most of his letters, he says that he is praying for his readers, usually in a context of giving thanks to God for them. In return, Paul often requests that his readers should also pray for him and for his work in the gospel (Romans 15:30; 2 Corinthians 1:11; Colossians 4:3). This mixture of prayer and thanksgiving is at the heart of his spirituality, which enables us to 'rejoice' and 'have no anxiety', knowing 'the peace of God which passes all understanding' (Philippians 4:4–7). James agrees on the importance of prayer, citing the example of Elijah (1:5–6; 4:2–3; 5:16–18), and insists that spirituality must be earthed in visiting orphans and widows, showing no favouritism to the rich in church and paying workers' wages (1:27; 2:1–7; 5:1–6).

Conclusion

Thus the spirituality of the early church also held together the relationship between prayer and

Spirituality inspires doctrine

Christian spirituality is grounded in the two key doctrines of the trinity and the incarnation. The theological understanding of God as three in one and of how Jesus is both human and divine is very complex. It took the early church several centuries of debate and argument to reach the classic expression of these beliefs in the creeds, while theologians and scholars have been debating them ever since. However, these beliefs arose not out of debate, but out of spiritual experience, worship and prayer. As Jews, Jesus' first followers believed in only one God. And yet, all they knew of the God of Israel was being made real and personal to them in Jesus – and this continued even more so after his death and resurrection. The early church found that 'where two or three are gathered in my name, I am in the midst of them' (Matthew 18:19).

From a very early period, they called Jesus *Mar* in Aramaic, the term 'Lord', previously reserved only for God, as is seen in prayers like *Maranatha*, 'Our Lord, come!' (1 Corinthians 16:22). Paul goes so far as to call Jesus 'God' in an outburst of prayer and praise in Romans 9:5. Meanwhile, Jesus had taught his disciples to pray to God as Abba, Father. Now, in their worship, they found that it was the Spirit of God who brought them this 'spirit of sonship', to be adopted as 'children of God' (Romans 8:14–17). The Spirit of God was experienced in prayer, 'helping us in our weakness… interceding for us with sighs too deep for words' (Romans 8:26). Thus this religious experience of God as Father, being revealed in Jesus through the fellowship of the Holy Spirit, led to these central Christian beliefs. It was early Christian spirituality which produced the later theological doctrines. Prayer comes first.

◆ *The Two Trinities*, by Bartolomé Esteban Murillo (1617–82), depicts Jesus as both human and divine at the intersection of his earthly family, with Mary and Joseph, and his heavenly trinity, with God the Father and the dove of the Holy Spirit.

practical action, individual devotion and corporate
fellowship, sacramental acts and scriptural study
which we noted in Jewish belief and practice. As
the Hebrew scriptures and the New Testament
writings were combined into the Christian Bible,
they provided an enormous spiritual resource
which would inspire Christians for thousands
of years to come as they developed many and
different ways of praying and worshipping. At
the very centre of it all is the person of Jesus
of Nazareth, who brought his followers into a
relationship with God the Father through his life,
death and resurrection and who continues to
inspire their life and spirituality through his
Holy Spirit.

1

The Early Church Fathers

(1st to 6th centuries)

John A. McGuckin

Timeline

	95	*First Letter of Clement*
100	95–100	*The Shepherd of Hermas*
	d. c. 100	Clement of Rome
	early 2nd c.	*Didache*
	early 2nd c.	*The Shepherd of Men*
	2nd c.	*The Epistle to Diognetus*
	2nd c.	Montanus, Prisca and Maximilla
	c. 106–107	Ignatius of Antioch (writing)
	c. 130–200	Irenaeus of Lyons
	c. 150–215	Clement of Alexandria
	d. c. 156	Polycarp of Smyrna
	c. 160–225	Tertullian
	d. c. 165	Justin Martyr
200	c. 185–249	Origen of Alexandria
	early 3rd c.	*Didascalia Apostolorum*
	early 3rd c.	*Passion of Perpetua and Felicity*
	early 3rd c.	Hippolytus
	3rd c.	*Martyrdom of Polycarp*
	200–58	Cyprian of Carthage
	251–356	Antony of Egypt
300	c. 296–373	Athanasius
	4th c.	*Codex Sinaiticus*
	4th c.	Eusebius
	4th c.	Jerome
	306	**Constantine the Great's rule begins**
	313	**Edict of Milan recognizes Christianity as a legal religion**
	325	**Council of Nicea**
	c. 339–97	Ambrose
	c. 344–407	John Chrysostom
	348–c. 410	Prudentius
	c. 353–431	Paulinus (Bishop of Nola)
	354–430	Augustine of Hippo
400	late 4th c.	Pelagius
	c. 400	*Confessions of Augustine*
	early 5th c.	*Codex Alexandrinus*
	410	**Sack of Rome by Alaric the Goth**
	476	**Romulus Augustus, the last Western Roman emperor, is deposed**
500	c. 480–c. 550	Benedict of Nursia
	6th c.	Romanus the Melodist
	c. 530–c. 610	Venantius Fortunatus
	c. 540–604	Gregory the Great
	632	Death of Mohammed
	c. 675–c. 749	John of Damascus

The focus of this chapter is on some of the main episodes in early Christian writing that mark the church's reaction to internal controversies and external hostility. The evidence that lies within our grasp is, of course, largely 'reactive' in character and not entirely descriptive of the inner spiritual life that would have marked the normal Christian experience, such as might be observed, for example, in a typical regular worship service of the early Christians. The normal aspects of spiritual life, then as now, tended to be unstated in text until much later. The surviving literature is only a partial glimpse of the life issues that concerned early Christians in the period following New Testament times. This period is generally called the 'patristic' era. It is a word that originated as a title for spiritual elders in early monasticism, and was later attributed to bishops. These were the 'fathers': Abbas in the words of the early Coptic monks, or *patres* in the Latin, which gave the word patristic to the vocabulary. It soon became a technical phrase with other associations. The Christian 'fathers' became not just any bishop or spiritual leader, but those who were regarded as carrying a universally recognized weight.

In a time when Christianity was undergoing extensive controversies over the nature of its essential identity – and that time should be seen as including almost all the period from the New Testament itself to the end of the era which we are looking at in this chapter – the concept of appealing to 'the fathers' was used as a way of organizing and describing the fundamental Christian character. So, the appeal to the fathers became a way of deciding what was substantive in the Christian tradition, and what was peripheral, dangerous or unacceptable. The latter were called 'heresies'.

The word 'heresy' first meant just a legitimate division of opinion, but Christians began to use it precisely as a way of describing someone's views which were seen to be opposed to the authentic church. Orthodoxy was used as a contrast to heresy. 'Orthodoxy' meant 'correct teaching' while heresy increasingly came to be invested with hostile associations, even in the text of the New Testament itself (cf. 2 Peter 2:1; Titus 3:10; 1 John 2). The heretics were those who marked out deviations from the right path (understood as fidelity to the gospel teachings) and the fathers were those who marked out the correct (or orthodox) path, one that commented on present crises in continuity with, and fidelity to, the gospel record. To this extent, then, the notions of orthodoxy and patristic thought were terms that claimed an authentically evangelical (they would have said 'apostolic') character for post-scriptural Christian developments.

Our discussion of the spirituality of the early church in the first six centuries can usefully follow the track of looking at the leading writers and intellectuals of the day: those who were the 'fathers'. It is a clear way of introducing the main shape of the Great Christian Tradition that grew up in controversy in the early generations and passed on its message to later centuries. However, it is not the whole story, or even the only way of telling the story: the real life of the Christian church was always far richer and more complex than the surviving writings can suggest. These can only hint at it rather than summing it up. The surviving texts are like the archaeological remains of a once-great city. One

needs imagination to use them correctly. For example, if we follow the writings of the fathers alone, we largely miss out on what Christian women were contributing during this period, as the women of that time were rarely literate. The dynamic contribution of women in these early centuries (and certainly their important impact on Christianity) was made by other means than writing, and if one only looks at texts, one becomes 'blind' to women's significant activity in the early church.

Another drawback of the patristic method is that the church's spirituality is always chiefly expressed in the manner in which it worships. Christian worship was called in ancient times the 'holy liturgy', meaning, in the main, the Eucharist or communion rituals of Christianity and its baptismal ceremonies. Early liturgical texts are in still evidence, and for completeness we need to look at these. They are not usually associated with any particular individual but grew up as corporate expressions of Christian communities. For the earliest period they are relatively silent, in the backstage shadow, where much of what is deeply important in the public domain, paradoxically, often prefers to remain.

The patristic writings, on the other hand, are usually centred around controversies. They reflect great arguments that grew up between individuals and different churches as to the correct interpretation of the Christian life in a given context. Insofar as they are 'controversial'

◆ A devout woman depicted in a mosaic pavement (dating from the 4th century), in the Basilica Aquileia, Udine province, Italy.

literature, they often have imbalances in their approach, and tend to focus on the argument in hand rather than seeking to give a more comprehensive view of the actual condition of general Christian life. If it is the case, as it is here, that we are looking mainly at Christian spirituality (rather than, for example, at the history of Christian theological ideas in general) then apologetic or controversial literature is often limited in its value. We need to look beyond the writings in many instances, to see what was happening in the development of forms of worship and prayer in early Christianity. We need to take the written evidence and press it for what it is *not* saying, as much as for what it is.

We shall take a patristic method in what follows, a method that will look at the work of some of the leading writers and theologians of the time. But we shall also try to take into account the significant developments that were happening in this period as represented by 'movements' that were not necessarily individual: for example, the growing ascetical tendency in Christianity represented by monasticism, and the importance of spiritual visionaries and martyrs (women prominent among them). Our concern is to provide a simple and clear introduction to the main shape of Christian spirituality in this era. Some of the chief thinkers of the patristic age, in its middle period, are also being considered in chapter 4, 'The Eastern Christian Tradition', and readers will wish to consult there for such influential figures as Athanasius and the Cappadocian fathers (the early Eastern patristic theologians after Origen).

The apostolic fathers
(2nd century)

The apostolic fathers is a collective name for those early theologians, mainly (but not always) bishops of ancient Christian communities, who wrote in the second century, and whom the church regarded as the generation of teachers succeeding the apostles. It is a term that marks the beginnings of Christian literature outside the canon of New Testament writings. Of course, at that time the very canon determining what was definitely 'scriptural' or not was not everywhere clear and fixed. Some of the most important writings from this collective designation of apostolic fathers are a case in point. Both the *First Letter of Clement* and *The Shepherd of Hermas* were, for some time, regarded as ranking alongside scripture, even as part of the New Testament. In the *Codex Alexandrinus*, the early fifth-century biblical manuscript kept in the British Library, the Clementine letters come immediately after the book of Revelation, and can be found in some Syriac manuscripts of the Bible, copied as late as the twelfth century.

The Clementine letters (c. AD 95)

The so-called Clementines are one of the jewels of early Christian writing. The larger of the two works is the *First Letter of Clement to the Corinthians*. It is, in form, an exhortatory treatise of the Roman church to the Corinthian church advising them on matters of spiritual discipline. The church at Corinth had undergone some kind of 'revolutionary' disturbance (such is the view from Rome) and the author, who is traditionally named as Clement, one of the early Roman bishops, writes to them to urge peace and concord. The author is writing in the last years of the persecuting Emperor Domitian, that is in AD 95. Clement's call to reconciliation, and to a renewed respect for order and charitable mutuality, is very characteristic of the Roman church, which had already by this stage gained a reputation for 'Christian orderliness', and whose pattern of organization was to command great sway among subsequent Christian communities. The central concept of obedience to authorities represents the traditional Roman and civilized appeal to the virtues of home and hearth: the so-called 'household code', but given a new Christian interpretation under the aegis of self-denying love:

Who among you is noble? Who is compassionate? Who is filled with love? Let such a person say: 'If it is my fault that there are rebellion and strife and schisms, then I shall give way.'[1]

In the writer's understanding of the inner nature of the church he gives priority to loving concord, and in this, the *First Letter of Clement* (the first of all the Christian non-biblical writings) is very comparable to the pastoral letters of the New Testament, 1 and 2 Timothy and Titus. Apart from writing the letter of reconciliation, Clement sent on mediators to assist the Corinthian church to return to unity. The letter is far too long to be an epistle in the standard meaning of that term; it is more of a biblically elaborated moral treatise. Constant examples are given from the scriptures to argue that humility and the desire for spiritual concord are virtues that God values, and that arrogance and pride are met with a refusal of God to hear them. The text often reads, as a result, as a generic kind of appeal to 'order and concord'. It also represents the principle that was held to be central by many early Christian communities, that the social organization of the churches, their discipline, was not an accidental part of the faith, but that the principle of order was dear to God and those in 'holy orders' whose job it was to preside over the organization were similarly close to God. He makes the argument that good discipline and the proper exercise of regulating authority within the church are part of the very inner fabric of its spiritual life. For the author of the *First Letter of Clement*, spiritual insight could not be opposed to obedience to the community elders constituted by God. In later times, just as it was in Clement's own generation, this principle was to be severely tested in periods of internal controversy.

The writer often seems to be appealing to a Christian congregation that was composed of many of the lower classes of slaves and servants. His prayer for forgiveness depicts God as the merciful owner who will not be too harsh to his slaves:

◆ **A 4th-century painting of a slave serving food and wine, from the House of Cellio.**

Through your works you have revealed the everlasting structure of the world. You, Lord, created the earth. You are faithful throughout all generations, righteous in your judgments, marvellous in strength and majesty, wise in creating and prudent in establishing what exists, good in all that can be seen, and faithful to those who trust in you, merciful and compassionate. Forgive us our sins, Lord, and our injustices, our transgressions and shortcomings. Do not take into account every fault of your slaves and serving-girls but cleanse us with the scouring of your truth and direct our steps to walk in holiness and righteousness and purity of heart.[2]

The *Second Letter of Clement*

The *Second Letter of Clement* is not by the author of the *First Letter of Clement* and has caused modern scholarship many difficulties in trying to find its proper context. It is certainly one of the earliest of all Christian liturgical sermons to survive. The author, another of the earliest-known 'bishops', is expounding on the text of the prophet Isaiah, to encourage his listeners to repent. The Christian who is alive can repent before the face of God, and God will look upon the faults of that person as a potter looks upon a mistake he has made while the clay is wet. The clay can be reformed to the proper image, and all will be well. But after a time, when the clay is hardened, repentance will no longer be possible, and the deformed pot will be cast away. In celebrating penitence as a primary aspect of the true Christian's spiritual life, the author was making a considerable advance in moving the early church towards a realistic 'ethic'. At first it was believed that the early community would be a totally pure elect within a corrupt world. As time exposed many of the flaws in the early Christian community, the doctrine of repentance had to be elaborated, without denying the essential insight that the church was indeed a community of the elect, rendered holy by Christ's saving grace. *The Shepherd of Hermas* is concerned with much the same thing. The *Second Letter of Clement*, with a vivid sense of the impending day of judgment – still expected to be imminent – prioritizes prayer, fasting and almsgiving as the central activities that constitute true Christianity, and which can turn the hearts of believers back to their God:

The day of judgment is already coming as a blazing furnace (Malachi 4:1) and some of the heavens will dissolve (cf. Isaiah 34:4) and the whole earth will be like lead melting in the fire, and then the works of men, both secret and public, will be made manifest. Charitable giving, then, is a good thing, and so too is repentance from sin. Fasting is better than prayer, while almsgiving is better than both, and 'love covers a multitude of sins' (1 Peter 4:8), while prayer arising from a good conscience delivers a man from death. Blessed is everyone who is found full of these things, for almsgiving relieves the burden of sin.[3]

For the author, prayer, fasting and almsgiving constitute the regular and essential structure of Christian spirituality. There can be no true inner life in the service of Christ which is not marked by them. Such an approach gives Christian spirituality a character of profound 'relatedness' to the real world: care for others and a deep sense of humility are necessary in the believer, even though such a person has received the election of the loving God. It was this that kept Christianity in the early period from becoming just another elitist spiritual movement concerned with inner purity, or a mystical individualism disconnected from society.

◆ **A Romanesque depiction of the last judgment, by Niccolÿ and Giovanni (11th to 12th centuries).**

The Shepherd of Hermas (c. AD 95–100)

In the ancient *Codex Sinaiticus* in the British Library *The Shepherd of Hermas* can be seen bound together with the New Testament books, even though by the late fourth century it had largely fallen out of favour, and was regarded as so archaic that it lost its place in the commonly recognized canon of scripture. The writer was Hermas, an apocalyptic preacher from the early Roman church. His work tells us much about the stern and charismatic character of the early Christians.

The book was written in stages between AD 95 and 100. The author was a freedman living in Rome, a former slave, who was most likely of Palestinian origin (possibly one of the slaves brought back from the capture of Jerusalem by the Romans in AD 70). Hermas gives a view of Christianity in Rome when it was still heavily influenced by Jewish religious tradition. Hermas is very concerned with matters of purity. His spirituality is visionary and prophetic in character. The book is organized as an account of a series of visions which the author experienced, written up in three main sections: Visions, Mandates (or commands) and Similitudes (or parables). The first part of the book (Visions 1–4) is the oldest. A female figure, an old woman, appears to him announcing revelations. The woman is the symbolic figure of the church, who later grows successively younger, as a symbol of how the church's earthly members must renew themselves in seeking after purity of life.

Hermas's visions lead him to move more and more to a celibate lifestyle (he was married with children though he seems to have been unhappy with his wife) and he understands this renunciation of sexuality as a more perfect lifestyle, suitable to someone who wishes to search after God.[4] God reveals to Hermas in his dreams that he is unhappy with him because of his reckless children. The disruptive family is clearly meant as an extended symbol of the 'children' of the Christian community over whom he is called to exercise a directive ministry. Like Hosea, the Old Testament prophet, Hermas's own life is used as a parable of judgment over the church, to whom he addresses his prophetic appeal to reform.

The earlier visions are marked by a strong sense of the expectation of a universal end to the world order (he calls it the 'Great Tribulation', in terms reminiscent of Mark 13, a text which was published not long before). This active sense of an imminent end (allied with a deep awareness of God's judgment hanging over the world and individuals) is often called apocalyptic or eschatological thought. It is no coincidence that in Hermas it is connected so strongly with matters of great concern over the church's purity, both individual and collective, for an apocalyptic method in religious teaching is itself a way in which to frame a message of repentance.

◆ **A 3rd-century wall-painting from the Catacombs of St Priscilla, Rome, depicting Christ as the good shepherd.**

Apocalypticism is essentially a call to the religious community to draw back to a fervent lifestyle: to renew itself in prayer and disciplines such as fasting, or in his case sexual abstinence. In other words Hermas is designing his book as a method of preaching urgent repentance. In the later sections of the book (from Vision 5 to the end) the Revealer-Guide changes and appears as an angel disguised as a shepherd. This, it appears eventually, is none other than the great Angel of Repentance. The author is playing with the religious ideas of readers who might have pagan backgrounds: the old woman he meets in Italy is superficially similar to the Sibyl, and the Shepherd is superficially similar to the pagan religious-philosophy of Hermetic mysticism, with its (surviving) treatise, *The Shepherd of Men*.

The centrality in the book of the interpretation of religious dream-visions was also another point of contact between Hellenistic, Jewish and early Christian religious circles, all of whom held such spiritual techniques to be important. The author makes resonances with such ideas to attract a wider audience into his Christian message. At the time Hermas wrote, Christians were faced with a considerable problem: trying to remain a fervent community of the pure elect (a self-definition which gave great coherence to the earliest Christians living surrounded by a polytheist and much more morally diffident Roman culture) while simultaneously trying to cope with the problem of lapses among the increasing number of church members. It was thought that sins would only be forgiven once by God, when the Christian converted and was baptized in the Holy Spirit. What to do about sins committed after baptism was a worrying problem. Did falling into sin mean that the baptism was meaningless, or that the individual could seek God's forgiveness and find it again? Hermas suggests, from his visions, that God would grant forgiveness a second time. He is very far away from the idea that God would give forgiveness readily and easily – and to this extent he can be described as a rigorist thinker.

The claim for inspiration which he makes through his book, and his choice of a visionary method of telling the story, along with the apocalyptic and moral fervour of the content, all demonstrate that Hermas was acting as one of the early Christian 'prophets' that are sometimes mentioned as operative in this period of ancient Christianity. He is speaking to his fellow Christians in the region of Rome, calling out to them to renew their moral purity by a return to a more rigorous lifestyle, and offering them in the process the hope that God would be lenient to their sins, even those committed after baptism, since the end of the ages (as he thought) was finally drawing near. It is a sobering reminder of the severe character of early Christian communities, when we consider the forbidding nature of this text (even though it is concerned with preaching forgiveness), to find Tertullian, a third-century African writer, later denouncing the work for laxity and calling it 'The Shepherd of Adulterers'.

◆ **A 3rd-century fresco of a baptism, from the Catacombs of St Calixto, Rome.**

Ignatius of Antioch (c. AD 35–c. 107)

One of the most famous of the apostolic fathers, roughly contemporary with Hermas, was again a Syrian – the Bishop Ignatius, who had charge of the Christian community of Antioch. Nothing is known of him except for his celebrated journey across Asia Minor to stand trial in Rome for the charge of being a Christian. Towards the end of the Emperor Trajan's reign, sometime around AD 105, Ignatius was arrested and taken to Rome. On his way he met and stayed with several Christian communities, and wrote to them, in the persons of their bishops. He stayed with Polycarp the Bishop of Smyrna (Izmir) and had a deep effect on him. Polycarp was to regard him later as a man of stature in the rank of the apostles. In his turn, Irenaeus, the Bishop of Lyons who came from Asia Minor, regarded himself as a disciple of Polycarp and, as such, personally linked with a generation

◆ One interpretation of the martyrdom of Ignatius: this baroque painting of Ignatius of Antioch by Francesco Fracanzane (c. 1616–56) presumes he was thrown to wild beasts.

that had apostolic character. The idea of associating with significant heroes of the early church was already quite clear, and can be assessed by the manner in which these early churches preserved and treasured Ignatius's letters. There is no certain evidence as to what actually happened to him. He again slips out of history, but the story of his (presumed) martyrdom (he wrote to the Roman church pleading with them not to arrange his release since he desired to be proven a true disciple by his martyrdom for Christ) became one of the most powerful images of Christian heroism in the face of the threat of totalitarian oppressors:

I am writing to all the churches and am insisting to everyone that I die for God of my own free will – unless you prevent me. So do not be 'unseasonably kind' to me. Let me be food for the wild beasts, through whom I can reach God. I am God's wheat, and I am being ground by the teeth of wild beasts that I might prove to be pure bread... Pray to the Lord that through these instruments I might prove to be a sacrifice to God.[5]

All in all, Ignatius left seven letters to the churches of Asia Minor, written first from Smyrna, and then from Troas (letters to the churches of Ephesus, Magnesia, Tralles, Rome, Philadelphia and Smyrna, together with a letter to Smyrna's bishop, Polycarp). Ignatius is a very important figure in the developing character of Christianity, for before him little is known of the office of bishop in the church. His letters do much to establish a pattern of leadership across a wide part of the Christian world, one that was soon to become standard: the pattern of leadership of the single bishop who governed the church, assisted by a council of presbyters (or priests) and deacons. This was, in future centuries, to have a very large impact indeed on the character of Christian spirituality. The figure of the bishop was given a prominence over the other offices. To some extent this prioritized the need for the community's internal unity and organizational coherence over its charismatic functions, though at first the bishop is described in strongly charismatic terms – the one who could lead the 'great prayer' of the church in purity of heart and under the inspiration of the Spirit. The bishop was now the senior office, and other forms of spiritual authority such as that of the prophet or the confessor (someone who had publicly suffered for the faith) were increasingly subordinated. The rise of the bishop's office to prominence, as witnessed in Ignatius, shows how the highest functions of leadership within the Christian community were organized around the liturgy. The bishop was the chief celebrant of the solemn eucharistic worship of all the Christians together in one church. This is Ignatius's insistence: one city, one bishop, one altar, and around that altar one heart and mind constituting the church.

The bishop, then, was expected to function as high priest of the community, interceding with God, and composing the great eucharistic prayer that recalled the last supper of Jesus. Ignatius's concept of the necessity for the church to be one with the bishop echoed and developed the arguments of the *First Letter of Clement*. This unity with the bishop is far from being a merely organizational or bureaucratic concept for Ignatius. He sees the bishop as the charismatically appointed leader, the chosen of Christ at the heart of the elect body. As the bishop is one with the Lord, the 'bearer of God', so the church must find its unity with God, and with one another, through the bishop. The bishop is like a sacrament (an efficient and mystical sign) of unity. For Ignatius that realization of unity among the Christian community is a mystical symbol of the way to unity with God, especially as ensured by the celebration of the Eucharist. The individual Christian is mystically associated with Christ's life and death in the unity of the Eucharist. It is no accident that Ignatius describes his own expected death as grinding like bread in the teeth (of lions): his destiny is to be transfigured eucharistically into Christ.

Ignatius's point originally was to call the church together in the face of dissension and divisions, such as those he heard about as he passed through the various churches of Asia. In his writings to Philadelphia he specifically censures Docetism: the view that Jesus' flesh was merely apparent. The complex of ideas goes together. Although he writes a set of very 'occasional' documents, his general views – that the reality of God is authentically found only in a concretely grounded gathering in unity around the celebration of Jesus' lordship over the church, and also that experience of God in Christ is necessarily rooted in the incarnation into true flesh and blood, and discovered again in the liturgy – were elements that were to mark all conceptions of Christian orthodoxy to come. The search for a unity with God, through Christ in the

Eucharist, as celebrated in a community of one heart and one mind gathered around the bishop, became an ideal of Christian organization, but also an ideal of the Christian spiritual life considered as a sacramental experience of peaceful and constructive wholeness.

Ignatius's career also showed how vividly the early church celebrated its martyrs. Those who died for the faith were regarded as gathered around the throne of God in heaven, and still exercising intercessory power for the church on earth, as part of Christ's glorification of his great saints. In the first three and a half centuries of the church's life the symbol of the martyr, time and time again, proved to be a rallying symbol for fervour and renewal, even though the persecutions themselves produced major problems in their wake, as they inevitably produced as many recanters as they did heroes.

Polycarp of Smyrna (d. c. 156)

Polycarp, who had given Ignatius hospitality at his church in Smyrna, is also one of the apostolic fathers. The account of his martyrdom survives as the very first Christian writing to celebrate martyrs' deaths as memorial feasts. This martyrdom account, written soon after the events it describes, so closely parallels the gospel passion narrative that we see in it a clear spiritual message that the true disciple (the martyr) must imitate the suffering Christ even to the point of death. Polycarp's letter, which served as a cover for those of Ignatius which he had sent on to the church at Philippi, shows the strongly moral character of the Christianity of this period. He stresses love for the poor as the transcendently important mark of Christian religion, and attacks those who make Christ into a mere intellectual symbol. He warns against lending a ready ear to 'speculations':

Let us leave behind the worthless speculations of the crowd and their false teachings, and return to the word delivered to us from the

◆ **A representation of Christian martyrs, from a Byzantine manuscript.**

beginning. Let us be self-controlled with regard to prayer, and let us persevere in fasting, earnestly asking the All-seeing God not to lead us into temptation since, as the Lord told us, the spirit is willing indeed but the flesh is weak. Let us hold steadfastly and without ceasing to our hope and the guarantee of our own righteousness, none other than Christ Jesus who bore our sins in his own body upon the tree.[6]

The Christian life, for Polycarp, must be one of active compassion, kept together and kept alive by prayer, and by a respect for the traditions that have been inherited. Like Ignatius, he shows the context of a church under assault from the moral

and doctrinal relativisms of the surrounding culture. In his letter Polycarp gives an early indication of the importance of the group of women called 'widows' for the daily spiritual life of the early church. These, who had probably originated as a group of widows who were being helped by the church's welfare programmes, soon developed into a powerful Christian order, something like societies of continual prayer and mutual support. Polycarp encourages them in what he describes as their priestly ministry of spiritual sacrifice:

> The widows must think soberly about the faith of the Lord and pray without ceasing for everyone, and stay far removed from all malicious talk, slander, false testimony, love of money, and any kind of evil; knowing that they are God's own altar, and that 'all sacrifices shall be scrutinized' and nothing escapes God whether thoughts or intentions or even the secrets of the heart.[7]

◆ **A woman at prayer, from the tomb stele of Theodora, a 5th-century Coptic burial stone found in Egypt.**

It is a small reference but one that indicates the great importance Christian women had in the earliest origins of the church's structures of organization, prayer and asceticism. One might presume, though it is largely left unstated, that the order of widows played a dominant role (as was later the case with the order of female deacons) in church catechesis for women and children, perhaps the most important of all the roles of evangelical proclamation that can be envisaged.

The Epistle to Diognetus (2nd century)

The apostolic fathers did not all enjoy a universal fame and an enduring influence. One of them, the unknown author of *The Epistle to Diognetus*, is only known to have existed because of a single thirteenth-century Greek manuscript, and even that was burned and lost in the Franco-German war of 1870. It was a text that only came to be read widely in the twentieth century, after its modern edition and English translation. The letter's date is uncertain and estimates have ranged from AD 117 to 225. It marks the transition between the apostolic fathers and the works of the apologists, or those who defended Christianity against political and intellectual attacks from pagans, a genre of literature that was to predominate in the period when Christianity became more publicly known, in the third century onwards. This letter is, in its form, a defence of Christianity against unnamed persecutors. It is a text that describes Christianity as the truest and most reasonable of all forms of philosophy. The religion of Christ calls humanity to live in an authentically pure manner which other philosophies only aspired to achieve, and this religion can make the effects of a true ethical life available even to the simplest members of society – something that cannot be said for any other philosophical school. Moreover, the Christians, however simple they may seem to be, cast aside with unerring instinct all the useless myths and false deviations of the pagan world. In a famous passage the letter speaks of the Christians living in the world but, by their manner of life, forming a contrast to it:

> While [Christians] live in both Greek and barbarian cities... and follow the local customs in dress and food and other aspects of life, at the same time they demonstrate the remarkable and admittedly unusual character of their real citizenship. They live in their own countries but only as aliens; they participate in everything as citizens yet endure all things as foreigners. Every foreign country is their fatherland, and every fatherland is foreign. They marry like everyone else and have children, but they do not expose their babies [to kill them]. They share their tables freely, but not their beds. They are in the flesh, but they do not live according to the flesh... In a word, what the soul is to the body, Christians are to the World.[8]

The tone of the letter is marked by elegant simplicity, and deliberately presents Christianity as a religion whose inner attractiveness will serve to convince all those who are not darkened by vindictive prejudice against it. The depiction of the Christian way as a philosophy was to have a great destiny ahead of it as the church moved more and more in the light of publicity (and frequently hostile interest) in the third century, and this presentation of the evangelical life as 'true philosophy' became a powerful method of evangelization and missionary strategy. It serves to underline how important the idea was to the early Christians that Christianity, if not lived out as an ethical way of life, became falsified, and lost its mystical quality.

The apologists
(late 2nd to 3rd centuries)

Christian literature and the life of the churches in the earliest period after the New Testament are profoundly Jewish in character, as we have seen in *The Shepherd of Hermas*. In the century following, as the Christian movement began to attract the attention of interested gentiles who were more highly educated and literarily skilled, the character of its writings begins to change. The signs given in *The Epistle to Diognetus* are developed more universally. These writers (late second century onwards) who put Greek literary methods (rhetoric) at the service of defending the church against its detractors are called the apologists: from the word *apologia*, which means a considered legal and intellectual defence of one's position.

The context of most of these writings is controversial, and that usually meant one of three scenarios:

(1) Writings addressed to 'the authorities' to argue that persecution of Christians was both unjust and unnecessary since they were good citizens.
(2) Writings addressed to pagan intellectual opponents to argue that Christianity was not a sub-rational religion of superstitious mystics, but a religion where reason and deep moral sense played a major part, and where the religious instinct proved superior to that of the local population.
(3) Controversial arguments addressed to the Jewish communities (who formed a large section of many ancient cities) which mainly turned on the nature of the interpretation of the 'Old Testament' and how it had meaning only as concerned with the foretelling of the story of Christ. In fact the conception of the Hebrew Bible as an 'Old' Testament (which had given way to, or been fulfilled by, the New) was a major theological idea developed in the time of the apologists, and is one of the marks of how early Christianity was moving more and more away from its Jewish roots to become a predominantly gentile religion, thinking and writing in Greek.

Gnosticism

The word 'Gnostic' signifies a person who has been 'initiated', or someone who possesses the secret 'knowledge' as an enlightened one. It is used today to summarize a widely diffused tendency in the ancient world to approach religious experience from an intellectualist starting point. This tendency can be seen within the texts of the New Testament, but is also attacked within other New Testament writings. Paul sometimes uses Gnostic-resonant phrases while at other times he pours scorn upon intellectualist religion, advocating a simpler faith that is firmly rooted in the historical acts of salvation centred upon the cross (see 1 Corinthians 1:20–25). The author of 2 Peter also shows clear signs of the struggle that was taking place at the end of the first century with some kind of Gnostic teachers who were already present in the New Testament church (2 Peter 1:16 – 2:22).

The Gnostic movement remains very difficult to define, precisely because it was more of a tendency than a movement. It combined philosophical speculation with religious mysticism. Certain aspects of the approach were common and identifiable, namely a desire to advocate a universalist religion rather than a particular one; a fascination with myths of redemption which also explained the creation and the fall of spiritual beings into materiality; a belief that materiality itself was punishment for sin; and (consequently) a radical form of dualism that often (at least in Christian Gnostic circles) issued in a belief in two gods: the supreme God who was beyond all material care, and the lesser god (the demiurge) who was a corrupt and embittered divinity who first caused the material world and then tyrannized over it. The demiurge was a god from whose clutches the true God and the true Saviour (Christ) came to deliver humankind. Several Christian Gnostics posited that this evil demiurge was none other than the God of the Old Testament, and that the 'Father of Our Lord Jesus Christ' was a radically different being, the true God, who stood in opposition to the demiurge, just as the New Testament stood in opposition to the whole of the Jewish law. These general attitudes of religious pessimism and dualistic aversion to the body were common aspects of many pre-Christian religious systems.

The Christian Gnostics taught an esoteric doctrine for the few. They regarded the larger mass of Christians as ignorant and prejudiced, not part of the higher elite. They were not as bad as the great mass of humanity who evidenced no enlightenment, but were certainly of a lower order in salvation.

Gnostic theories about the cosmic effects of the redemption achieved by Christ's sacrifice took Christian speculation into a wholly different order of thought. Before the Gnostic crisis of the second to third centuries the church was characterized by a simpler and more literalist understanding of the events of salvation. Jewish biblical categories predominated in Christian thinking. After the Gnostic era, the church emerged as a much more sophisticated society that was ready to present the Christian hope as a doctrine of grace for the entire world of Greco-Roman culture, and prepared even to describe it in philosophical terms that the ancient world would recognize. In short, the Gnostic movement, for the first time, advanced the Christian missionary strategy onto a world platform.

In specific terms of resistance the Gnostic crisis also shaped Christianity by forcing it to define what it was precisely that it did not like about Gnostic approaches. The Gnostic arguments brought the anti-Gnostic theologians such as Irenaeus of Lyons (c. 130–200) to a point where they could elaborate on the chief points of 'authentic' or 'orthodox' Christian teaching. The notions of heresy and orthodoxy become clarified from this point onwards.

Irenaeus's arguments against the Gnostics

In Irenaeus's overall argument against the Gnostic positions he advanced to the forefront three extremely important anti-Gnostic principles (or 'canons') over which he had spent much careful thought.

The first was the importance of having a definite 'canon of scripture', and an agreed list of authoritative books that were commonly agreed to be the definitive list of revealed scriptures. This not only 'closed the covers' on the concept of the Christian Bible, which was to make Christianity henceforth a definite religion of the book, but it had a precise effect in cutting off the variety of new texts, known as 'apocryphal' or 'non-canonical' gospels and treatises, that were increasingly being produced in this period.

The second and third anti-Gnostic positions were (a) the importance of having a single authoritative leader for each Christian community who could make immediate decisions about Christian authenticity based upon (b) the received tradition. This double principle of owing obedience to a single bishop who would defend the integrity of a universal (or 'catholic') tradition was to define the shape of Christianity for centuries to come. The tradition was itself articulated into short anti-Gnostic charters of belief. These were the first creeds, called the 'rule of faith', and were later used at baptismal ceremonies to ensure the shared beliefs of new Christians. All the opening sections of the ancient creeds are clearly anti-Gnostic in their design, concerned to stress the unity of God and the harmony of the material order within the divine plan:

I believe in One God,
the Father Almighty,
Who made heaven and earth
And all things visible and invisible...

◆ **A 17th-century engraving by Michael Burghers, a Dutch engraver, depicting Irenaeus.**

Justin Martyr (d. c. AD 165)

The Epistle to Diognetus is a good example of the first type of apologetic writing. But it is Justin Martyr who represents all three elements in his work, and who was one of the most influential of the early apologists. Justin has been described as one of the most original thinkers Christianity has produced. He was an itinerant philosopher-teacher, a gentile of Roman tradition, born in the Roman province of Syrian Palestine (modern Nablus on the West Bank). After reviewing several different schools of philosophy he became a Christian, seeing it as 'the only safe and beneficial philosophy'.[9] He was deeply affected by the courage of Christian martyrs which he personally witnessed,[10] and an encounter with an old Christian who showed him the Christian signification of the scriptures finally led to his conversion. 'A fire was immediately kindled in my soul,' he says.

His writings, although often addressed to an external hostile world, and thus describing Christianity to 'the outside', always remain deeply inspired by his biblical sensibility. To this extent he gives important indications of the inner life of Christians in his period. He came to Rome and taught there during the reign of the Emperor Antoninus Pius (AD 138–161). It was to this emperor that Justin addressed his *First Apology* in AD 155. Christianity, he says, must not be judged on the basis of ignorant prejudice. He describes Christianity as a religion of the highest moral character, whose adherents were devoted monotheists, and who also served the Christ, who was the pre-existent Son and Word of God. Justin used many well-recognized philosophical themes of his day to describe Christian doctrine, but his inspiration is decidedly biblicist. The Son of God who came to save the World is the *Logos* mentioned at the beginning of John's Gospel, who is also the divine Word or divine spark in the material cosmos which the pagan philosophers had spoken of without properly understanding it.

Justin uses philosophical ideas in the manner of an evangelistic missionary. He addresses the persecutors with an invitation as much as a rebuke: 'You are our brothers, come to know the truth of God.'[11] His chief concern is to stress two things: first, the truth which God has sent into the world for its salvation in Christ is a universal force that progresses along its mysterious way and cannot be frustrated by the hostility or apathy of human beings; and secondly, the spread of Christianity, despite all attempts to destroy it, is a sign of God's new plan of salvation. The church is, therefore, the mystery of God's loving power at work in the world. Christ is a universal saviour, who is also the central principle of the unity, and meaning, of the very cosmos.

Justin's concept of Christ is vast in its scale, but he argued strongly against the Christian Gnostics, especially the Valentinian party in Rome. These wished to approach Christ more as a cosmic symbol than as a material reality, thinking that materiality was irredeemably corrupt and that the Saviour-God only 'appeared' to enter into flesh, while in reality he was a bodiless spirit trying to pull his church out from the horror of material existence. Justin argued to the contrary that Christ was indeed the pre-existent Wisdom of God, who set the pattern for the very creation of the world but, even so, genuinely entered into a human life within history, and worked out the salvation of human beings through his teachings and miracles.

For Justin, the Eucharist is central to the life of the believer. In the eucharistic transformation believers find a pattern of union with the Lord and their own transformation into his life. Justin is one of the most important witnesses to the state of the early Christian liturgy. For him the sacraments were important in a way they were not to Christian Gnostics, who could never escape their deep suspicion of material reality. Justin represents an 'incarnational' theology which sees materiality not abandoned or condemned by God, but rescued and transfigured by its original maker through the mysteries of the life and death and resurrection of Christ. He wrote an important work addressed to the Jewish community in Rome, *Dialogue with Trypho the Jew*, arguing that Christianity was also the fulfilment of all their religious aspirations. It is a key text for the way in which it shows the modern reader how early Christians approached biblical exegesis

Enraged by the blatantly unjust execution of three Christians in Rome Justin addressed his *Second Apology* to the senate, by this means publicly identifying himself as a leading Christian teacher. He wrote this sometime during the reign of the 'philosopher–emperor' Marcus Aurelius, who held Christianity in profound scorn. The prefect of Rome, Junius Rusticus (162–68), arrested Justin along with six others, and demanded that they should sacrifice to the gods. Justin said he would worship only Christ, and was scourged and beheaded outside the city walls of Rome. His martyrdom made his writings a very influential source for many of the later apologists. Several of these were skilled Latin writers, who had trained rhetorically as lawyers before their conversions, and were now eager to put their education to the service of the gospel. They continued the themes of Justin: that the inner life of Christianity was intrinsically superior to paganism, and that Christ is the central truth to which all other tangential approaches to truth, such as philosophy, or Judaism, or the better forms of world religion, were all groping towards in various defective forms, waiting only for the light of Christ to lead them into fullness. The writings of the apologists gave to the Christian church the missionary impetus which it was to develop with such force and vitality in the succeeding centuries.

Tertullian (c. AD 160–225)

The leading Latin thinker among the apologists was undoubtedly Tertullian, writing at the very beginning of the third century. He was a North African of a rigorous cast of mind. The fourth-century church historians Eusebius and Jerome tell us that he came to Rome as a lawyer and was converted to Christianity in middle age, becoming a presbyter or elder of the Roman church, but his

◆ **Tertullian, from a collection of 16th-century engravings.**

own writings reflect the context of the North African church, at Carthage. To work in Rome and have estates in Africa was no uncommon thing for the wealthy class of the day, and he was certainly a wealthy and well-educated man, whose professional training brought a strong legal cast to his theology. At the end of his life his rigorism grew, and he came to be a defender of the Montanist movement, which was later regarded as a heresy. In Tertullian's time it was not universally 'excluded' and both Tertullian and Irenaeus could be its advocates without us necessarily presuming they ceased to represent the 'main' character of their local churches.

Tertullian is one of the most important of all Latin theologians before the time of Augustine. He strongly defended the principle of Christ's saving work in the flesh against Gnostic thinkers who thought divinity and incarnation were incompatible things, and who diminished the significance of Christ's earthly life. Accordingly, he passionately argued for the doctrine of the resurrection of the body which some Christian intellectuals wished to replace with a doctrine of the survival of the soul only.

In his great work *Against Praxeas* he attacked a tendency in the Roman church to teach a unitarian doctrine of God, arguing for the first time in clear language that the Christian doctrine of God as threefold unity was its fundamental biblical heritage, and that this form of monotheism could not be reduced, however difficult it might be to conceive otherwise, to the form of belief where God the Father and Son were just two names for the single same reality. Tertullian was the first theologian to try to supply technical terms to Christian doctrine. His influence was to last for a very long time as Christians developed their thought on the nature of God as trinity across the following centuries.

Tertullian's context was not only one of conflict with the church from without, but definitely a time when internal arguments over basic ideas of what defined Christianity were highly active in the churches. His approach was to clarify and simplify the lines of battle. Roman religions and Judaism were his main 'external' partners in the argument, but to Christians whom he thought were lax in their lifestyle, or who had questioned the explicit historicity of Jesus' life, he was equally hostile, regarding them as wolves within the fold. Tertullian articulated the concept of how to recognize the true tradition of Christian belief by speaking of the 'apostolic tradition' and the 'rule of faith'. Tertullian regarded this simple statement or profession of belief (the basic structure of the baptismal creed, that is, belief in one creator God, and in the saving life and works of Christ, and in the Holy Spirit) as the possession of the true church alone. It was like a legal inheritance which no one else could claim. In legal terms this 'ruling out' of false claimants was called a 'prescription', and in his important work *On the Prescription of Heretics* Tertullian was one of the first thinkers, along with Irenaeus the Bishop of Lyons, to lay down a system for defending the inner coherence of the Christian community at a

time when internal division (heresy) was threatening to disrupt it.

Ecstatic prophecy: Montanism and after
(2nd to 3rd centuries)

In Phrygia (the central part of modern Turkey, known as Asia Minor in antiquity) a movement grew up that was to have large repercussions. It was begun by a group of early Christian prophets: Montanus, and two women, Prisca and Maximilla. These Christian teachers began to preach in around AD 170. Women teachers were by no means unknown in earlier Christianity. They had formal positions among the community in the form of the widows and virgins. We have already noticed the order of widows, but the virgins were another group of women (sometimes widows and sometimes younger unmarried women) who were formally dedicated as the brides of Christ. They lived singly or in small groups near the church buildings, and during the liturgy they stood apart, wearing a veil that was the sign of their consecrated status. Many early Christian texts, from the late New Testament letters onwards, show a certain degree of conflict: on the one hand encouraging these orders of female ministry in the church, and on the other hand restricting the extent of the 'teaching' they were allowed to give. Many texts restrict the right of the women's orders to teach publicly. By this we must presume that there were moves to restrict them in the exegesis of the scripture and the public preaching that took place in the churches themselves, but they probably had an extensive teaching role in the villages and houses of the community, especially among the women and children of the locality, and those restricted to the household: the sick and the aged. In ancient city life this was no small function.

The three prophets stressed the apocalyptic nature of Christianity, and taught that theirs was the last generation. Christ was coming again at the end-time. He would descend on a tiny village in

Asia Minor, called Pepuza, and transform it into the heavenly Jerusalem. The preaching of these prophets seems to have been ecstatic in character. That is, they were 'seized' by the Spirit and spoke in a way that was outside their normal senses. This corresponds with what is known of some of the Hellenistic prophetic cults. It was an aspect of the Montanists' doctrine that many of their Christian opponents resisted, accusing Montanus of having carried into Christianity foreign practices from his previous life as a pagan priest.

This resistance was highly influential on the larger church. With the wide-scale renunciation of the Montanist theology, Christianity took a definite stand on the nature of the inspiration of the Holy Spirit of God that has characterized it ever since. The ecstatic states of mind common to Hellenistic religious enthusiasm were frowned on more and more after this controversy, and the Holy Spirit was believed to be characterized by the clear-headedness it produced in those who were most clearly moved by it. Just as Jesus was

◆ **The city of Jerusalem, from an early Christian mosaic pavement at Ma'daba, Jordan, Israel. The Montanists were preoccupied by the concept of the heavenly Jerusalem.**

inspired by the Holy Spirit, and the apostles and martyrs, so it was believed (in reaction to the Montanists) that Christian believers would never be violently 'possessed' by the divine Spirit, like the 'sons of the prophets' in the books of Kings, or taken out of their senses like the Montanists. On the contrary, they would show a refinement of the gifts of the mind, rather than their abandonment. In most Christian spiritual thought ever since, the action of the Spirit of God on a man or woman has been thought never to dispossess them of their senses, and ecstatic spirit-filled states that claim otherwise have, generally speaking, always been regarded with deep suspicion in Christian circles. The anti-Montanist reaction is one of the chief reasons why Christian mysticism is predominantly characterized by sober rationality through all its subsequent history, and ecstatic cults have been in the minority and short-lived.

Like other apocalyptic movements which stressed the end of history, Montanism had a rigorous view of the church's nature as a pure elect, and of its relation to culture (one of withdrawal and renunciation). It called for a renunciation of ordinary relationships and advocated severe fasting, radical purity of lifestyle, forbade second marriages and encouraged celibacy. Martyrdom was elevated as the supreme Christian witness, and if a persecution came near, the Montanists encouraged their disciples to volunteer for martyrdom. This was a source of friction with the non-Montanist Christians of the locality who felt that such a desire for death was foolhardy and over-zealous and endangered the lives of the large majority of Christians who legitimately tried to keep out of the hands of persecuting authorities. In keeping with their original teachers, Montanism seems to have allowed clergy of both sexes from an early date. Many local Christians in Asia Minor were impressed by the rigorous character of the Montanist lifestyle. However, many opposed the movement, not only because they wished to argue for the rational character of Christian inspiration by the Spirit, but also because they were suspicious of the visions and ecstasies which the Montanists favoured as continuing signs of a dedicated believer. For this reason a spirituality of ecstasies, visions and out-of-body states was soon regarded as 'suspect' to Christianity as a whole. It was always an aspect of Christian life, as the Montanist movement itself shows, but it would rarely appear again in Christian history without lively opposition.

In reaction to the Montanist movement, the leaders of Christian churches in Asia Minor called together the first province-wide meetings of bishops. This set a precedent for centuries to come. When Christianity was felt to be in crisis these 'synods' of bishops were a way to address problems. After the Asia Minor synods met, the Montanist movement was denounced as a threat to unity. The movement itself, however, had a considerable effect. In its call to fasting and celibacy it had a great influence on the emerging forms of 'catholic' Christianity and advanced Christianity's ascetical tendencies. It also brought forward in the catholic churches (as a reaction against Montanism) the regulatory aspects of the offices of bishop and presbyter, greatly to the disadvantage of the larger circle of other offices in the early church, such as virgins, widows and prophets. After this time the office of prophet all but fades away and is replaced by the office of the scriptural teacher and preacher, which was claimed as the preserve of bishops or presbyters alone, and remained so for many centuries. The Montanist movement endured as a smaller sect of the church, and was active in Rome and North Africa in the third century, and still visible in Asia Minor in the sixth century, for when the Roman Emperor Justinian tried to suppress them in the name of church unity, a large number committed mass suicide in protest.

Martyrdom accounts
(3rd century)

The earliest Christian texts had spoken of martyrdoms and persecutions, but these were often sporadic and very localized. As the church became more socially visible it began to attract more interest from political authorities. From early times the Christian martyrs had been regarded as great heroes by their communities. Ignatius's letters were given their status because of his martyrdom, and similar reverence is shown for Polycarp in the account of his passion. The genre of martyrdom texts grew to have increasing importance. As with the *Martyrdom of Polycarp*, the parallelism with the gospel passion narrative is often underlined. There are several 'martyrdom accounts' surviving from Christian antiquity, some of them closely related to the actual accounts of the trial, to which the church sent witnesses to make a record. Some of them relate to the heroic resistance of women, such as Blandina and Fausta, or Perpetua and Felicity (see box, p. 51), and numerous other women who feature prominently among the early Christian martyrs, and were given the highest possible status in the church. Martyrs were believed to gain crowns in heaven next to Christ, as spoken of in Revelation 7:9–17.

The unyielding resolve of these women, and the other martyrs, struck pagan society with a profound fear of Christianity as a deranged fanaticism, a religious system that was so determined not to be absorbed into the surrounding culture that it transgressed the fundamental structures which held ancient society together: obedience to the patriarchal head of the household and submission to civic authorities in all public matters, including religious conformity. Private religious sentiments might be held around a wide basis of cults and beliefs, but religion was universally believed to be socially formative, and to inculcate civic virtues that underpinned the stability of the household and city. To have a religious principle that could so blatantly transcend household values, and which so questioned civic religion, was something that marked a stark conflict between North African Roman society and the early church. The idea of the martyr as the true disciple left its impress on Christianity for ages afterwards. Not all might be called to follow their way of suffering, but those who had been tried and executed for the faith

Perpetua and Felicity

The story of the death of the young Roman woman Perpetua, and her Christian slave Felicity, in the province of North Africa during the third-century persecutions is an unusual text of great interest. Their story is contained in the *Passion of Perpetua and Felicity*. It was probably compiled by a Montanist theologian. It contains within its overall framework the prison diary which a young mother, Perpetua, kept in Carthage in AD 203. Her father was a pagan who could not comprehend the apparent madness and stubborn disobedience of his daughter. She had recently converted to Christianity and was undergoing a period of instruction prior to her baptism when she was arrested for her Christian beliefs. Although offered her freedom if she renounced Christianity, she refused to compromise and was baptized in prison.

Perpetua had just given birth, and the description of her arrest is one of the most vivid of the early accounts of martyrdom. Her father pleaded with her not be so unreasonable, and to consider her family obligations, but she opposed him. The concept of a young woman standing against her father and husband's wishes, and ready to leave even her newborn baby struck the church as an incredible witness to her tenacity and courage. The servant Felicity was pregnant and delivered her child while in prison. She too gave up her baby to the care of a Christian woman shortly before her execution.

◆ A contemporary icon showing Perpetua and Felicity.

became the supreme symbols of the disciples who had entered into a profound imitation of the suffering Lord. The martyr cult, in turn, emphasized the radical face of an emergent Christianity that was not content with merely resting quietly in the face of opposing cultural and religious systems, but was ready to withstand them and offer alternative social and moral visions, even at the cost of appalling personal suffering.

Perpetua's diary is a record of her dream-visions while in prison. She and another 'confessor' (a title given to those in prison for the faith),

Saturus, had visions of the afterlife, and how their prayers as confessors could persuade Christ to forgive the faults of both the living and dead. The concept of the church as a cosmic 'communion of saints' is very apparent in the texts; so too is the high role and status afforded by the early church to its martyrs. They were not just heroic witnesses, but heavenly intercessors, whose prayers could ensure the purity of the church on earth. Soon festivals were regularly instituted to mark their deaths; this was the beginning of the Christian calendar of saints, and the belief in the sanctity of

SCS PANCRATIVS SCS CELSO GONVS SCS PROTVS SCS IAOVINTVS S

◆ **Procession of the martyrs, a 6th-century mosaic from Sant'Apollinare Nuovo, Ravenna, Italy.**

their relics. The anonymous compiler of these martyrdom texts is believed to have been a North African Montanist, and one can see within the writing the underlying theme that visions and prophetic dreams are important as continuing signs of the Spirit of God's guidance of the church.

The stern quality of the Christianity here is also reminiscent of aspects of the Montanist movement, which elevated martyrdom as the supreme aspect of Christian discipleship, and which also afforded women a more enhanced status within the organization of the church than the 'catholic' body had hitherto allowed. It is difficult to know to what extent the martyrs themselves were part of the majority church of Carthage or a smaller sectarian movement of surviving Montanists. Their martyrial 'witness', however, fired the church of this era and made its sense of identity all the more certain, even as the forces of opposition grew more and more severe.

Cyprian of Carthage (200–58)

The African church of the mid-third century is
revealed to us in an especially clear light by the
surviving letters and short treatises of one of the
early bishops of Carthage. Cyprian was a successful
rhetorician and man of political influence who
(like Justin) was converted to Christianity by the
personal influence of an old presbyter around
AD 245. He resolved to adopt a life of celibacy and
simplicity, and gave away a large fortune in social
aid to the townspeople. As a result, he was
immediately thrust into the limelight, for the
people acclaimed him as a new Christian leader
and benefactor, and very quickly he was elected
as a presbyter, and then bishop of the city. His
theological works are interesting as examples of
how a recent convert began to make Christianity
understandable to himself in the process of
preaching it to others.

His rapid rise to leadership made him an object
of envy to several of the leaders who had been
passed over, and for the rest of his life his period
of governance over this important African church
was controversial. The conflict was made worse by
the fact that the Roman authorities in the time of
the Emperor Decius opened a persecution against
Christians that demanded public sacrifice to the
gods of Rome on pain of legal penalties. Its effect
was to cause many Christians in the community to
fall away. Some sacrificed to the gods, others
bribed officials to give them certificates saying
they had sacrificed, even though they had not.
Cyprian, who was a marked man because of his
social prominence as well as his role as Christian
bishop, withdrew from the capital and directed
church affairs from hiding.

The persecution was soon over, but the clergy
of the church of Rome sent a letter to Africa
denigrating Cyprian's caution as unworthy of a
bishop. The ideal of martyrdom had, as it were,
been rejected. The Roman clergy called him (using
the words of a parable of Jesus about good and
bad shepherds – cf. John 10) a 'hired man' who
had no care for the flock. Cyprian made a counter-
argument that the Lord had sanctioned flight from
one city to the next in the case of persecutions (cf.
Matthew 10:23), and that seeking out martyrdom
was not required of the faithful, only patient
endurance if one was captured. His return to the
city after the persecution waned caused much
unrest. He wished to apply some sanctions to
those who had offered sacrifice to the old gods by
refusing them communion in church, but his strict
policy was undermined by others in the leadership
who turned to the 'confessors' for guidance
instead of the bishop. These were those who had
been imprisoned or punished in the persecution.
They were regarded now as having a status
comparable to martyrs; their stand against the
authorities had shown that, if necessary, they
would have offered their lives to remain faithful.
The confessors recommended a more lenient
approach to those who had lapsed from
Christianity in fear of their lives, and the stage
was set for great disruption in the affairs of the
North African church.

Cyprian's writings from this time became
classic letters about the role of the bishop in the
church. His work also considers, for the first time
specifically, the issue of how church unity can be
guarded in the complexities of social life. For
Cyprian, the church is a great 'sign of unity'.
This unity reflects the cosmic atonement won by
Christ in the world, and the church cannot be
divided among itself and still proclaim its central
message of divine reconciliation which it must
embody if it is to be faithful to the gospel. In
this context of argument he defended his own
behaviour, distinguishing caution from cowardice –
exemplifying, as the saying goes, that 'discretion
is the better part of valour'.

The work he produced on this topic, *On the
Unity of the Catholic Church*, became a standard
reference for later generations in the Eastern as
well as the Western Christian world when they
wished to consider the spiritual significance of
unity among Christians. For Cyprian the true
church possesses the abiding presence and gifts of
the Holy Spirit; those who break from it, whatever
the reasons, lose the validating power of the Spirit
of God, and their sacraments (he is thinking of

◆ A 6th-century mural depicting Cyprian (on left).

attached to the 'spiritual' communion of the faithful, but rather an essential embodiment of the physical and moral salvation won by Christ. The church was not only the sign of salvation in the world, but also the focus of the ongoing work of the saving Spirit. Cyprian's model of church unity became a highly influential standard for the ancient churches. In our time, when Christianity has been divided into a bewildering array of factions and denominations, his central point to the argument – how a divided church is a contradiction in terms – is perhaps even more significant than when these books were first written. Soon afterwards, another persecution began under the Emperor Valerian. Cyprian was arrested, and when brought for trial he confessed his Christian faith and refused to sacrifice to the false gods. He was beheaded and so ended his days as a martyr.

The Christian tradition of Alexandria

If the churches of northern Africa were marked by a character of passionate enthusiasm, then the churches around Alexandria, at the mouth of the Nile, were to become famous for their development of Christian intellectual life and mystical theology. Alexandria was one of the most important centres of secular learning in the ancient world. Its library held precious texts, and its medical schools were world renowned. It was also probably the largest centre of diaspora Judaism then in existence and had a distinguished record of Jewish intellectual life. The Christian community in Alexandria, from an early time, had learned from this ambience.

By the late second century we see in the city a remarkable character, now known as Clement of Alexandria (c. 150–215), who functioned as a teacher of philosophy in this city full of philosophers. He strenuously presented the religion of Christ as the highest fulfilment of all the varied philosophies of the ancient world. Christ

baptism especially) are completely invalid. He was echoing some of the theology of Irenaeus, but on a more practical level. His writing, like that of the apostolic fathers, shows how the actual church organization was regarded by Christians of the time. It was not merely a bureaucratic apparatus

was the highest truth present in all true insight, and the universal centre and goal of all existence. Clement taught that Christianity was a religion capable of being lived on many varied levels. One could approach Christ through a simple life, observing the moral requirements laid down in the gospels, and either stay content with this or from that point enter into the deeper mysteries by studying the scriptures until one came to glimpse the esoteric mysteries offered by Christ to the initiated. Clement's Christianity is a system, one of the earliest forms of systematic thought about Christianity, offered in a trilogy of three closely related writings: *The Exhortation to Greeks*, *The Pedagogue* and *The Miscellanies*. Each volume takes the reader further into his overarching cosmic Christianity, and probably represents the varied levels of his instruction offered to pupils in Alexandria.

The first volume is an attempt to interest outsiders and provide simple moral arguments why right living is necessary and how Christianity can fulfil society's need for a true religious philosophy. The second volume concerns guidance in living the ethical life amid temptations and difficulties. He describes how the Word of God informs all created order, but most especially the human mind and heart, and how the ethical life is a progressive 'ordering' in a person's life which allows the true self to emerge. The true self, for Clement, is in harmony with the divine Word of God, and this harmonious encounter anticipates the union with God on a higher level, which the gospel offers as its deepest level of truth. *The Miscellanies* is meant as a book of higher aphoristic wisdom for advanced pupils. Clement challenges the insight of his Christian students and encourages them through an array of riddles and clues to think out the higher implications of religion and philosophy: it is like a book of 'case studies'.

This beginning by Clement was taken to new heights by one of his successors in the Alexandrian church: a man who was undoubtedly the greatest intellectual the early church ever produced, and one of the most influential thinkers ever to shape

the future of Christianity: Origen of Alexandria. There were several Christian teachers, at Alexandria and Rome particularly, who were representing Christianity as a mystical other-worldly religion. Some of them were heavily influenced by oriental traditions of the illusory (or even corrupt) nature of the material world, and so wished to represent the gospel story as a mythic and symbolic account of the struggle of good against evil. This complex movement, which can be noticed in Christianity from earliest times, has often gone collectively under the name of 'Gnosticism', a word that connotes higher knowledge or initiated insight (see box, p. 44). Many aspects of the Christian Gnostic systems were so anti-material that even the physicality of Jesus was held in suspicion by some groups. Early bishops such as Irenaeus and Ignatius had warned against this mythical de-historicizing trend, but the Christian Gnostics were among the church's first intellectuals and had an irresistible influence in the very way they were prepared to think out

◆ **Engraving of Origen from 1584.**

implications outside the text of the scriptures. To them the Christian communities who used only the scriptures to articulate their religion seemed underdeveloped. Thinkers such as Clement and Origen tried to present an acceptable form of 'Christian Gnosis', holding firmly to the historical tradition of the gospels, the centrality of Christ's redemptive work within the created order, and to the identity of the creator with the God of salvation (a link that many Gnostics had severed, instead seeing the creator as a hostile God and the redeemer as a deity who rescued creatures from the punishment of material imprisonment). While the Gnostics tended to cut off the Old Testament from the New, and radically distinguished the God of Israel from the Father of Jesus Christ, the Alexandrian school fought diligently to preserve, and explain, the problematic unity of the whole biblical corpus.

Origen of Alexandria (c. 185–254)

Origen was the first great Christian thinker to write extensively on the principles of biblical interpretation in the church. For him, the Bible was a book of mysteries. Every word was significant. God had inspired the biblical text from centuries past. In it he had placed the story of creation, and even intimated mysteries that had taken place before the human race had been born. The biblical text appeared at times extremely strange and even unworthy of the great majesty of God. This was largely its mysterious design. God had set the text as a threefold 'sacrament'. It was meant to teach historical realities about God's existence and his plan of salvation for an elect people. But it was also meant to be read at a higher level for the moral truths it contained, such as the basic requirements not to kill or commit adultery, and the more advanced requirements of the gospel. It was also meant to teach those who had a mind open to the inspirations of the Spirit the higher mysteries of the divine life.

To sustain his point that the Bible had this threefold progressive character, Origen used an allegorical method. Stories in the scriptures which seemed to have a straightforward reading were, in his system, also charged with secret meanings of a symbolic order. The ultimate story contained within the Old Testament and the gospel parables was the cosmic story of salvation: how God saw his creation fall away from its spiritual destiny, lose itself in the material order, and decline so far from spiritual wisdom that the divine Word had to come to earth to call spiritual beings back to their true selves. Those who live in accordance with Christ's commandments now rise up once more to spiritual maturity, through prayer and the increasing purification of their spiritual intelligence. For Origen, all the stories of the Bible contained this higher tale of spiritual ascent hidden within the narrative. Even those stories which seemed to have a straightforwardly simple historical point (such as the capture of Canaan, or the description of the temple rituals) were full of higher mystical revelation. Origen was so influential in his 'spiritualized reading' of the scriptures that this pattern of interpreting the sacred books became standard in the church even though it was moderated (and often rejected) by successive generations of Christians.

Origen represents the final triumph of the so-called *Logos* theology. For the early church Jesus was the eternal Wisdom of God who had patterned the creation in its very origin, and who, accordingly, could be found in the fabric of the cosmic order as the central pole around which all existence turned. In Origen this all-embracing Christ mysticism was also given a profoundly personal and passionate intensity. He speaks often of 'my Jesus'. He retells the story of the Song of Songs, where the young bride is desperately seeking her lover in the night-scented orchards, in an allegorical way that makes it read as an account of the Christian soul seeking the passionate love of the *Logos* within its deepest essence. Origen has been called the 'father of Christian mysticism' and indeed there is hardly any great Christian intellectual of the early period that comes after him (especially in the Eastern church) who does not owe him a great debt.

Eastern monasticism: the desert fathers and mothers

In his writings Origen insisted that the human spirit could ascend to the presence of God only if the turbulent desires of the body were brought into check. He was an ascetical thinker. He saw the body and mind and soul as so intimately related that spiritual progress could only take place if the body was disciplined, and the mind was purified by study. His writings were highly influential in the century following him, when the movement of ascetics that soon came to be called 'monasticism' began. This movement was discernible in the earliest days of the church, and was particularly influential in Syria, where celibacy and ascetical forms of life were expected as a normal part of Christian activity from the newly baptized. By the fourth century the movement had developed in the Syrian countryside and the semi-desert lands around the Nile in Egypt. Christians were leaving the towns and searching out places of solitude. The quest for solitary asceticism led to the new name of monk (*monachus*) or 'solitary person'. The early monastic movement, as tradition recounted it, was summed up by Antony.

Antony was a moderately wealthy Christian in Alexandria who one day heard the gospel being read which spoke about possessions: 'Sell all you have and come follow me' (Mark 10:21). Antony took this literally, and sold all his property, dispersed it among the poor, and left the city. He eventually made his way into deeper and deeper solitude, where his fame as a Christian hero for a new generation began to spread. He attracted disciples to his radically simplified lifestyle, and soon he emerged as a Christian teacher of the practical ways to achieve a high standard in a Christian lifestyle. Disciples began to gather around him, themselves seeking a 'solitary' life, and so the monastic movement soon had two forms: one in which a person lived in complete seclusion, sometimes being approached for wise

The Jesus prayer

The earliest indications of monastic spirituality represent extreme simplicity and, at least among the Coptic teachers, a dedicated attempt to change one's mind and heart by constant recitation of short texts from the scripture. These 'sentences', favourite short passages of biblical texts, were repeated as short prayer invocations, or incantations, throughout the day and used to simplify the mind and imaginations of the early monks. It was a method through which they tried to calm the restlessness of their minds and hearts so that they could focus on the presence of God in their lives.

The repetition of these short texts led soon to the establishment of the most famous of all monastic prayers, which became one of the main spiritual practices of the Eastern church: the practice of the invocation of the name of Jesus. The monk would slowly repeat the same simple prayer many hundreds of times as he went about his daily business: 'Lord Jesus Christ, Son of God, have mercy on me a sinner.'

To this day the 'Jesus prayer' is used both by Eastern Christian monastics and lay people as an important form and method of prayer; a way to focus attention on the task of sustaining a prayer life across a longer period of the day than the formal times of fixed prayers. The phrase is repeated slowly in groups of a hundred invocations (centuries).

spiritual advice, but generally committing themselves in extreme simplicity of life to dispossession, celibacy and constant prayer; the other in which a group of monks gathered in a loose form of community around a famous teacher. The older teachers became known as the

◆ **Antony the Hermit, by an artist of the medieval Tuscan school.**

Lives and sayings of the desert mothers and fathers

Books began to circulate in the early church telling the stories of these 'heroes of the desert'. The tales are simple and direct, with all the colour and directness of folk tales. They were gathered into two forms: the 'wise sayings' of the desert elders who gave advice about the spiritual life, and the stories about their lives. The Lives became the successors to accounts of the Christian martyrs, and as the time of persecutions was now clearly giving way to a period when Christians were in the social ascendancy (soon to have a publicly pro-Christian emperor after 312, Constantine the Great), the exploits of the monks were used to capture the popular imagination as a kind of replacement heroism. The manner in which the martyr was thought to have powers of intercession was replaced by the conception of ascetical monks as holy intermediaries with God, people who could heal the hurts of the heart and soul and pray for the forgiveness of sins for ordinary Christians.

The first widely popular Life of a monk was the Life of Antony written by Antony's contemporary, Athanasius (c. 296–373), the Archbishop of Alexandria. This was soon translated into Latin and had as much popularity in the Latin world as it did in the Greek. The concept of the Lives began a large-scale practice in subsequent centuries for hagiographies: tales describing the exploits of saints. These focused on ascetical feats and were full of references to exorcism of demons and other miraculous powers exhibited by the new generation of ascetic saints. Many later generations have regarded them as unhistorical, and even distasteful in their emphasis on ascetical renunciation. Used with caution, however, these later hagiographies provide

'old men' (Abbas) who emerged almost as a parallel authority structure to the bishops of the Christian communities in the cities. At first the episcopal city churches and the nomadic or rural monastic communities were quite separate, but throughout the fourth and fifth centuries the monastic movement gained such popularity and importance in Christianity that it more or less successfully took over the role of the bishops, and by the fifth century more and more of the important bishops directing the church were

important evidence about the state of the life of the churches of the so-called 'Dark Ages', and offer an interesting view of the manner in which society at large still (like the generation of the gospels) regarded power over demons as a principal prerequisite of an authentic religion.

The following extracts from the collection of tales of the desert fathers and desert mothers give a flavour of the whole. These sometimes moving and sometimes fantastical stories proved to be immensely popular as folk-tale collections serving to inspire the early Christians. Some have described them as the last example of wisdom literature that Christian Egypt produced.

◆ **A 3rd-century Coptic relief of two saints holding a cross.**

Tales of the desert fathers and mothers

Thieves once came into an elder's cell and said: 'Whatever you have here we have come to take away.' And he said to them: 'Take whatever you see my sons.' So they took up all that they could find in his cell and left. But they overlooked a little bag that was hidden in the cell. So the old man picked it up and followed after them shouting: 'My sons, you forgot this! Take it with you.' And the thieves, touched in the heart at the marvel of the elder's patience, brought everything back into his cell and all of them did penance, saying to one another: 'This is indeed a man of God.'[12]

One of the brothers went to the cell of Abba Arsenius in Scete and looked through his window. He saw the old man as if he had become a single great flame. (Understand that the brother was worthy to look upon such things.) So he knocked, and the old man came out and questioned him: 'Have you been knocking long? Did you see anything?' The brother said: 'No.' So Abba Arsenius talked with him for a while and then sent him away.[13]

The holy mother Syncletica used to say: 'A treasure that becomes public knowledge is quickly spent up. Just so a virtue that is commented on and publicly known, is soon destroyed. Just as wax is melted in the fire, so is the soul made feeble by praise and soon loses the resilience of its virtues.'[14]

◆ A Coptic painting on wood of Abba Mena with Christ,
dating from the 6th or 7th century.

contexts, became more and more represented by its radical element: those who demanded a strict abstinence from sexuality and marriage and possession of worldly resources. The renunciation of the world was elevated as a central principle of the ascetical movement, and this spirituality of renunciation or asceticism became a dominant aspect of Christianity from the fourth century to the present, coming to mark all manner of Christian attitudes to ethics and politics and spiritual reflection. In the late medieval Reformation, the Western church made this religious philosophy one of the major points of contention, so much so that in the Latin world monasticism is now largely restricted to Roman Catholic Christian experience. In the Christian East, however, monasticism retained its mainstream influence over the church at large, and nearly every spiritual writer of the church after the fifth century wrote from the presuppositions of a monastic lifestyle.

The cult of the saints
(4th century onwards)

The increasing focus on the importance of saints in the life of the church led to a growing desire to preserve their tombs. Devotion to a range of saints became a definite mark of the churches from the late fourth century onwards; this had expanded from the first category of martyrs into a wide variety of other holy men and women who were believed to have exemplified fidelity to Christ during their earthly lives.

From the sixth century onwards the cult of relics came to have great popularity among Christians. The relics, the physical remains of saints from the past, were believed to be specially potent focal points of spiritual power. The grace of the Lord, once at work in the earthly life of the saint, was believed to be operative even after death in the form of heavenly intercessions which the saints could bring about – especially for those who prayed before their tomb, or who venerated their memory. In time, popular Christian devotion to the saints

drawn from the ranks of the monks. To this day, in Eastern Christian practice, a bishop must be a monk.

The monastic movement gained a third form very soon afterwards. Several leaders organized communes of Christian radicals. The key element was a celibate lifestyle, an ascetical form of daily routine revolving around manual labour, and the recitation of the psalms. Monastic founders, such as Pachomius or Shenoute in Egypt, formed large colonies of monks, and from then on there was a threefold pattern of Christian ascetical life: *Eremitic* (living alone in seclusion), *Lavriotic* (living in a small colony of hermits) and *Cenobitic* (living in a large household of monastics who shared common resources on a daily basis). These varied patterns became popular all over the ancient Christian world.

The Christian religion, which had in earlier times been especially successful in urban

culminated in an intense devotion to the one regarded as the greatest of all the saints: the mother of Jesus. Devotion to Mary began to gain popularity, especially from the late fourth century onwards. She was given the title *Theotokos*, or 'Mother of God', and devotion to her was used to express the church's deep sense that her son, Jesus, was no mere man but the incarnation of the divine Word himself. Her title, Mother of God, was used as a theological definition in its own right, to defend this fundamental Christian allegiance to the notion of Jesus as the divine Son of God, incarnate. It was the subject of intense theological debate in the international synod of bishops held at Ephesus in 431 – the Third Ecumenical council.

The monastic movement in the West: Benedict (c. 480–c. 550)

Benedict, from the Italian town of Nursia, has been called 'the father of Western monks'. He is the subject of the whole of Book II of Gregory the Great's treatise *The Dialogues*, and it is from this later study of a pope who admired him as his chief monastic hero, as well as from the famous Rule of Benedict, that his fame as the leading monastic legislator of the Western church has grown.

Despite this, Benedict remains a shadowy figure for historical research. He was born sometime around 480. He was the son of a wealthy landowner in the region of Nursia and was sent to Rome to complete his studies in the capital. He discovered in the city a vital society of ascetic Christians which had been active for a century, and probably learning from them, though certainly reacting to his own experiences of life in the capital, he soon turned away from the city as a hopelessly corrupt place. As a result of this strong aversion to life in Rome, he abandoned his studies and left for the village of Enfide (now Affile) where he wanted to pursue a solitary monastic life.

◆ **Fresco of Benedict in Sacro Speco, Subiaco, in the Romanesque style by an unknown artist.**

Benedict founds his first monastery

Soon after this move he decided to settle in the region around the town of Subiaco, forty miles east of Rome. For a time he became the leader of a communal monastery near Vicovaro and then decided to found other monasteries, to work out in practice his own ideas on the best way to organize the daily life of a dedicated monk. In the neighbouring Aniene valley in Italy he founded, within a short space of time, twelve monasteries each with twelve monks, each one under the authority of its own abbot (the father of the monastic household, who had the governance of all the spiritual lives of his monks). His model was obviously influenced by the example of Jesus and his twelve chosen disciples.

There was, at first, some resistance to his ideas of monastic order. In the East, monasticism had allowed a great degree of freedom to its individual adherents. Benedict's ideas were far more organized and disciplined. In response to some agitation directed against him, Benedict left Subiaco around 529 and settled on the remote mountaintop of Monte Cassino, where he used the ruins of an abandoned pagan temple and built a monastery that still functions today as the centre of the worldwide Benedictine monastic family.

The Rule of Benedict

It was on Monte Cassino that Benedict probably decided to set into a written form his Rule, which has since evolved into the blueprint for most of the older monastic families of the Western church. The Rule of Benedict was probably based upon the earlier prototype of the 'Rule of the Master', as well as on a variety of other monastic writings such as the works of Basil and excerpts from the desert literature, but Benedict's gift for simplicity, humanity and order gave these writings a new dynamism and life for the Western church.

Benedict conceived of the perfect monastic life as one lived in a community which was the family of God. He had little time for solitaries or for daring acts of asceticism, which he saw as self-indulgent and undisciplined. The exploits of the solitaries, as witnessed in the Lives of the desert fathers and mothers, were subordinated in his system to the ongoing daily round of quiet and humble asceticism that he believed a community life lived in poverty, chastity and obedience would foster. For each of his monastic houses he envisaged a large degree of autonomy, with a society and communion provided by common adherence to the same principles outlined in the Rule. Liturgical life would play a central part in the daily activities of each monastery, and the abbot, or the single 'head of the family', was given a great prominence. His authority as interpreter of the Rule was the last word in all matters of spirituality and discipline.

Benedict thus propelled to the foreground the virtue of obedience. For him, obedience was the ultimate ascetical act: a monk in promising strict obedience to the monastic father, under God, was almost laying down his life in a sacrifice of self-will, for the sake of the kingdom of God. Allied to this centrality of common obedience was the demand for stability (*stabilitas loci*). The Rule required that each new entrant to monastic life would promise to stay in the house he entered until death. Before this many monastics had followed a common Eastern practice of wandering from monastery to monastery. Benedict regarded these 'nomads' as seriously detrimental to the discipline and order of a religious household, and was determined to abolish the practice. His daily life in the monastery was conceived as a synthesis where a balance of intellectual, spiritual and manual labours took place.

Benedict's legacy

In the course of subsequent centuries Western monastics came to regard the Benedictine Rule as a wise and compassionate synthesis of all that was best and admirable in the monastic movement. The Benedictine monasteries became veritable oases of culture and spiritual life for a church entering the difficult period of its progressive alienation from the protection of the Roman emperor in Byzantium. They were often the last repository of culture for the long centuries between the Classical Age and the Renaissance. For this Western society owes to Benedictinism an inestimable debt.

Christian liturgical development

In times past, the history of the church has largely been studied in terms of the stories of significant personalities or religious controversies, and understandably so, given the nature of the surviving evidence. The various large councils or international gatherings of bishops that occurred from the fourth century onwards, later called the Ecumenical Councils, offer a chart of the development of Christian thought, especially in relation to central doctrines about Christ and the trinity. It is, however, the quieter aspects of Christian life, precisely those things which escaped controversial attention for a long time, that perhaps more intimately and accurately capture the essential spirit of the early Christian community's life of prayer. Surely there could be no clearer indication of this than to study the form of the primitive Christian liturgy, the church's public prayer and worship services.

The New Testament contains many indications of important aspects of the prayer life of the earliest Christians, especially the focus on the memory of the passion of Jesus, and communal gathering around the table at which the death and resurrection of the Lord were celebrated in a 'Eucharist' ritual. The precise details of early Christian liturgy, however, remained more 'off the page' than on, in the centuries following, and it is not until the fourth century that more and more details were given of Christian liturgy, as the church emerged more publicly. The indications of the early liturgies that remain, in the writings of the second-century writer Justin, the third-century North African author Tertullian, the Roman theologian Hippolytus, the Egyptian Bishop Serapion (whose altar book survives from the mid-fourth century), and the compilation of Syrian liturgical practices that survived in the texts called the *Didache* and the *Didascalia Apostolorum*, all provide a body of early data about the Christian liturgy that show how it was taking shape in the years immediately after the New Testament. The

stress in formal Christian prayer meetings was on the giving thanks to God for the life and salvation offered to the world in Jesus. The *Didache* describes the essence of the early eucharistic prayer in the following terms:

> We give you thanks, Our Father, for the holy vine of David your servant, which you have made known to us through your child Jesus. To you be the glory unto the ages. We give you thanks, Our Father, for the life and knowledge which you have made known to us through your child Jesus. To you be the glory unto the ages. Just as this broken bread was scattered upon the mountains and then was gathered together into one, so may your church be gathered together from the ends of the earth into your kingdom. For yours is the glory and the power, through Jesus Christ, unto the ages.

The communion of bread and wine, of course, was rooted in the account of the last supper, and the 'giving of thanks' became symbolic of the whole spiritual journey to God. The rite thus came to be called the Eucharist (Greek for 'thanksgiving'). The bishop of the community was expected to lead the gathering of the whole community on the Lord's Day (Sunday or the first day of the week). In honour of the resurrection he organized the reading of scriptures and psalms, received offerings of bread and wine from the people, set aside offerings of money which would be applied to the relief of the poor, and then gave thanks in an extended and extemporized prayer over the bread and wine, which were then distributed among the community as a communion (a sharing or fellowship) in the life and death and resurrection of Christ.

Hippolytus, an early third-century Roman church leader who wished to reform the manner of prayer in his city, suggested how the bishop ought to offer thanksgiving. He did not wish to restrict the freedom of the Christian leader to extemporize (for this was precisely his primary role as leader of prayer, to witness to the faithful the quality of his own gift or *charism* as a new Moses, a new

prophetic channel of grace to the community
under his spiritual care), but Hippolytus wished
to point out what common elements ought to
characterize a good Christian at prayer, and so
although his work, *The Apostolic Constitutions*,
probably does not represent any 'particular' liturgy
from the ancient church, it certainly represents
an exemplar, or common character, of the formal
prayer of the early communities. These early
eucharistic prayers are moving in their simplicity
and spiritual intensity. The bread of Christ's body
is taken as a symbol of unity and ingathering.
The Eucharist emerges as the central action of
the Spirit which creates and ever renews the
vitality of the disciples of Jesus and constitutes
them as the elect church of God.

As time went on, especially from the fourth to
sixth centuries, the liturgy gained in ceremonial
grandeur. The text of some of the intercessory

◆ **Blessing the bread, a 3rd-century Christian wall-painting
from the Catacombs of St Paul and St Marcellius in Rome.**

prayers remained alive, however, to the times when
there were suffering members of the community
who must not be forgotten. In the Eastern liturgy,
there exists to this day a moving prayer of loving
and communal intercession that vividly reflects
the conditions of the ancient church, as well as
the conditions that characterize the essence of
Christian prayer that seeks to go beyond itself:

O Lord, accept this sacrifice for the forgiveness
of sins of all our community in Christ, and for
every troubled and grieving Christian soul that
has need of your mercy and help; for the
protection of this nation and those who live
here and for the peace and stability of the holy

John Chrysostom (c. 344–407)

John Chrysostom was born of prosperous parents in Antioch and baptized in his early twenties. He was ordained soon afterwards, eventually (and against his will) being made Archbishop of Constantinople in 398. His powerful preaching there alienated the imperial family, though it also earned him the name 'Chrysostom' (literally 'golden mouth'). He was exiled in 403 by the emperor and died in exile in Armenia.

His preaching conveyed a powerful and vigorous Christian spirituality which sought to hold together prayer and ethics, this world and the next. In particular he defended the poor, often referring to Matthew 25, and urging his hearers to see Christ among the poor around them (this too was not popular with the ruling families). His reflections on love capture the heart of his spirituality:

> We need to see that the love of God is intertwined with our own love, and bound to it as though by a chain. And so it is sometimes said that there are two commandments, and sometimes only one; for a person who accepts the first (to love God) cannot but accept the other (to love one's neighbour) also.[15]

◆ **Emperor Nicephorus III Botaniates (1078–81) flanked by John Chrysostom (on the left) and the Archangel Michael; on vellum.**

churches of God; for the salvation and help of those who serve and minister zealously and with the fear of the Lord; for ascetics, for missionaries and for travellers; for the healing of the sick; for the deliverance of the enslaved; for those taken before tribunals or condemned to the mines; for those in exile or want; for those who hate us and for those who love us; for those who are merciful to us and who minister to us, and for those who govern us.[16]

Latin Christian poetry
(4th to 6th centuries)

Other non-controversial literature was also being written. Some was written to represent Christianity to the elite classes. This was especially true of Christian poetry, which became increasingly popular after the fourth century. The New Testament itself contains many hymns within it.

These are mainly short pieces reflecting on Christ and his redemptive work. They were possibly part of the liturgies of the apostolic age from very early times. The main body of Christian poetry was a later literary development. The lawyer, rhetorician and politician Ambrose (c. 339–97) was converted to Christianity in the fourth century and soon became the bishop of the major imperial capital of Milan. He was the first important writer to bring into Latin church practice the Eastern custom of singing hymns, and so he composed several short and pithy poems for recitation in church. One of his works, 'Eternal Maker of All Things', celebrates the first light of day with a prayer of repentance:

> *Jesus look upon our frailty,*
> *and, seeing us, set us right.*
> *If you look down our sins shall cease*
> *And guilt be washed by tears.*

This new style of writing hymns proved so popular that Ambrose set off a veritable avalanche of imitators. Some of them might not be great literature, but they proved to be very memorable, even though their original authors are now unknown:

> *O Blessed Light, the trinity,*
> *Source of all true unity,*
> *Now, as the fiery Sun declines,*
> *Pour in our hearts your light that shines.*
> *At dawn we sang you hymns of praise*
> *As evening falls our prayers we raise.*
> *It is our glory to serve you, our glory,*
> *Giving glory through all the ages.*
> *Amen.*[17]

Ambrose's influence was so great that he is called the 'father' of Western hymn-writing. His authentic hymns celebrate the changing hours of the day in the light of Christ's sanctifying presence within them. He was trying to evoke the sense of the Lord's presence for Christians in the various occupations and changing stages of normal daily life. Some of his compositions retain their dynamic character in translation, but the Latin originals were rhythmically powerful and were tailor-made for congregational chanting. It was the beginning of a long and successful practice of Christian devotion that is still popular in the churches today. The Christian hymn proved to be a dynamic medium of prayer. It has often been said that if you really wish to know the heart of a Christian's belief, look at the hymns that he or she sings regularly.

Other important Latin Christian poets in the fourth to sixth centuries were Prudentius, Paulinus (Bishop of Nola) and Venantius Fortunatus. Their works all tend to consecrate the passing hours of the day to the service of Christ. They strengthened the tendency to divide up the day into various 'hours' of prayer: notably the evening and morning services of psalms and hymn-singing which extended the eucharistic rite and became the basic structure of all subsequent Christian worship services.

In the Greek-speaking world, religious poets such as the sixth-century Romanus the Melodist or the eighth-century John of Damascus composed a large body of lyrical poetic theology that was like a carpet of biblical allusions, retelling the scriptural stories in a manner designed to captivate and entertain the popular imagination.

These religious songs, along with psalms, eventually came to form the warp and woof of the Eastern church's structure of the offices of prayer. In Eastern Christian tradition the services are still, in general practice, sung rather than 'read', and there can hardly be a Western church service that does not contain some singing. The church's poetry, generally speaking, combines 'high theology' with a deep sense of personal devotion. In harsher times, especially later in the Eastern church when Christians were to find themselves under oppression and religious restrictions of many kinds, these hymns preserved their sense of identity even when schools of thought and the very churches were forcibly closed.

Augustine of Hippo
(354–430)

In the Western church at the end of the fourth century a formative age was coming to an end and a long period of 'consolidation' was about to settle in, as the fabric of Western society began to break down under harsh economic and political conditions. In the middle of the fourth century the heart of the Roman imperial administration moved eastwards to Constantinople, leaving the Western provinces at times feeling defenceless before the increasing pressure of waves of Germanic tribes crossing the Danube into Roman territory. It was to be a long period of dissolution of many aspects of Roman societal life in the Western world, changes which were to affect the church intimately.

In this period, Western Christianity witnessed the appearance of its greatest theologian of the early period, an intellectual whose writings dominated all Western Christian thought from his own time even to the present century: Augustine. His life story became famous from the autobiographical account of his early years – his *Confessions* – in which he recounted the story of his conversion to the service of Christ. This story, so vividly written and with such fine regard for the inner workings of the human mind and heart became, almost from the outset, one of the classics of Western world literature.

Augustine believed that the inner state of a human spirituality (the secret heart of a person) was a mirror of the divine presence of the Creator. God, in making the world, had partly imaged himself in it. In making the human heart he had particularly imaged himself. As the Word of God was himself the image of the unseen God (cf. Colossians 1:15), so the human soul was an image of the Word. This had been a traditional Christian understanding of the biblical doctrine of the image of God in previous Christian times, but Augustine, coming from a philosophical background of late Platonism, took the idea to new psychological depths. The act of introspection

Controversy over divine grace

In their own time Augustine's *Confessions* began a large debate about the way in which God works in human lives. This became known as the controversy over grace. The divine grace was seen by Augustine as the power with which God initiated every movement of a human creature towards the good. All that was good in a Christian was attributable to God. All that was defective was attributable to the person's failure. A Christian thinker in Rome, a Briton named Pelagius, thought that such a view denigrated the need to preach a more simple and robust call to Christians to 'self-improve'. Pelagius was a famed moral preacher and from this perspective he criticized Augustine for his doctrine of the complete pre-eminence of God. Pelagius argued that Christ had set moral standards and challenged his disciples to meet them. If God had set those standards then they were surely attainable by men and women of good will. From a local disagreement this controversy grew to become one of the largest arguments over theology in the church of late antiquity. The implications of the controversy over grace surfaced again in the late medieval period and were a powerful element in the Reformation divisions of Western Christendom as Protestant and Catholic theologians interpreted Augustine's legacy in different ways. The following passage illustrates part of Augustine's teaching on the necessity of divine grace for salvation:

> We, for our part, maintain that the human will is so divinely aided towards the doing of righteousness that, besides being created with the free choice of our will, and besides that teaching which instructs us how to live, we also receive the Holy Spirit, through which there arises in the human heart a delight in and a love for that supreme and unchangeable Good which is God: and this arises even now while we still walk by faith and not by sight. This pledge, as it were, is

given that a person may burn to cling to the Creator, and be on fire to attain to a share in the true light, so that we may derive our blessedness too from the one who has given us our being. A person's free choice effects only to lead into sin, if the way of truth lies hidden. And when it is made plain to us, what we should do and to what we should aspire, even then unless we feel delight and love for the prospect, we do not perform our duty, do not undertake it, and do not attain to the good life. But, so that we may experience this affection, 'the love of God is shed abroad in our hearts', not by means of 'the free choice which springs from ourselves', but rather 'through the Holy Spirit which has been given to us' (Romans 4:5).[18]

Augustine's critics argued that his great stress on the divine grace coming before, during and behind every human activity for the good, effectively diminished or even destroyed the human freedom of will that was absolutely necessary for moral choice. Augustine took the criticism seriously but countered with the idea that there can be no freedom at all, only psychic and material enslavement to evil habits, unless God's grace first gives us that freedom, which then we exercise. So, even the freedom to choose the good is a gift of God. Without it humans can only have one course of action, and that is enslavement to the bad, which is the negation of all freedom. He argued this position in his great work on religion, culture and politics, *The City of God*:

> It does not follow that the saints (in heaven) will not have free choice, because sins will no longer have the power to attract them. On the contrary [our will] shall be more truly free when we are set free from the delight of sinning, so as to enjoy the steadfast delight of not sinning. For the first freedom of choice, which was given to the Man (Adam) when he was created standing upright, conferred the ability

◆ **Augustine preaching to his disciples, shown in an illustrated text of *The City of God* dating from the 11th or 12th century.**

not to sin and also the ability to sin. But the new freedom (of the City of God) will be far more powerful, simply because it will not have the power to sin: and this not by its own unaided natural ability, but by the gift of God...

> The first immortality, which Adam lost by sinning, was the ability not to die; the new immortality will be the inability to die. In the same way, the first freedom of choice conferred the ability not to sin, whereas the new freedom will confer the inability to sin... We would surely not conclude that because our very God is unable to sin, therefore God has no freedom of choice?[19]

became, as it were, the primary means of divine awareness. The story of a life, therefore, was also the account of the secret workings of divine providence in the innermost fibres of the heart, and within the tangled webs of world history. Christian autobiography could thus carry a force comparable to a biblical narrative. When he released his life story, it had an impact on the church far greater than all of his works of theology, important though these were.

Augustine in his mid-life became Bishop of Hippo Regius, and produced a veritable stream of theological works concerned with almost every aspect of the church's life. He wrote on the nature of the church, on sacraments, on biblical interpretation, on the nature of the trinity, prayer and grace (see box, p. 68). His works were so profoundly to impress his Western readers (though he never gained anything like a comparable reputation in the Eastern church) that he became undoubtedly the most important single thinker in Western Christianity since the time of the apostle Paul. He was the supreme theological authority for the church after him, and his works were copied and commented on as the theological foundations of the medieval world.

Despite his massive influence on the intellectual and theological structure of Western Christianity ever after him, Augustine remained vivid in popular imagination largely for his autobiographical accounts in the *Confessions*. Here, with searching honesty, described in a luminous prose style, he tells of his heart torn between groping towards God and living for decadence, until that moment when God seized him, and in a moment flooded his life with grace and mercy.

There are few ancient authors who can so lyrically describe the inner processes of God's rescue of the human heart from its own perversities:

O Lord you are eternal, but you will not always be indignant with us (Psalm 84:6) because you take pity on our dust and ashes. You saw me and it pleased you to transform all that was misshapen in me. Your spur rode into my heart,

giving me no peace until the eye of my soul could discern you without mistake. Under the secret touch of your healing hand, my swelling pride subsided, and day by day the pain I suffered brought me health, like an ointment which stung but cleared the confusion and darkness from the eye of the mind.[20]

Augustine's *Confessions* had a major influence on most forms of Western Christian spirituality that were to follow, and gave the concept of 'conversion' a high priority in the West, comparable in importance to the notion that, correspondingly, organized most of Eastern Christian spiritual thought – the idea of transfiguration in Christ. He died after he had asked for the psalms to be painted on the walls of his room so that he could recite them on his deathbed. As he lay dying the Vandal nomadic warriors were besieging the city walls of Hippo Regius, a sign of much that was to happen in succeeding centuries in the West as the old Roman order gave way before the waves of tribal migrations from the East: the so-called 'Dark Ages' were beginning.

Gregory the Great
(c. 540–604)

Augustine was a complex individual, and a genuine intelligence of towering proportions. His ecclesiastical readers, however, were not always up to the mark. The last great figure we shall look at in this present chapter, Pope Gregory the Great, shows the way things were heading. Gregory was no great intelligence himself, but an admirable compiler, and a political administrator of genius. Theologically, he simplified Augustine's works and left them in a state which could serve as an authoritative handbook for generations to come.

◆ **Opposite: Gregory the Great and his deacon, Peter, from the Codex Cassinensis (1022–35).**

Politically, he stepped into the breach of the declining power of the Roman political protection of the Western provinces and made sure that the church would be able to stand, in future years, as a more independent agent. In strengthening the prestige of the church in this way, and demonstrating himself as one of the most capable of all the previous bishops of Rome, Gregory left the papacy in a position of holding an incredibly enhanced reputation. He began the process that was to lead to the increasingly centralist role that the Roman church would exercise in the administration of church affairs in Western Europe afterwards. In many respects Gregory the Great is the last pope of the ancient world, and the first of the medieval period.

He believed he was probably the last pope before the end of the world, so apocalyptic and doom-laden seemed his own society. In spite of his apocalyptic mindset he collated a highly influential guide to pastoral care – a kind of handbook for Christian rulers: princes and bishops. It became the pastoral theology of the later Christian world, and the source of most of the church's understanding of its role in society in the early Middle Ages. In this book, called the *Pastoral Rule*, he sketched out the essential requirements for Christian leaders: that they should give a spiritual model for all who looked to them, in their own lives, and especially in the care they gave to breaking the bread of the scriptures to all the different levels of their audiences within church and society. Gregory stressed the clergy's duty of effective preaching, and laid out an influential guide to a biblical style of teaching, simplifying the rules of exegesis so that the biblical text could be readily 'applied' to the congregation's needs by the preacher. In many respects it was his work that was influential in making Western Christianity a religion that readily turned to the biblical text and wished to live by it. In this respect he was the father of the medieval biblical mind, and reformed Protestantism restated his biblicism in the late medieval period, with profound effects on Christianity which are apparent to this day.

Conclusion

This is only a partial account of the spirituality of the early church in this patristic period. It was a time of great changes, many of which were to become 'constitutive' of practices and attitudes in Christianity for centuries to come. Chapter 4, 'The Eastern Christian Tradition', continues many aspects of this patristic period with its discussions of the work of the Greek monks and ascetics, and of the great patristic theologians such as Athanasius or the Cappadocian fathers. Insofar as there are common themes in the spirituality of this early period we could perhaps sum them up as follows.

There was a profound Christ-centred devotion, visible in all the writings we have looked at, one that expressed itself in a recurring desire for unity and socially active charity. Ascetical ideas were much expressed. The patristic period was highly realistic about the vacillating state of the human heart, and its constant tendency to decline from single-minded commitment to the gospel and its values. Facing their own inadequacies, they kept a deep sense of trust in the mercy of their God. Confident of their own forgiveness by a gracious Lord, they tried to live out the sense of unity and wholeness to which they believed all creation had been newly called in Christ Jesus. As their own faith was new (the majority of the church still being composed of recent converts) so their sense of evangelism was active and alive. It all contributed to making them a generation of Christian believers who can command our interest and admiration even today.

2

Celtic and Anglo-Saxon Spirituality

(4th to 10th centuries)

Douglas Dales

Timeline

Christianity took root in Roman Britain quite early, perhaps in the second century AD. There were several martyrs during the era of persecution, notably Alban, and by the fourth century British bishops were attending church councils in the Mediterranean area. Archaeology has also uncovered evidence of Christianity in villas in Dorset and Kent, and in the Water Newton and Mildenhall treasures. When the Roman government and armies were withdrawn in 410, the church remained, even though organized town life and industry rapidly collapsed.

◆ Figure of Christ, with 'Chi-rho' symbol in mosaic, from the 4th-century Roman villa at Hinton St Mary, Dorset.

Patrick (c. 390–c. 460)

The only Romano-British Christian about whom anything substantial is known is Patrick. He grew up as Roman rule was coming to an end, and was kidnapped from his father's villa by pirates to work as a slave in the west of Ireland. After some years he escaped, returning to Britain to become a priest. His suffering in exile deepened his faith, and he felt called by God to return to the very people among whom he had been held hostage.

◆ Patrick and a king, miniature from a manuscript, the *Golden Legend of Jacopo da Voragine* (c. 1260).

I heard in my dream the voice of those who were by the wood of Voclut which is near the western sea, and this is what they cried as with one voice, 'Holy boy, we are asking you to come and walk among us again,' and I was struck deeply to the heart and woke up.

Patrick remained for the whole of his ministry as a missionary bishop to the Irish, despite misgivings among his own people at home in Britain. Fortunately two of his writings survive – a letter to a British chief who had abducted some Irish whom Patrick had recently confirmed, and his *Confession*, which is an autobiographical defence of his activities and vocation. In this he echoes directly the writings and vision of the apostle Paul. He believed that God had called him to preach the gospel to people on the very edge of the known world, and that his sufferings among them had

Martin of Tours – monk, bishop and missionary (316–97)

In both Celtic and Anglo-Saxon traditions, the figure of Martin of Tours looms large. The way the story of his life was told moulded the way other saints' lives were described, and his example served later as a role model for many bishops.

He was a Roman soldier before becoming a Christian monk in the middle of the fourth century. His generation was still haunted by the memory of persecution, and vulnerable to the hostile presence of paganism at the door of the church.

Around the year 371, Martin became bishop of Tours, where he remained until his death in 397. He continued to live the life of a monk while a bishop, which caused some resentment among the other bishops of Gaul. His lifestyle was ascetic and simple, and he was an active missionary among his own people, often challenging pagan shrines and even destroying them.

Martin also played an important political role, challenging the Western emperors for their corruption and cruelty. He was a prophetic figure, who attracted the active support of many wealthy landowners and their families. He was remembered for his many miracles of healing and exorcism, and for his active sympathy towards the poor. One of the most famous of these actions became a popular symbol of him throughout the Middle Ages: Martin riding into a city while still a soldier, and cutting his cloak in half to give it to a beggar, who later appeared in a dream as Christ himself.

brought him very close to Christ. His was a living martyrdom in obedience to the missionary command of Jesus in the gospels. He was also a man of deep contemplative mysticism:

> Another night I saw him praying in me earnestly with groans. I was in amazement, wondering who it could be who was praying within me; but at the end he told me it was the Spirit: 'He who gave his life for you; he it is who speaks within you.' At that I woke up full of joy.

◆ **St Oran's Chapel, Iona Abbey, Scotland. The 12th-century chapel and the burial ground are dedicated to Oran, a cousin of Columba and one of his twelve companions on the voyage to Iona.**

The spread of monasticism

Despite heavy pressure from the invading Germanic tribes in the lowland east of Britain, the British church remained strong in the western parts. Many British fled across the sea to Brittany and northern Spain, while connections with southern Ireland remained close. By the year 500, small monasteries were being established all along the western British coasts, directly influenced by developments in the Mediterranean, Egypt and Syria. A major centre of this monastic life was at Llaniltud Fawr in south Wales. The Life of St Samson, from the early sixth century, tells the story of how Samson was educated there by Illtyd (450–535), before leaving first for Ireland and Cornwall, and then for a very active missionary career in Brittany.

In the next generation, Gildas (c. 500–c. 570) played an important role in fostering monastic discipline in Ireland and Wales. He composed the first penitential codes, which were practical tables of guidance for priests hearing confessions:

> The Lord calls blessed not those who despise their brothers, but the poor; not those who hunger and thirst just for water in order to disparage others, but who genuinely seek righteousness; not men who cause war, but those who endure persecution for the sake of the truth.

The Irish church became a brilliant centre of Christian culture and monastic spirituality. The most famous of its leaders was Columba (c. 521–97), an Irish prince who took refuge in western Scotland in the middle of the sixth century. On the island of Iona he created a monastery whose influence was to bring Christianity to much of Scotland in his own time, and in the next generation to northern England also. His life was recorded by one of his most able successors as abbot, Adamnan, writing a century after his death. More immediate impressions are found in ancient Latin and Irish poetry remaining from the monastery after his death:

> *Beloved of God, he lived against a stringent rock,*
> *a rough struggle, the place of his bed.*
> *He crucified his body, left behind sleek sides;*
> *he chose learning, embraced stone slabs, gave up bedding.*
> *He possessed books, renounced fully all claims of kinship:*
> *for love of learning he gave up wars and strongholds.*[1]

This captures well the spirit of Irish monasticism. It was both ascetic and educated, and often sought in exile abroad the life of a pilgrim, seeking the kingdom of heaven. Columba himself was a charismatic figure, believed by many to be a healer and prophet; and a visionary in touch with heaven, visited by angels, being transfigured by light.

Many followed Columba's example, most notable of whom was Columbanus (c. 543–615). He left Ireland for the continent with some companions, and founded famous monasteries at Luxeuil in France, and at Bobbio in Italy. The intensity of the monastic life which he fostered made a lasting impression on the French church, and led to many new churches being created in marginal areas and among the Germanic invaders in the north of the country. Columbanus was a poet, teacher and scholar, and in touch with Pope Gregory the Great. He was fearless in his approach to the 'heathen', as well as towards rulers and fellow churchmen. His inner life was inflamed by

◆ **Figure of St Luke from the Canterbury Gospels, sent by Pope Gregory the Great from Rome with the first missionaries.**

The spirit of Irish monasticism

Monasticism struck a deep root in Irish society, and abbots became more important than bishops. Families of monasteries mirrored the tribal structure of the land, and many religious houses became important centres of learning and art. Latin was studied to a high level, and outstanding manuscripts were created, such as the *Book of Kells*. Throughout the early Middle Ages, the travels of Irish monks took them far and wide across Europe, and their diligence did much to disseminate Christian and classical learning. The search for the 'desert' led them to colonize with hermitages many isolated hills, islands and headlands, often now remembered in place names, and to generate a strong tradition of saints' Lives, of which the Life of St Brigid is the most famous. They regarded nature as a mirror of God's glory, as these words of a ninth-century poem express:

> *A hedge of trees surrounds me,*
> *A blackbird's voice sings to me;*
> *Above my lined book*
> *The call of birds chants to me.*
>
> *In a grey mantle from the topmost bush*
> *The cuckoo sings:*
> *Truly may the good Lord protect me;*
> *At peace I shall write under the green canopy.*[2]

Irish monasticism never lost its vigour and power of renewal. In the eighth century, the Culdees flourished; these were groups of hermits, often thirteen in number, living an apostolic life of great austerity in Ireland and Scotland. The ardour of their vision is well captured in these maxims from a Rule associated with them:

> *Be always naked in imitation of Christ*
> *   and the evangelists.*
> *Have a mind steadfast for white martyrdom.*
> *Forgiveness from the heart for all.*
> *The measure of your prayer shall be until*
> *   your tears flow.*

This 'white martyrdom' of ascetic life and exile for Christ made its mark on the Welsh church too. The richest memory of these centuries are the numerous and beautiful carved stone crosses found throughout Wales, and the many place names that recall often obscure saints. The Welsh and English churches influenced each other throughout the Anglo-Saxon period. In the eleventh century, Rhigyfarch composed the Life of St David at the important centre of Llanbadarn Fawr. A lovely illuminated psalter also remains from his hand.

John Scotus Erigena (c. 810–77)

The most outstanding luminary of Irish Christianity was John Scotus Erigena. He migrated to the court of King Charles the Bald in France, where he presided over the school at Laon. There he taught Greek, and contributed to various controversies over predestination and the nature of the Eucharist. His knowledge of Greek enabled him to translate works of Dionysius the Areopagite, Maximus the Confessor and Gregory of Nyssa. His own most important work, *Periphyseon*, combined neo-Platonic and Christian understandings of God and creation:

> For God only truly exists by himself, and he alone is everything which, in the things that are, is truly said to be. For none of the things that are truly exist in themselves: true being comes only by participation in him.

◆ **Opposite: Christ, from the book of Matthew in the Book of Kells.**

the Spirit, believing that the 'love of God renews his image in us, wounding us by his love':

> Be kindled with the fire of divine love, that the flame of his love, the longing of his so-great charity, would mount above the stars, burning forever within. For he who loves drinks of him: he drinks who burns with the love of wisdom.

The spread of Christianity

Christianity came to the Anglo-Saxons from two main directions: from Rome and France, and from Iona and Ireland. In 597, missionaries arrived from Rome, led by Augustine and sent by Pope Gregory the Great. They arrived in Kent and established their headquarters at Canterbury. From there they were able to extend Christianity to London, and later for a time to York. The vision behind the mission was the pope's: it is said that it was kindled when he encountered some English slaves on sale in Rome, and declared them 'not Angles but Angels'. Gregory's example and teaching supported the mission, and moulded the ethos of the earliest English church (see box, p. 81). By letter and in his writings he offered practical and spiritual guidance: 'miracles are the greater the more spiritual they are'; people are drawn by them to 'inward grace'. The preaching of the gospel is about 'the healing of souls, because it is in them that we are made in the image of God'. To a bishop in Alexandria he reports the progress of the mission, reminding him that 'your prayers are where you are not, your holy works are evident where you are'. The first generation of English Christians regarded him as their father-in-God. Gregory's *Dialogues* endorsed the spiritual authority of Benedict of Nursia, whose Rule became increasingly respected among monasteries throughout the seventh century. Gregory's *Pastoral Rule*, which outlines the principles of exercising Christian authority, also proved highly influential in England during the Anglo-Saxon centuries, being translated into English by King Alfred the Great.

Christianity came to the northern Anglo-Saxons from Iona at the request of the king of Northumbria, Oswald, who had himself become a Christian while in exile on Iona. Aidan was sent from Iona to be a missionary bishop, and he founded a monastery upon the tidal island of Lindisfarne. Bede, a biblical scholar and monk of the eighth century, in his *Ecclesiastical History* paints a glowing picture of Aidan as a man of 'outstanding gentleness, devotion and moderation'. He tells famous stories of Aidan's simplicity of life, and resilience towards kings and nobility:

> Such were his love of peace and charity, temperance and humility that his soul

◆ **Statue of Aidan on Lindisfarne, the Holy Island in Northumberland.**

Gregory the Great, apostle of the English (c. 540–604)

When Gregory sent the prior of his own monastery in Rome to lead the mission to England in 597, he was acting in an unprecedented way as pope. He was also fulfilling a personal vision, which he sustained in the midst of the many pressing crises which beset his reign. Anglo-Saxon Christians regarded him with profound affection and respect as the apostle who had brought them to Christianity. The first Life of Gregory was written by a monk at Whitby, and Bede saw himself as Gregory's disciple.

The English church was profoundly marked by the ethos of Gregory's teaching and approach to authority. He was a skilled preacher of the gospel, and also a spiritual guide to the contemplative life. His *Pastoral Rule* was used as a practical guide to Christian leadership by bishops and kings. From Bede to Aelfric (c. 955–c. 1020), Anglo-Saxon scholars and artists developed the vision of Christianity which Gregory expounded.

Gregory gave to the papacy the title 'Servant of the servants of Christ'. But this concept also applied to any who exercised authority in the church. He was concerned to enhance the authority and confidence of all the many bishops to whom he wrote, and he gave precise guidance to Augustine in Canterbury as to how he should proceed in the conversion of the English. The most important thing was that there was to be no compulsion, nor were pagan shrines to be destroyed automatically; instead they were to be transformed into Christian churches.

Gregory also articulated, and to some extent resolved, the tension between the active and contemplative aspects of Christianity. He was an aristocrat-turned-monk, reluctantly drawn into discharging the highest office of the Western church at a most difficult time in its history. The desire to pray seemed to conflict with his sense of duty. His spiritual writings, which did so much to mould Western monasticism over many hundreds of years, demonstrated how, by faith and love, a Christian might be able to discover perfection in the midst of imperfection.

◆ **Gregory the Great at his writing desk; German ivory panel from the end of the 10th century.**

triumphed over anger and greed, and despised pride and pomp. He was diligent in study and prayer, and by his priestly authority reproved the proud and mighty. His tenderness in comforting the weak and protecting the poor was constant.

◆ **Cuthbert's pectoral cross.**

Cuthbert (d. 687)

In the life and cult of Cuthbert, the Roman and Irish currents of Christianity among the Anglo-Saxons were reconciled and united. He rapidly became the foremost of the English saints throughout the Anglo-Saxon centuries.

He was born in Northumbria, and became a monk at Melrose in 651 after a vision of the ascent to heaven of the soul of Aidan. His early spiritual life was moulded by his spiritual father, Boisil, from whom he also learned how to be an evangelist among his own people. He used to spend many weeks away from the monastery among very poor and dangerous villages in the hills, where he was a charismatic preacher. From Melrose he moved to become prior at the monastery of Lindisfarne.

After a time he felt called to become a hermit, and for a while he combined this with his pastoral duties by retreating to a tiny tidal island beside the monastery. But in due course he withdrew altogether to the island of the Inner Farne some miles away, which Aidan had earlier used for a retreat. He gave this reason for his seclusion:

> Even if I could possibly hide myself away in a tiny dwelling on a rock, where the waves of the swelling ocean surrounded me on all sides, and shut me in completely from the sight and knowledge of men, not even there should I consider myself to be free from the snares of this deceptive world; but I should fear lest the love of wealth might tempt me and somehow still snatch me away.

Cuthbert built a small chapel and cell on the Inner Farne, and a shelter for visitors. He delighted in the bird life of the island, and laboured at raising some crops. His contemplative life did not cut him off from his own community at Lindisfarne, nor from the wider life of the church in Northumbria. In 685 he was persuaded by the king to become a bishop, much against his inclination, and he operated from Lindisfarne until his death in 687.

◆ **The news of Cuthbert's death on the island of Inner Farne is conveyed to the island of Lindisfarne using burning torches; 12th-century English manuscript illumination, *The Life of St Cuthbert*.**

Cuthbert's significance was as great in death as in life. He died of tuberculosis in the midst of a March storm on the island of Inner Farne, and his body was buried at Lindisfarne. In 698 they wished to translate his remains into a shrine in the church; when they opened the tomb they found that his body was completely incorrupt. This was regarded as a great miracle: the holiness of the saint during his life, and the completeness of his suffering before death, had steeped his body in the presence of the Holy Spirit. It became a sign of the reality of the resurrection, and the nearness of eternal life, and miracles continued to occur at his shrine. Large fragments of the carved oak coffin created at the time of this first translation still remain in the treasury of Durham Cathedral.

Cuthbert's life and memory were also commemorated in writing: first by an unknown monk of Lindisfarne, then by Bede himself in a poetical life and in a later prose life; and also in Bede's *Ecclesiastical History*. Beautiful artefacts were laid in or near his tomb: his pectoral cross and portable altar, precious silks and later vestments, and possibly also the famous *Lindisfarne Gospels* which may have been commissioned by and produced at Lindisfarne to adorn his cult. All these treasures accompanied the relics of the saint on their prolonged pilgrimage from Lindisfarne to Durham after the sacking of the monastery by the Vikings at the end of the eighth century.

Bede (c. 673–735)

Most of what may be known about the church of the English during these early years is found in the pages of Bede's *Ecclesiastical History*. He was a monk who lived for almost all his life in the double monastery of Wearmouth-Jarrow on the banks of the River Tyne. He was a great teacher and scholar, and is the only Englishman to be regarded as a Doctor of the Church. His *History* is his most famous work, and at the time of King Alfred the Great it was translated from Latin into English. He wrote it towards the end of his life, collaborating

with other churchmen in England far and wide, and notably with the church at Canterbury. But Bede was not only an historian; he had keen interests in mathematics and science, in poetry, and above all in the study of the Bible. He was a theologian whose spirituality was influenced very much by the teaching of Gregory the Great. This prayer at the end of his *History* encapsulates his vision:

> I pray thee, merciful Jesus, that as thou hast graciously granted me to drink deeply and sweetly from the word which tells of thee; so wilt thou of thy goodness grant that I may come at length to thee, the fountain of all wisdom, and stand before thy face forever.

◆ **Bede writing, from an English manuscript dating from c. 1175.**

The *Lindisfarne Gospels*

The *Lindisfarne Gospels*, which are now in the British Library in London, are the most outstanding work of Anglo-Saxon art. In the middle of the tenth century, a priest called Aldred recorded the tradition that:

> Eadfrith, Bishop of the church of Lindisfarne, originally wrote this book, for God and for St Cuthbert, and for all the saints whose relics are in the island. Ethelwald, also Bishop at Lindisfarne, impressed it on the outside and covered it by his great expertise. Bilfrith, the hermit, forged its ornaments, adorning it on the outside with gold, gems and silver-gilt, all of the purest metal. Later, I Aldred, an unworthy priest, glossed it in English between the lines with the help of God and St Cuthbert.

The gospels are written on vellum derived from a large number of calves. It was a work which commanded extensive material resources, including colours imported from the Middle East. There are fifteen elaborate and fully decorated pages. Each gospel is faced by a full picture of its author, and starts with an intricate and majestic decorated initial. Its style is derived from Ireland, where there are gospels of comparable artistry. The many birds incorporated in the designs may reflect the natural life of Lindisfarne.

This was a sacred text to be laid on the altar, or carried in procession, and it became the single most precious treasure at the shrine of Cuthbert. A glimpse may be gained of the spirituality lying behind such artistic dedication and skill in these words describing an Irish craftsman at work in a Northumbrian monastery, which had been founded from Lindisfarne:

◆ **Ornamental page from the *Lindisfarne Gospels*, illuminated by Bishop Eadfrith in Lindisfarne Monastery.**

He could ornament books with fair marking, and by his art made the shapes of the letters most beautifully, one by one, so that no modern scribe could equal them. It is no wonder if a true worshipper of the Lord could do such things, when already the Creator Spirit had taken control of his fingers, and had fired his consecrated mind towards the stars. Thus he taught his brothers so that they might seize the light from above.

Bede describes in some detail how the English church was built up in the seventh century by such notable bishops as Wilfrid and Theodore. Wilfrid was an energetic Englishman who for a time ruled as bishop over the whole of Northumbria. Because of numerous quarrels with the king and later with the archbishop of Canterbury, he made several trips to Rome to appeal to the pope. He was an active founder of churches and monasteries who did much to promote the use of the Rule of Benedict. Theodore was a Greek bishop sent by the pope to Canterbury to reform and develop the church in England, which he did with great energy despite his advanced age. He founded an important centre of learning at Canterbury, and one of its most learned pupils was Aldhelm of Malmesbury. Aldhelm was a scholar as learned as Bede, being a theologian and poet of some skill, as well as an active bishop. In his *History*, Bede describes how Christianity began to permeate Anglo-Saxon culture at every level. Symbolic of this is the story of the poet Caedmon at the royal nunnery of Whitby who suddenly found in a dream that he could render Christian theology into Anglo-Saxon poetry.

The missionary impetus

Christianity in England was born of missionary initiative, and in the eighth century the church of the Anglo-Saxons continued the tradition by sending a steady stream of missionaries to the Low Countries and Germany. Foremost among these were Willibrord (658–739) and Boniface (680–754). From Boniface's many letters, a vivid picture may be built up of his activities, his relationships with kings and popes, and his reliance on support from his friends at home. He sought urgently their prayers for the conversion of the Germans:

> We beg you to be instant in prayer to God and the Lord Jesus Christ, that they may convert the hearts of the pagan Saxons to the faith. Have pity on them, for their repeated cry is – 'We are of the same flesh and blood as you!'

Boniface worked closely with several popes, and actively reformed the French church, as well as founding monasteries, many of which were led by fellow English men and women. He was killed while on a mission to Frisia on the North Sea coast, and was immediately hailed as a martyr by the English church. His memory was treasured by the next generation of English churchmen working on the continent. The most notable of these was Alcuin (c. 735–804), who sums up well the ethos of this mission from England, which was inspired by the example and teaching of Gregory the Great:

> Faith is a matter of will, not constraint. A person can be attracted to belief, he cannot be forced. The teachers of Christianity must be schooled in the example of the apostles. They must be preachers, not predators, trusting only in the goodness of God.

Alcuin himself exercised a profound influence upon Christian culture and church life on the continent. He was the personal adviser of Charlemagne, and with his support worked actively to revive Latin learning, making many copies of the Bible, and preserving Christian and classical texts. He also left his mark on the liturgy of the Western church.

Alfred the Great
(849–99)

The onslaught of the Vikings throughout the ninth century posed the gravest threat to Anglo-Saxon church and society. The kingdoms of Northumbria and East Anglia were destroyed, and half the Midlands was overrun by invaders and settlers. In the 870s, the kings of Wessex were hard-pressed to maintain their independence, and the church of Canterbury was pillaged. The turning point came in 878, when King Alfred the Great managed to defeat a Viking army at Edington in Wiltshire. Thereafter, he and his successors gradually rolled back the Viking threat, and by the middle of the tenth century they had created an united English kingdom under their rule as far as the river Humber.

Alfred was a devout Christian and a self-taught scholar. He took in hand the restoration of morale within the church, and commissioned scholars to translate into English several fundamental texts of Latin Christian theology. His own Life was written by a Welsh priest, Asser, and Alfred includes some biographical details in the prefaces to the translations he inspired. He set a pattern for Christian kingship and leadership, and commitment to education and monastic life, which was to exercise a profound and lasting influence upon the reform and development of church and society throughout the tenth century.

Dunstan (909–88)

The career of Dunstan provides a comprehensive framework for understanding what was achieved in the life of the English church and society in the tenth century. He died in 988, having served as archbishop of Canterbury for twenty-eight years. Immediately after his death he was regarded as the foremost English saint at Canterbury, until the Norman Conquest displaced his memory for a while. It was Anselm who in due course restored his cult there.

Dunstan grew up at Glastonbury, where he was educated by English and Irish scholars. It was an ancient holy place, dedicated to the Blessed Virgin Mary, and formerly a monastery of British foundation. Like many such places it had suffered during the Viking raids, but it was probably restored as a centre of education by King Alfred the Great. From there Dunstan went to Winchester, where he was persuaded by his uncle the bishop to become a monk. After a severe illness he agreed, and returned to Glastonbury to serve as a teacher, and to pursue a contemplative life of prayer under the direction of a holy woman there.

◆ **The Alfred Jewel, now in the Ashmolean museum in Oxford. It portrays Christ as the Wisdom of God; its surround carries an inscription asserting 'Alfred made me.'**

He had connections at court, but was the butt of envy and intrigue, and was about to go into exile in Germany when a new young king had a change of heart, and appointed him to be abbot of Glastonbury, with a view to restoring the Benedictine monastic life. This he did, backed by considerable endowments from the royal family. The footings of some of his buildings have been discovered, and the place rapidly became a lively centre of learning and art. Dunstan himself was a scholar and artist, and also a musician.

After about twenty years as abbot, he fell foul of another new young king, and narrowly escaped death by fleeing into exile in Flanders, where he stayed at the newly reformed monastery in Ghent. The kingdom divided and civil war threatened. During this time Dunstan was recalled to be bishop, first of Worcester, then of London. Another change of king led to his becoming archbishop of Canterbury in 960.

As primate of England, Dunstan presided over many developments in the church, and exercised a steady influence upon the legislation of the country; the Coronation Order in England is largely of his creation. He was in regular touch with the continental church and with Rome, and during his time missions were sent to Scandinavia. He soon gathered around him a congenial group of bishops, some of which were drawn from his own monastery at Glastonbury. They embarked upon the wholesale restoration of Benedictine monastic life throughout southern England and East Anglia. Nearly thirty monasteries were created, many of which lasted until the Reformation. They were regulated by a unique national act of uniformity, which applied the Rule of Benedict to the English situation. This *Regularis Concordia* is a text of great historical interest and spiritual richness, and

Some Anglo-Saxon prayers (c. 9th century)

*O God, the maker and recreator of human
nature, the creator uncreated:
You spread the heavens and founded
the earth;
You planted Paradise and formed man
from the dust.
You recall man from error to the way of life.
You are truthful and without deceit,
You are one and omnipotent, the fountain
of immortality.*

*O Christ, the height of humility and
strength of the weak,
By your humiliation you have raised up
our fallen world;
You permitted the cruel hands of sinners
to raise you on the cross.
I thank you, and pray that you will stoop
to lead me from all self-will.
Draw me from earth to heaven –
do not forsake your sheep,
But carry me in your arms
that I may be found within your fold.*

*Lord Jesus Christ, the way, the truth, the life:
We seek eternal life that you may make us
your friends.
You came from heaven to pour life into
the world;
We know you to be the bread of life,
the loving bond of human hearts.
Grant us peace in our hearts and minds
always,
For you are our true peace, preserve us in it,
O God.
When there is peace, you yourself draw near;
Where you are may your own be also.
Come to us, O Lord, and possess us with
your joy
That we may become a temple for your
Holy Spirit.*

was drawn up and agreed upon at Winchester around the year 970. Its ethos is well captured in this prayer included within it:

*Most loving God,
You brought forth from the rock a spring of
living water for your thirsty people:
Bring forth from the hardness of our hearts
sincere tears of repentance,
That we may be able to weep for our sins and
obtain by your mercy forgiveness.
Listen graciously to our prayers, and deliver
our hearts from all temptations to evil;
That we may become fit to be the dwelling-
place of your Holy Spirit.*

Dunstan's life is full of interest, as his abilities were manifold. Manuscripts remain which he edited, either at Glastonbury or at Canterbury. He was a skilled worker in metal, and the picture which he drew of himself as a monk at the feet of Christ may have been the outline for a creation in metal, or the illumination for a manuscript. In the picture Christ appears, perhaps on the Tor at Glastonbury, as the wisdom of God, holding the budding rod of God's kingdom, with a tablet inscribed with words drawn from the prologue of the Rule of Benedict. In his own hand, Dunstan has inserted a little prayer for protection from 'the storms of the underworld'. This may allude to the conflicts he experienced in his own spiritual life while at Glastonbury, described in

◆ **Picture by Dunstan of himself praying at the feet of Christ, from St Dunstan's Classbook in the Bodleian Library, Oxford.**

the first Life of the saint. He was a deeply contemplative person, who throughout his life had visions of heaven, in some of which he learned music which he later turned into plainchant. For centuries after, the setting called 'Kyrie Rex Splendens' was attributed to him:

Christ our King enthroned on high, whom
the ranks of angels praise sweetly:
always have mercy.
Christ whom the one church throughout
the world praises,
Whom sun and moon, stars, earth and sea
serve:
always have mercy.

O King of kings, our blessed redeemer,
offspring beloved of holy Mary,
By the power of your most precious death:
always have mercy.

Conclusion

The Anglo-Saxons created a kingdom remarkably united and well organized – hence its attraction to the Normans, who took it over in 1066. The English church remained, with its own character and strong monastic core, and in the twelfth century its churchmen felt free and confident to research and affirm their own roots and language. The *Ecclesia Anglicana* created during those four centuries of Anglo-Saxon culture and belief persisted throughout the Middle Ages, to find expression in both the Anglican and Roman traditions until the present day.

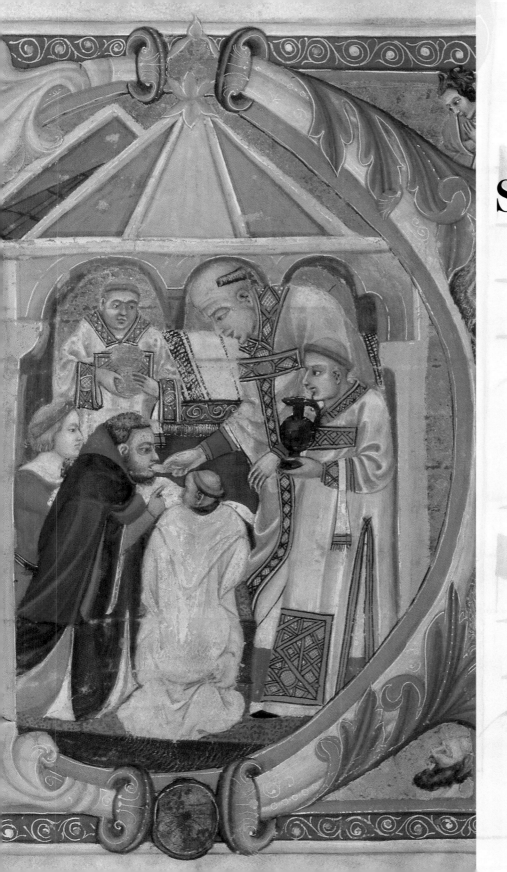

3

Saints and Mystics of the Medieval West

(11th to 16th centuries)

David Farmer

Timeline

A subtitle to this chapter could be 'From Anselm to More'. These first and last personalities of the period from 1060 to 1535 both lived in Canterbury and were famous, one as archbishop of Canterbury, the other as chancellor of England. Both suffered at the hands of Christian kings for their fidelity and their faith, one by exile, the other by execution. There were also significant differences: Anselm, an Italian who became a monk at Bec in Normandy, was soon on a collision course with William Rufus, the king of England. Thomas More was a lay scholar, lawyer and writer, a Londoner and a devoted family man. He, too, was unable to support his king, Henry VIII, in his divorce plans and rejection of the papacy.

During the 400 and more years that separated Anselm and More, society changed greatly, and the church experienced important renewal, especially through the various religious orders. The devastation caused by plagues and wars and the scandal of the Great Schism – when for forty years two rival popes, from Rome and Avignon, were claimants to the allegiance of Christendom – was also a catalyst for change. At the beginning of the period few people were literate; by the end of it many were, especially in the towns which had sometimes grown out of recognition through the impact of trade, defence or even ecclesiastical institutions. The consequent growth of a professional middle class is one of the most important changes in the period.

Anselm, More and many who lived between them showed in different ways the abiding influence of God in their lives. More's human achievements would have been impossible for a layman in 1100; Anselm's might have seemed dated to some in 1535. In all ages, mystics and martyrs are comparatively few, but very significant, as they indicate the development of convictions and values that are challenging to contemporaries. In very different contexts this minority could say with Paul: 'I live, now not I, but Christ lives in me' (Galatians 2:20).

Spirituality of the Early Middle Ages

(1060–1300)

During this long period great changes took place in society. The most obvious of these is the progress of literacy. But the growth of towns (related to educational progress) and the advent of repeated plagues, wars and consequent famines all affected human life and the ways that people related to God, Christ and the perceived or unperceived divine influences in their lives. Side by side with these came the growth in human consciousness, sometimes called individualism, which we all take for granted, with its consequent emphasis on individual mystical experience. Throughout the whole period, the Eucharist, in different settings and perceived in different ways, was the most important daily link between God and man.

Benedictine monasticism

If we look at Christian institutions at the beginning of the period, we are faced with the deep and permanent influence of Benedictine monasticism. Anselm, Peter the Venerable and Bernard are all examples of this. The usually silent example of monasteries dedicated to the public prayer of the whole church, varying considerably in size and wealth, composed of men and women who had chosen this form of consecrated service through a regime of community life in poverty, chastity and obedience, was for long dominant. But, during the twelfth century, variant forms of self-dedication developed: some of these, such as the Austin (Augustinian) and other regular canons, were more concerned with educational and pastoral matters, but others, such as the Carthusian monks, developed a form of greater solitude in community. These last, who presented a life of extreme austerity, flourished to a greater degree during the later Middle Ages, reaching their statistical

maximum in the sixteenth century, by which time both Benedictines and Cistercians seem to have passed their peak. But it is important to note that each of these ways of religious life survived not only into the sixteenth century, but also into our own times, and each has contributed powerfully to the good of the church as a whole through its varied and eminent representatives.

◆ **German illuminated manuscript from 1473, depicting a novice joining a monastery.**

Anselm (1033–1109)

Born at Aosta (Italy), Anselm lived in Burgundy with his mother's family after quarrelling with his father. He was attracted to the monastery of Bec in Normandy, already famous for the wisdom of his compatriot, Lanfranc of Pavia. Here Anselm became a Benedictine monk at the age of twenty-seven. Highly intelligent, charismatic, with a gift for friendship, Anselm soon became prior (an office he held for fifteen years), then abbot for another fifteen years before he was appointed Archbishop of Canterbury in 1093.

He had an intuitive and perceptive mind, mainly concerned with the truths of faith. He saw reason as being at the service of faith and its mysteries, some of which, he believed, could be proved by rational argument rather than by an appeal to authority alone.

His famous 'proof' for the existence of God followed this theme. As God is unique, Anselm believed there must be a unique argument capable of demonstrating that God exists and is the sovereign good on which everything depends, but who himself needs nothing. The very nature of God, expressed in his name, leads to acknowledgment of his existence. His two works on this theme, *Monologion* and *Proslogion*, were written while he was still prior.

Over 400 of his letters survive; so too do many prayers and meditations (see below). These are

characterized by a deep sense of sin, combined with personal warmth and commitment. Some are addressed directly to God, others to individual saints.

Anselm's unwillingness to become Archbishop of Canterbury, his subsequent refusal to accept the anti-pope whom William Rufus supported, and Anselm's resulting exile, are all events familiar to historians. His exile was distinguished by his contributions to the understanding of the mysteries of the incarnation in his book *Cur Deus Homo* and that of the trinity: at the personal invitation of Pope Urban II at the council of Bari, he defended the doctrine that the Holy Spirit proceeds from both the Father and the Son against the Greeks.

Throughout his life he was a persistent and courageous witness to the primacy of the spiritual. In his last years at Canterbury, when the quarrels about investiture had been settled, he devoted himself to a treatise on the origins of the soul. Fortunately we can know many details about this very distinguished man through his Life, written by the English monk Eadmer, his companion, admirer and friend.

◆ **Contemporary statue of Anselm, standing in the grounds of the Monastery of Sant'Anselmo, Rome.**

Extracts from Anselm's 'Prayer to Christ'

Lord Jesus Christ,
my Redeemer, my Mercy, and my Salvation:
I praise you and give you thanks.
They are far beneath the goodness of your gifts,
which deserve a better return of love;
but although I requite so poorly
the sweet riches of your love
which I have longed to have,
yet my soul will pay its debt
by some sort of praise and thanks,
not as I know I ought, but as I can.

Most merciful Lord,
turn my lukewarmness into a fervent love
of you.
Most gentle Lord,
my prayer tends towards this –
that by remembering and meditating
on the good things you have done
I may be enkindled with your love.
Your goodness, Lord, created me;
Your mercy cleansed what you had created
from original sin;
your patience has hitherto borne with me,
fed me, waited for me,
when after I had lost the grace of my baptism
I wallowed in many sordid sins.
You wait, good Lord, for my amendment;
My soul waits for the inbreathing of your
grace
in order to be sufficiently penitent
to lead a better life.

He then proceeds to a very personal consideration of the passion:

So, as much as I can, though not as much as
I ought,
I am mindful of your passion,
your buffeting, your scourging, your cross,
your wounds,
how you were slain for me,
how prepared for burial and buried;
and also I remember your glorious resurrection,
and wonderful ascension.
All this I hold with unwavering faith,
and weep over the hardship of exile,
hoping in the sole consolation of your coming,
ardently longing for the glorious contemplation
of your face.

Consideration follows for Mary and her sorrows at the suffering and death of her Son. This meditation ends as follows:

… Let me be fed with griefs,
and let my tears be my drink;
comfort me with sorrows.
Perhaps then my Redeemer will come to me,
for he is good;
he is kind, he will not tarry,
to whom be glory for ever. Amen.[1]

Traditional Benedictine life, with its blend of prayer, study and work, has long proved attractive and fruitful for many. The Rule of Benedict, famed for its discretion and prudence, is both a spiritual guide and a directory to how the monastic day is spent. The balanced alternation of its principal elements has seldom been bettered as a regime of enlightened self-discipline: prayer in the church several times a day, communal meals, reading in the cloister, work in the garden, orchard and kitchen, or care for novices, guests and the poor. The oft-repeated claim of Benedict that it was a 'little rule for beginners' actually hides the exacting nature of Benedictine obedience, year in and year out, which is the touchstone of the monk's dedication to Christ.

Anselm was an eloquent teacher of this truth and exemplified it in his own life (see box, p. 92). His single-minded commitment to Christ and to the 'Vicar of Christ' (the pope) led him to oppose courageously and persistently the claims of King William Rufus to domination of the church. He was not, however, only a man of obedience; he was also a man of wisdom, friendship and perceptive intuition. His deep understanding of Christian doctrines such as the trinity and the redemption earned him acclaim in his lifetime and nomination as a Doctor of the Church long after his death. He was also the author of prayers and meditations, while his conversations about spiritual matters were recorded by his English biographer, Eadmer. His many-faceted mind, formed by long study of Augustine and other Christian writers, was equally at ease with educational problems (he reproved contemporary abbots for their frequent use of corporal punishment), with the cults of English saints (he recommended the continued cult of Alphege as a martyr for justice), and with the problem of how God could be known by unbelievers as certainly existing from the very concept of God himself. Often regarded as the greatest Christian thinker between Augustine and Aquinas, he was formed primarily by monastic life and the duties of prior and abbot. The late archbishop Michael Ramsey regarded him as the greatest archbishop of Canterbury ever.

Monastic reforms

With the passing of time, Benedictine monasteries sometimes seemed to suffer from their own 'success'. If the latter is regarded in worldly terms, one can point to too much wealth, too close an identification with rulers and aristocrats (who were often the founders of their monasteries), too comfortable a regime. To remedy these imperfections, various reform movements arose in the monastic order, mainly in Burgundy and Italy in the late eleventh century. Numerically, the most important of these was the Cistercian Order. Its most charismatic member was Bernard of Clairvaux (see box, p. 96), but it is arguable that Stephen Harding (d. 1134) was the most important of the three founders of Cîteaux, near Dijon, the first house of this reform. The Englishman, Stephen, was the author of the *Carta Caritatis* and other early Cistercian documents, and it was he who appointed Bernard abbot of their foundation at Clairvaux while still in his late twenties. This reform movement aimed at a restatement of monastic life in its primitive elements of solitude, poverty and simplicity. It was a new start, with monasteries in the country not the town, and with inmates who aimed at following the Rule of Benedict to the letter. Meat was excluded from the monastic diet and manual work was restored to a place of honour. Simplicity of architecture and ornament was fundamental. Even more important in the long term were the legislation about monasteries' relations with each other and the admission of lay brothers into the monastic community, which enabled the illiterate (the vast majority of society as a whole) to become monks. Another factor in the rapid expansion of the Cistercian Order (in England a growth from none to fifty monasteries from 1129 to 1153, some of them, such as Rievaulx and Fountains, of exceptional size) was that their policies of bringing marginal land into cultivation and developing sheep-farming on a large scale met, without intending to do so, the economic needs of a rapidly rising population. The Cistercian expansion took place all over Europe from Spain to Poland and Scandinavia to Italy.

The rhetorical genius of Bernard was partly the cause of this development, and his influence has been significant in every century. A recent biography of him by an admirer has the title *The Difficult Saint*.[2] No such description is attached to Peter the Venerable, the contemporary abbot of Cluny, whose letter of condolence to Heloise, the former lover of Abelard, on the death of the latter, is one of the most moving documents of the medieval period. Bernard's treatise on the love of God is still read with profit nowadays, while his perception of the human characteristics of Christ and his mother with the consequences for the devotional life of believers has proved enduring and beneficial.

The crusades

This series of armed conflicts which began with the preaching of the first crusade by Pope Urban II in 1095 can be considered in several different ways. The crusades can be studied as examples of war history, or as the first attempts to establish a European 'empire' in the Near East, or as attempts by younger sons and the comparatively poor to better their lot in a society which offered few opportunities for doing so.

Here they will be considered as elements of medieval religious sentiment with the goal of Jerusalem in the first place, rather than the aspect of a militant Christendom defending itself against

◆ **A battle between the crusaders and the Muslims, from a 14th-century French manuscript.**

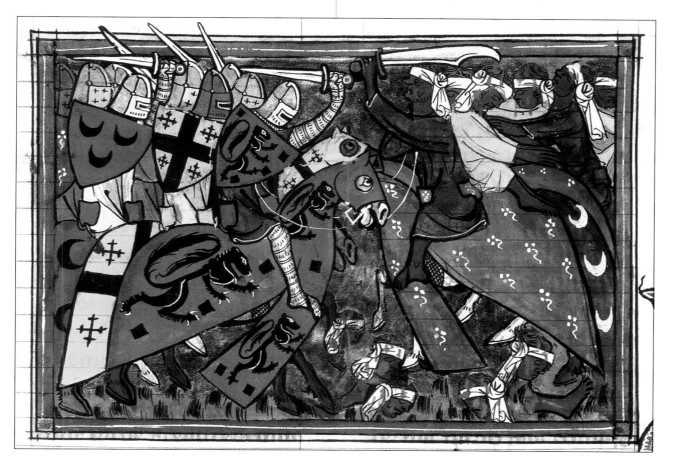

Bernard of Clairvaux (c. 1090–1153)

Bernard came from a family of Burgundian knights. One of his uncles had been on the first crusade, which had achieved its aim of taking Jerusalem for Christendom in 1099. In his early twenties he became a monk at the poor, reformed monastery of Cîteaux, near Dijon in Burgundy, which was in the process of expansion. Bernard brought with him numerous friends and relatives, about thirty in all, who made profession to the abbot, Stephen Harding. Their way of life was deliberately austere: they renounced many traditional sources of wealth and followed a very frugal lifestyle. They aimed at living the Rule of Benedict to the letter, but in point of fact made various modifications which contributed to their phenomenal success. One was the concept of a 'mother-house' of the whole order, from which, directly or indirectly, all the other abbeys were founded. The admission of lay brothers and new methods of farming added to the impetus for growth. Bernard's community of Clairvaux made numerous foundations but still numbered about 700 (including lay brothers) at the time of Bernard's death. By then the order had 400 abbeys, of which over 50 were in Britain.

Personality

Austere yet emotional, Bernard acquired a phenomenal knowledge of the Bible through constant reading. He brought with him from earlier studies a mastery of rhetoric (based on Jerome and Augustine) which makes many of his works a joy to read. His letters are among the most accomplished of the Middle Ages, but their author was sometimes unjust or unfair to those who thought differently from himself, and they bear witness to repeated attempts to obtain the nomination of his own candidates as bishops. Pope Eugenius III had been one of his monks, but Bernard did not always obtain from him all that he wanted. By temperament he was pugnacious, a trait that became clear in his criticism of Cluny, of Peter Abelard and of Gilbert de la Porrée, the last two of whom were respected intellectuals. It must be admitted

that some of the causes for which Bernard fought so hard are less attractive to Christians of our day than of his, but his immense importance as a spiritual writer remains.

Teachings on God

Fundamental to all his teaching is his treatise on the love of God. This starts from the biblical perception that God loved us first, freely and without reserve; hence men should love God without any limit:

> My God, my help, I shall love you as much as I am able for your gift. My love is less than is your due, yet not less than I am able, for if I cannot love you as much as I should, still I cannot love you more than I can, I shall only be able to love you more when you give me more, although you can never find my love worthy of you...
>
> You want me to tell you why God is to be loved and how much. The reason for loving God is God himself; and the measure of love due to him is immeasurable love. He gave himself for us, unworthy wretches. Hence, if one seeks for God's claim upon our love, here is the chiefest: because he first loved us.[3]

Intensely Christocentric and affective in his outlook, Bernard preached warmly about the name of Jesus some centuries before Bernardino of Siena popularized this devotion:

> The name of Jesus is more than light, it is also food. Do you not feel increase of strength as often as you remember it? What other name can so enrich the man who meditates? What can equal its power to refresh the harassed senses, to buttress the virtues, to add vigour to good and upright habits, to foster chaste affections? Every food of the mind is dry if it is not dipped in that oil, it is tasteless if not seasoned by that salt. Write what you will, I shall not relish it if you exclude the name of Jesus. Jesus to me is honey

in the mouth, music in the ear, a song in the heart.[4]

Sometimes the search for God becomes tedious:

When men grow weary of studying spiritual doctrine and become lukewarm, when their spiritual energies are drained away, then they walk in sadness along the ways of the Lord. They fulfil the tasks enjoined on them with hearts that are tired and arid, they grumble without ceasing. If, when we are subject to these moods, the compassionate Lord draws near us on our way… I am sure his happy talk will drive away all tension from the hearer's mind and weariness from his body.[5]

◆ French illuminated manuscript from c. 1490 showing Bernard preaching the second crusade in the presence of King Louis VII of France at Vezelay in 1146.

torrents of grace. She is also star of the sea, uplifted over those who struggle in the stormy ocean of this world: 'When the winds of temptation arise, and you run on the rocks of tribulation, look at that star, think of Mary, call on her by name.'[7]

Teachings on Mary

Bernard wrote also about the saints, and in particular about the Blessed Virgin. Dante called him 'Mary's Bernard'. He praised her both for her role as mother of Christ and as intercessor for Christians. The annunciation was seen by him in terms of all people awaiting her answer to the angel Gabriel, consenting to be mother of the redeemer:

On your word depends the consolation of the desolate… the salvation of all the children of Adam… Make haste to answer the Angel or rather to answer the Lord through the Angel. Say the word and receive the Word.[6]

Elsewhere he describes her as the aqueduct through which the fountain of grace reaches us with drops or

Bernard and the second crusade

Bernard's life became gradually less 'enclosed' and he never lost the knightly instinct for conflict. In his case it was reflected in controversy, with other monastic orders, or with notable thinkers of the time, or with the crusades. He was deputed by the pope to preach the address inspiring the second crusade. His famous sermon at Vezelay united Christian kings and peoples into this common enterprise, which he passionately believed was willed by God. The subsequent military disaster was not his fault, but he was blamed for it and lost much credibility. At the end of his life a preaching tour against Catharism met with only partial success. These reverses need to be placed in perspective. His acclaim as a living saint and (later) as a miracle-worker, not to mention his monastic achievements, led to his canonization in 1174. His treatises and letters reveal his personality and outlook in a way and to an extent seldom matched by other writers.

Islamic penetration. Over the centuries Islam had eliminated many churches in northern Africa, Spain and in the areas of the Byzantine empire; it was this empire's appeal for help to the pope that had triggered the first crusade.

The quest for Jerusalem, with its close connection with the life of Jesus and with Old Testament salvation history, was an aspect of pilgrimage described elsewhere (see below). People were ready to leave all in search of the holy city, thought of as Christ's own city. But if there was to be free and easy access, it needed either Christian rulers, or, at least, effective agreement that pilgrims would not be harassed or killed on the way. This attraction for Jerusalem and the Holy Land led to many relics of earth, trees, stones and so forth being brought back from there to Europe. These were secondary to relics of what was believed to be the True Cross of Christ, brought by the Empress Helena in the fourth century to the Roman basilica of Holy Cross. Church dedications in England and elsewhere to Holy Cross usually reflect crusader interest and links with the orders of Templars and Hospitallers founded for defending or providing care for wounded or sick pilgrims. The principal hospital in Jerusalem was one of the largest and best anywhere and it used the services of Jewish and Islamic doctors.

While realizing the immense importance of Urban's appeal to Christian leaders to cease fighting each other and unite instead against a militant Islam, enemy of all Christendom, it has to be admitted that we have no strictly contemporary account of what he said. Four accounts were written about fifteen years after 1095 and they all reflect developments in crusader ideology since that time. The dominant account was Frankish, but another was German. The first crusade was largely, but not exclusively, Frankish in character, and it is interesting to note that Islamic sources refer to the crusaders as Franks, whom they detested for distracting attention from the real purpose of extending their own dominions into areas ruled by other Islamic leaders. Then, as now, Islam was divided by sectarianism, and, similarly, it was extremely difficult to unite the Christian armies under different leaders with different ideas.

The attraction of Jerusalem, however, was not allowed to become total. Monks were forbidden by Bernard to go on crusade because they had attained Jerusalem ('city of peace') already, in their monasteries. Even more important was the fact that most people were badly needed at home to till the ground and gather the crops. Those who went physically on crusade were always a small minority, and many of them never returned. Voyages into the unknown were often disastrous. Although they and their families found consolation in the belief that they were likened to martyrs and their baptism in the Jordan was regarded as remitting all punishment due to sin, the fact remains that casualties were grievous and widespread. Some of them were the result of popular and fanatical preachers telling the people that they were the poor, and God would prosper their cause even without proper precautions – such as weapons and strategy. On the other hand the official crusade was more realistic in such matters, although the leaders sometimes made crucial mistakes – a problem in all wars.

The euphoria which followed the taking of Jerusalem in 1099 was widespread. Here, it was thought, against all the odds, was a victory for Christ. The massacre it entailed was regarded as being within the conventions of war for the time. However, the pogroms of Jews in the Rhineland on the way were not: Bernard and the papacy vigorously condemned such events.

Later centuries saw the crusades modified – some would say deformed – by political involvement, sometimes against other Christians and their regimes. Nevertheless, a number of saints regarded the renewal of the crusade, with its unitive fervour, as necessary to defeat the current dangers. Crusades against the Albigensians, or against the tribes of the Baltic, were less compelling than the fights to save Austria and Hungary from Turkish invasion. Perhaps the last example of crusading zeal, the battle of Lepanto in 1570 under the leadership of Pope Pius V and Don John of Austria, was one of the most impressive in

◆ *The Battle of Lepanto* (7 October 1571),
by Paolo Veronese (1528–88).

its achievements. This sea battle, in which Spanish, Venetian and papal forces decisively defeated the Turkish navy, broke their power in the Mediterranean.

It is interesting to note that crusading mentality is by no means dead. The Second World War was called a crusade, and even the more recent Gulf War attracted the same rhetoric. In a quite different field, the Red Cross and the Knights of Malta are examples of benevolent organizations which can trace descent from the Templars and Hospitallers of medieval crusades.

Lay illiteracy

One of the many problems associated with investigating medieval spirituality is the illiteracy or near-illiteracy of the vast majority of the population. Up to the end of the twelfth century the clergy had a near-monopoly on literacy. This meant that, on the one hand, clerics filled important positions in government and in teaching which we rightly expect to be filled by lay people today, while, on the other hand, there is very little surviving influence on which to base a picture of lay spirituality. That is why lives of hermit saints are of special importance. Many hermits were lay people and one of them, Godric of Finchale (c. 1069–1170), not only exercised in his later years a considerable local apostolate but also found, through his strong contact with Durham, a friend and confidant, Reginald, who produced a Life of Godric based on their combined memories. This reveals much about Godric's early life as a pedlar, a sailor and a pilgrim to the main shrines of Christendom, as well as details of how he learned a little Latin, built his hermitage, prayed assiduously and experienced visions, natural disasters and unwelcome visitors.

Much of medieval history is inevitably concerned with literate and wealthy members of society, so records of Godric and of Christina of Markyate (c. 1097–1161), who came from a merchant family of Huntingdon, are precious indeed. She was a notable example of a strong-minded young woman, who married unwisely under parental pressure, obtained a decree of nullity, and became a hermit and later a prioress. She was a visionary and became confidential adviser to the abbot of St Albans. She also embroidered mitres as a present to the only English pope, Adrian IV, and owned the St Alban's Psalter, a masterpiece of Romanesque illumination.

Friars

The next milestone in the development of the organized religious life was the founding of the friars in the early thirteenth century. For the purpose of this book we need to concentrate on their two principal orders. Francis and Dominic, the founders, were very different in character and outlook, but each provided a new way of life which attracted thousands of followers. Francis of Assisi (see box, p. 101) is the better known of the two and has inspired much popular admiration in our own times; Dominic, a man of organization and government rather than charisma, made a different but equally important contribution to the needs of the time.

Francis as a young man led a worldly but not dissolute life. He was taken prisoner in a local war against Apulia and was for some time seriously ill. Soon after this he experienced a conversion which led him to care for the lepers and the destitute and also to restore three ruined churches. He sold some of his father's cloth to raise funds, but the bishop of Assisi told him to pay it back. This Francis did, and divested himself of his clothes. Now his poverty was absolute, and he gathered followers around him who preached repentance, peace and salvation. It was unusual for laymen to preach, even informally, outside the churches. Some laymen had tried, but did not entirely avoid heresy in so doing. Francis's orthodoxy and his respect for priests, bishops and popes differentiated him from these movements. He remained a deacon all his life, practised corporate as well as individual poverty, and his truly evangelical message and attitude attracted many.

Francis of Assisi (1181–1226)

Francis, the son of a wealthy Italian cloth-merchant, is probably the most popular of medieval saints. Poet as well as mystic, founder of a brotherhood which became a religious order, his ultimate significance is surely that he, perhaps more than most saints, reflected Christ more extensively. His aim was simply to live the gospel as closely as possible to the life of Christ: in voluntary poverty, in the care of the sick, in preaching to others the message of the gospel. Another characteristic was a love of nature and the whole of creation, which went together with a deep perception of the passion of Christ and its importance. It is especially this last and quite fundamental point that is neglected by some modern portrayals. It may indeed be asserted that Francis has suffered more than most from unperceptive admirers who have seen in him only what they wish to see. It must also be admitted that his followers were deeply divided, that he himself lacked the qualities to govern a numerous and widely spread following, and that the papacy for the needs of the church encouraged his order in a direction which made change inevitable.

In his short life Francis achieved much. His writings are comparatively sparse, but very significant. His *First Rule* is mainly a series of excerpts from the gospel. His famous 'Canticle of the Sun' reflects his love of creation, manifesting God the Creator (see below). Written probably at San Damiano, Assisi, its poetry and praise came into being amid the exquisite scenery of that area.

Francis's final years

Francis's last years were both sad and joyful. The government of his order was in the hands of Brother Elias, but he was able to experience divine mysteries (perhaps as never before) and to draw up his spiritual testament. He inaugurated the Christmas crib at Grecchio (an event of considerable devotional importance), but, even more important, he experienced the stigmata on Mount Alverna in 1224. Bonaventure's Life of Francis describes his astonishment at seeing the seraph:

> At length he understood that this vision had been thus presented to his gaze by divine Providence, that the friend of Christ might have foreknowledge that he was to be wholly transformed into the likeness of Christ crucified, not by martyrdom of body but by enkindling of heart… ▶

◆ **Francis of Assisi, Italian painting on wood from the first half of the 13th century showing the stigmata.**

Forthwith there began to appear in his hands and feet the marks of the nails, even as he had just beheld them in that figure of the Crucified.[8]

These marks could not be entirely hidden, nor could the prophecy about his death be suppressed. He suffered from blindness, but even more from the primitive surgery meant to alleviate his sickness. He died at the Portiuncula, Assisi, at the age of only forty-five.

Francis's legacy

His *Testament* (1226) began with an account of his own sinfulness, but also of his total attachment to the Holy Roman Church and its ministers, and, above all, to the divine mysteries. He then detailed his ideal of evangelical poverty: few clothes, no buildings to be given or accepted, mendicancy and manual work. But there was also a deep concern for orthodoxy, and the local superior was enjoined to guard those who strayed from the way like prisoners until they could be handed over to the cardinal of Ostia. The minister-general and all concerned were enjoined not to add anything to Francis's own words.[9]

The wonderful personality and achievements of Francis did not, unfortunately, prevent bitter quarrels arising among his disciples, especially concerning the interpretation of poverty and its importance. Subsequent efforts, of the Holy See and various Franciscan luminaries, were only partially successful in healing the divisions. In spite of these, the Franciscan Order gave immense service to the church as a whole. It had become much bigger than Francis foresaw, and its many fine churches, especially in Italy, witnessed to the example and inspiration of the one called the 'Poor Man of Assisi'.

'Canticle of the Sun'

Most high, omnipotent, merciful Lord,
Thine is all praise, the honour and the glory and
every benediction, to thee alone are they confined
and no man is worthy to speak thy name.

Praised be thou, my Lord, with all thy
creatures, especially for brother Sun, who gives
the day and lightens us. And he is beautiful and
radiant with great splendour: of thee, most high,
he reflects the glory.

Be thou praised, my Lord, for sister Moon and
the stars, in the heaven thou hast formed them,
clear and precious and comely.

Be thou praised, my Lord, for brother Wind
and for the air, the cloud, the serene and all kinds
of weather, by which thou givest thy creatures
sustenance.

Be thou praised, my Lord, for sister Water, who
is very useful and humble, precious and chaste.

Be thou praised, my Lord, for brother Fire,
by which thou dost illuminate the night; he is
beautiful and joyful, robust and strong.

Be thou praised, my Lord, for our sister mother
Earth, who sustains and rules us, and produces
different fruits and coloured flowers and herbs.

Be thou praised, my Lord, for those who
pardon for thy love, and endure sickness and
tribulation. Blessed are they who endure them
in peace, for by thee, most high, shall they be
crowned.

Be thou praised, my Lord, for our sister bodily
Death, from whom no living man can escape.
Woe to those who die in mortal sin; blessed be
those who are found in thy most holy Will, for
to them the second death will bring no ill.

Praise and bless my Lord, give him thanks
and serve him with great humility.[10]

The order he had founded rapidly attained a total of 5,000 friars, and there were more adherents in the Poor Clares (an order of nuns founded in partnership with the Franciscans), and a third order of lay penitents.

In 1220 Francis resigned from ruling the order, but the last six years of his life contained some of its best-known elements. Making the first Christmas crib, experiencing the stigmata or marks of Christ's wounds in his hands, feet and side at La Verna (1224) and composing the justly famous 'Canticle of the Sun' (1226) should remind us, together with his sufferings of blindness and stomach ulcers, that his life was hard, austere and uncompromising. Unsentimental joy and complete identification with Christ in his sufferings are the authentic elements of Francis's outlook.

Preachers

Francis and Dominic were contemporaries who came from very different backgrounds, but made somewhat similar contributions to the needs of the church in the thirteenth century. Dominic (1174–1221) was Spanish by birth. After his education at Palencia university, he became a canon of Osma and helped staff the cathedral there. He was an Augustinian (or Austin) canon, one of the fastest growing but comparatively unspectacular orders in the twelfth century. At Osma he learned the regular monastic discipline of prayer, work and study under Bishop Diego. Ordained priest at twenty-five, he soon became sacristan and then subprior, and eventually became Diego's chaplain and companion on long journeys, including one to Denmark on a marriage mission for the king of Castile's son. This opened their eyes to the needs of the church in northern Europe and to the dangers of Catharism in the south. These sectaries had flourished in southern France for about fifty years. Their doctrines in their undiluted form were extremely subversive.

Bishop Diego and Dominic realized that what was needed was the example of orthodox itinerant preachers, living in poverty like Christ. At least some of the Cathars were austere, and their heretical beliefs called for serious intellectual refutation. This was provided by Dominic and Diego, who united orthodox teaching with a severely ascetic regime. The Cathars had obtained support from the wealthy, while the orthodox clergy seemed ineffective, both intellectually and spiritually. The so-called 'perfects' among the Cathars included a number of devout women: Dominic founded at Prouille a 'second order' of devout women, whose asceticism matched that of the Cathars and whose convent (endowed by Simon de Montfort) provided a necessary base for the mendicant preaching friars.

◆ *Dominic*, by Bernardo Daddi (d. 1348). Originally a side-panel from a polyptych (c. 1340).

The Cathars

Not all Cathars formally subscribed to the belief that the material world was evil and that two equally powerful forces, of good and evil, were locked in a dualism without resolution. Their teachings – that Christ was an angel with a phantom body who did not suffer on Calvary or rise again after it, that the sacraments were unnecessary, that marriage was condemned (along with the forbidding of meat, milk and animal produce) – were fundamental indeed, with a wide range of practical consequences. These beliefs were too austere for most Cathars, so there developed two classes of believers: the 'perfect' who undertook the whole programme, and the ordinary 'believers' who lived more normal lives but would receive the *consolamentum* or quasi-sacrament when in danger of death. The role of Christ for them was reduced: he had preached good doctrine, but had not suffered redemptive death and resurrection. A number of upper-class heretics and some local rulers subscribed to all or some Cathar beliefs, but the ordinary clergy lacked both the intellectual strength to resist these ideas and the austerity of life comparable to that of the 'perfect'. Diego and Dominic realized the need for intellectual and moral example to be provided by itinerant preachers who, as in the gospel, spoke directly to the people and presented an austere and committed way of life. Their success was varied, but a new way of life was born and soon developed in a much wider context than that of southern France. Dominic himself had no share in the violent and repressive measures adopted against the Cathars, but rather looked to the long-term improvement in the spiritual quality of clerical life for the solution of the problems posed by the heretics.

The Order of Preachers

Dominic's principal title to fame was his foundation of the Order of Preachers. Although the idea first surfaced in southern France, Dominic soon showed awareness in practice of a wider apostolic need than that of reconciling Cathars in Languedoc. When his order was still in its infancy he took the bold step of dispersing his followers, two by two, to Paris, Bologna, Spain and elsewhere. Contact with Pope Innocent III soon followed. This was absolutely necessary for the establishment of an order devoted to preaching, as preaching was regarded as the prerogative of bishops alone, and those to whom the bishops delegated this task. The most important sector was now that in Italy. Dominic worked in both Bologna (where he later died), and in Rome itself, where Pope Innocent III gave him three houses (two for friars and one for nuns), besides providing both guidance and numerous privileges vital for the order's development. Dominic's achievement was to found or, as a modern Dominican has said, to be midwife to the birth of a new institution. Soon the Dominicans' numbers increased dramatically and they worked in Scandinavia, Poland, England and Hungary as well as in mainland western Europe.

Dominic, from the first, saw the importance of strong intellectual life, not only for refuting heresies but also for building up a sound, well-informed spirituality. Dominic was above all a man of prayer, and in an extant treatise suggested different bodily postures for its exercise. He took a prominent part in the foundation of Toulouse university, modelled to some extent on that of Paris. Elsewhere, too, Dominicans were active in universities and a considerable number of their new members came from this milieu, as well as from the new urban professional classes. For Dominicans, learning, preaching and spiritual direction – both inside and outside the sacrament of confession – completed the traditional liturgy, somewhat simplified, which they offered publicly for the needs of the church. They were soon in demand in parishes and at court as mission-preachers and as confessors and directors. They were strongly supported by and improved the quality of spiritual life of the growing professional classes in cities and towns. Among their most famous teachers were Thomas Aquinas and Albert the Great (his tutor). The Thomist synthesis of

◆ *Christ Welcomes Two Dominican Friars,* **fresco by Fra Angelico (c. 1387–1455).**

philosophy and theology has strongly influenced Christian thought from the thirteenth century until the present day.

There is a persistent tradition that Dominic and Francis met each other. Positive historical evidence is lacking, but the tradition reflects a reality that each of their orders learned something from the other and adopted its practices. In the course of time they both emerged as mendicant preachers and teachers, who did much to raise the standards of clerical education in the church as a whole and to foster the development of a more sophisticated laity in the context of greater wealth and literacy in society. While Francis had been concerned for poverty and Dominic for learning, the Franciscans later repudiated Francis's rejection of learning, while the Dominicans adopted something of Franciscan mendicancy, although Dominic himself had practised this and forbade the enlargement of his friary at Bologna.

Aquinas and Bonaventure

In the later thirteenth century, the intellectual giants Thomas Aquinas (c. 1225–74) and Bonaventure (c. 1217–74) (one Dominican, the other Franciscan) contributed decisively to the development of Christian theology and spirituality. While Aquinas emphasized the rational approach, with the influence of Aristotle's philosophy and Augustine's theological penetration behind him, he nevertheless quietly corrected much of the work of his predecessors and produced a synthesis of Christian doctrine of permanent as well as contemporary value. A prodigious worker, who started lecturing in 1252 and continued almost

until his death in 1274 at the age of forty-nine, he taught in Paris, Rome, Naples and other centres. In 1272 he experienced a revelation of God which made all he had written to be 'like straw' in comparison with what he had then seen. This experience in no way invalidated his theological conclusions, which ranged in different works from *Summae*, for theologians, to more homely commentaries on the Creed, the Our Father and the Hail Mary. He died on his way to take part in the Council of Lyons.

His exact contemporary, Bonaventure, lived to take part in the same council, and prepared the work for reconciling the Greeks, but did not live long enough to see Constantinople repudiate it. Like Aquinas he died comparatively young, but not before expounding an affective rather than a rational approach to the mysteries of God. This can be read in his *Journey of the Soul to God*, which soon became a classic. He was also important in the history of the Franciscan Order, of which he became minister-general at the early age of thirty-six. He wrote a Life of Francis (which later became official) and stressed the need for study, and hence books and buildings for the friars to live in to accomplish their mission of teaching and preaching in universities and elsewhere. He rejected the claims of the Franciscan spirituals to prefer poverty to learning, while giving a notable example in his own life of simplicity,

◆ **Above:** *Thomas Aquinas Teaching*, **by Zanobi di Benedetto Strozzi (1412–68).**

◆ **Below:** **Christ walking on the waves from an illuminated copy of** *Meditations on the Life of Christ,* **by Bonaventure; mid-14th-century Italian manuscript.**

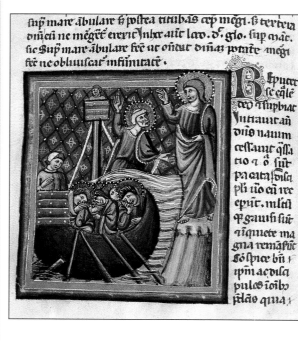

diligence and detachment. He was nominated archbishop of York in 1265, but declined this honour.

Meister Eckhart
(c. 1260–1328)

Born at Hochheim (Thuringia), Johannes Eckhart became a Dominican friar early in life, and studied at Paris and subsequently Cologne (under Albert the Great). He then lectured in theology in various places and held important offices within his order such as prior, and later was provincial of Saxony (1303–11). This summary might easily apply to several other Dominicans, but what made Eckhart famous (or notorious) were his original and speculative theological works. He wrote in both German and Latin, which, together with the intrinsic difficulty of his thought, made interpretation especially difficult. He was accused of heresy in Cologne, but appealed from the bishop's court to the papacy. He died during the proceedings. After his death some of his propositions were condemned in 1329 by Pope John XXII, but with the proviso that Eckhart had recanted and had never had heretical intentions. His writings were and are attractive to many.

Some of the propositions are certainly surprising: he argued that we are totally transformed into God's being; that whatever God the Father gave to his Son in his human nature, he gave totally to the believer, with no exceptions. Whatever scripture says about Christ, he stated, is verified in every good and holy person. But all creatures are simply nothing; that is, not anything or a little thing, but quite simply nothing.

For him, the simple ground of reality, where God and the soul are inseparably one, is the ultimate abstractedness, whose perception is the highest virtue, including charity and humility within it. This produces intimate union with God, from which the Word is born in the soul and the soul gives birth to the Word. These ideas are taken out of context, but indicate something of the difficulties in his writings. Eckhart's thought has been much studied, but the definitive work on him has probably not yet been written.

The Later Middle Ages

(1300–1535)

If the thirteenth century has been greatly esteemed, the fourteenth and fifteenth have usually had fewer admirers. Nevertheless they had many admirable spiritual writers. Ruysbroeck, Suso and the Rhineland mystics, as well as four justly famous English writers (see box, p. 116), can be seen as beacons of light in comparative obscurity. The fourteenth century included in its span such different disasters as the Black Death, the Great Schism and frequent wars and famines. These events did not suppress spirituality but gave it a different emphasis. Survival in the face of disaster was indispensable, and a greater perception of the immediacy of death coloured much writing and many artistic works of the same time.

The later Middle Ages are often regarded as times of disaster and corruption. There is some truth in this assertion, but, like most generalizations, it needs substantial modification, especially as applied to spirituality. There were indeed repeated outbreaks of plague and disease, compounded by comparatively primitive medical knowledge. The Black Death is credibly estimated as the killer of between a third and half of the whole population, and its first major outbreak was between 1347 and 1351. In England it led to a number of villages being deserted, but perhaps the most striking statistic is from St Albans, one of England's largest and richest abbeys. There the community numbered one hundred on Palm Sunday 1378, but by Easter Sunday, only a week later, the monks were reduced to fifty. Comparable heartbreaking experiences were known elsewhere. The Black Death kept on reappearing at intervals, but never on the same scale as in 1378–79. Social changes, such as a renewed demand for higher wages in rural areas as well as a movement to the towns soon followed. One of its lasting results was a growing realization of the brevity of all human

Dante Alighieri (1265–1321)

Born at Florence but later rejected by the people of the town for political reasons, Dante became an outstanding poet and philosopher, famous especially for the curiously named *Divine Comedy*. This long dramatic poem was written towards the end of his life, mainly when he was in exile at Ravenna, where he eventually died and was buried. The poem, which displays the highest culture of his age with regard to many subjects such as history, classical literature, ethics and theology, was of great importance in the development of Italian language and literature. Its subject is the afterlife, as experienced in hell, purgatory and heaven. His guide in the earlier part was the poet Virgil, who was succeeded by Beatrice, a Florentine lady whom he knew in early life but never married: she is idealized in a platonic relationship as the embodiment of faith, revelation and the church of faith. She died in 1290, the wife of Simone del Bardi.

Visions of the damned

Medieval spirituality was much concerned not only with death but also with the last judgment. This was portrayed, with the punishment of the damned, in graphic, sometimes gruesome fashion by painters, sculptors and mosaic artists. The depiction of the 'Mouth of Hell' goes back to Anglo-Saxon times, and so do comparatively short accounts of the details of the afterlife. Both Bede, in his account of Drythelm, and Boniface (apostle of Germany) in his *Vision of the Monk of Much Wenlock*, as well as the late twelfth-century *Vision of the Monk of Eynsham*, provide examples of the type of literature which culminated in Dante's outstanding poem. These accounts begin with the visionary experiencing a death-like trance in which he remains for a considerable time. After this, he returns, as it were, from the dead, and relates to others what he

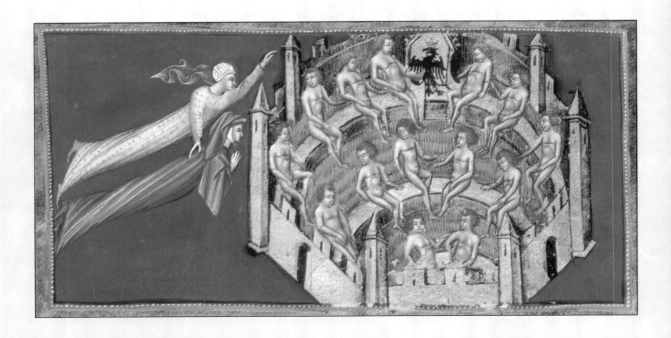

has seen. Usually, there are three states in the afterlife: Hell, Purgatory and Heaven, but sometimes a fourth is added, called Paradise (subsequently Limbo).

In interpreting this literature, several points have to be borne in mind. First, a vision is experienced by a particular person with all sorts of preconceptions: in the words of Aquinas, the thing received is received according to the mode of the receiver. This means inevitably that the experience is in part subjective, even if genuine. Moreover, it usually comes to us through another intermediary, the relator, who also has his own preconceptions and convictions. Sometimes visions were used to convey unpalatable or unacceptable messages. Thus, in the case of the *Monk of Eynsham*, a Bishop of Coventry who had expelled monks from the cathedral is shown experiencing great suffering in the afterlife. Few people nowadays would accord total confidence in the record of the visions; this applies to Dante as well as to the earlier, less sophisticated visionaries. Dante, as a great poet, inevitably added much of his own to the experience. It cannot be an accident, for instance, that he placed Pope Boniface VIII in hell, when we learn from elsewhere that in life Dante opposed the papal policies of Boniface and supported the emperor against him.

Lay sanctity

For the purposes of this volume one point should be stressed. This was that Dante encouraged and appreciated lay sanctity. This was very much a contemporary concern. In the later Middle Ages few kings or emperors were canonized, and even bishops were comparatively few. Instead candidates were brought forward from the ranks of the friars and from the third orders inspired by them. Homobonus of Cremona (1120–97), Elizabeth of Hungary (1207–31) and local hermit saints are examples of this trend. Dante might consign to hell important popes such as Gregory VII and Boniface VIII, but his quite legitimate concern was that sanctity should be recognized wherever it occurred: among merchants or farmers, queens or nuns or housewives. Like William Langland, the author of *Piers Plowman*, he favoured and appreciated the humble and hidden examples of sanctity. They, rather than certain prelates or rulers, would be recognized on the day of judgment as true disciples of Christ.

Dante's other works, on politics or language, do not concern us here. Nor should we necessarily accept his claim to have experienced the 'beatific vision' in his life. It is interesting to note that he claimed this for Bernard as well, who in the *Divine Comedy* presented Dante to the Blessed Virgin who obtained this singular grace for Dante himself. Over the centuries Dante's works have been much studied, more so than those of many another medieval writer.

◆ **Opposite: Illustration by Giovanni di Paolo (c. 1445), from Dante's *Divine Comedy*.**

life, causing the portrayal of death and corruption in its grislier aspects in funerary monuments. The underlying fear and insecurity are shared in our own day by victims of AIDS and of the more malignant cancers.

Another problem of the times was the renewal of wars and their consequent destruction. French historians have emphasized this aspect, but rightly avoid obsession with the crusades as cause. In reality, the crusades, although important, represent just one example of the losses inevitable in all wars, most of which were between states or were examples of rebellion. Society was youthful and the population comparatively sparse. Life was to be lived to the full while there was still time and health to do so. This resulted both in a cult of

pleasure and a readiness to hear calls to conversion. Meanwhile the towns and their merchants grew in importance as well as wealth, and contributed to the expansion of religious orders. The canonization by Innocent III of Homobonus, a merchant of Cremona who lived a devout life and was generous to the poor was also significant: a lay saint in an age when such was rare, if not unknown.

Heresy

In the field of religious belief, there were heresies (more or less important) on the continental mainland, but England was free of heresy for

◆ Kings contemplating death, from the 14th-century psalter of Robert de Lisle.

the whole period between Pelagius (late fourth century) and Wycliffe (c. 1330–84). Wycliffe's importance was considerable, because of his determined and destructive criticism of doctrines and of institutions within the church of his time. He maintained that the Bible was the only criterion of doctrine, that both the authority of the pope and the organized religious life were ill-founded in scripture. His followers (usually called Lollards) lost credibility through attempting rebellion against the Crown and went underground; but Wycliffe's influence was strong, not least in Bohemia, where Jan Hus initiated similar protests. In England he was the precursor, not of the Anglican Church but of the dissenters of the seventeenth century. Wycliffe indeed, although for some time parish priest of Lutterworth, was never one of the establishment, although he did have some academic support. The main targets of his attacks were the church authorities who, in his view, lost all authority if they were in a state of serious sin: in this case the civil power had the right (or even the duty) to deprive them of it. Members of the organized religious life, especially the friars, were also targeted by him for supposed hypocrisy and immorality. His repudiation of traditional doctrine on the Eucharist was the decisive event in his loss of widespread support. Nonetheless he was an influential catalyst of future change, through his encouragement of his disciples' translation of the Bible and the propagation of vernacular religious tracts under his name. His doctrines were condemned in England in 1382, 1388 and 1397, as well as by the council of Constance in 1415, but they persisted in rural areas of the Chilterns, Essex and Kent.

Another influential writer of the later Middle Ages was Jan Hus of Bohemia (1372–1415). A notable philosopher of Prague University, he was ordained priest at about the time when Wycliffe's teachings were becoming known there, partly through the marriage of Richard II of England to Anne of Bohemia. At first he was supported by the Archbishop of Prague, Shinko von Hasenberg, not least for his condemnation of a supposed eucharistic 'miracle' at Wilsnack, but opposition

to Wycliffe increased at Prague. Notwithstanding this, and in consequence of deep Czech resentment at German domination, as well as widespread controversy over which pope should be supported in the Great Schism, Hus emerged as Rector of Prague University, appointed by royal decree in 1409. This became a notable centre of Wycliffite teaching and aroused papal opposition. Hus then published his chief work *On the Church* which owed much to Wycliffe. This was not merely a vigorous denunciation of clerical corruption, but also a positive plea for greater lay access to the scriptures, greater lay participation in church matters, a vernacular liturgy, and communion of all under both kinds. It is interesting to note that several of these policies have been adopted by the church since Vatican II.

His views on both predestination and on the supposed loss of clerical jurisdiction and ownership in case of sin were widely condemned, and both Franciscan and Dominican involvement in his last imprisonment and death at the stake, following his condemnation by the council of Constance (to which he had appealed against the pope), left much resentment. The Czechs treated him as a martyr and his case is currently the subject of revisionist history with some support from the modern papacy.

Jan Ruysbroeck
(1293–1381)

An almost exact contemporary of Wycliffe, and like him a parish priest of northern Europe who loved his vernacular tongue, was Jan Ruysbroeck from Brabant in Flanders. Ruysbroeck, however, became a hermit for some years, but then with his small community joined the Canons Regular of St Augustine. A prolific and influential writer and director, he gave new emphasis to works of mercy as an integral expression of contemplative life, not as a separate but praiseworthy activity. At one and the same time, he wrote, in the same moment love acts and rests in the beloved: the two things (internal and external) strengthen each other. The complete mystic, he believed, is not an abstract contemplative, incapable of human activity, but rather one who possesses his life in both repose and action. In each he is whole and entire without division because he is entirely in God. He saw this integration of action and enjoyment as being founded on the life of the holy trinity. Moreover, an ordinary man who is raised into God and descends into charitable action shares fully in the life of the God–Man, Jesus Christ. But Ruysbroeck was also aware of the dangers of false mystics whom he condemned as pantheistic caricatures, as they believed they did not need to practise virtue.

He was in close contact with other new movements of devout believers in the Rhineland and elsewhere, together with the Beguines in Flanders and Gerard Grote, founder of the Brothers of the Common Life and an originator of a new devotion popularized by Thomas à Kempis in the *Imitation of Christ*.

Pope Urban V
(1310–70)

Another contemporary of Wycliffe was the little-known pope, Urban V, a Benedictine monk and abbot of Marseilles before his promotion. Francesco Petrarch, Italian poet and humanist (1304–74), called him 'a great man, without equal in our time and whose equals in any age are rare'. A student, moralist and jurist all his life, he found himself in the situation of awarding student-grants at a time when many thought that there were too many students and too many clerics. He agreed that large numbers of those provided by him with grants would not become clerics but would stay in the world and become fathers of families. Whatever state of life they chose, even in professions where manual skills predominate, it would always be useful to them to have studied. With this conviction documented from his own words, it is no surprise that he understood the ideals of men of the court as well as those of monks, who chose contempt for the world. He

stands as an example of the renewed vigour of Benedictine monasticism in the fourteenth century, exemplified in England by Adam Easton of Norwich, Uthred of Boldon in Northumbria, and Simon Langham, archbishop of Canterbury.

Revival of the friars

Meanwhile the friars, in spite of contemporary criticism, showed remarkable examples of vitality. Bernardino of Siena (1380–1444), theologian and popular preacher as well as a reformer of his own order, was a phenomenon in his own day. His tiny cell can still be seen at Fiesole, while artists loved to depict him holding the IHS symbol for the holy name of Jesus.

His Florentine Dominican contemporary, Bishop Antoninus (1389–1459), gave a wonderful example of evangelical poverty in his household but also commissioned Fra Angelico to decorate Florence's priory of St Mark. The best of these paintings mark one of the highlights of medieval religious art.

Yet another near-contemporary was John Colombini (1304–67), founder of the Jesuates (not to be confused with the later Jesuits), a married man with two children, and a magistrate, who experienced a dramatic conversion and devoted himself to preaching penance and poverty. This he did by example as well as words. Stripped of good clothes and dressed in rags, he went through the streets like a criminal condemned to death. He claimed that the name of Christ was forgotten in places where he is most honoured in appearance, but is more widely betrayed than by publicans. If Christ returned to earth, he believed, he would seek out sinners, usurers and robbers for salvation even more than before. If there is some element of fanaticism here, at least it shows that there was positive criticism and desire for genuine reform amid widespread corruption.

◆ **Opposite:** *Bernardino of Siena Preaching*; painting attributed to Bertodi Giovanni (d. c. 1529).

The flagellants and Vincent Ferrer
(1350–1419)

A somewhat analogous movement is found in the flagellant confraternities, criticized by Jean le Charlier de Gerson (1363–1429), a French spiritual writer, for imposing heavy burdens not willed by Christ's law of love. These strange lay people carried crosses, scourged themselves and went on pilgrimages from one city to another for thirty-three days (representing Christ's thirty-three years on earth). Voluntary expiation was substituted for the sacrament of penance; their instant anti-clericalism went with a keen sense of sin and an acute need for protection against the Black Death and subsequent plagues.

The famous Dominican preacher, Vincent Ferrer shared some of their concerns but provided for their needs in an orthodox way. Half Spanish and half English, Vincent became widely known and appreciated in France, Spain and Italy. Although widely known as a preacher of the Last Judgment, this theme was far from being the whole of his message. This was one of repentance through devout living in voluntary poverty, silence, obedience and abstinence. Despising of self, returning to God through the humanity of Jesus, and penance were all part of his teaching. To the flagellants he emphasized the need for the sacraments; to those afflicted with fear he emphasized the mercy of God. He recommended the Way of the Cross as a pilgrimage in spirit to Jerusalem, linked in spirit with crusader idealism. The 'second baptism' should result in joining religious orders or at least confraternities for religious theatre or opposing heretical sects. For all, penance was necessary, leading to contemplation of the divine mysteries. He lived in the time of the Great Schism, when rival popes from Rome and Avignon claimed the allegiance of believers. Vincent supported Pedro de Luna (of the Avignon line), and tried but failed to persuade him to be reconciled with Rome.

Carthusian monks

Meanwhile, as in other times of crisis, there was a return to monastic life by a small but significant minority. This time, however, it was the austere hermits of Chartreuse who attracted a comparatively widespread following. The Carthusian Order now experienced its greatest expansion. Their high reputation, even with a sceptical observer like Erasmus, ensured the respect and admiration of many. Their solitude matched the individualism of the age; their extreme austerity appealed to people who needed penance as well as prayer, and their isolation from the world recalled the earliest days of Christian monasticism and symbolized the near-exasperation reached by those tempted to despair at laxity and corruption. It is

◆ Flagellants depicted in an illustrated book (c. 1349).

interesting to note, in the same period, an increase in artistic portrayals of hermits and the hermit life.

Women mystics

Evidence of spirituality is difficult to find in the largely illiterate society of the early twelfth century. With the passing of time and the development of town life and education from the top of society down, it becomes easier to find examples of articulate women saints and mystics in the fourteenth and fifteenth centuries than before. To be sure, one can invoke from an earlier age the examples of Margaret of Scotland, a famous and devout Englishwoman, Hildegard of Bingen, a remarkable polymath and visionary rediscovered in our own times, and Christina of Markyate.

The women mystics that emerged in the late medieval period sometimes took a prominent part in movements of the time (Catherine of Siena and Bridget of Sweden), while others, enclosed in contemplative nunneries (Rita of Cascia and Julian of Norwich), were very little known in their lifetimes.

Bridget (c. 1303–73), a noble Swedish lady, founded an order of nuns and monks and was also famous for her revelations concerning details of Christ's life on earth. These have been immensely popular but are also problematic, insofar as they were written by her directors who sometimes altered or interpreted these visions. One mission which Catherine and Bridget had in common was the attempt to persuade the popes of Avignon to return to Rome. They were not the only people who advised this, but they were ultimately successful.

Catherine of Siena (c. 1340–80), a Dominican tertiary, was the most notable and unconventional woman mystic of the fourteenth century. The youngest of a very large family of a Sienese dyer, she refused marriage and devoted herself to prayer, penance and solitude. This she ended after some years by nursing the sick in hospitals and gathering a group of male and female disciples around her, some of whom were already members

◆ *Catherine of Siena*, **by Fra Bartolommeo (1472–1517).**

of religious orders. In her short life she preached persistently on the need for prayer and for repentance, not (it would seem) in churches, but through her principal work, the *Dialogue*, and her 380 surviving letters. These were dictated by her, as she never learned to write. They are characterized by an ardent love of God and of Christ, matched by strong, repeated criticism of abuses which hurt her deeply, as she regarded them as betrayals of Christ, whose active presence in the church she never doubted. She could be personal in her strictures: 'Bloated with pride,' she said of some of the priests of her time, 'they devour money meant for the poor and spend it on their own pleasures.'[11]

But even as she saw the church going from bad to worse, she nevertheless recognized this as the

English mystics

Four English writers, all of the fourteenth century and all orthodox, are usually called the English mystics. They were linked with the practice of the hermit life but also with the Dominican tradition of spiritual writing, coming from Thomas Aquinas through the Dominican Rhineland mystics such as Henry Suso (1295–1366). Each of them, nonetheless, was original and personal.

Richard Rolle (1300–49)

Richard Rolle studied at Oxford but became a hermit in early life and continued in it near the Cistercian nuns' house at Hampole, Yorkshire, until his early death. A prolific writer in Latin and English, his best-known works are the *Fire of Love* and the *Emendation of Life*. He was greatly esteemed for 200 years and more and, although criticized for subjectivity and emotionalism, is widely read today. 'The name of Jesus', he wrote, 'is in my mind as a joyful song, in my ear a heavenly music, and in my mouth sweet honey.' And elsewhere: 'Some are deceived by too much abstinence from meat and drink and sleep. That is a temptation of the devil... so that they do not bring it to an end as they would have done if they had known reason and maintained discretion.'

The Cloud of Unknowing
(14th century)

The second writer is anonymous: his main work is called *The Cloud of Unknowing*. Between God and us, he believed, there is always a cloud of unknowing, which can be pierced only by love. A 'naked entent', in which our being is simply offered to God, is a form of prayer preferable to that of discursive meditation. This teaching, according to David Knowles – with the nights of sense and spirit, the desire for union with the Word of God, and the signs by which the true spirit of prayer can be known – anticipates the teaching of John of the Cross, and is superior to that of contemporaries, not excluding Suso and Ruysbroeck.[15] The author's own words include the following: 'As the cloud of unknowing lies above you, between you and your God, you must fashion a cloud of forgetting beneath you, between you and every creature.' And: 'In anticipation of eternal glory, God will sometimes inflame the senses of his devoted friends with unspeakable delight and consolation even here in this life. And not just once or twice, but perhaps very often, as he judges to be best.'

Walter Hilton (1343–96)

Walter Hilton, a Cambridge graduate, also became a hermit, but later an Augustinian canon at Thurgarton, Nottinghamshire. In teaching and in spirit he more closely resembles the author of *The Cloud* than any other writer. Both wrote with authority as directors and enjoyed true liberty of spirit within a context of perfect orthodoxy. Although they lived in an age of controversies and scandals, when the Great Schism divided Europe and Wycliffe was a divisive force in England, they remained serene in their own pursuit of spirituality, which helped others tread a similar path: 'Set in thy heart wholly and fully that thou wouldst have nothing but the love of Jesus and the spiritual sight of him... for to that only art thou made and bought; that is thy beginning and end, thy joy and thy bliss.' Again: 'Anyone who thinks himself a perfect follower of Christ's teaching and way of life... but who cannot follow Christ in having love and charity towards all, both good and bad, friends and foes, without pretence or flattery, contempt, anger or spiteful criticism, is indeed deceiving himself.'

Julian of Norwich (1342–1417)

Last, but by no means least, of the English mystics is Julian, the anchoress of Norwich, greatly esteemed nowadays, but whose writings were scarcely known in her own lifetime. She may have been a Benedictine nun and certainly settled as a recluse in a noisy and insalubrious area of Norwich. There she experienced impressive visions or 'showings', which she described in two recensions which reflect considerable theological skills. She found in the passion of Christ the key to understanding all that is sinful in this world: creation and redemption are united in predestination of the elect. In a justly famous saying she wrote, 'It is true that sin is the cause of all this pain; but all shall be well, and all shall be well, and all manner of things shall be well.' And elsewhere: 'Of all the pains that lead to salvation, this is the greatest, to see your love suffer. How could any pain be more to me than to see the one who is all my life, my bliss, my joy, suffer? Here I truly felt that I loved Christ so much more than myself that there was no pain I could suffer that could match the sorrow I had in seeing him in pain.' Thus her Christian optimism in the first extract is not divorced from perception of acute suffering, nor is it an unrealistic withdrawal from evil and sin.

occasion for the gift of reform. As the guilt of the world drew the saviour of humanity to its need, so the church's sin draws to its poverty this same redeemer whose power alone can heal and restore it as his poor and humble community. God will not refuse the very intercession he inspires: 'You cannot resist giving it to the hardened hearts of your creatures.' Again God was invoked: 'O boundless, gentlest charity! This is your garden, implanted in your blood... watch over it... set our hearts ablaze and plunge them into this blood.'[12]

Her deep love for the church impelled her to attempt to improve it by working in the world of ecclesiastical politics. She tried hard and ultimately succeeded in persuading Pope Gregory XI to leave Avignon and return to Rome. She could not, however, be held responsible for the character of his successor Urban VI, nor for the consequent Great Schism which lasted for about forty years. Her own 'living martyrdom' for the church lasted until her death and her description of other faithful reformers exactly matched herself: 'Their hearts were vessels of affection that carried God's name to the world and proclaimed it with burning love.'[13] Her director described her death as 'not for any natural cause, or for any other reason than the sheer intensity of her love for God, she breathed her last'.[14] In 1970 she was declared a Doctor of the Church, an honour attained by very few bishops and priests.

Margery Kempe of King's Lynn (c. 1373–1440) must also be mentioned. The daughter of a mayor, she married a burgess of Lynn, by whom she had fourteen children. Her life was unusual, yet she is in some ways easier to understand than some of the other mystical writers, if only because she is more accessible. This is due in large measure to her autobiography, *The Book of Margery Kempe*. This relates her visions, but also her temporary madness, the support and the criticism she received from the clergy, her many pilgrimages to the Holy Land, to Canterbury, Compostela and elsewhere. Devout and sincere, she could also be trying, not least for her outbursts of weeping and howling. But her experiences included close communion with Christ and strong sorrow for widespread sinfulness. With her long-suffering husband she took vows of chastity in 1413. She once met Julian of Norwich (see box, p. 117), but unfortunately no adequate account survives of what passed between them.

The women mystics in their search for union with Christ, both then and later, seemed to concentrate on the passion of Christ, whose sufferings they reproduced in their own lives, offered in expiation for the sins of the times. The majority but not the totality of people who experienced the stigmata, that is, the imprint of Christ's wounds in their own bodies, were women. The first stigmatist was Francis of Assisi and several of these women mystics were influenced or directed by Franciscans.

Lay piety

Mystics and stigmatists were important but inevitably few. What of the religious outlook of the majority in the late Middle Ages? With the growth of literacy and the emergence of the professional middle class, more has survived to enable us to hazard a few tentative judgments. The immense number of surviving Books of Hours tell us about their habits and preferences at prayer. It is interesting to note that the contents of the Books of Hours (often beautifully illuminated) were almost exactly those of the supplementary monastic liturgy of earlier centuries. The Hours of the Blessed Virgin and those of All Saints, the Office of the Dead and the Litany of Saints were now the preferred prayers of kings and queens, barons, merchants and their wives. These books are significant evidence of how the monastic life still appealed to many. It might be said that they represent in abbreviated form the monastic day of prayer in a somewhat similar fashion to the flagellants' attempt to extract in 'tabloid' form the austerities of monastic life.

At this distance of time much must remain obscure, but it is clear that saints and their shrines remained of great importance. This is further shown by the great popularity of the famous *Golden Legend* (1255–66), a collection of saints' Lives throughout the calendar, together with sections on the principal Feasts of Our Lord in the liturgical year. Although uncritical and sometimes romantic, the large numbers of copies printed by William Caxton and others (both in Latin and the vernacular) make it clear that it was in great demand right up to the Reformation.

Pilgrimage

Pilgrimage is an activity common to most of the world's great religions. In Islam, pilgrimage to Mecca is compulsory (if you have the means), at least once in a lifetime. In Christianity it has always been voluntary, unless imposed as a penance.

The oldest recorded Christian pilgrimage to the Holy Land dates from the fourth century: the vivid account of it is due to a Spanish lady called Silvia of Egeria and it is an important source for the liturgy of Jerusalem in c. 380. Constantinople, Edessa (in Turkey) and Egypt were also part of her pilgrimage route.

From about the same period, or even earlier, pilgrimages were made to shrines of the martyrs in different parts of Europe, but the Middle Ages are widely regarded as the great age of pilgrims and pilgrimages. The Holy Land, Rome, Compostela and Saint-Gilles in Provence were all established pilgrimage centres, and all were visited by the English traveller Godric in the early twelfth century before he became a hermit at Finchale, near Durham. He died in 1170, the same year as the martyrdom of Thomas Becket, an event which caused Canterbury to become one of the most important centres of pilgrimage in Europe. Later it was immortalized by Chaucer in the *Canterbury Tales*, a fictional satire which chronicled the sayings and doings of some not very devout men and women of the fourteenth century.

In medieval times pilgrims were specially

blessed by the church and set off in their pilgrim's garb of cloak, hat and staff; their badges of pilgrimage are now much prized by archaeologists. The dangers of the journey were very considerable and a number of them never returned. The church protected them as far as it could and the local church helped their spouses and families to escape exploitation. Crusading was originally an armed pilgrimage to the Holy Land: arms were necessary for self-defence and for those religious orders such as the Templars and Hospitallers which were founded for this very purpose.

It is often asserted that most medieval people seldom left their towns and villages. There is much truth in this view, but the general picture is modified considerably by the practice of pilgrimage, whether overseas or at home. Pilgrimages to the cathedral of the diocese were well established, while the greater abbeys often housed the relics of a saint which would draw the people. In England, St Albans, Bury St Edmunds, Westminster, Lincoln, Durham, York and Chichester all had shrines of important and well-known saints, although none of these centres could rival Canterbury for numbers or revenue. Western Europe's principal shrines (besides those mentioned above) included Fleury, Tours, Lyons, Venice, Cologne and Merida. The possession of a shrine could be an important financial asset for a town as well as for a church. The presence of pilgrims, all in need of food, drink and accommodation enhanced revenues, providing employment and opportunities for producers rather like the modern presence of crowds for football or other sporting events. The main difference to bear in mind, however, is the comparatively tiny size of the medieval population, so that domestic pilgrims at any one time would have numbered (very likely) tens or hundreds rather than thousands. It must also be emphasized that these churches were not primarily pilgrimage centres or exercises in architectural skill, but the places of the church's public prayer. That is why, to be appreciated properly, they need to be seen in active liturgical use.

◆ **Imaginary view of Constantinople from a 15th-century German book. Constantinople was a major pilgrimage destination, despite the destruction wrought by the fourth crusade, until it was captured by Islamic forces in 1453.**

Discussion of pilgrimage journeys must include some consideration of relics. Practically all cults of saints began at their tombs where it was believed the influence of the saint was especially strong, both as protector and as healer. Innumerable 'miracles' were claimed and often verified, but it has to be admitted that the idea of miracle in Christian antiquity did not have its present-day, more precise sense. In antiquity a miracle was a *small* example (*miraculum*) of a wonderful great truth or event such as the creation and providence of God, exercised through the intercession or the relics of one of his special friends. These friends of God were invoked as patrons (in a world of extensive secular patronage) and commanded strong local or professional followings, in times of

war as well as of peace. Churches were dedicated
in their honour and the distribution of dedications
to a particular saint tells us something about the
popularity of their cults. To this day some local
saints (such as Cuthbert of Lindisfarne, Roch
of Montpellier or Antony of Padua) are seen as
exemplars and patrons of particular districts.
Similarly national patrons' feast days such as
Patrick's or Stephen of Hungary's are occasions for
asserting national identity, especially in countries
far from home.

In early centuries, bodies of saints were not
divided but were kept intact in their tombs.
Constantinople abandoned this practice long
before Rome. Everywhere demand for saints'
relics (comparable to the present-day search for
souvenirs) outstripped the supply. Relics most in
demand were those of saints closely associated
with Christ when on earth. Particular churches
wished to have on their altars (or in their
treasuries) concrete visible links with Jesus:
hence demand for relics of the apostles, John the
Baptist, Mary Magdalene and others. Particular
places claimed to have the tombs of these saints,
and strong desires linked with national patriotism
overcame any scruples about historical accuracy
in a pre-scientific age. Thus it was that when King
Canute gave to Canterbury a relic of the arm of
Bartholomew, it was accepted with honour and joy,
although Canterbury had plenty of historically
authentic relics of their own local saints. It must
also be stressed that the earliest relics were
'secondary' relics: pieces of cloth, dust from
the saint's tomb or other objects associated with
the saint. In this connection some secondary relics
such as St Dunstan's Class-Book from Glastonbury
or the Gospel book of Margaret of Scotland are
to some devotees more attractive than pieces
of bone.

Relics of saints were sometimes bought and sold
for very high prices. Here, too, there is a modern
equivalent in the enormous sums of money paid
for the clothes or effects of celebrities such as the
Duchess of Windsor (formerly Wallis Simpson),
Diana, Princess of Wales, Elvis Presley or Marilyn
Monroe. The memory and the attachment to
particular people sometimes seems to bear little
relationship to monetary values.

Over the centuries, the papacy and conscientious
bishops tried hard to regulate the cults of saints.
They were not always totally successful in eliminating
abuses. It may be worth citing a remark of Martin
Luther in this connection. 'Of course there are
abuses,' he said, 'but are they eliminated by
destroying the objects abused? Men can go wrong
with wine and women. Shall we then prohibit wine
and abolish women? Such haste and violence betray
lack of confidence in God.'[16]

What of the motivation of medieval pilgrims?
Doubtless they were many and varied. Perhaps
some were like modern tourists in search of
novelty and change; others were more devout
and at considerable cost and danger visited
shrines to satisfy devotion and thus express their
commitment. Others again went on pilgrimage for
penance and expiation: the Irish called this 'the
green martyrdom'. But, whatever the motivation,
pilgrimage was an established devotional practice
which has left memorials in our own day. Pilgrims
are still found at Canterbury and at Compostela,
where the European Union has designated
pilgrimage routes. Rome, in repeated Jubilee or
holy years, attracted and still attracts very many
pilgrims. Equally important is the way the idea of
pilgrimage inspired the Pilgrim Fathers as well as
John Bunyan's *Pilgrim's Progress*. Nowadays most
Christian churches stress that the whole of the
Christian life on earth is a pilgrimage with many
hazards, disappointments and rewards. And in
teaching the importance of perseverance, they
echo, perhaps unconsciously, the ideals of medieval
pilgrims, who are thus much closer to us than
might at first appear.

Thomas à Kempis
(1380–1471)

The most widely read spiritual writer of the
fifteenth century was Thomas à Kempis, author
(it seems certain) of the famous and influential

Cult of Mary

The cult of the Virgin Mary, as pre-eminent among the saints for her unique privilege of being the mother of him who was both God and man, was firmly established in East and West from early centuries. It was based on the liturgical feasts of the Annunciation (25 March) and the Assumption or Dormition (15 August). By common consent, however, the cult of and devotion to Mary developed considerably in the medieval centuries.

The deeper perception of Christ's humanity by Anselm, Bernard and Francis was matched by similar understanding of the Blessed Virgin. In the general reaction against overemphasis on Christ as judge came the twelfth-century *Miracles of the Virgin* stories which had, as a common feature, stories about the intercession of Mary being decisive in obtaining God's mercy rather than his justice. This went together with artistic representations of Mary as a human mother rather than as a distant queen; her motherhood extended from Christ to all who believed in him. Medieval depictions of Mary are innumerable and varied. Byzantine icon-painters continued to produce stylized portraits, while Western artists and sculptors developed more human and emotive representations, such as the roundel of Chichester (in the bishop's chapel) or the carvings of Gislebertus, a twelfth-century sculptor of capitals at Autun and elsewhere.

Architectural developments followed. Many cathedrals and larger parish churches in England added a Lady chapel at the east end of the building (e.g. Winchester, Long Melford and elsewhere), while all Cistercian churches were dedicated to her and so did not have need of an extra chapel. Famous French shrines such as Chartres and Notre Dame at Paris were likewise in churches dedicated to her. Eloquent sermons were preached on her by the friars, sometimes on the aspect of Our Lady of Sorrows, suffering at the foot of the cross yet accepting in John her patronage of all believers. The *pietàs* sculpted by Michelangelo are the supreme examples of this devotion.

Also in the Middle Ages came the development of the rosary as a devotion. This series of meditations on the life and mysteries of Christ was accompanied by the praying of the Hail Mary with the Lord's prayer and the *Gloria Patri*. English bishops' legislation made it obligatory for all Christians to know the Hail Mary:

Hail Mary, full of grace, the Lord is with thee.
Blessed art thou among women and blessed is
the fruit of thy womb, Jesus.
    Holy Mary, mother of God, pray for us sinners,
now and at the hour of our death. Amen.

Honour was paid to Mary for Christ's sake, as his supreme and unique friend both on earth and in heaven.

◆ **Mary shown enthroned with Francis of Assisi and angels,
by Cimabue (c. 1240–1302).**

Imitation of Christ. As its name indicates, it instructs the believer through following Christ as a model both in general terms and in interior attitudes and through Holy Communion. Full of good advice and insisting strongly on humility and piety formed by the gospels and Paul's epistles, it is pietistic rather than doctrinal in inspiration. Holy Communion was seen in terms of the real presence for the individual rather than as an integral part of the sacrifice offered by Christ and the church. The piety reflected by the *Imitation* is individualistic rather than communal.

It is an orthodox work, but one which has been criticized for what it omits rather than what it says. What it does say is often pithy and very much to the point: 'Jesus now has many lovers of his heavenly kingdom, but few bearers of his cross.' In his statement that he would rather feel compunction than know how to define it, one can sense an anti-intellectual bias which has indeed been very influential. Again: 'A humble knowledge of yourself is a surer way to God than an extensive search after learning.' No doubt the statement is true, but it does not stress, as Dominic and others did, the importance of sound learning in the pursuit and practice of the spiritual life.

Perhaps his most characteristic meditation is the one on death. The Christian should be ready for death at all times, presuming on life's continuance neither in the morning nor in the evening:

> While you enjoy health, you can do much good; but when sickness comes, little can be done. Few are made better by sickness, and those who make frequent pilgrimages seldom acquire holiness by so doing... Who will remember you when you are dead? Who will pray for you?... While you have time, gather the riches of everlasting life. Think only of your salvation and care only for the things of God. Make friends now, by honouring the saints of God and by following their example, that when this life is over, they may welcome you to your eternal home.[17]

The *Imitation of Christ* was immensely popular up to and after the Reformation period.

Reform movements

There had long been movements of reform within the church, and not least within its hierarchy. The famous Gregorian Reform, of the eleventh to twelfth centuries, had resulted in a greater insistence on clerical celibacy, on the emergence of active lay participation in various movements, on the clearer definition of church–state relations and, at its best, on the clear primacy of the spiritual. Later medieval writers seemed very conscious of sin in their world and preachers repeatedly called the people to repentance. The need for this evangelical change of heart was heightened, on the one hand, by the experience of sudden death and disaster in plagues and wars, and, on the other, by the abuse of power, the greed and extortion in high places and the widespread sins of theft and sexual irregularities, especially in the towns. Superstitious practices of various kinds were not unknown, some ludicrous and others scandalous. However, it must be remembered that there have been and are abuses in every age of the church's history, from the time of the disciples, when one betrayed and another denied his Lord, and even in the patristic period (often hailed as a 'Golden Age' but whose reality was very different, as the Church Fathers themselves tell us).

In the Middle Ages there was likewise much to praise and much to blame. In the reality of widespread but diminishing illiteracy (from the top of society down), through the sometimes excessively emotional input in prayer and sacred art, the reality can be glimpsed of a spiritually better-educated clergy and laity, whose ideals are revealed in the Eucharist, the cathedrals, the pilgrimages, the sermons and the lecture halls of the time. Here the influence of the friars was both substantial and impressive. The attraction of the older monastic orders, however, was not dead, as has been shown above, while the rarer but more important input of mystics, hermits and stigmatists could be perceived by those who had eyes to see. In public life, however, the overall impression is much less attractive.

◆ ***The Arrest and Supplication of Thomas More*, by Antoine Caron (1520–99).**

Erasmus of Rotterdam (1469–1536) is usually regarded as the greatest scholar and the most outspoken critic of abuse in his age. Several of his friends were English, not least John Fisher (1469–1535), vice-chancellor of Cambridge university and bishop of Rochester. King Henry VIII claimed that no other kingdom had such a distinguished prelate as Fisher, while the ambassador of the Emperor Charles V declared him a paragon of bishops for his learning and holiness.

The then chancellor of the kingdom, Thomas More (1478–1535), was also a distinguished scholar, lawyer, wit and family man. He too was a friend of Erasmus and very likely appreciated his satire more than Fisher. Both refused to approve of the king's divorce from Catherine of Aragon and both refused to acknowledge Henry as supreme head of the church. They paid for their convictions with their lives shortly after the Carthusian monks of London had gone joyfully to their deaths for the same reasons. On the scaffold Fisher quoted the gospel of John: 'This is life eternal to know thee, the only true God and him whom you have sent, Jesus Christ. I glorified thee on earth and have accomplished the work you gave me to do.' More, for his part, declared himself 'the King's good servant, but God's first'. Each was a fine representative of the church of their time: they were the first English martyrs of the Reformation period.

Conclusion

In the 400 years covered selectively in this chapter, some elements of spirituality remained unchanged while others were considerably modified. Life, in medieval times in general, changed much more slowly than it has in our own day, but the interaction of several layers of different influences produced long-lasting developments.

The constant elements in medieval devotion were the sacraments. By baptism, people became children of God and members of the church: this was taken for granted as much as membership of their nation. In the Eucharist, celebrated daily in large cathedral or humble parish church, the life-giving food of the soul was perceived through the Real Presence, depicted by Lanfranc and Thomas Aquinas in different terms centuries apart. If people fell into sin, help was at hand through the sacrament of penance which brought pardon and peace. The twelfth century was the time of special importance for this practice; sometimes it led to austere penances, including pilgrimage, being undertaken. Apart from chance encounters in these journeys, most medieval people had little or no direct contact with devotees of other religions.

Emphasis on the humanity of Jesus and Mary led to greater attention being paid to Christ's sufferings and death, sometimes at the expense, it would seem, of the resurrection. It also led to a more emotional spirituality and to the practice of vicarious suffering. To be sure, these elements had some basis in the scriptures, but the emphasis was rather different in 1500 from that in 1100. The experience of the plague contributed to this development.

Developments and changes were neither necessarily good nor necessarily bad: individuals, famous or obscure, could and did provide admirable examples of Christian living in often precarious and difficult conditions. Sudden death

and incurable illness were constant reminders of the uncertainty of human life, while the considerably improved education did not of itself provide the cures achieved centuries later by more advanced medical science. Saints' intercession was often believed to be the best remedy against diseases that were seldom understood. Often the same saints, especially the local ones, provided succour and sanctuary in times of acute need as well as more general protection outside them. Guilds, in particular, were often associated with saintly patrons and protectors. Preoccupation with suffering and death was balanced by vivid faith in heaven and the resurrection, well portrayed in Fra Angelico's paintings of angels and saints.

Knowledge of the Bible was mediated through preaching in the vernacular, through the related images on walls of churches and through the mystery and miracle plays which were a popular feature of medieval religion. Nor should the contribution of vernacular poetry from the eighth-century *Dream of the Rood* to the fourteenth-century *Piers Plowman* be forgotten. The later invention of printing made possible what had been impossible in earlier centuries: the diffusion to the many of biblical texts and other works of spirituality.

Medieval Christianity was important both for what it retained and what it was modified. In many ways, sometimes unexpected, it influenced for good or ill much of the spirituality of the Catholic 'baroque' age, but also that of several Protestant churches which were the fruit of the Reformation.

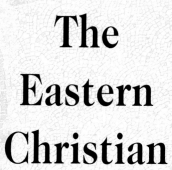

4

The Eastern Christian Tradition

(4th to 18th centuries)

John A.
McGuckin

Timeline

c. 185–254	Origen of Alexandria
c. 290–346	Pachomius
c. 296–373	Athanasius
c. 306–73	Ephrem the Syrian
325	**Council of Nicea**
c. 329–91	Gregory of Nazianzus
c. 330–79	Basil of Caesarea
c. 335–94	Gregory of Nyssa
c. 346–99	Evagrius of Pontus
5th c.	Dionysius the Areopagite
c. 400–86	Diadochus of Photike
writing c. 420	Palladius
d. 444	Cyril of Alexandria
451	**Council of Chalcedon**
d. c. 466	Shenoute (or Shenudi) of Atribe
6th c.	Barsanuphius and John
6th c.	Dorotheus of Gaza
c. 580–662	Maximus the Confessor
638	**Conquest of Jerusalem by the Arabs**
c. 660–740	Andrew of Crete
c. 675–749	John of Damascus
d. c. 700	Isaac of Nineveh
c. 810–77	John Scotus Erigena
949–1022	Symeon the New Theologian
1054	**Schism between Roman and Eastern Orthodox churches**
1202–1204	**Fourth Crusade culminates in the conquest of Constantinople**
c. 1255–1346	Gregory of Sinai
1296–1359	Gregory Palamas
1453	**Conquest of Constantinople by the Ottoman Turks**
1722–94	Paisy Velichovsky
1782	**The *Philokalia* published in Greek**
1815–94	Theophan the Recluse

Timeline markers: 300, 400, 500, 700, 1200, 1700

The Eastern Christian tradition of spirituality begins in antiquity and extends to the present day as the underlying fabric of a large family of churches. Until very recently, Western Christians rarely encountered the Christian East and, as a result, the patterns of Christianity determined by the Reformation controversies often seemed to be the 'norm' when it came to a consideration of the Christian religion. In recent years, however, extensive patterns of emigration or personal travel, and increasing media coverage of world events, have made it clear that the Eastern Christian churches have a vitality all of their own. Their endurance, and sometimes even heroism, have been tested in years of survival under hostile and oppressive political regimes. The Eastern churches are bound together by common inner attitudes, even where they differ on aspects of doctrine.

The largest of the families of churches is the Byzantine, which includes the Greek Orthodox, Russian, Romanian, Bulgarian, Georgian and Serbian; in short all the Greek and Slavonic churches which share the common heritage of a Byzantine past. There are also the churches of Armenia, Egypt (the Copts), Ethiopia and Nubia (destroyed in the late medieval Islamic wars), which show how the common tradition of the Christian East has always extended far beyond the boundaries of Europe. To this we may add the Oriental churches, that even in antiquity extended through Syria and Persia (Iran) and had made inroads by the sixth century into imperial China and Buddhist India. There are variations in form and detail, but these Eastern churches (both Orthodox and Oriental) share a common character, often venerating the same saints and teachers. For all of them, the liturgical nature of their prayer and worship is very distinctive, and they adhere to a common ascetical discipline, where individuals try to live out the personal demands of Christian discipleship in a practical way of life that is intimately bound up with day-to-day 'exercises' such as fasting or physical forms of prayer, involving prostrations, regular vigils and services lasting many hours at a time.

The overarching spiritual climate of the Christian East gives to the distinctive spirituality of the Orthodox and Oriental churches an inward-looking and mystical character that is, at the same time, firmly rooted in community life. It bears a highly realist character that tries to make the individual soul own up to its numerous weaknesses, yet still dares to look into the face of God with confidence in the divine mercy. This central twofold pattern of loving reconciliation and the ever-deepening approach to the mystery of God that is found in the life of disciples who open their lives to the presence of Christ is summed up in the two key concepts that dominate the entire Eastern spiritual tradition: repentance and communion with God. In all the writings of the many different teachers who have shaped that ancient and extensive spiritual history, these two ideas, so central to the experience of the salvation offered in the gospel of Christ, recur time and time again. Let us look at some selected teachers from that tradition. They will be taken, in the main, from the early Egyptian, Syrian and Byzantine writers.

◆ **Cyril of Alexandria; 17th-century Greek-school icon.**

Athanasius and Cyril of Alexandria

Athanasius (c. 296–373) and his later successor as Archbishop of Alexandria (the capital of Hellenistic Egypt) Cyril (d. 444) are undoubtedly the two most important theologians of the Greek tradition in the early church, whose teaching centred upon the person of Christ. Both men were active and dominant politicians and used their position as bishop as a means of exercising significant power in the international affairs of both church and empire. I have paired them together, though they worked three generations apart, because Cyril's teaching represents the logical fulfilment of Athanasius's work, and he was able to spread his controversial predecessor's doctrine widely over the whole ancient Christian world.

Both men wrote extensively on the questions:

Who was Jesus of Nazareth? What significance does his person have for the spiritual life of the Christian? For both, the controversial issues that made the question come alive had little to do with external criticism of Jesus (either from the surrounding Greek polytheistic culture, or from the Jewish community in Alexandria, a city that was at the time the chief intellectual capital of Judaism). Both thinkers were more immediately concerned with internal Christian arguments. Some wished to present Jesus as an object of veneration to the church, but as a figure who was primarily an 'example' to be followed, while disciples engaged directly with an invisible and immaterial deity. Athanasius's and Cyril's rejection of this apparently harmless idea as, at heart, something that saps the essential energy of Christian spirituality, has become relevant once again in the present age. Many of the same issues have re-emerged in Christian debate: a surrounding climate of distaste for Christianity, a multicultural challenge to Christianity's claim to ascendancy in terms of religious truth, and a context within Christianity itself which frequently presents Jesus as first and foremost a human example of the godly life.

From the time of Origen of Alexandria (d. 254) onwards, the notion of deification came to be used by Greek theologians to synopsize the dynamic effect of the divine encounter with humankind through the incarnation of the Word. The doctrine was based on its biblical appearance in John 1 and 2 Peter 1:4, but it also used extensively the image of the bodily form of Jesus radiating unearthly light on the mountain of his transfiguration (Mark 9). From such a perspective, Athanasius and Cyril argued that Jesus was not a human being who had been elevated to a high spiritual condition by the visitation of the Spirit of God; rather he was the very person of God, the Word of the Father, the second person of the divine trinity, who had chosen to live a human life.

◆ **The transfiguration; 11th-century mosaic from Daphni monastery, Greece.**

For both Athanasius (*On the Incarnation of the Divine Word*) and Cyril (*That the Christ is One*) this choice to live in the body (the incarnation, or the 'coming into the flesh') formed a turning point in the history of the world. It marked the end of old systems of religion where God revealed divine truths or the divine presence in partial manifestations, and instead stated a dynamic and startling new fact: that God had committed himself to the human race in a profoundly intense and definitive manner. The event of the incarnation, for them, became nothing less than the new creation of a world order. The human flesh of Christ was not 'old Adam', they argued, using terms drawn from the apostle Paul, but 'new Adam'. In other words, though Christ had an authentic human body, he had transfigured his own flesh to make it radiant with the life-giving divine presence. What he had achieved in his own person, he offered to disciples as the new (and paradoxical) condition of an authentic human life that would be defined henceforth no longer by separateness from God (the stark gap between creature and Creator), but rather by the possibility of an intimate and mystical union with the divine presence.

Athanasius set out the idea of this Christ-centred transfiguration of natural life quite clearly as the centre of his theology of incarnation: the divine Word assumed flesh so that all humankind could be lifted up into the mystery of his divinity. He conceived the incarnation as a real physical bringing together of the hitherto distinct natures of God and humanity.

Cyril of Alexandria clarified Athanasius's implications further. That which could not happen, that is the 'natural' reconciliation of divinity and humanity, had in effect been demonstrated, in the incarnation of the Word as the God–Man Jesus Christ. By stressing that this whole mystical transaction 'in the natures' came about not solely in the person of Christ or merely for Christ's sake, but rather as a pattern for the human race, and as something that brought about the divine re-creation of the very foundations of human nature, Greek patristic thought thus conceived the incarnation as having reconstituted the human person as a divinely graced mystery.

Athanasius put it into a memorably concise Greek phrase, that needs more 'stretching out' in translation:

He (God) became what we are (human) in order that we (humans) might become what he is (divinized).[1]

Or, as Cyril restated it: 'What he is by nature, he makes us by grace.'[2]

For both Athanasius and Cyril this was the heart of the 'economy of salvation', or the reason why God became incarnate. They use the term 'economy' to signify the dynamic work going on in the incarnation. At one stroke it broadens the whole perspective on the life, death and resurrection of Christ. Instead of mere reliance on the older biblical categories of atonement by sacrificial substitution, it suggests that, in addition to the motive of sacrificial redemption, the divine Word was making new the fundamental nature of humankind.

The heart of the matter was a mysterious form of transference of attributes (eventually to be known as the 'communion of properties'). In their teaching, the divine Word assumed human nature without losing his being and power as God. Once he assumed human life, however, he was subject to its limitations. So, in his own divine person, he experienced the dual conditions of suffering and limitation (as a man) and also godly power (as the architect of the universe). Athanasius, and even more so Cyril, loved to apply the paradoxes in this view to the full, so as to stress the mysterious

nature of the transaction (the economy): so, the immortal God died on the cross, but being immortal rose again to show his supreme victory over death. Their opponents, then and later, argued that by stressing such paradoxes they ran the risk of rendering the human life of Christ somewhat unreal. To counter this, Athanasius and Cyril argued that, far from showing the life of Christ was unreal, the theology demonstrated how the incarnation was a dynamic process designed for others which modelled how an ordinary human life, that of the believer, could be caught up intimately into the divine condition. What the divine Word achieved as a natural result of his incarnation, they said, he gave to the human race as the grace of its new liberation. So, humanity which had once been defined by its mortality, and corruption, and divided separateness from God, was now redefined as a state of being with the potential for immortal life and for perfect communion with the God who had entered into a 'natural' union with the human race.

Through the forceful work of Athanasius and Cyril, this dynamic understanding of Christology (the theology of the incarnation) became the official teaching of the church as it was reaffirmed by the first five Ecumenical Councils. It thereby affected every major thinker of the early period. Its net result was to imbue the whole manner of early Christian spirituality with a profound Christ-centred mysticism of dynamic transformation. As and when the believer drew close to the risen Christ, through prayer and the sacramental life of the church, so – inexorably, it was believed – the believer's very essence as a human being was slowly transfigured into a new condition of light, and grace, and growing stability, and the fullness of life: an ever-radiant growth that would be completed in the next age of the kingdom, but was already sensed in the spiritual life here and now. We have begun, at length, with this idea because it dominated the entire early Christian world and underlies all its other spiritual theologies. The Christian East was always, and entirely, possessed by the concept of this Christ-centred mystical transformation.

The Cappadocian fathers

After Athanasius's death a generation of younger theologians based in Cappadocia (in present-day Turkey) took on his work and gave it a stronger basis by drawing out its various ramifications in the liturgy and prayers of Christians. All of them were closely related friends or family and all communicated with each other as a cooperative team. They were Gregory of Nazianzus (c. 329–91), one of the most learned men in the history of the early church who had been educated as a classical rhetorician; his closest friend Basil of Caesarea (c. 330–79); Basil's elder sister Macrina (c. 327–80), an important figure in the history of female monasticism; and Basil's younger brother Gregory of Nyssa (c. 335–94).

The doctrine of the trinity

The Cappadocian men used their position as bishop to propagate the Christology of Athanasius, and in the process also developed the doctrine of the trinity. The Christian God, after them, was seen as a communion of three personal realities who shared the single divine nature that was communicated to the Son and the Spirit by the One Father. It was then, and remains now, a difficult intellectual aspect of the Christian faith, but one that was eminently 'approachable' through the trinitarian prayers of the liturgy, where it found its abiding home, and in some of the poetry which Gregory of Nazianzus, among others, wrote on this theme.

> Grant Immortal Monarch
> That we may hymn you,
> Grant we may sing of you
> Our ruler and lord;
> Through whom is the hymn,
> Through whom is the praise,
> Through whom the chorus of angels
> Through whom the endless ages...
> Through whom the great beauty of the stars,

> Through whom our noble race was made
> That as rational beings we could perceive
>   our God.

> For you have created all things
> And given order to each,
> Governing all in your providential care.

> You spoke a Word and it came to pass,
> The Word was God your Son,
> Of the same being as yourself,
> Of the same honour as his parent.
> He has kept all things together
> That he might rule over all.

> And the Holy Spirit, who is God,
> Embraces all things round,
> Guarding all things in his providence.
> O living trinity I name you,
> One and only Monarch
> Unchangeable nature that has no beginning,
> Nature of ineffable being,
> Impenetrably wise intelligence,
> Unshakeable strength of the heavens...
> Be merciful to us,
> For glory and thanks are yours
> To the endless ages of ages. Amen. [3]

The advanced theology of the trinity had at least one profound result – that perfection (the divine being) was understood now not as the splendid isolation that had constituted the ancient philosophical belief in the one God, but rather as a profoundly interrelated communion of persons. The notion that the perfection of identity was constituted in communion rather than solitude ensured that Christian spirituality ever afterwards prioritized the concept of loving relationship as the supreme image of God, and the ultimate way to experience the divine presence.

The path of prayer

Apart from their purely theological works, Basil and the two Gregories also left behind extensive writings relating to the way in which a dedicated disciple can advance in the paths of prayer. All of them stressed that the essential stages of the journey involved initial repentance and a desire to purify one's lifestyle. After that came a period of consolidation through application to prayer, a life lived in relative peacefulness with study of the sacred scriptures. There was then a developing period of growing insightfulness until, in the end, the person was sensitively attuned to the promptings of the Spirit of God and was like glass that had first been cleaned and then became itself radiant as the divine light passed through it. In a famous passage Basil of Caesarea put it as follows:

The Paraclete takes possession of a pure eye, as the sun does, and will show you in himself, the image of the Invisible One… It is he who shines in those that are cleansed of every impurity to make them spiritual through communion with him. Just as bright and transparent bodies themselves become scintillating when light falls upon them, and reflect another brightness from themselves, just so Spirit-bearing souls, illuminated by the Spirit, become spiritual themselves, and send forth grace to others.[4]

This theology soon became standard in all the monastic communities of the East; their intellectual life was founded on the ascetical and theological writings of these earlier fathers, especially the writings of Basil and Gregory of Nazianzus.

◆ Liturgy of St Basil; Macedonian wall-painting from the middle of the 11th century.

Pachomius (c. 290–346)

Pachomius was an Egyptian convert to Christianity. Well before the lives of the later and more celebrated 'organizers' of the monastic life, such as Basil the Great or Benedict, he is generally credited as being the first to plan for centrally organized 'common life' monasticism, with a Rule and a regulated schedule for the day that revolved around communal meetings for prayer, work and table fellowship under the overall control of an abbot. This monastic lifestyle was named *cenobitic*, the Greek term for 'common life'.

Conversion

As a young man, Pachomius was conscripted from his village to serve in the army. When passing through a small Christian village in Egypt, at a time of severe personal depression, he experienced the practical charity of a Christian benefactor and he later ascribed to this his conversion to the 'new religion'. When he was dismissed from military service in 313 he returned to the Upper Egyptian village of Chenoboskion and was baptized into the Christian community there. Shortly afterwards he took up the ascetical life under the guidance of the hermit Abba Palamon. A nearly contemporary *Life of Pachomius* takes up the story and tells us that in the early 320s he was collecting firewood at the deserted village of Tabennesi, in the Thebaid, near to the River Nile, when in a heavenly vision he heard a voice telling him to settle and build a monastery in this place. He seems to have been a charismatic leader and soon attracted many disciples to live the ascetical life as a family. After six years he had to establish a second foundation nearby at the village of Pbou.

◆ **A painting of the area around Thebes;** *The Thebaide,* **by Starnina Gherardo (1354–1413).**

The spread of the movement

This second foundation was destined to grow in importance as the largest monastery and would become the centre of a chain of Pachomian 'federated' houses, as other monastic groups further afield began to associate themselves with his system along the great river in Upper Egypt. This chain of organized Christian communes, some occupying old Roman forts and each capable of harnessing the collective work of their members (and so growing in economic and political weight while at the same time offering their members secure protection), was an important factor in the establishment and growth of Christianity in Egypt in this era.

Pachomius's military background is often said to have shaped his ideas of group organization and discipline, though some recent scholarship has pointed to the possible influence of already existing Manichaean communities in the area. Pachomian settlements were

characterized by a strict insistence on communal poverty, and the discipline in the houses we might regard as excessive. However, in comparison with ancient military camps, or even such alternative contemporary monastic leaders as Shenoute of Atribe who was later to be active higher up the Nile, Pachomius was positively moderate.

The influence of Pachomius's ideas

In 346 Pachomius died in the severe plague that ravaged the settlements along the Nile. At that time he held nine male and two female monasteries under his authority. Palladius the Greek historian, writing c. 420, estimated that 3,000 monastics belonged to Pachomius's federation in his lifetime.[5] By the fifth century the federation had entered into a process of dissolution, a break-up that was accelerated by the Christological controversies that divided the church in the period after the Council of Chalcedon (451). Pachomius's ideas about the organization of cenobitic life, however, had by that time strongly influenced the monasteries at Sinai, Palestine and Cappadocia, and would have long-lasting effects within international Christianity.

The Rules of Pachomius are highly practical and based on common sense and an active concept of the common good. They were, perhaps, not written down until after Pachomius' death, but they certainly represent the essential tenor of his system. They not only influenced Basil of Caesarea, but, after being translated into Latin by Jerome (c. 342–420), were a strong influence on the Western theologians and monastics John Cassian, Caesarius of Arles and Benedict of Nursia, and so they played a role as something of an archetypal guide to cenobitic founders both in the Eastern and Western churches.

Monastic teachers

The monastic life, by the late fourth century, had established itself in a most successful way. Even in the earliest stages of monasticism, the tradition of teachers who would pass on their insights to selected disciples was strong. As the monastic life spread and stabilized in key centres such as Egypt, Palestine and Syria this tradition of spiritual advice was consolidated and evolved into the more permanent form of written manuals of spiritual advice. These works, for over a thousand years, were the predominant Christian writings. Today they are just beginning to be rediscovered as they emerge from Latin, Greek, Syriac and Coptic, to have their first modern translated editions. We have space here only to look at a few of the leading teachers of the ascetical life.

Evagrius of Pontus
(c. 346–99)

Evagrius was a disciple of Basil and of Gregory of Nazianzus. He was one of the most important monastic writers to set down extensive advice on the stages of the spiritual journey. His doctrine is related to that of the Cappadocians in many respects, but he specialized in giving practical and detailed advice about the life of prayer, and as a result his writings served as guidance manuals for generations of monks after him. Shortly after the council of Constantinople in 381 Evagrius left a promising career in the capital and took refuge in the Palestinian desert with the spiritual teacher Melania the Elder (c. 342–c. 410). She advised him to go to Egypt to experience the monastic life there, and he did so in the two great centres of the movement: first in the desert of Nitria, and then (in 385) in the area called Kellia, where he studied with two of the most famous of the early monks, both of whom were called Macarius.

Evagrius's teachings presented the Christian life of prayer in the form of philosophic discourses. He was heavily influenced by Pythagorean and Platonic ideas about the ascent of the soul when released from bodily concerns and, in his own lifetime, his Christianization of this philosophic approach was both famous and controversial. He argued that any image which the mind entertained in prayer necessarily falsified the reality of God which, by definition, transcended any earthly thought or sensation. To instruct his disciples he wrote highly dense 'sentences' that have the form of a terse instruction or sometimes a riddle. His books are comprised of many pages of these strings of aphorisms. The monk was not meant to read the whole book in one sitting, rather to repeat a chosen sentence many times, meditating on it until it opened the mind into understanding. The practice of repeating a simple phrase over and over in the course of a day was already standard prayer-practice in the desert, but usually it was the simple invocation of the name of Jesus, or a short phrase from scripture. Evagrius developed the form by making the sentences ascend in increasing difficulty, in the cause of advocating the practice of 'imageless prayer'. Evagrius's two most popular books were his *Praktikos* (as its name suggests, a practical manual of guidance on the practice of mental prayer) and his book of *Chapters on Prayer*. Here are a few selected sentences to give the flavour:

> Prayer is the constant communion of the spirit with God. Can you imagine the condition of soul that will be required for a spirit to strain after its Master, without faltering, and to live constantly with him as if face to face?[6]

> Moses attempted to draw near the burning bush (see Exodus 3:5) but was forbidden until he had taken the shoes off from his feet. It is the same with you – you must take off every thought that is coloured by your passions, since you wish to see the One who is beyond all thought and all perception.[7]

> Struggle to make your mind deaf and dumb at the time of prayer, for only then will you be able to pray.[8]

In his *Praktikos*, Evagrius provided a veritable treatise on psychology, and it was to be read and reread for centuries by practitioners who came to respect its insights and usefulness:

The demons strive against people who live in the world mainly through their external deeds, but in the case of monastics, mainly through their thoughts; for life in the desert cuts off many deeds. But just as it is easier to commit sin in thought than in deed, so also is the warfare conducted on the field of the thoughts more severe and difficult than the warfare over things and deeds. The mind, you see, is very easily moved, and difficult to control when sinful fantasies approach it. Consider this. We were never commanded (in scripture) to pass the night in vigils or to fast severely; yet we were commanded to 'pray without ceasing'.[9]

This potent mix of down-to-earth comment with high metaphysical theory is typical of all Evagrius's work.

Diadochus of Photike
(c. 400–86)

Another highly influential monastic teacher was Diadochus, Bishop of Epirus in northern Greece. He was a careful reader of Evagrius whose traditions he wished to synthesize and correct. He did this most notably by giving a theological primacy to love, something which Evagrius only touched upon. In making adjustments to Evagrius he propelled to the forefront of his teaching the biblically grounded conception of the primacy of the heart. For him the heart and the *nous* (the spiritual identity of a person) have been harmonized, in Christ. The intellect is the organ of attentive perception; the heart is the location of the inner self where the meeting with God takes place. Diadochus emphasized the 'embodied' character of true prayer. He did not believe either that prayer should be purely an emotional thing,

or that it should be so intellectualized that it did not take into consideration important things such as bodily feeling and bodily posture. He was also a strong advocate of the Jesus prayer, teaching that the repetition in quietness of the phrase: 'Lord Jesus Christ, Son of God, have mercy on me,' slowly, over many hundreds of times, would inevitably lead to the heart of prayer. His influence was felt all through the later Greek church.

Many writers in his time approached the issue of the human heart as if it were the centre of all that was corrupt and unreliable in the life of a disciple. Not so with Diadochus. He turned this pessimistic idea around, and argued that the heart was, by contrast, the holy place which God had chosen as the ground of encounter between the divine and the human:

When the whole person has turned towards the Lord, then grace reveals to the heart its presence there with a feeling which words cannot express; once again waiting to see which way the soul will incline… God may allow the arrows of the devil to wound the soul at the most inward point of its sensitivity but only so as to make the soul search out God with warmer resolve and a more humble disposition. If, then, a person begins to make progress in keeping the commandments and calls unceasingly upon the Lord Jesus, then the fire of God's grace spreads even to the heart's more outward organs of perception.[10]

The person who dwells continually within the heart is detached from the attractions of this world, and such a person lives in the Spirit and cannot know the desires of the flesh.[11]

Whenever we fervently remember God we feel the divine longing well up within us, from the very depths of the heart.[12]

His doctrine centres on the idea that the person who wishes to find God in prayer must try to dwell within this sacred shrine, or temple, of the heart, focusing its attentiveness like a worshipper waiting for the revelation of God's presence, and using the invocation of the holy name of Jesus to achieve this, until the light makes itself known, illuminating the whole person in the process:

> It is written that none can say Jesus is Lord except in the Holy Spirit (1 Corinthians 12:3). Let the spiritual intellect, then, continually concentrate on these words within its inner shrine, with such intensity that it is not turned aside to any mental images. Those who meditate unceasingly upon this glorious and holy name in the depths of their heart, can sometimes see the light of their own intellect. For when the mind is closely concentrated upon this name, then we grow fully conscious that the Name is burning off all the filth that covers the surface of the soul.[13]

Shenoute of Atribe (d. c. 466)

Shenoute, the Coptic Master of the White Monastery at Akhmim in Upper Egypt, is reminiscent of Diadochus when he too teaches about the importance of quiet and peaceful invocations of the name of Jesus forming the

◆ **Christ on a donkey surrounded by angels; a decoration from the White Monastery at Akhmim.**

substructure of simple heartfelt prayer. He advised the villagers in Upper Egypt to invoke the divine name in all aspects of life so that life and prayer would run together:

> *When entering the house say: God!*
> *and when leaving say: Jesus!*
> *When resting say: God!*
> *and when rising say: Jesus![14]*

Shenoute is putting the ancient biblical 'doctrine of the name' in a simple Christian form, teaching that calling on Jesus is nothing less than an invocation of the name of God, with all its power, into the heart of the believer:

> *Seek the meaning of these words, and you will have them in your mouth and find them on the lips of your sons.*
> *If you are joyful and celebrate a feast say: Jesus!*
> *If you have worry and suffering: Jesus!*
> *If the sons and daughters laugh: Jesus!*
> *Those who touch water: Jesus!*
> *Those who flee from barbarians: Jesus!*
> *Those who see monsters or other frightening things: Jesus!*
> *Those who have pain or illness: Jesus!*
> *Those who have been taken captive: Jesus!*
> *Those who have been unjustly judged and suffer injustice: Jesus!*
> *The name of Jesus alone is on their lips and is their salvation and their life; he and his Father.[15]*

Shenoute was a powerful Christian leader in his own time, and continued to have an importance for the Coptic church in Egypt, as he wrote in that language. But it was this that also made his work slip away from the interest of the Greek church until its translation and wider 'rediscovery' only late in the twentieth century. But if Coptic was becoming less well known by the sixth century, there was an abundance of texts being produced in Greek that were destined to have a long and abiding influence.

Barsanuphius and John
(6th century)

Little is known about the historical lives of Barsanuphius and John, who were two hermits who lived near one another and close to a desert monastery near Gaza in Egypt. They represent the mature stage of Egyptian monastic spirituality and in their own lifetimes had a high reputation as masters of spiritual guidance. They are a good example of how the monks often looked for a spiritual elder (a spiritual father or mother – later to be known in the Russian tradition as a Staretz) who would undertake the skilled task of guiding them in their spiritual development and to whom they would reveal the innermost workings of their mind, and confess their whole lives. The two hermits were known as 'the great old man and the other old man' and they served as the guides for many monks in their locality, including Barsanuphius's celebrated disciple Dorotheus of Gaza. After their deaths their works came to be regarded as one of the primary sources of desert spiritual wisdom and had a deep influence on the later Byzantine Hesychasts, those who focused on the tradition of inner prayer and quietness.

Unusually, the two old men refused to interrupt their hermit lifestyle in the course of giving instruction, and it is because of this that we have our knowledge of their teachings, for one of the disciples of Barsanuphius, Seridus, was abbot of the nearby monastery. He saw to it that all questions for the elders were gathered and submitted to them in writing, and they gave their replies back later, also in writing. Their collected teachings soon grew, and as they were both teachers in a very similar tradition, they were later edited together to form one literary source. Today about 850 questions and answers survive.

Barsanuphius and John were an important force in balancing the popularity of Evagrius and his highly speculative spiritual tradition that looked back to Origen. They represented a simpler and more practical form of wisdom that emphasized the necessity of keeping to a regular and humble method of prayer, rather than seeking after ecstatic imageless states. They insisted that the usual Christian practices of vocal prayer – the repetition of set forms of prayers such as the Our Father, or the recitation of the Psalms, were not inferior aspects of prayer, meant only for beginners, but critically important to all disciples at every stage. The recurring refrain of their teaching is the Pauline dictum that prayer should be unceasing. To help the disciple towards a state where prayer would be as regular as breathing, they recommended the use of the Jesus prayer, short heartfelt cries that used the name of Jesus as a prayer in itself. Their recommended formulae were varied but based around a common theme of the invocation of the holy name:

Lord Jesus Christ, have mercy on me.[16]
Lord Jesus, protect me and help my weakness.[17]

This spiritual tradition of extreme simplicity, humble obedience to experienced guides, and the focus on the presence of Jesus, soon came to be a dominant force in Eastern Christian spiritual tradition. In later years it was associated with techniques of aligning the actual words with the rhythms of breathing and heartbeat, and in this final form it came to be known as the Jesus prayer, a method or discipline of prayer which is, to this day, central to the spiritual activities of the Eastern Christian monks.

Dorotheus of Gaza
(6th century)

The Jesus prayer, when associated with the teaching to focus the heart on the presence and mercy of Christ, can also be described as 'the prayer of the heart'. One of its chief representatives is another great sixth-century teacher of the Egyptian desert, Dorotheus, the Archimandrite of Gaza. Dorotheus had been born in Syrian Antioch around 506 and died in Gaza sometime after 560. He consciously combines the teaching tradition of the Cappadocian fathers,

Evagrius, and the sayings of the desert fathers and mothers. He was personally acquainted with Barsanuphius and John. Like Diadochus of Photike, he was to be an important link in the combining of the Egyptian and Syrian Christian spiritual traditions.

Dorotheus speaks in a very personal way of how the heart moves in prayer with God. He encouraged his disciples by telling them of a lengthy time of spiritual deadness he experienced, which ended when he could endure it no longer: for God never abandons the faithful disciple to a trial that cannot be endured. He described an epiphany of Christ in terms of an encounter with a mysterious visitor who gave his heart the grace to rise from heaviness into joy:

My heart was heavy, my mind was dark, nothing could comfort me and there was no relief anywhere… The grace of God comes swiftly to the soul when endurance is no longer possible. Suddenly I turned towards the church and saw someone who looked like a bishop entering into the sanctuary… Something drew me powerfully after him, so I went into the church behind him. He remained standing for some time with his hands stretched up to heaven, and I stood there in great fear, praying, for I was very alarmed by the sight of him. When his prayer was finished he turned and came towards me, and as he drew nearer to me I felt my pain and dread passing away. Then he stood in front of me and, stretching out his hand, touched me on the breast and tapped my chest with his fingers saying the words of the psalm: I waited. I waited on the Lord and he stooped down to me; he heard my cry. He drew me from the deadly pit, from the miry clay. He set my feet upon a rock and made my footsteps firm. He put a new song into my mouth – praise of our God (Psalm 40:1–2). He repeated all these verses three times, tapping me on the chest as I have said… Then he departed. And immediately light flooded my mind and there was joy in my heart, with comfort and sweetness. I was a different man. I ran out after

him hoping to find him but I could not. He had vanished. From that moment on by God's providence, I have not known myself to be troubled by fear or sorrow, for the Lord has sheltered me up till this moment through the prayers of the old men.[18]

For Dorotheus, like Diadochus, the heart is all that matters in the movement of the spiritual life. If it is ready, then its very eagerness and willingness ensure the presence of God:

If anyone really and truly desires to do the will of God with all their heart, God will never leave them to themselves, but will constantly guide them according to his own divine will. If someone really sets their heart on the will of God, God will enlighten a little child to tell such a person what is his will. But if a person does not truly desire the will of God, even if they were to go to search out a prophet, God would put into the mouth of that prophet a deception similar to that which was in that man's own deceiving heart.[19]

His was an insistence that is present in the best of Christian teaching on the spiritual life – that prayer is not a task for holy people, or experts, but an activity for all, something that should be as natural as breathing, and burning in the heart like the flame that fuels the whole life of Christian discipleship. He teaches that if the heart is ready and eager, the grace of God will never be slow. It became a fundamental rule of the Christian spiritual life.

The Syrian spiritual writers
(4th to 8th centuries)

The Syrian Christian writers may not seem immediately to belong in this present section that looks at the Greek Christian traditions of prayer, but two of their most famous writers need particular mention, for they were translated into

Ephrem the Syrian (c. 306–73)

Ephrem was an important defender of the theological tradition of Athanasius of Alexandria. He lived on the far eastern border of the Roman empire, and was a deacon in the churches of Nisibis and Edessa. He was a hymn-writer and choir-leader for a convent of Syrian nuns, and also organized relief work for his church and city in times of need. In one of his hymns he has a vivid image describing prayer and how people learn how to pray, when he compares God's patience in teaching creatures to be aware of him to a man who tries to teach a parrot to speak[20] using a mirror to fool it into thinking it was chatting with another bird. Human language was something that could not come naturally to the bird. Only the squawk arose spontaneously, but the gracious discourse with God was, even at its heights of achievement, something laughable, and yet touchingly wonderful: awesome in what it revealed of the patient attentive care bestowed on the dumb animal by an ineffably transcendent power who had compassion on the creature's weakness. The parrot's primary problem in learning this strange syntax was its lack of attentiveness; its lack of awareness of the divine milieu to which it was being summoned by the presence. In wandering away from the sense of that presence time after time, it kept falling back from its task. On the occasions when it learned by heart, or rather from the heart, it was capable of addressing its master – in that moment it saw its Lord face to face, just as a human does when the heart dares to lift itself up in the presence of the Holy One, and, at that moment, is in the full conscience of his presence. Ephrem's image of the disciple in prayer, communicating like a parrot under the amused gaze of its devoted owner, is a salutary reminder of the need for constant humility in the spiritual life.

◆ *The Sepulchre of Ephrem*, **including scenes from his life, by Emanuel Zanfurnari (15–16th century).**

Greek at an early stage and exercised a great influence on classical Byzantine spiritual theology.

Isaac of Nineveh (d. c. 700)

Isaac came from Qatar, and was a monk at the monastery of Beth Abe in Kurdistan. He was consecrated Bishop of Nineveh, but soon after he retired to live the solitary life in Khuzistan. Becoming blind in his old age, he moved back into a monastery and here, at the end of his life, he edited his spiritual teachings in the form of the *Ascetical Homilies*. These were translated into Greek in Palestine and published in Constantinople in the ninth century and have exercised a deep influence on the Greek Christian world ever after. Isaac is important in the history of Christian spirituality, not only for his own writings, but also because he is a synthesist, a bridge-builder between the intellectualist mystical tradition of Evagrius, who spoke of the ascent of the mind to God, and the traditions of Syria and Egypt, which spoke of the descent of the mind into the heart where the disciple met God. Isaac's vivid and likeable personality emerges on every page:

> Often when I was writing these things my fingers failed me in setting down all onto paper; they were unable to endure the sweetness that descended into my heart and silenced my senses.[21]

The heart under the eye of God is a primary symbol of Isaac's theology. He lays high stress on the essential requirement of purity of heart in the person desiring true prayer.

He also taught that the revelation of the presence of God within the heart produced an inevitable sensation, and in *Ascetical Homilies* he gave a taxonomy of spiritual sensation, a guide for the disciples: how to recognize the difference between ordinary psychological experiences and the kind of sensation that the Spirit of God caused in the soul as a sign of his presence and working.[22] Like many of the earlier desert fathers, he taught that the chief sign of the divine presence was peacefulness and joy and a sense of humility. The chief sign of a false spiritual experience was disturbed or excited agitation, and self-satisfied pride. Isaac describes the soul in the presence of God as comparable at times to an ecstasy like the 'drunkenness' of Pentecost:

> The love of God is fiery by nature and when it descends in an extraordinary degree onto a person it throws that soul into ecstasy. And so, the heart of the person who has experienced this love cannot contain it or endure it without unusual changes being seen... the face becomes lit up, full of joy; the body becomes heated; fear and shame depart from such a person who thus becomes like an ecstatic... The gaze of this

Dionysius the Areopagite (5th century)

There is another Syrian writer, someone who stands historically midway between Ephrem and Isaac, who certainly demands a place in the Greek spiritual tradition. His works if not written originally in Greek were translated into that language very quickly, and had a major impact on the subsequent history of both the Eastern and Western churches. Dionysius the Areopagite (or Pseudo-Areopagite) is a peculiar instance in Christian history of a wholly unknown character whose works nevertheless gained a widespread following, and had a deep influence on the Christian tradition of mysticism. In the Eastern church he was a powerful force on the doctrine of Maximus the Confessor (c. 580–662) who popularized and 'systematized' him for a wider readership. The medieval West rediscovered him later when he was translated into Latin by the Irishman John Scotus Erigena (c. 810–77), and afterwards he became a veritable founding father of the medieval mystical renaissance. His writings first appeared in a theological conflict in the Eastern church in the sixth century, and were rejected out of hand as forgeries, for someone claimed them as the surviving treatises of the Dionysius whom the apostle Paul had converted in Athens (on the hill of Areopagus) as recounted in the Acts of the Apostles.

The writings, however, have all the marks of being works of a fifth-century Syrian bishop–monk, teaching for the benefit of his small community and explaining how the sacred rituals of the liturgy mirror the cosmic structure of the universe. The chief works of this anonymous writer (*Mystical Theology, Divine Names, The Celestial Hierarchy* and *The Ecclesiastical Hierarchy*) can now all be read in English translation and range from very short sermons, to longer and more complex discussions.

The spiritual teaching of Dionysius

Within God's plan of the universe spirits ascend and descend to and from the supreme glory of God. The Christian, caught up in the mystical rites of the church's sacraments, shares with the angels (who surround all that the earthly church does) this glorious ascent which can be experienced in many ways. Chief among them is the ascent of the mind and heart, which rise naturally to their divine source once the clamour of material passions and conflicting desires has been quietened by discipline and prayer. Dionysius is much occupied with 'hierarchies' or the orders and forms of making progress and ascent. He discusses the ranks of the angels, and his work seized the imagination of the ancient world as well as having a great attraction for medieval thinkers and Gothic architects who were equally exercised by hierarchies, but he was more concerned with drawing a picture of the Christian life as something that could not be experienced 'all at once' or claimed as a static state. He pictured true Christian life as an ongoing maturation, and at various stages certain things spoke to the believer more directly than at other times. A believer might not only progress, but even fall away from the progress, but the person whose heart desired God would be led ever more profoundly into union with God – from faith towards vision, from belief towards knowledge.

Three stages of growth

A marked aspect of Dionysius's writing is the way in which he used the idea of negation of language and experience (we have already seen this in Evagrius) to depict the spiritual life. God is the One beyond all names or images or categories of being. The Christian experience of God, according to Dionysius, is essentially 'unknowable'. To enter into this 'knowledge of unknowing' is to use language which deconstructs itself even in the process of making affirmations. He puts it like this:

> God is known in all things and apart from all things... and therefore everything can be affirmed of him at one and the same time, and yet he is none of these things.[23]

Dionysius presented an overall scheme in which the spiritual ascent was marked in each individual case by a progress over three stages. The first was a moving away from selfishness by discipline, ethical fidelity and increasing devotion to prayer. This was the initial stage – purification. For those who became stabilized by the willingness to adopt the disciplines required by the life of conversion, God increasingly opened their minds, and hearts, and inner spiritual eyes, to the secrets of his nature and purposes in the world. This was the second stage – illumination. Once the faithful disciples had been initiated in these two stages there came an ever-deepening and peaceful state that transcended formal words or prayers, in which searching gave way to finding, and belief gave way to direct experience. This was the third stage – union.

This schema of the spiritual life as a threefold ascent had a profound influence on most spiritual writing that followed. It was based on the work of the Cappadocian fathers but gave more stress to that state of wisdom that passes beyond speech. To this extent it became known as 'apophatic' theology (from the Greek word for 'turning away from speech'). Maximus the Confessor was to spread this style of theology widely in the Greek church, where it became a well-used medium, or style, for trying to describe transcendent experience in the limits of language.

person's intellect is fixed inseparably and delightedly upon Him. Though he is distant he speaks with Him as one who is near at hand... This vision is natural, but inaccessible to sense-perception. In his actions as well as in his appearance, such a one is enflamed... This is the spiritual passion which inebriated the apostles and martyrs.[24]

This Syrian tradition of the 'sensed' experience of God in the heart was very prominent in the spiritual writer Macarius, and through the translation of his works that appeared in England in the eighteenth century, it came to have a deep influence on the young John Wesley.

Maximus the Confessor
(c. 580–662)

The late sixth and seventh centuries were a time of great transition for the church and for wider Roman society. The Greek and Latin worlds were growing apart, and Maximus is one of the last theologians of the Greek patristic age to have regular correspondence with, and knowledge of, the Latin world, mainly because he was exiled to the West (North Africa and Rome) by Persian invaders who drove him from his monastery in Palestine. He was a highly intelligent commentator and wrote extensively on theology and on the spiritual life. His works came to have an important influence on the whole of the later Greek Christian world, though they were less well known in the West until the twentieth century. Maximus resisted the church policies of Emperor Constans II who was trying to settle a foment of Christological arguments by propagating a view of Jesus that said he had only one divine will (monothelitism). The emperor's party thought that this transcendentalist view, where the divine nature of Christ so absorbed the human characteristics that there was no possible room for any development of a human will in Jesus, would properly account for the perfect life of the Saviour.

◆ **Jesus; an illumination from an 11th-century Byzantine manuscript.**

For Maximus, the teaching that Jesus had no human will, only the divine will of God, made his humanity into a sham, and rendered his human life completely worthless as offering any example to disciples who were tempted. Maximus argued strongly that Christ had two wills, each belonging to its own 'nature'; in other words, a divine will as the eternal Word of God, and a human will as the man Jesus. To affirm this, he thought, made Jesus truly, and really, both human and divine. But, as Maximus went on to argue, the unique thing about Jesus considered as human was that his will as a man was entirely in harmony with the divine will. And this was exactly how he was a pattern for believers to find their salvation – as they too learned to make their own human wills, choices and deeds come into harmony with the will of God.

Maximus suffered for his political resistance; he was tortured and mutilated by the state authorities, and died prematurely as a result of his injuries. This was how he earned the title 'Confessor', which signifies someone who has survived a martyrdom. The debates culminated after his death in the sixth Ecumenical Council at Constantinople (681) where his teaching was confirmed. It is often regarded as an obscure period and is an area of theology which many find too 'mechanical' for their tastes, but in a real sense the work of Maximus was an important philosophical defence of human freedom. Maximus saw the perfection of human persons, their sanctification, to be inextricably linked to their growth into full human freedom. The concept of the neurotic saint was, for him, something incompatible, since Christ had become human precisely in order to bring healing to a dangerously unbalanced humanity which had lost its freedom in the pursuit of self-centred desires. His work implies that God requires the exercise of freedom as a fundamental element in the process of salvation, and he characterizes the experience of holiness as a profound liberation of the human psyche, a growing into the image of God. As he put it:

> The mind that is joined with God and abides with him through prayer and loving desire, will become wise, and good, and powerful, and merciful, and long-suffering. In a word, it will come to know in itself almost all the characteristics that are Godlike.[25]

If more Christians had considered such arguments from this hero of Christian resistance, perhaps the use of oppressive and authoritarian measures in the history of Christianity might have been considerably reduced, and the concept of the spiritual life as a natural path towards healing and wholeness could have been stressed more fundamentally. Maximus is notable for what has been called a 'cosmic theology'. His vision of the healing of humankind embraces the whole cosmos, which he sees as finding its meaning and joy in the paradox of the God who entered into material life at a particular moment in history. This supreme mystical communion serves as a luminous key to the understanding of the meaning of life, and its direct expression is given in a mysterious experience of loving communion which, therefore, stands as the quintessence of Christian truth. His main spiritual writings are the *Centuries on Charity*, *The Ascetic Life* and *Commentary on the Lord's Prayer*. He also wrote a commentary on the liturgy and numerous works of doctrinal criticism.

The Greek Christian poets

We have so far been looking at theological teachers or monastic elders in the Greek Christian tradition, but perhaps we ought not to neglect the fact that in antiquity, just as today, Christians expressed their faith and spirituality in the kind of hymns they sang or the traditional prayers they recited. Hymns were an important element of Christian life from the very beginning and several of the earliest hymns have survived in the text of the New Testament itself.[26] In later times the hymn

◆ **Virgin and Child with the archangels Gabriel and Michael; 7th-century mosaic in the Church of Panagia Angeloktistos at Kiti in Cyprus.**

was greatly developed in the Latin church by writers such as Ambrose, Prudentius and Sedulius. In the Greek East the hymn became a standard part of the worship services of the church at an early date, but in the sixth century a great poet and musician, Romanus the Melodist, took the form to new heights which affected the Greek church services ever afterwards. Prayer services, such as Matins or Evensong, in the Greek church consist of large amounts of these hymns written by Romanus, or his later successors such as Andrew of Crete, Joseph the Hymnographer, Cosmas of Aitolas and John of Damascus.

The Greek hymn-writers share common aspects of style. They delight in putting together biblical paraphrases, retelling the biblical stories (often for a non-literate audience) with added details and comments of their own to highlight the key issues. These long biblical hymns have rightly been described as 'homilies in verse', and were an important teaching device in the early church. Frequently the writers – and Romanus is a case in point – put together adjacent sentences throwing a sharp focus on the apparently incompatible elements of the life of Christ the divine Word. They follow the doctrine of Athanasius and Cyril, but express it in more popular and poetic forms – alluding to the Virgin who is also a mother, the child wrapped from head to toe in swaddling bands who was also governing the course of the stars, the death of the immortal God on the cross, and so on.

The abundant piling up of these paradoxes of theology stressed the need for wonder in the face of mystery when contemplating the essential story of Christianity. The central place of hymns in Greek Christian spirituality served an important function in keeping the element of wonder and mystery to the fore, and prevented the Eastern church from turning theology into a sterile rationalist exercise. The easiest way to comment on these poets is to present a very few extracts from some of their works. The riches of this tradition of medieval Greek poetry remain to be discovered by the wider world, as many of the writers have not yet been translated into English.

Christ the light

A beautiful and ancient Greek hymn, called 'The Gladdening Light', still sung today in every evening service of the Orthodox Church, compares Christ to the light that never fails. It takes its theme from the fact that the evening services traditionally began when people in their homes, or in church, had to light oil lamps because the daylight was beginning to fade:

Jesus Christ,
the gladdening light
of the deathless Father's holy glory;
the heavenly,
holy, blessed one.

As the sun reclines
we see the light of evening
and sing our hymn to God,
the Father, Son and Holy Spirit.

Worthy are you, O Son of God,
through each and every moment,
that joyful songs should hymn you.

You are the giver of our life,
and so the world gives glory.
(Anonymous, c. 3rd century)

We can begin with Romanus's famous hymn on the Virgin Mary, at the point where he describes the annunciation:

I cry to you: All Hail Unwedded Bride!
An angel of the highest rank
Was sent from heaven above,
To say to the Virgin: All Hail!
And at this bodiless sound, O Lord,
He saw you come into the body's form.

He stood astounded and amazed,
And cried out to her saying:
Hail, through whom comes radiant joy,
Hail, through whom the curse has ceased.
Hail, lapsed Adam's restoration…
Hail to you, the royal throne,
For you carried the One
Who himself sustains all things.[27]

One of the later Greek poets, who was also an important theologian, John of Damascus (c. 675–749), was a political leader of the Christian community in Damascus at the time it was ruled by the Islamic Caliphate. He abandoned his career and became a monk in the monastery of Mar Saba near Bethlehem. In his theological work he defended the theological tradition of Athanasius and the trinitarian tradition of the Cappadocian fathers. He was engaged in a lengthy theological debate over whether icons (religious images) were legitimate for Christians (the iconoclastic dispute) and here he argued that the proper veneration of religious images of Christ, the Virgin or the saints was a useful and important aspect of a living faith that took the fact of the material incarnation of the divine Word seriously. His teachings heavily influenced the Orthodox Eastern world where icons still play a far greater role than in Western Christianity. It is in his hymns, however, which he wrote in the company of his half-brother Cosmas, also an accomplished poet, that he had his greatest effect on the Eastern liturgy. His hymn on the feast of the cross (14 September) is an example of how the Greek theologians habitually see the passion and death of Christ as the dynamic transference of life to the world:

> *Ceaselessly we bow, O Christ our God,*
> *Before your cross that gives us life,*
> *And glorify your resurrection,*
> *Most powerful Lord,*
> *When on that third day you made anew*
> *The failing nature of humankind,*
> *Showing us so clearly*
> *The way back to heaven above:*
> *For you alone are good,*
> *The Lover-of-Humankind.*
> (John of Damascus, 'Hymn on the Life-giving Cross')

The Hesychast movement
(11th century onwards)

John of Damascus's largest single work, *On the Orthodox Faith*, was a massive synthesis of all the doctrines of the Eastern church that had been defined up to his time. It was a book of reference that was used as a source by Thomas Aquinas in the medieval West. Systematic and summative works like this were indications that the Christian East was already entering a long period of consolidation and (in some places) radical decline, when ancient Christian centres such as Egypt and Syria passed permanently out of the political world

◆ **John of Damascus flanked by John Climacus and Arsenias; Russian icon from the 15th century.**

Symeon the New Theologian (949–1022)

One of the precursors of the Hesychasts was Symeon the New Theologian, an aristocrat who abandoned his political career and entered a monastery in Constantinople. He tells us in remarkably vivid autobiographical accounts how his spiritual life had been careless and sporadic, but God, through the prayers of a kind old monk who had become his spiritual father, seized him violently one day with the first of a series of visions of the divine light. He goes on for the rest of his life to insist that Christianity can only be 'caught' from living saints (like one candle flame lighting another), not found in books.

Symeon's deep devotion to his spiritual guide, whom he describes as an angel of light who prays for him in the presence of God, together with his remarkably intense theology of the light of Christ that enveloped and transfigured him, marked out the path of much Hesychastic thought that was to follow. The 'theology of light' began to focus on the figure of Jesus transfigured on the mountain (so radiant in his form that the disciples could not bear to look upon him) as a symbol of how the true disciple who really comes close to Christ in prayer, will similarly be transfigured in light. It is a new form of the old doctrine of deified communion with God which we saw in the Alexandrian fathers Cyril and Athanasius. Profound and luminous 'transfiguration' thus comes to be the dominant motif of the whole Hesychast school.

Symeon had a long and controversial career as a monastic elder himself, and left a considerable body of work. His *Hymns of Divine Love* are among the most extraordinarily personal and intense documents in all of East Christian spiritual writing. The emotional charge of these writings had not really been witnessed before in the monastic texts from late antiquity which had hitherto been standard authorities. One of his hymns describing his reception of the Eucharist will serve to give a taste of his passionate and personal style, and his theology of luminous 'communion' with the divine:

> *My blood has been mingled with yours,*
> *And I know I have been merged with your Godhead.*
> *I myself have become your most pure body,*
> *A member, dazzling bright, a member truly sanctified,*
> *A member glorious, transparent, luminous...*

What was I once?
What have I now become?
Where shall I sit? What shall I touch?
Where shall I rest these limbs that have now become your very own?
In what works or actions shall I now employ
These members that are so terrible and divine?[28]

His experience of this ecstatic communion with Christ led Symeon to insist vigorously on the need for all Christians to experience for themselves the life-giving power of God. He taught this doctrine insistently, and caused great arguments in the capital. Nevertheless, in his opinion, if one could not claim the personal experience of God in one's life it was tantamount to admitting one had not yet become a Christian. He had no time whatsoever for those who counselled against the advisability of 'seeking the experience':

Do not say: It is impossible to receive the Holy Spirit;
Do not say: It is possible to be saved without Him.
Do not say that one can possess the Spirit without being aware of it.
Do not say: But God does not appear to men.
Do not say: But men do not see the divine light –
Or at least it is impossible in this current generation.
This is a thing, my friends, which is never impossible, at any time.
On the contrary it is entirely possible for those who long for it.[29]

◆ **Interior of the Hagia Sophia, the Church of**
the Holy Wisdom in Constantinople, where
Symeon the New Theologian worshipped.

of the Christian rulers. The great successes of Islam and its expansion in the territories of the old Roman empire would progressively reduce many Christian communities, especially those outside the Slavic world, into the position of struggling religious minorities. The centre of the East Christian world passed definitively now to Constantinople. The great capital, founded by Constantine the Great in the fourth century, would remain the Eastern hub of Christian art and theology until its conquest by the Ottoman Turks in 1453; a time that finally spelled the end of the Byzantine empire.

But Byzantium was long in its twilight, and before it lost its independent political reality, it successfully disseminated its influence far and wide: from Armenia to Ethiopia, from Italy even to Saxon England. One of the most notable achievements of this late Byzantine period, a time which saw a wonderful flowering of art, and a good deal of development in the rich Eastern liturgies and prayer services, was a spiritual movement that has come to be known as Hesychasm, a word that means 'quietness'. The movement stretches from the eleventh century to modern monasteries all over the Orthodox world, where it is still the dominant spiritual tradition.

Most of the Hesychast tradition is a restatement of the spiritual masters of the desert, as exemplified in writers such as Barsanuphius and John, or Diadochus of Photike. The same stress on the need for inner quietness is there; the central position of the Jesus prayer; the importance of finding an experienced spiritual guide who could interpret one's inner life; and the teaching that the heart is the very centre of the spiritual intelligence of a person, the focal point of the encounter with God. The Hesychasts, however, offered a newly intensified statement of all those different elements from the ancient tradition, and their resultant synthesis formed a powerful renaissance in the spiritual tradition of the East.

The ideas that can be seen in Symeon the New Theologian (see box, p. 146), merged in succeeding generations to form Hesychasm proper. This movement has been for ever associated with two leading theologians of the late Byzantine period – Gregory of Sinai (d. 1346) and Gregory Palamas (1296–1359). Gregory of Sinai was a hermit monk on Mount Athos, the monastic republic that still exists in the Halkidiki peninsula, almost unchanged from Byzantine times. Gregory advocated the Jesus prayer as the surest method of arriving at intense union with the luminous Christ. He recommended that the physical posture of the body ought to be made to assist the practice of prayer. He suggested the disciple should sit on a low stool, and 'drag down the intellect into the heart'. The breathing was to be controlled and slowed so that it could correspond with the ingoing and outgoing of the phrase: Lord Jesus Christ, have mercy on me, a sinner. The breathing technique and the slow repetition of the words were meant to help in stilling the thoughts that often run wild in times of prayer, and also to concentrate the monk on the approaching presence of the merciful Christ, a presence that is announced by a definite 'warming of the heart'.

Gregory Palamas was the most noted theologian of the whole Hesychast movement. The doctrines which Hesychasm represented caused great controversy, not least from thinkers who insisted on the utter unknowability of God. People who claimed to have 'seen the divine light' were dismissed by the latter group as cranks. Some of a more rationalist temper (and there have always been many of those in the Christian religion) dismissed the Hesychasts as ignorant mystics who had nothing to contribute to the 'modern world'.

◆ An 11th-century gold and enamelled reliquary showing Mary raising her arms to Christ who looks down from the sky. It would have been worn around the neck to protect the owner from harm.

It was Palamas who defended the Hesychast tradition on the intellectual front. If God cannot be approached or experienced directly in this present world, he argued, then the whole theology of the incarnation was not being taken seriously. The immaterial God, having entered into a profound relationship with his own flesh, uses the flesh to reveal his true divinity to the chosen, just as Christ once revealed the glory of his true divinity to the three apostles on the mountain of transfiguration. For Palamas, Christians who entered into a profound relationship with Christ through prayer, themselves became the apostles of his presence in the current generation. They were the elect, chosen for the end of ages.

Like Symeon the New Theologian, Gregory Palamas used his spiritual doctrine to insist that Christianity is nothing unless it is the direct and personal experience of believers who can witness the truth of the risen Christ in and through their own life experience. Those who pray, and know the power and presence of God in and through their prayer, form the living flames who will save their contemporaries. Far from being a side issue, a kind of pious introversion, prayer, for Gregory Palamas, was the lifeblood and entire point of theology, and the *raison d'être* of the Christian church.

Gregory of Sinai spent his last years near the borders of Bulgaria, and by the time of his death his followers had already started to take his teachings throughout the Slavic world, where Hesychasm was to have an immense effect on the life of the Orthodox Church, in Bulgaria, Russia, Serbia and Romania. Gregory Palamas was himself so successful in his lifetime that the emperor sponsored and encouraged the spread of his teachings widely in Greece. They especially came to take hold on Mount Athos, the centre of Orthodox monasticism.

The *Philokalia*
(18th to 20th centuries)

The successful spread of Hesychasm was to reach its peak in the production of the *Philokalia*. This was a large collection of all the previous Greek Christian writings, from the fourth to the fifteenth centuries, relating to the practice of the spiritual life, and approached from the perspective of a Hesychast. It was all collated by three monks – Macarius, Notaras and Nicodemus – and was first published in Greek in Venice in 1782. Subsequently translated into Slavonic by Paisy Velichovsky (1793) in Romania, and then into Russian by Theophan the Recluse (1876–90) it spread throughout the whole Christian Slav world. In the latter part of the twentieth century it appeared for the first time in English translation, in part through the labours of the British bishop–monk and Hesychast Kallistos Ware, and so came to begin its long path influencing the spiritual life of countless people in these islands too. One can find the writings of almost all the

◆ **Gregory Palamas; an icon from 19th-century Russia.**

masters of the spiritual life that we have touched upon in this present section, now easily accessible in the volumes of the translated *Philokalia*.

Conclusion

This has been a rapid survey of the spiritual traditions of the Eastern Christian church. It has left out far more than it has included, and done scant justice to the great teachers it has mentioned. There are common ideas, however, that emerge clearly enough from all the Eastern Christian writers of the past. The dominant theme is Christ. Prayer to the absolute divinity, for a Christian, begins in the movement of the Holy Spirit of God, and moves unerringly through Christ alone. Christian prayer, therefore, has a profoundly trinitarian character in its monotheism: 'To the Father, through the Son, in the Holy Spirit.' All the writers equally stress how essential a vivid and faithful life of prayer is for the continuing health and effectiveness of the church. It is not a pious add-on for a Christian, but the very lifeblood of the faith, and the purpose for the existence of the church in the world. Through its prayer, the body of Christians becomes light for its generation. The writers also point to deep mysteries of the discovery of the self through prayer. Most of them teach the necessity of entering the depths of the heart and, through discipline and perseverance, finding purification and enlightenment through the practice of prayer. All of them are agreed that once one embarks on the journey of prayer, nothing, and no one, ever remains the same.

5

The Russian Spirit

(10th to 19th centuries)

Sergei Hackel

Timeline

I t was not until the seventeenth century that anyone devised the term 'Holy Russia', and even then they must have been referring to an ideal rather than a reality. Nonetheless, there were individual Russian saints in plenty by that time, and their numbers have continued to grow.

Russia received her Christianity at the hands of the Byzantine church. There are confused records of how this all happened, and precisely when. The

◆ The baptism of Vladimir (c. 988), from a 15th-century Russian manuscript, the *Radziwill Chronicle*.

baptism of the pagan Russian ruler Vladimir in about 988 may be seen as a critical event. But it would be misleading to link it with a conversion of his people. This was to be a lengthy process, and it was never to be as comprehensive as church leaders liked to claim.

Nor was medieval Russia as coherent or as powerful an entity as its later publicists insisted: it was a loosely assembled series of confederated states, too often vying with each other for primacy of status. When Vladimir was baptized he was the prince of the then-dominant city-state of Kiev. But this was not to ensure Kievan pre-eminence as a centre of Russian Christianity throughout the centuries to come. In any case, the senior Russian bishop might be variously located at Kiev, Vladimir or Moscow. But until 1448 he was nothing other than the representative of the patriarch in distant Constantinople, and often a subservient one at that. Only in that year did Russian churchmen elect their own presiding bishop.

Of course, power politics has never engendered or ensured holiness. The local saints, who acted as the models and the guarantors of the Christian way of life were far more important. In fact, we need to speak of saintly figures, not just saints. Not all were ranked as saints within decades of their death. Some were not canonized for many years and others never received official recognition. But here was a communion of saints, whose intercessions might determine the resolution of their neighbour's problems. Had not the Lord undertaken to be merciful to Sodom, they might have asked themselves, if as few as ten righteous should be found there? (Genesis 18:26–32)

Boris and Gleb (d. 1015)

Righteousness could be perceived even beyond the obvious boundaries of church life. Princes could be singled out for praise and veneration. In 1015 Vladimir's two young sons, Boris and Gleb, were assassinated. Vladimir had died that summer, and Boris and Gleb were seen as rivals by their half-brother in the contest for the throne. According to the stylized tales which have survived, both suffered their deaths in all humility and in a Christlike manner. Boris, in particular, deliberately leaves himself defenceless in the southern steppes. He dismisses his numerous supporters and refuses to resist his foe. All this, he makes plain in one of his last prayers to his Lord, is done 'out of love for thy word: it is for thy sake that I am stricken'. Above all, he prefers 'the path of peace which leads to thee'.

So perished the first two Russian saints to be canonized. A new title had to be devised for their stance, which was not simply that of martyrs. They were to be known as 'passion-bearers'. Even in a squalid contest for the throne they were able to uphold the claims of the new moral code. Its remorseless logic demanded nothing less than non-resistance to evil.

Tolstoy and his followers were to take this teaching further in due course (see box, p. 163). But the Russians of the Middle Ages preferred to transform the cult of these two princes into something more mundane. Boris and Gleb retained their popularity, but merely as heavenly defenders of the Russian lands. In effect, public opinion required them to renounce their pacifist stance, and it was not long before icons showed them bearing arms.

◆ **Russian icon depicting Boris and Gleb bearing arms.**

Theodosius of the Kievan Caves (d. 1074)

It was not long before Russia had its monks. Some chose to withdraw from the secular world with its perpetual tensions and temptations. The young Theodosius chose to live a life of poverty in caves near Kiev. Here, high above the River Dnepr, was founded one of the most influential of monastic communities. It was always to be known as the Kievan Caves monastery. Yet it had its greatest impact once it had outgrown the actual caves. It was Theodosius who settled the monks above ground, and Theodosius who saw to it that his community, however dedicated to a life of prayer, should not ignore society at large.

His was not a formal obedience to a Rule. According to his biographer, 'Such was the compassion of our good father Theodosius, that if he saw a beggar or a pauper in distress and poorly dressed, he would grieve on his account and be greatly troubled over him and would go past him in tears.' Furthermore, this sort of encounter was not left to chance. A church on the monastery grounds was set aside, together with its courtyard, where 'he ordered that beggars, the blind, the lame and the sick should be housed. He supplied their needs from the monastery, and gave a tithe from all that the monastery possessed.' Not that others were forgotten. On Saturdays, for instance, 'he would send a cartload of bread to those who were in prison or in bonds'.

He preferred to be poorly dressed. Because of his tawdry clothes, there were many who failed to recognize him as the abbot, but 'mistook him for one of the cooks'. One impoverished widow came and asked for his support. 'Tell me, monk, where is your abbot?' she asked him. 'What do you want of him?' asked Theodosius: 'The man is a sinner.' He undertook to plead her case before a judge 'when our abbot arrives'.

As an abbot, Theodosius was tolerant, even tender-hearted, hence effective. His biographer noted that any monks who had absconded from the monastery would meet a ready welcome from

Extract from a sermon of Theodosius

I beg you, brothers, that we should labour in prayer and fasting and be concerned about the salvation of our souls. Let us turn away from our sins and deceitful ways – adultery, theft, slander, idle chatter, strife, drunkenness, gluttony, and hatred of brethren. Let us shun these things, brothers, and abominate them, so that thereby we do not defile our souls. But let us travel along the Lord's road leading us to paradise, and let us seek God with tears and sobs, with fasting and vigils, and in humility and obedience, so that we may receive mercy from him. Let us also hate this world still more, always bearing in mind the word of the Lord: 'If any man will not forsake father and mother, and wife, and children and such for my sake and that of the gospel, he is not worthy of me'; and also, 'He that findeth his life shall lose it: and he that loseth his life for my sake shall find it.'

So, brothers, as we too have rejected the world and renounced those living in it, let us hate every kind of unrighteousness and do nothing that belongs to this world, and let us not return to our former sins like a dog to its vomit. 'For no man', said the Lord, 'having put his hand to the plough, and looking back, is fit for the kingdom of heaven.' How shall we escape eternal torment if we complete the span of this life in idleness and without repentance? For us, brothers, who are called monks, it is fitting to repent our sins daily, for repentance is the key to the kingdom of heaven. It is not fitting for anyone to live without it; repentance is the way leading to paradise. Let us keep firmly to this way, brothers; let us keep our footsteps fixed on it. The wily serpent does not approach this road. The stages of this road are now beset with afflictions, but in the end they will be full of joy.'

him whenever they returned. But he reacted firmly to possessiveness or greed. Thus, when he visited his disciples in their cells and 'found something, whether food or clothing, beyond what was permitted by the Rule, whether food or clothing, he would take these things and cast them into the stove'. For it was Theodosius's conviction that 'it is wrong for us who are monks and have rejected worldly things to collect possessions in our cells. How can we offer a pure prayer to God if we hoard possessions there?'

'Pure prayer' was to remain an abiding concern for Theodosius himself, as well as for Russian monks throughout the ages. But inward-looking though it could become, here it had its social repercussions. It motivated the simple works of compassion to which the Caves community had a firm commitment. It also undergirded its abbot's stance in respect of government and public affairs.

Theodosius refused to accept the overthrow of Iziaslav, the ruler of Kiev, by the latter's younger brothers, one of whom usurped his throne in 1073. Moreover, he went out of his way to publicize his views. Sometimes he conveyed them orally to the usurper. On one notable occasion he summarized his views in writing.

Theodosius's letter enraged the usurper, who flung it to the ground. Whether Theodosius would be left in peace was increasingly in doubt. But even the likelihood of imprisonment would not deter him, 'for nothing in this life is dear to me'. When his secular well-wishers urged restraint, he used imagery which they might understand. 'Should deprivation of wealth and prosperity constrain me? Or the loss of villages? We brought none of these things into this world. We were born naked and so it is also fitting that we should depart naked from it. Therefore I am prepared for imprisonment or death.'

In the event, confrontation was avoided. This was some time before Theodosius's death in 1074. Indeed, the ruler even agreed to visit the Caves. A more peaceful dialogue was in prospect. But the basis for it remained unchanged. In Theodosius's words, 'It is our duty to reproach you and to tell you what is needed for the salvation of your soul. And it is your duty to listen.' In effect, he was commending a prophetic role for the church, no matter what the cost.

◆ **The Kievan Caves monastery.**

Sergius of Radonezh
(c. 1314–92)

'Pure prayer' was to be the central concern of
another humble monk of the early Middle Ages,
Sergius of Radonezh. But the setting for it had
changed radically from the time of Theodosius.

The invasion of the Russian lands by Mongol
hordes in the thirteenth century involved
devastation and dislocation for most local
institutions. It also enmeshed most of them in a
tightly controlled system of taxation. The church
was the only institution exempt from this. The
Mongols had arrived with a deeply ingrained
tolerance of all religions which outlasted the
fourteenth-century conversion of the Mongol
rulers to Islam.

This tolerance, matched with tax exemption
for all church foundations, created favourable
conditions for those who were disposed to set up
new monasteries in the wilds. Sergius was a pioneer
in this respect. His first venture was a lonely one.
His brother Stephen, who had accompanied him
into the uninhabited forests beyond Moscow, found
life too hard and left him to it.

Sergius's first trials were therefore those of a
solitary. He shared his meagre portions of bread
with a bear. However, rumours spread of his
steadfast vigils in the chapel and the cell which
he had built from logs. Within a matter of years a
palisade enclosed a settlement of various followers
who sought the guidance of the saint. Not that
Sergius sought precedence or recognition. It was
necessary to persuade him to accept the role of
abbot and of priest. To his newly established
community, which became known as the
monastery of the Holy Trinity, he said simply,
'If you come to live in the desert, the beginning
of all virtue is the fear of God.'

In all humility he refused to be promoted more
than this. He was sufficiently well known to the
principal bishop of the Russian Church to be
approached by him as his possible successor. He
had certainly shown his mettle more than once on
political assignments. But his answer was firm:

◆ Sergius of Radonezh overseeing construction of a cell and
church at Sergeiv Posad in a 16th-century Life illustrated
by a follower of Andrei Rublev.

'Who am I, but a sinner and the least of men?'

He had no intention of asserting his rights
even as an abbot. Once the community was well
established, his older brother returned to live
by his side. Stephen was ill at ease with the role
Sergius now played. During one of the services,
at which Sergius was the celebrant, a book was
handed to the director of the choir. When Stephen
was told that it came from 'the abbot', he
responded, 'Who is abbot in this place? Was I not
the first to settle here?' Sergius heard the remark,
but refrained from any comment. After the service
he simply left the monastery. Before long he had
set up another hermitage in the wilds. It took
some time before he could be persuaded to return.
But he had needed to purge the community of
envy and of pride. In due course he was to found
forty monasteries.

Sergius's concern for purity of prayer may
well have involved him in the practices of those
specialists in inward prayer whose teachings were
spreading at this time from Athos and other
monasteries of the Greek world. All-important in

Icons

Icons have been a feature of Russian Orthodox church life since the very beginning. The great battles about whether it is permissible to represent the divine or the holy at all had already been fought in the Byzantine world over the preceding centuries. So Russians were able to import a teaching on what icons mean together with the works themselves.

At the very least they gave visual expression to Christian beliefs – they had an educational role to play. The thoughts of an individual Doctor of the Church – 'If people ask me what I believe I show them the inside of my church' – were shared by all. The visual presentation of the faith was vital in a time when few could read.

It was believed that the icons also provided access to the sacred persons represented. Therefore worshippers would venerate the image which they saw before them. Their attention was not limited to the representation; it was addressed to the person represented. Icons were windows on the other world, revelations of the kingdom of heaven.

Communication with that 'other world' was helped by the direct gaze of the revealed and incarnated Christ. Christ was usually presented in a frontal pose, as were his saints.

Rublev's icon of Christ

One of the greatest Russian icon painters was Andrei Rublev (c. 1360–1430), who painted a famous icon of Christ in the 1420s. The icon by which he is best remembered, however, is a more mysterious work, *The Old Testament Trinity*. He is not the first artist to use the image of angels who came to Abraham (Genesis 18) as a type of the triune God, but his depiction can hardly be excelled.

The three figures are bound together in an understated circle, subtly differentiated though they are. Here is an eternal contemplation of a sacrificial chalice, whose challenge one of them is willing to accept in concert with them all.

It is an icon which is the product and the prompter of contemplative prayer. So it is not surprising to learn that it was produced for the monastery of Sergius of Radonezh, under whose auspices the icon painter lived and worked.

◆ *The Old Testament Trinity* **(c. 1422–27), by Andrei Rublev (c. 1360–1430), Tretiakov Gallery, Moscow.**

this teaching was a belief that mankind had access to the divine light, the light by which Jesus had been transfigured. Sergius did not write on this (or any other) subject, but there are aspects of his life which suggest that his prayer life had allowed him access to this very light. There was talk of an awesome light which hovered over the chalice when the saint celebrated the communion service. 'I saw the grace of the Holy Spirit cooperating with you,' said an astonished witness. But Sergius was clearly anxious to avoid any sort of cult: 'Tell no one what you have seen until the Lord calls me back to him from this life.'

Within a few years of his death the cult of Sergius could no longer be contained. He was canonized in 1422 and his tomb is visited by countless pilgrims to this day.

Nilus of Sora
(1433–1508)

By the middle of the next century, we find a saint who was obviously committed to the way of prayer, and, unlike Sergius, wrote of it as well.

The fifteenth century had seen the expansion of monastic life and the proliferation of solid and well-regulated foundations. So prosperous had some of them become that a basic question needed to be asked: Ought monks or monasteries to own property at all? Nilus of Sora argued that the answer was 'No.' For this very reason he left one of the most prosperous monasteries and ventured into the wilds. There he set up a small community of like-minded monks. These were 'brothers', rather than 'disciples', he insisted. A lifetime of dedicated poverty and prayer confirmed him in the wisdom of his ways. To the end of his days he was anxious to have them debated by the church at large, not promoted merely by a group of dissidents like his. At the Moscow church council of 1503 he intervened to ask: Did not the basic vow of poverty decide the question once for all, and for each and every monk? This was his strongly held belief. The council saw things

differently. In its aftermath, Nilus's followers were to be marginalized, even persecuted, by the established church.

Even more important for the community was the determination not to be defeated in their innermost strivings. This, too, was a struggle. But, more than any other, it had to be pursued in perfect silence. Feeding the silence was the prayer of prayers: the Jesus prayer of their Near-Eastern masters. Nilus quotes several variants of it, each of them authentic, but at the core of each is the invocation of the holy name: 'Lord Jesus Christ, Son of God, have mercy on me'; or 'Lord Jesus Christ, have mercy on me, a sinner.'

Such prayer should indwell the individual, each in his own way; each spiritual exercise should be performed 'with discretion and within due measure'. But 'when reason fixes both the time and the measure, then the resulting benefit can be truly marvellous'. Indeed, the prayer could give way to encounter with its very source and destination, God himself. Nilus borrowed the following words from an earlier visionary, Symeon the New Theologian (949–1022), but borrowed them with authority, as if they were his own:

> I behold a light which the earth does not possess, glowing in my cell. I see it as I sit on my couch. Within my own being I gaze upon the Creator of the world, and I converse with him, love him and feed on him, nourished only by this vision of God. And uniting myself with him, I rise above the heavens. Where the body is at such a time I do not know.

Nilus was demanding of himself. He insisted that, 'We must observe this general rule of life – to be about the work of God perpetually, and in every undertaking, in body and soul, in word, thought and action, according to the measure of our strength.' Yet he was tolerant of others. At a time when death penalties were demanded for heretics, Nilus urged that 'those who have strayed from the path of virtue should not be reviled or reproached'. At all times 'we must love our neighbours in obedience to our Lord's commandments'.

Joseph of Volokolamsk

(1439–1515)

Joseph of Volokolamsk was foremost among those who opposed Nilus in 1503 at the Moscow church council. He argued that monasteries were not only justified in owning land, it was their duty to do so. How else could the community be at the disposal of the needy? Joseph's community at Volokolamsk could provide refuge for thousands at a time of famine. Even on ordinary days, six or seven hundred needy people could be sustained there. As Joseph reminded his monks in the Rule which

Fools for Christ's sake

The sixteenth-century Muscovite establishment was scrupulously concerned for precedence, proprieties and rules, following in the tradition of Joseph of Volokolamsk. It is therefore not surprising that this period sees the flowering of a peculiar protest movement. Its leaders were to be found in the streets, even in the gutters of the city. Their practice was to mock and attack all social norms and conventions. For this reason, they adopted the role of simpletons or madmen: 'fools for Christ's sake'. As often as not, their very folly acted as a safeguard even when they addressed the tyrants of their day. As an English visitor to Moscow noted in the late sixteenth century, such holy men 'note their great men's faults that no man else dare speak of'.

One of these 'fools', Nicholas of Pskov (d. 1576), is reputed to have faced up to Ivan the Terrible himself. This tsar had already massacred thousands in Novgorod, a neighbouring town of Pskov, and was threatening the citizens of Pskov with the same fate. The local authorities tried to pacify the Russian tyrant and met him with due deference. But Nicholas refused to beat about the bush. He confronted Ivan with what the local chronicle described as 'awesome words to stop this great bloodshed'. Another account gives these 'awesome words' a dramatic setting. Nicholas is supposed to have received Ivan with raw meat. Not only was it raw (an affront in itself), it was a forbidden food that season. Ivan immediately objected: 'I am a Christian, and I therefore eat no meat in Lent.' 'Yet you drink Christian blood?' answered the fool. In the event, no 'great bloodshed' was to follow here.

◆ Ivan the Terrible arriving at a monastery at Sergeiv Posad, from a 16th-century manuscript.

he composed, their service of the hungry, thirsty, homeless, sick or imprisoned involved nothing less than service of the Lord himself. And he gave the necessary reference to the passage in the gospels where this is all spelled out (Matthew 25:35–40). Thus, in the service of the poor, he followed in the tracks of Theodosius. But Theodosius would not have welcomed the rigour of Joseph's new Rule, which was directed at the inner and the outer life of each person. Patterns of behaviour were taken to determine spiritual understanding: 'Let us concern ourselves first of all with the proper aspect and the proper ordering of things, and [only] then with inner attentiveness and obedience.'

This is an attitude which contrasts starkly with the flexibility of Nilus, who recognized the integrity of the individual seeker. Nilus urged that anyone who might know of better or more effective ways of achieving spiritual aims than those which he proposed 'may do as he sees fit'.

The defeat of Nilus's position at the council of 1503 was symptomatic. In general the Muscovite establishment of the sixteenth century was to prefer the ways of Joseph.

Avvakum (c. 1620–82)

The pious norms of the sixteenth-century establishment were to be questioned again in the century which followed. There were many who resisted any modifications, let alone reforms, of the inherited tradition. They saw themselves as the defenders of authentic tradition and were prepared to suffer and even die for their beliefs. One of their leaders, Archpriest Avvakum, was scornfully dismissed as a fool by the church council which tried him. He immediately responded in Pauline terms, 'We are fools for Christ's sake. We are weak, but you are strong. You are honourable, but we are despised' (1 Corinthians 4:10).

Avvakum was imprisoned in an arctic subterranean dungeon for the succeeding sixteen years and died at the stake. But the fortitude with which he faced his sufferings (his autobiography survived) reveals the extraordinary strength of the 'weak', the unblemished honour of the 'despised':

> Take note, my listeners. Our troubles are inevitable, it is impossible to avoid them. This is why God permits offences, that the elect may be revealed, that they may be purged by fire and rendered pure, that all those who passed their trials shall be in your midst. Satan has persuaded God to let him have radiant Russia that he may render her crimson with the blood of martyrs. Good for you, devil. But we also are happy to suffer for our dear Christ's sake.

Avvakum sought to safeguard his church against alien influences of all kinds. Not even the Greek world could serve it as a model in his estimation, no matter how Orthodox it claimed to be, and Western European churches had no claim at all.

Tikhon of Zadonsk
(1724–83)

By the end of the century Peter the Great was to encourage, even to enforce, all kinds of westernization. The administration of the church became firmly subordinated to the state on Western lines. It also affected the education of the clergy: new seminaries were established with programmes borrowed from the West. The frontiers between church traditions were blurred, causing some confusion. But there was also creative interplay between traditions. Thus, one Russian bishop, Tikhon of Zadonsk, drew on several Western authors in his writings, most prominent among them Joseph Hall, an Anglican bishop, and Johann Arndt, a Lutheran theologian. Avvakum would have tolerated no such thing. Yet Tikhon's Orthodoxy was undoubtedly enriched thereby.

Tikhon's writings are not the hallmark of his holiness, however. His personal life shows him at his best. When he resigned from his official duties he lived in a provincial monastery as humbly as he could, the counsellor and benefactor of the poor in

◆ **A Russian church dating from 1649–54.**

spirit. But he was never complacent. A local 'fool for Christ's sake' (see box, p. 159) found him in the yard, slapped him in the face, and shouted, 'Don't think highly of yourself.' The former bishop accepted the rebuke and rewarded the fool with a regular payment of several copper coins a day. The fool may have erred in the wrong direction, however, as Tikhon often thought too little of himself. He had to urge himself to believe in hope against hope (Romans 4:18):

> I do not despair of salvation in Christ. He does not pass judgment on sinners, but on unrepentant sinners. When the thought overpowers us: how can we ever be numbered with the apostles, prophets, martyrs, and other great saints who shine with such virtues? let us resolve our doubts in this way: we desire to be with the thief, who at the very end of his life uttered only one cry of repentance, and was heard.

Tikhon urged simplicity of life on all who came to see him. One of his visitors objected that he was not obliged to follow suit: he had never taken any vows, nor did he intend to be a monk. Tikhon responded with the gentlest of rebukes: 'My dear, all those words of love, poverty and service were uttered before there were any monasteries at all.' Of Tikhon's own commitment to 'those words' there was never any doubt. His charity was boundless. Hence the conclusion of his will: 'As I have no possessions, I leave nothing behind.'

Seraphim of Sarov
(1759–1833)

Seraphim spent his entire adult life in or near a single monastery at Sarov. Above all, he sought solitude. For sixteen years he lived as a solitary in a forest hermitage nearby. Even when he was required to live in the monastery proper he immured himself in his cell. This second isolation lasted for five whole years. Throughout this time Seraphim committed himself to inner prayer. 'With this prayer in your heart,' he said of the Jesus prayer, 'you will find inner peace and sobriety of body and soul.' At the same time, it would be dynamic in its impact, becoming 'like a spring of living water' flowing ceaselessly in the soul.

Seraphim did not intend such grace to be harboured and safeguarded for himself. In 1815 the moment came for his cell door to be opened. It was rarely to be closed again. So began an extraordinary ministry to all and sundry. As many as 2,000 pilgrims might seek to consult him on a given day. Seraphim anticipated many of their needs. It was not his wont to offer general guidance to the many; he addressed the individual and provided answers to specific problems without waiting for them to be put. Some were healed and most received new strength. He lived by the words of Isaac of Syria, whom he quoted with affection: 'Let a cheerful heart precede the gift you give.' Hence it was his custom to greet visitors throughout the year with the gladsome Easter greeting, 'Christ is risen!' and to address each and every person as 'my joy'.

At the core of Seraphim's teachings was the conviction that a Christian should aim at nothing other than 'the acquisition of the Holy Spirit'. He insisted that prayer, vigils, fasting and works of mercy, however good in themselves, serve only as a means to that end. When Nicholas Motovilov, an educated layman, visited him in the winter of 1831 he was shown what Seraphim's own living 'in the fullness of the Holy Spirit' might mean.

Motovilov tells of how he perceived a mysterious light emanating from Seraphim. He spoke of this to the saint: 'Your whole face has become brighter than the sun, and my eyes ache.' But he was to receive a startling response: 'You too have become as radiant as I am myself. You yourself are now in the fullness of God's Spirit, else you would not be able to see me as I am.'

None of this would have been unfamiliar to Nilus of Sora. Together with Seraphim he would have urged that the inner equilibrium which undergirds a revelation of this sort is all-important for the mission of the church. As Seraphim had urged elsewhere, 'Learn to be at peace, and thousands all around you will be saved.'

There is nothing better than peace in Christ, for it brings victory over all the evil spirits in creation. When peace dwells in someone's heart, it enables that person to contemplate the grace of the Holy Spirit from within. Whoever dwells in peace collects up spiritual gifts as if with a scoop and sheds the light of knowledge on others. All our thoughts, all our desires, all our efforts and all our actions should make us say constantly together with the church, 'Lord, give us peace.' For God reveals mysteries to those who live in peace.

Macarius of Optino
(1788–1860)

The idea of a spiritual elder, who could supervise the spiritual life of people less experienced than himself, was much favoured in the age which followed Seraphim of Sarov. No one officially instituted such an order – the elders simply met the needs of the faithful, whether they were monks or not. Most prominent among the centres where elders could be found was the monastery of Optino near Kozelsk. As with Seraphim, countless individuals came long distances to consult a given elder, but others corresponded. The letters of an elder such as Macarius provide us with immediate access to the counsels of such holy men. These reveal how demanding they are to themselves, while yet sensitive to the needs and limitations of their flock.

Thus Macarius has no doubts about the value of the Jesus prayer, and bases his own devotions on it. Yet he writes to one of his correspondents to warn against it: 'It is beyond your strength, outside the scope of your capacities, incompatible with your circumstances.' Instead, he writes, 'live humbly, according to the admonitions of your

Leo Tolstoy (1828–1910)

Tolstoy devoted the last three decades of his long life to his reassessment of Christianity. Fiction occupied only a modest proportion of his life at this time. He pruned the gospel narrative of everything supernatural and even prepared his own Greek 'edition' of the text. On rational grounds he adopted a deist attitude to life. But he became an implacable prophet of public morality. Like some of the earlier 'fools for Christ's sake', he campaigned against society's defects. As a novelist, he had already gained the hearing of the world at large, and the Russian state could not suppress him, anarchist though he showed himself to be. But the Russian Orthodox Church distanced itself firmly from its errant former member, and Tolstoy was excommunicated in 1901.

Tolstoy's teachings therefore had to speak for themselves. He added to their force by living as best he could in accordance with his teachings.

This involved 'simplification', as he called it. As a landed aristocrat, he was ashamed of the way ordinary people were exploited. 'I can never cease to feel myself a partaker in a crime which is continually being committed,' he wrote, 'so long as I have superfluous food while others have none, so long as I have two coats while there exists one man without any.' So he dressed as a peasant and worked in the fields. He limited his diet in line with his vegetarian beliefs. He was convinced that the bearing of arms was wrong. He urged everyone to love their fellow human beings and to renounce violence. He also advocated non-resistance to evil. This teaching was to have lasting repercussions, as it was taken up by Gandhi, and then by Martin Luther King.

Tolstoy was convinced that 'he alone is superior to others who humbles himself and is the servant of all'. But for all his 'simplification' it is doubtful that he ever achieved peace in himself. On the contrary, his was a life of service which offered him no solace – all the more reason to admire his lonely stance.

◆ **Above: Portrait of Leo Tolstoy (1884),**
   by Nikolai Ge (1831–94).

conscience; and carefully, according to the commandments of our Lord. In other words, live the life of an ordinary, God-fearing member of the Christian laity.' In the process, 'avoid making idols of either things or practices' for fear of pride. 'All good things come from humility,' therefore 'humble yourself and find peace'. Only then will prayer prove productive, wrote Macarius:

Bear in mind that prayer alone, unaccompanied by moral improvement, is useless. St Macarius of Egypt says of such prayer that it is unreal; that it is a mask of real prayer. As to your longing for solitude, bear in mind that, as Nilus of Sora tells us, it does not profit everyone. Our love finds expression in our love of people. And even when people hate us we should thank them for it, because they are then the tools of our correction.

Pilgrims came to Optino from every walk of life. Among them was the novelist Fyodor Dostoevsky (1821–81), who portrayed one of the great elders, Ambrosius Grenkov (1812–91), as Father Zosima in *The Brothers Karamazov*. More surprising a visitor was another great writer, Leo Tolstoy (see box, p. 163), as he had long broken with Orthodox Christianity when he made his fateful, since final, journey to Optino, near which he died.

John of Kronstadt
(1829–1908)

The saintly John Sergiev, a contemporary of Tolstoy, spent all his working life as priest of the busy island-fortress of Kronstadt. The impact of his work reached far beyond the boundaries of his parish. Like Tolstoy, he was concerned for the needy and founded many workshops. However, his main concern was for the spiritual welfare of his congregation, which, with his increasing fame, was drawn from far and wide. For him this did not involve a retreat into private prayer, but the sharing of each person's prayer in public. Above all, this meant active sharing in communion.

Out of sheer awe, Russians came to communion only rarely. This had been the case for several centuries. John could not accept this passivity. He encouraged regular and frequent communion, and modified the practice of preliminary confession. Since John could not possibly expect to hear the personal confession of the thousands who wished to receive communion, he encouraged them to make their confessions no less fully, but together and aloud. In a conservative church this was a startling innovation. Only the authority of John could bring it into play or keep it under control, and it was not to outlast him.

Although John wrote that 'we must keep in view the utility of sicknesses' since 'not a single malady remains without profit to our soul', he also accepted that his ministry should include healing, for 'lively and unshaken faith can accomplish miracles in the twinkling of an eye'. He was able to record healings in his 'spiritual diary' which were utterly unexpected from a medical point of view. Here were prayers 'in bold trust' which were answered. Not that this involved any praise of self, he assured himself in his diary. As with any such prayer, 'it is not I who prayed for God's people, but

"the Spirit itself" within me making intercessions for them "with groanings which cannot be uttered" (Romans 8:26).' John's careful reservations were not to prevent his widespread acclaim as a healer.

Unlike Theodosius of Kiev, John of Kronstadt never sought to criticize his ruler. Nor was he a monk, being married and a simple parish priest. He therefore had no reason to dress in tawdry clothes. Yet the silken cassocks which he favoured could not disguise or diminish the man who wore them. Hence his counsel: 'Do not look at someone's garment (or the body which is someone's "garment" for a time): look at the person who is clothed therein.'

Conclusion: the tradition under threat

John of Kronstadt was soon to be posthumously disgraced under Soviet rule. But so was every saintly figure, every religious institution. Relentless persecutions were unleashed, and millions were martyred. A new period of Russian history began under atheist rule. It could hardly have been more costly to the church. But there are no limits to glory: as one of the Russian bishops, Metropolitan Arsenius of Novgorod, was able to perceive from the outset (1918), 'The host of martyrs illumines our path and demonstrates that strength which no persecution can undermine.'

6

The Protestant Tradition in Europe

(16th to 19th centuries)

Herman J. Selderhuis

Timeline

The Reformation of the sixteenth century is not the story of a simple monk longing for a pure church and a religion of the heart. Not only was Luther a learned professor of theology, his reforming activities were intertwined with political and cultural, as well as theological, events. For example, the speed with which his ideas were spread in Europe was only made possible by the invention of the printing press some fifty years before. Without the printers and booksellers, Luther's ideas might only have been heard in a restricted area. Taking into account the political context, one should say that it is certainly doubtful whether the Reformation would have become such an immense success if so many German princes had not backed Luther as an instrument in their political fight against pope and emperor. Their support of the Wittenberg professor did not in all cases result from religious convictions. However, both these aspects give the spirituality of the Reformation some extra dimensions, since it can be characterized not only as a spirituality of the book, but also as a spirituality that directly addresses social and political issues. This can also be said in a different way: Protestant spirituality is fed by literature, yet stays in direct touch with the world it lives in. The essence of this spirituality is theological, namely the relationship between the gracious God and the saved sinner.

The spirituality of the Reformation

Although the Reformation of the sixteenth century has many themes and aspects, the decisive theme is clear: justification through faith alone. The term

◆ Opposite: *Last Judgment,* by Hieronymous Bosch (1450–1516). Luther's ideas challenged contemporary thinking about death and judgment.

'justification' appears to introduce a legal aspect into religion which could develop as a threat to spirituality. However, quite the opposite is the case.

On the eve of the Reformation the experience of faith was for many dominated by fear – the constant fear of being eternally damned, of ending up in hell or at least spending many years of agony in purgatory. What this fear amounts to can best be illustrated by the collection of almost 19,000 relics, owned and cherished by Elector Frederic of Saxony. Everyone reverently visiting these relics would receive a reduction in punishment of almost two million years!

Since the answer to the question of whether one goes to heaven or to hell largely depends on one's own lifestyle, people would do anything to be as sure as possible of salvation. Martin Luther's success can be largely explained in terms of this fear. He pointed out long-forgotten words of scripture which said that people were justified by faith and not by works.

Luther's doctrine that salvation is no task but a gift relaxed the spiritual life immensely. People started to see God less as Judge and more as Father, and to see themselves less as slaves and more as children. The fear of God was replaced by love of God. It was evident that this 'new' doctrine had fundamental consequences for spirituality.

Communion with Christ

The reformers regarded communion with Christ as the aim of justification, and in this there is some resemblance to medieval piety. A fundamental difference, however, is that this piety is not just communion with God, for that would mean a form of mysticism which had no room for Christ.

Another difference is the fact that this communion is grounded in God's predestination, meaning that it is trustworthy because it depends on God's choice and not on that of human beings. Communion means that what has happened to Christ, happens to me. I also die and I also rise from the dead: my old life of sin dies and a new life arises. Reformation spirituality is characterized by

◆ **Opposite: Martin Luther (left) and Philipp Melanchthon, by Lucas Cranach the Younger (1515–86).**

the desire to make myself less in order that Christ can grow in me. Yet it is a communion in which Christ and I keep our individuality. This communion with Christ and with one's fellow Christians, as celebrated in the Lord's Supper, is characteristically Protestant; it was strongly stressed by the Swiss reformer Ulrich Zwingli (1484–1531) (see box, p. 174).

'Let them preach, let them preach!'

This is the message the Strasbourg reformer Martin Bucer (1491–1551) proclaimed. The new doctrine also changed the church service. Many characteristics of Roman Catholic piety such as candles and statues disappeared, and the pulpit was moved from the side of the church building into the centre. The altar, where the mystery of transubstantiation was believed to take place, was replaced by the table of the Lord's Supper, where the communion of reconciliation is celebrated. Faith focuses only on the Word, that is, on God who comes to people through his Word. The priests become preachers. Ulrich Zwingli pointed to the importance of good training for preachers and he was the first to set up such training in Zurich.

The result of all this is that spirituality is no longer restricted to the *experience* of faith, but now includes the *knowledge* of faith. Reformed preachers were convinced that a spiritual life which is not nurtured by knowledge will slowly die. The church service becomes dominated by the sermon, for there lies not only the true source of piety, but also the theological truths by which piety must be guided. The Reformed message has to be heard first and then experienced. The message has a deep personal touch: Christ has died for me so I must give my heart to him.

The monastery is the world

Once human beings are freed from the obligation to take care of their own salvation, they can pay more attention to the world around them. To be truly pious, one does not have to leave the world and enter a monastery. The world becomes the monastery – God can be served in everyday life. The work of a farmer is no less pious than that of the cleric. For spirituality this means an expansion to other aspects of life. It also means that spirituality comes to stand squarely at the heart of society. The Reformation thus led to a strong impulse for the development of science and trade.

At every point in society human beings are able to serve the Lord and to experience faith. Reformed piety does not take place somewhere between heaven and earth, but seeks to practise the heavenly calling on this earth. Politics also become important. Zwingli, Calvin and Bucer, among other reformers, strongly argued for the fact that it is the task of government to turn God's law into political and social laws.

Church, home, school

For the sake of posterity, the contents of faith as well as its experience have to be taught. Luther's colleague Philipp Melanchthon (1497–1560) wrote his *Loci Communes* ('Commonplaces') to that end, and it became a best-selling handbook for students of theology. Placing trust at the centre of faith, Melanchthon also defines faith as a matter of the heart:

> Accordingly, faith is nothing else than trust in the divine mercy promised in Christ, and it makes no difference with what sign it has been promised. This trust in the goodwill or mercy of God first calms our hearts and then inflames us to give thanks to God for his mercy so that we keep the law gladly and willingly.[1]

In the Reformed tradition the catechism became the ideal handbook for the people in the pew. Catechisms were summaries of biblical doctrine and were used to teach the Reformed faith in school as well as in the home. Worldwide recognition has been accorded to the Heidelberg Catechism which is characterized by a close connection between faith as knowledge and faith as experience:

Question: What is your only comfort in life and death?

Answer: That I, with body and soul, both in life and death, am not my own, but belong unto my faithful Saviour Jesus Christ; who with his precious blood has made full satisfaction for all my sins, and delivered me from all the power of the devil; and so preserves me, that without the

Martin Luther (1483–1546)

The founder of the Protestant Reformation in Germany was born in Saxony, the son of a miner. In 1505 he joined the Augustinian order within the Catholic Church, and in 1508 became a professor at the University of Wittenberg. In 1515 he was appointed to a senior position within the Augustinian Order.

The events that led to his break with Rome were triggered by his own growing conviction that human beings cannot save themselves by their own efforts, however religious, or simply by being members of the church: they can be saved only by the gift of God's free grace which he makes available to us through the death of Jesus, which establishes a new relationship between humanity and God by taking away the effects of our sins.

This belief (called by theologians 'justification by faith') seems to have developed before 1519, partly in response to Luther's growing opposition to the Roman Catholic doctrine of indulgences, by which individuals could (in his view) purchase their own salvation by paying for remission from the effects of their sins either in this world or the next. In 1517 Luther made his opposition public by nailing his '95 theses' to the door of the church at Wittenberg Castle.

Roman Catholic reaction to Luther's Wittenberg theses led to Luther being tried for heresy in Rome in his absence. Refusing to recant, Luther went further and in 1519 publicly denied the supreme authority of the pope. By this time Luther had attracted the attention and support of some of the German princes, who had their own reasons for rejecting Roman authority. Luther was formally excommunicated in 1521, reputedly declaring before a tribunal at Worms: 'Here I stand; I can do no other.'

During the years that followed Luther developed his Reformed theology, together with a programme for moral and spiritual renewal for the German people. In 1524 he finally discarded his Augustinian habit and in 1525 married an ex-nun. In 1530 the Augsburg Confession established the basic principles of what came to be called Lutheranism. Luther died in 1546 and was buried at the castle church at Wittenberg, where he had effectively begun the Reformation.

◆ **Altar front from Torslunde, Denmark, showing Luther preaching to the faithful (1561).**

will of my heavenly Father not a hair can fall from my head; yea that all things must be subservient to my salvation, wherefore by his Holy Spirit he also assures me of eternal life, and makes me heartily willing and ready, henceforth, to live unto him.[2]

All reformers stressed the idea that piety preached and taught in church should also be shaped and fed at home and at school. The family came to be seen as a small church within the large church; and this explains why, ever since the sixteenth century, scripture-reading and prayer

Luther's great discovery

Luther was convinced that we could not achieve our own salvation. For him, human beings are walking paradoxes, a wild mixture of goodness and evil: 'A Christian is both righteous and a sinner, holy and profane, an enemy of God and yet a child of God.'[3] Instead we needed to believe in a God loving and gracious enough to do that for us – and a God who still left us the freedom to refuse his offer: 'Christians are not made righteous in doing righteous things, but being now made righteous by faith in Christ, they do righteous things.'[4] But Luther still believed that our lives should reflect our faith. First we must receive God's free gift of salvation; and then our whole lives are transformed:

> In him we are by faith, and he in us. This bridegroom [God] must be alone with the bride in his secret chamber, all the servants and family being put outside. But afterwards, when he opens the door and comes forth, then let the servants and handmaidens return, to fulfil their ministry. There let charity do her office, and let good works be done.[5]

Luther believed that God could and would work a real change in human hearts, if we are willing to let him. And once God has wrought that change, our lives are transformed. We become *assured* of salvation. And that doesn't make us arrogant. It makes us aware of the amazing and undeservable privilege of being loved. Luther looked around him and saw the abuse of indulgences making Catholic Christians more anxious about where they would go after death. He believed that this was a perversion of Christianity. He wanted

to recover belief in a God big enough to change human lives, and loving enough to change human hearts. God is not a cruel judge but a loving father who can never do enough for his children.

The impact of Luther's ideas

Luther's influence was enormous. His reform began within his own heart. Then it spread, first to the academic world of Wittenberg University, and then to the secular world of sixteenth-century Germany before travelling to France, England and the world. The invention of printing helped to spread his ideas, as did the improvements in travel.

Why was he so influential? Partly because his challenge to the pope suited the German princes with their own political agendas. But partly too because Luther caught the mood of the moment. The sixteenth century was an age which witnessed a major growth of 'humanism' – a longing to recover the original state of humanity as it had been experienced in the Garden of Eden, in early Christianity, and in ancient Greece and Rome. Luther's 'back-to-sources' theology became hugely popular, because in a different way other famous contemporaries (such as Erasmus) were calling for the same thing. More important still, Luther made ordinary people feel they mattered, to God and thus to one another. Small wonder his influence was so immense.

have become a pattern in families around meals and at the beginning and the end of a day. In addition, the spiritual life of the believer was discussed with elders and pastors who made regular housecalls.

School came to be seen as the place where active Christian citizens were brought up, and so Bible reading and prayer were encouraged there.

The message of Martin Luther

The young student Martin Luther was so filled with fear of God that he abandoned his law studies and entered a monastery, to the surprise of his friends and relatives. There, in the cloister, he set himself the task to reach in Christian living such a level of holiness that God would be content with him. It turned out to be a hopeless task. Monastic life in fact took him further away from God, for Luther failed time and time again to live up to the demands he thought God was making. God demands the impossible and knows that we cannot do it. Luther ended up, he later recalls, hating God!

That hate did not disappear until, as he confesses, the gates of paradise opened for him. Searching the scriptures in order to find a way out of his spiritual misery, he suddenly realized that justification is not a command but a gift. Only then was his hatred of God replaced by love of God.

But this message had to be made public to all those around him who were also desperately trying to satisfy God. Once Luther had shared his spiritual experience and scriptural insight with others, he was on the way to becoming the most famous theologian in the world. Many in church and politics celebrated him as a liberator; others fought him as a dangerous heretic (see box, p. 170).

The merry exchange… and struggle

Luther had been looking for God for quite some time. He tried to find him in heaven and on earth, but could find him nowhere. That is to say, he could not find a way to climb up to God in heaven, and he certainly did not find God in himself or in humanity. Finally he found God in the cross of Jesus Christ. Luther's spirituality is a spirituality of the cross. Calvary's cross knocks me down, for there I see how disastrous my sins are and how deeply sin has taken root in me. Calvary's cross also raises me up, for there I see how Christ takes away sin and guilt from me and carries them himself. Luther calls this the merry exchange and struggle. Christ wants an exchange. I give him my guilt, he gives me his justice; I give him my death, he gives me his life. This exchange makes faith a merry enterprise. Luther knows how to enjoy faith in a light-hearted manner. And yet it is also a struggle. Faith has to fight against doubt, and against Satan who whispers in his ear that it's a beautiful gospel, but does not count for Martin Luther. Joy and struggle resound in all his letters and books, in all his sermons and prayers:

> Faith not only gives the soul enough for her to become, like the divine word, gracious, free, and blessed. It also unites the soul with Christ, like a bride with the bridegroom, and, from this marriage, Christ and the soul become one body, as St Paul says. Then the possessions of both are in common, whether fortune, misfortune, or anything else; so that what Christ has, also belongs to the believing soul, and what the soul has, will belong to Christ. If Christ has all good things, including blessedness, these will also belong to the soul. If the soul is full of trespasses and sins, these will also belong to Christ. At this point a happy exchange takes place.[6]

At the same time

Luther demands attention to the fact that a human being stands continually before God. All the time he has to deal with God. The Christian in this regard lives in strong dependence upon God, for he knows that he is at the same time both sinner and righteous:

We are in truth and totally sinners, with regard to ourselves and our first birth. Contrariwise, insofar as Christ has been given for us, we are holy and just totally. Hence from different aspects we are said to be just and sinners at one and the same time.[7]

Luther uses the example of a patient. The doctor promises that the patient will get well again. The patient trusts him and in this faith uses the prescribed medicine. This, however, does not mean that he is well again yet, although potentially he is healthy already. This situation makes human beings dependent on God, and explains a spirituality firmly founded on the promise of God. This is also the reason for Luther's fear and dislike of mysticism. Mysticism brings people face to face with themselves; and that causes panic, for one only sees one's own disease. Human beings, however, need the Word, in order to look not at themselves but to the Healer. Luther translates the Bible and he stimulates preaching, for in the Word we find the promise and in the promise we find health and life.

'We are beggars'

The transformation that Luther underwent was a radical one and fundamentally changed his spirituality. He started out as a monk, believing that he had to roll up his sleeves to earn salvation; he died as a preacher who had learned and taught that we have to hold out our hands to receive salvation. The last words he wrote were found right after his death, in the pocket of his coat on a scrap of paper.

The little note ends with the words: 'We are beggars. That is true.'

John Calvin's spirituality

'I do not like to talk about myself.' These words could give the impression that not much can be said about the spirituality of John Calvin. Yet quite

the opposite is true, since his way of speaking and writing on what true spirituality is reveals much about his own spiritual life.

Pilgrim

As soon as Calvin had declared his sympathy with the new Reformed movement, he was forced to leave his native country of France. After some wanderings he ended up in Geneva, the city to which he would give so much and that would demand so much of him (see box, p. 174). Not until a few years before his death did he obtain

◆ John Calvin; a portrait by the 16th-century French school.

The Swiss reformers

John Calvin (1509–64)

Calvin was a French reformer and theologian; born in Picardy, he studied law, and published a commentary on a work of the classical Roman author Seneca in 1532. This interest in ancient texts is important; it was part of the contemporary humanist fondness for a 'back-to-basics' approach to faith and learning.

In 1535, his growing enthusiasm for the ideas of the Protestant Reformation forced him to flee from France to Switzerland. In 1536 he was invited to help further the Reformation in Geneva. After a couple of years a conflict arose and the city council banned him from the city. However, after three years spent as a pastor to a French Protestant church in Strasbourg, he was invited by the city council of Geneva to take up residence there and establish a Reformed regime. Calvin duly accepted the invitation, and settled in Geneva in 1541.

Life was not easy for Calvin even then. He was consistently opposed, both by Catholics and by other Protestants who disagreed with him. His wife Idelette died in 1549, their only child having already died in childbirth. Only after 1555 was he effectively free of opposition and able to develop his ideas systematically. His *Institutes of the Christian Religion*, which first appeared in 1536, but was later revised by the author, became the single most influential text of the Protestant Reformation. Overall, Calvin's influence was enormous. For the hundred years from 1550 to 1650 he was the most published author in England.

The *Institutes* begin, 'Our wisdom... consists almost entirely of two things: the knowledge of God and of ourselves.'[8] Knowledge of God only underlines our own sinfulness and inadequacy. But, as Calvin goes on to say, knowledge *of* God is not the same as knowledge *about* God. True knowledge of God leads directly to true piety. 'By piety,' wrote Calvin, 'I mean that union of reverence and love to God which the knowledge of his benefits inspires.'[9]

Calvin's thought is rooted in the overwhelming grandeur and living presence of God. Faith is the means by which we appropriate that amazing reality, and experience his love: it is 'a firm and certain knowledge of God's benevolence towards us'. Faith is rooted in the conviction 'that we should not think of God's promises of mercy to be true apart from us and not in us, but rather make them ours by embracing them inwardly'.

Faith makes us members of the body of Christ, through the hidden power of the Holy Spirit. As with Luther, Calvin stresses the fact that God takes the initiative in saving us. From all eternity, he predestined some to eternal life and others to damnation. But, contrary to what is often thought, Calvin did not make this the centre of his faith: his emphasis lay on God's sovereign grace and freedom, and on the mystery of the divine love in calling us into an eternal and intimate relationship with him. By imitating Christ we are drawn into union with him, a union which for Calvin is 'a sacred marriage, by which we become bone of his bone, and flesh of his flesh'.[10]

And Calvin believes in a God who is free to surprise us by the wind and flame of his Holy Spirit, constantly at work in the world around us:

> The beauty which the world displays is maintained by the invigorating power of the Spirit... The mere fact of his not being circumscribed by any limits raises him above the rank of creatures, while his transfusing vigour into all things, breathing into them being, life, and motion, is plainly divine... By means of him we become partakers of the divine nature, so as in a manner to feel his quickening energy within us.[11]

It is the Spirit who brings human beings into a relationship with God, it is the Spirit who gives us the experiential knowledge of Christ, it is the Spirit who leads us to prayer and praise. It is also the Spirit who brings us back to appreciating the law as a means to serve God and our neighbour. The Calvinist accent on the sanctification of daily life results from its stress on the work of the Holy Spirit.

Ulrich Zwingli (1484–1531)

Ulrich Zwingli, the 'third man' of the Protestant Reformation (after Luther and Calvin), was born in 1484 in the Toggenburg valley of Switzerland. He became deeply learned in classical and scriptural studies, and in 1518 was appointed pastor and preacher at the Grossmünster church in Zurich. His preaching here, which became steadily more Protestant in theology, led to a climax when in 1523 Zwingli successfully defended his beliefs against the Roman Catholic vicar-general in a public debate before an audience of 600. The city council backed Zwingli, and declared their independence of Rome.

Zwingli's theology was in some respects more Protestant than Luther's, and he refused to accept that Christ was in any way present in the bread and wine of Holy Communion. But he believed deeply in the presence of Christ in the hearts and lives of those who worshipped him. Zwingli was killed in battle while acting as chaplain for the forces of Zurich in 1531.

◆ **Above: Portrait of Ulrich Zwingli, after Hans Asper (1499–1571).**

Zwingli's articles of faith

The following… articles and opinions, I, Ulrich Zwingli, confess that I have preached in the venerable city of Zurich on the basis of scripture…

II The sum of the gospel is that our Lord Jesus Christ, the true Son of God, has made known to us the will of his heavenly Father, and by his innocence has redeemed us from death and reconciled us unto God.

III Therefore Christ is the only way to salvation for all who ever lived, do live or ever will live…

IX Just as the members of a physical body can do nothing without the guidance of the head, so now in the body of Christ no one can do anything without Christ, its head…

XIII When we listen to the head, we acquire a pure and clear knowledge of the will of God, and we are drawn to him by his Spirit and are conformed to him.

XIV Hence all Christians should do their utmost that everywhere only the gospel of Christ be preached.[12]

the rights of a citizen; before that he officially remained a stranger and an asylum-seeker in a town full of hostility towards him. For Calvin that is the enduring situation of the believer on earth. Christians realize that they must be directed to what they do not see, since what they see and what they go through could bring them to lose their faith. The life of the believer is full of hardship, yet they bear their cross with joy and trust.

Yet Calvin's spirituality is a positive one; for the believer, on his way through the desert of this world, rejoices in the providence and grace of God and looks forward to entering the promised land.

Misleading portraits

The portraits we have show us a man who seems to be stiff, stoical and maybe even unfeeling. The portraits mislead us. Here is a man who knows physical and spiritual pain, a man who struggles with the hiddenness and incomprehensibility of God. Here is a man who knows from his own experience the sufferings so many of his flock underwent. He comforts them with the God with whom Calvin himself found comfort. It is the God of Israel who gives and takes, helps and hurts, but does all for the well-being of his children. His providence and predestination all aim at the salvation of God's people.

'I offer you my heart' – that motto of John Calvin defines Reformed spirituality. Human beings are on earth to serve and honour God, not with outward rituals, but with a loving heart. Faith is a spiritual matter, a thing to be experienced. This faith, this spirituality, however, needs nutrition and direction and because of that there should be a well-ordered church with an emphasis on good sermons, Bible studies and hymns.

Whereas Luther can be called the source of Reformed spirituality, Calvin can be said to be its organizer.

Lay spirituality and the Reformation

The effect of the Reformation was felt first and foremost in the cities of Europe. The early sixteenth century witnessed growing social unrest as the effects of food prices and economic deprivation made themselves felt. The call of Luther and others to stand firm for the integrity and independence of the individual and the community fell on ready ears; and it was taken up by the German princes, who had their own reasons for wanting to be independent of the papacy.

But there is much more to the impact of the Reformation than that. The great Protestant stress on justification by faith allowed individuals to feel that they mattered – before God, and thus before human beings too. The individual's standing before God, and the individual's own journey to faith, came to count for far more than hitherto. The Reformation also diminished the need for priestly mediation – and this too caught the mood of a society in which lay people were increasingly confident, articulate and literate. It has been justly said that the Reformation in England was a victory for the gentry over the clergy. And, although it may well have been the case that rural areas were far slower to adopt the practices of the Reformation than cities were, it is remarkable, even allowing for the power of local rulers, that the teaching of Luther and Calvin was rapidly adopted by immense numbers of people across northern Europe.

William Tyndale
(c. 1490–1536)

John Foxe's Acts and Monuments is the main source for our knowledge of the life of William Tyndale. He was an effective preacher of the gospel, but his outspokenness and evangelical zeal brought him into conflict with some of the higher clergy. He became convinced that the English people needed repentance and revival and that this could be brought about by giving them the Bible in their own language:

> So now the scripture is a light, and shows us the true way, both what to do and what to hope for. And a defence from all error, and a comfort in adversity that we despair not, and it fears us in prosperity, that we sin not. Seek therefore in the scripture, as thou readest it, first the law, what God commands us to do; and secondly, the promises, which God promises us again, namely in Christ Jesus our Lord. Then seek

Only an English Bible would make people into the Christians God wanted them to be. However, Tyndale's request to begin translation was rejected by the Bishop of London. Mindful of John Wycliffe (see chapter 3, p. 111), the bishop feared that an English Bible would foster heresies.

Tyndale knew that the only way to reach his goal was to do the job abroad, and so he went to study at Luther's university in Wittenberg. In 1525 the translation of the New Testament was finished, printed and smuggled to England, where it found many readers. His style made his translation very readable. How much this work was later valued is obvious from the fact that the King James Version

◆ Frontispiece of Tyndale's New Testament, revised edition published in Antwerp in November 1534.

examples, first of comfort, how God purgeth all them that submit themselves to walk in his ways, in the purgatory of tribulation, delivering them yet at the latter end, and never suffering any of them to perish that cleave fast to his promises.[13]

of the New Testament retains ninety per cent of Tyndale's words and syntax. The bishops, however, decided it should be burned. Tyndale then went to Antwerp, one of the publishing capitals of Europe. There he wrote a good number of commentaries on various biblical books. He published other

◆ The martyrdom and burning of Tyndale in Flanders, from *John Foxe's Acts and Monuments* (1563).

◆ Opposite: John Knox and Christopher Goodman (c. 1520–1603) haranguing Mary Queen of Scots; woodcut from the late 16th century.

works such as *The Practice of the Prelates* (1530) and *The Obedience of a Christian Man* (1528) in which he defends the authority of the scriptures and obedience to secular rulers, both in opposition to the authority of the church.

Tyndale also started the translation of the Old Testament. Just after completing the book of Jonah he was betrayed and imprisoned in Brussels. His one-year stay in jail was productive for he was able to continue working on his Old Testament translation. Yet his end was tragic: the church courts found him guilty of heresy and he was sentenced to death. The execution took place near Brussels in 1536 and it is reported that his last words were: 'O Lord, open the king of England's eyes.'

John Knox (1513–72)

Luther's message was soon well received in Britain (see chapter 8). In a certain sense the work of John Wycliffe and William Tyndale had prepared the soil for the seed of the Reformation. And undoubtedly one of the most remarkable products of this combination of seed and soil is the Scottish reformer, John Knox.

Since his own day John Knox has acquired a notorious reputation for his views on women in government. As a result not much more is generally known about this man who became a Scottish national hero. In fact not much is known of him before the 1540s when he emphatically appears on the scene. He was born in Haddington, East Lothian, studied at St Andrew's and was ordained as a priest in 1536. After his conversion to the Reformed conviction, he preached his first sermon, also in St Andrews, in 1547. In this sermon he vigorously attacked the church of Rome and the pope, identifying both as Antichrist and revealing himself as a man with strong convictions combined with often uncontrolled emotions.

In that same year the Roman Catholics took over St Andrews and Knox was sentenced to a harsh life at the galleys. After almost two years he was released and went to England to become a preacher, but after Mary Tudor became queen he had to flee to the continent. During this period he wrote his

His idea that subjects have the right to resist their rulers, and that rulers have no right to impose their religious convictions on their subjects, was modern and even revolutionary. Many Scots were willing to practise what Knox preached and this resulted in the 1559 rebellion leading to the withdrawal of the French from Scotland and to the final abdication of Mary Stuart in 1567. It is not surprising that when Knox was buried, his epitaph was: 'Here lies he, who has never feared the face of a human being.'

famous book with its revealing and provocative title: *First Blast of the Trumpet Against the Monstrous Regiment of Women* (1557). Although directed against Mary Tudor and Mary of Guise, who had both caused him many hardships, Queen Elizabeth, who came to power after Mary Tudor died, so much disliked the book that there was no possibility of Knox staying in England. No other choice was left to him than to move back to Scotland, where he became a minister in Edinburgh.

Scottish hero

Once in Edinburgh, Knox devoted all his powers to the Scottish Reformation. The impact he had on this movement and its people is documented by an English diplomat who wrote that Knox was 'able in one hour to put more life in us than five hundred trumpets continually blasting in our ears'. Knox's own documentation of his attitude and belief is to be found in his *History of the Reformation*, on which he began work in 1559 and did not finish until shortly before his death in 1572. This description of the road that God's church has to travel demonstrates a passionate love for that church mingled with unrestrained bitterness towards all those he saw as enemies. Knox's spirituality centres on the might of God and human beings' subjection to him. The stress on human depravity is balanced by the preaching of Christ as Saviour.

German Pietism

When the head gets too much attention, the heart feels neglected and beomes restless. This is a principal cause of the eruption of German Pietism, starting in the seventeenth century. The surging Enlightenment movement not only reasoned

An untranslatable word

The fascination of every language is that there are certain words which contain so much meaning and are so specific that they are untranslatable. The Latin *pietas* is just such a word. In the sixteenth century the humanists picked this word up from classical antiquity, and a little later the reformers applied it to their message.

Pietas might be translated as 'piety', if one keeps in mind that it means much more than just the inward, personal experience of faith. *Pietas* is piety that finds its centre in the communion with Christ and finds shape in a life that wants to serve God and neighbour in word and deed. The piety of the Reformation is a triangle in which God, the neighbour and the self each find their own place.

◆ **Engraving depicting August Hermann Francke, by S.R. Wolfgang (1729).**

important doctrines of faith away, but also threatened to suffocate the experience of faith. Apart from this, life in the church at the beginning of the seventeenth century was starting to be dominated more and more by dogmatic discussions which are rarely fruitful for the man and woman in the pew. As soon as sermons start to become speeches and preaching becomes debate, as soon as many are still only members of the church on paper and not in practice, then within some believers a desire starts growing, a longing for change, renewal and revival. This desire was the beginning of the movement that will come to be called Pietism. Pietism is the most important renewal movement since the Reformation of the sixteenth century. At the beginning this name was a nickname for the followers of the man who gave this movement its shape and content, Philip Jakob Spener (1635–1705) (see box, p. 181).

Even before Spener, Johann Arndt (1555–1621)

had pointed to the fact that Christian faith above all needs to be experienced, in his *Four Books on True Christendom* (1605–10). This work turned out to be a bestseller and stimulated spiritual life and the desire for revival enormously.

Practical piety

Pietism found a way to combine a sharp interest in personal faith with the building-up of the church; the church members, as well as the church itself, had to come to conversion and renewal. This could only be achieved by taking the Bible seriously. A characteristic of Pietism is that the Bible is not only read and studied, but also meditatively discussed in groups of believers.

August Hermann Francke (1663–1727) continued in the paths of Spener, although he emphasized penance more than Spener. Franck understood penance to be the spiritual struggle believers have to go through before regeneration can take place. At the same time, Francke broadens Spener's perspective: piety would only grow in people's hearts when their outward circumstances were suitable. The road to helping people to get rid of their unbelief is first to help them get rid of their poverty, loneliness or addiction. Francke saw it as the calling of every believer to take care of his or her neighbour in deed. Francke then turned his opinions into practice and, as a result, in the north-eastern German town of Halle where Francke was professor, an orphanage, schools and a home for the homeless were founded. Activities were developed to promote the spread of the Bible. Missionary work was undertaken and furthered. The 'Hallesche Stiftungen' (the Halle Foundations), famous even to our own day, were the fruit of the spirituality of Pietism.

Part and whole

Whereas Spener had the whole of the church in mind, his emphasis on personal faith-experience

Philip Jakob Spener (1635–1705)

Spener shaped the influential spiritual movement called Pietism. As a minister he was confronted and shocked by the immense distance between colleagues who spent their time discussing each other's viewpoints, and the spiritual need of the people in the pew. In 1670 he started out with his *collegia pietatis*, meetings of enthusiastic believers who together meditated on the Bible and shared their personal spiritual experiences. Through these groups, which actually functioned as little churches within the church, Spener was trying to reach all of the church. He defined his spiritual programme in his most famous work, *Pia Desideria*. Literally this means 'pious desires', but what Spener wanted to achieve was a common desire for piety. The full title makes this aim clear: *Pia Desideria, or a hearty desire for a God-pleasing improvement of the evangelical churches, accompanied with some simple Christian proposals to reach that goal*.

Spener longed to see people more existentially involved with the Bible, for fewer polemics in the church and for more sermons that touched the heart and strengthened the faith. Above all he wanted to attain a 'spiritual priesthood'. Every Christian has received the Holy Spirit and is therefore entitled and called to build up fellow Christians in the faith and pray for them. Spener's spirituality has a strong eschatological tone. He expected better times for the church and a mass conversion of Jews. After that the kingdom of Christ will come. *Pia Desideria* has been widely read, however, the renewal of the whole church was Spener's ultimate aim.

Spener on the inner life

While the whole of our being as a Christian exists in the inner or new man whose soul is the faith and for whom the effects of faith are the fruits of life, I find it most important that the sermons are directed at this inner life. God's precious benefactions, destined for the inner man, must be preached in such a way that faith as well as the inner man are gradually strengthened. On the other hand we must urge on to deeds, so that we are not really satisfied if we can bring people to stop outward calumnies and to perform outward virtues. For then we just have to do with the outer man, and heathen ethics can do that as well. But we must very solidly place a foundation in the heart and demonstrate that all that does not arise from this foundation is just hypocrisy. We must see to it that people get used first to paying attention to their inner being so that they stir up love for God and for their neighbour, and that after this they bring forth good works outwardly.[14]

risked devaluing the communion and fellowship of the church. Furthermore, a believer striving for inward transformation (sanctification) could fall victim to perfectionism. This danger became a reality with Jean de Labadie (1610–74), who set up such high standards for being a Christian that in the end all that was left of his movement was a small congregation meeting in a house.

The overemphasis on the life of the soul can be found above all in the writings of the German mystic, Gerhard Tersteegen (1697–1769). After his conversion he wrote with his own blood a declaration in which he promised to devote all of his life completely to the service of Christ.

According to Tersteegen, our aim must be to move the soul to a position of rest and resignation: the more passive, the better. This is the highest goal: to have nothing but God alone, to want nothing but to please him, to not be able to do anything by yourself and in yourself not being anything at all. These thoughts became influential after his death, when some of his poems were accepted as liturgical hymns. These hymns were translated and can be found in hymn books throughout the Protestant world.

Nikolaus Ludwig von Zinzendorf (1700–60) was the most important and creative representative of eighteenth-century Pietism. He kept his eye focused on the whole of Christianity. He travelled throughout Europe and America to convince Christians that they were one in Christ in spite of ecclesiastical differences, and that they should celebrate this unity as a gift.

In the congregation of Herrnhut in Saxony the vision of Zinzendorf became a reality in a colony of houses of prayer and workshops. From there the Herrnhutters accomplished their worldwide mission work to which they were inspired by Zinzendorf:

Herrnhut… must remain in a constant bond of love with all the children of God belonging to the different religious persuasions. They must judge none, enter into no disputes with any, nor behave themselves unseemly towards any, but rather seek to maintain among themselves the pure evangelical doctrine, simplicity and grace.[15]

Puritan spirituality

The Puritans certainly did not choose their own name. Apart from that unlooked-for title, there is some confusion about the use of the term 'Puritanism'. This confusion relates to the considerable diversity within this movement and the fact that it is a movement which extends over

◆ Sir Peter Lely's portrait of Oliver Cromwell (1653). Cromwell asked Lely to paint him 'truly… roughnesses, pimples, warts and everything'.

almost two centuries. When some members of the Church of England around 1560 organized their resistance against what they called 'papist' elements in the liturgy and in the government of the church and wanted to purify the church, they were labelled 'Puritans', a contemptuous term. They also received a lot of contempt from the official church. Because of the close relationship between church and king, Puritanism rapidly obtained a political dimension. Samuel Rutherford (1600–61) was a Scottish clergyman who vigorously defended Calvinist principles and not least those relating to political issues. Only after his death did he become famous through his letters, in which he described his piety and religious life. These letters were widely read in Puritan families as they were regarded as a good way to feed the spiritual life.

In his *Lex Rex* (1644) Rutherford defends his conviction that God has given political power not to the king but to the people. Under the leadership of Oliver Cromwell (1599–1658) Puritanism was devoted to political activities against the absolutism of the monarchy. The Westminster Assembly (1643–48) marked the zenith of this period, where a confession of faith and two catechisms were formulated. These have now been for centuries the carriers of Puritan spirituality. After their political influence diminished, the Puritans suffered heavy repression in the years from 1682 to 1689. After that Puritanism concentrated on the aim that has made the movement famous: the promotion of a practical and strict spiritual life, in private as well as in public.

Sin

As sin is the cause of all trouble in this world and causes God's wrath and sorrow, Puritanism directed attention to combatting public and personal sins. Regarding public life, one of the most decried sins was the secularization of Sunday, which the Puritans identified with the sabbath of the Old Testament. Of even more social interest was the Puritan fight against the abuse of alcohol. In the Christian's personal life the focus was on less conspicuous although very persistent sins such as bad desires and the slackening of faith and prayer. Puritanism strove for a purposeful Christianity, which meant a living faith and a conscientious way of life. Both of these elements – the inner fight against sin and the pious life – can be found extensively in the writings of one of the most famous Puritans, William Perkins (1558–1602).

In his book, *A Golden Chaine*, Perkins makes a rather unfortunate attempt to give a logical explanation of God's work of election, which dangerously threatened a vivid piety. But most of his works are filled with amazement over the incomprehensible love of God for fallen sinners and for the majesty and sovereignty of the Lord:

But when God's Spirit has by the light of God's word opened his eyes and touched his heart to consider his estate, then he seeth the frail bridge of this narrow life and how little a step there is between him and damnation, then he seeth hell open as the due for his sins and himself in the highway unto it: sin being the craggy rock and hell the gaping gulf under it. Then he wondereth at his miserable estate, admireth the mercy of God in keeping him from falling into the bottom of hell, wondereth at the presumptuous boldness of his corruption which so securely plodded on towards destruction; and being ashamed of himself and these his ways, he turns his heart to the God that saved him from these dangers and sets himself into more holy ways and more conformable courses and confesseth that ignorance made him bold and blindness made him so presumptuous.[16]

Perkins' leading theme is that a faith that is not experienced cannot be a real faith. This theme urges him to ask for careful self-examination, for a concern for a truly Christian life and to bring people to the insight that life is short and God's judgment is to be feared:

God smites the heart with legal fear, whereby when man sees his sins, he makes him to fear punishment and hell, and to despair of salvation, in regard to anything in himself.[17]

Characteristics of the Puritan

The Puritan believer is characterized by a steadfastness demonstrated by an uncompromising willingness to honour and serve God. Characteristic also is the tension between, on the one hand, a pleading for religious tolerance and, on the other hand, a zeal to shape society into a biblical model. In spite of all the criticism of the church, most Puritans never left the Church of England. They did not even want to establish a party within that church for fear of losing sight of the unity of the church. Puritans tried to compensate for the lack of spiritual food – as they experienced the church services – by getting together in small groups. In these 'conventicles' people opened their hearts to each other and discussed their religious affections. These groups were seen as containers that kept true religion fresh and alive.

International influence

Puritanism and Pietism were both European movements with locally different accents. The concentration on the inward, spiritual life made it possible to organize contacts that crossed church and national borders. These contacts became flesh in the translations of the important works of Puritans and Pietists. Puritanism has English, Dutch and American branches (see chapter 9,

p. 278ff). The branch that developed in the Netherlands is usually called 'Further Reformation', referring to the idea that the Reformation of the sixteenth century should be continued and extended in life and doctrine. This 'Further Reformation' was, like the Anglo-American Puritanism, a movement of piety aspiring to the spiritual renewal of the whole church. However, in a later phase, when it became evident that the national and ecclesiastical goal could not be reached, the inner feelings gained so much attention that this Dutch form of Puritanism resulted in an elite and almost suffocating mysticism. That phase had not yet arrived at the time of Gisbertus Voetius (1589–1676) and Wilhelmus à Brakel (1635–1711), to name the most influential theologians of this movement. But when it came to mysticism in their spiritual descendants it gave a negative stamp to the spirituality of many believers.

◆ *A Puritan Family Saying Grace Before the Meal* (1585), by the Flemish painter Anthuenis Claeissins (1536–1613).

◆ Elisabeth Fry visiting inmates of Newgate Prison.

A point of difference with German Pietism is the fact that Puritanism pays a lot of attention to the conscience, which results in accentuating the knowledge of one's sinfulness. In return, this awareness of sin accounts for a great longing for the glory of heaven where sin and guilt will be in the past – elaborately described in the widely read book by Richard Baxter, *The Saint's Everlasting Rest*:

Rest! How sweet the sound. It is a melody to my ears! It lies as a reviving cordial to my heart, and from thence sends forth lively spirits, which beat through all the pulses of my soul! Rest! not as the stone that rests on the earth, nor as this flesh shall rest in the grave, nor such a rest as the carnal world desires. O blessed rest! when we rest not day and night, saying Holy, holy, holy, Lord God Almighty! When we shall rest from sin, but not from worship; from suffering and sorrow, but not from joy! O blessed day! when I shall rest with God! when I shall rest in the bosom of my Lord.[18]

Non-doctrinal piety

As in every age, the seventeenth century also had its definitely extra-ecclesiastical groups. A specifically non-church form of spirituality is that found among the Quakers. Their founding father, George Fox (1624–91), was convinced that no true light was to be expected from the outside. More and more he heard the inner voice of God in his soul. Fox managed to convince others to follow the inward life as well, and so the Quakers began. Their spirituality is characterized by a non-doctrinal personal piety in which communion with God means everything, although there is no outward standard for that communion since even the Bible is an outward voice. That this attention to what is inward need not necessarily result in neglect of daily life and physical needs is best illustrated in the life of Elisabeth Fry.

Elisabeth Fry (1780–1845)

After a period of doubt a sermon by an American Quaker preacher brought Elisabeth Fry to the certainty that God was present and alive. Having grown in this conviction, she also became convinced that her personal faith should result in helping others: 'Charity to the soul is the soul of charity.' For this she received much opportunity through her marriage with a rich merchant, Joseph Fry, a prominent member of the London Quaker community. Their eleven children were also encouraged by Joseph and Elisabeth to partake in their enterprise – to give spirituality hands and feet.

Elisabeth was by then a deeply religious woman who knew the strength of prayer from experience, and this helped her to start her battle against

John Bunyan (1628–88)

In any list of the most read Christian books of all time, John Bunyan's *Pilgrim's Progress* is most likely to come second only to the Bible. In many Christian homes this book also received second place as a spiritual guide for the Christian. The success of this work is even more impressive when it is remembered that its author was a cobbler who could hardly read and write.

Puritan from birth, he chose to become a soldier for the cause, joining the Parliamentary army that fought King Charles I. This experience supplied him with the images he used to describe the spiritual battle in another famous work, *The Holy War*. Some years after returning from the war he married, and his wife brought into their home some devotional works. Reading these books, Bunyan experienced heavy spiritual agonies, fearing he had committed the unforgivable sin against the Holy Spirit. Bunyan was so depressed that he considered suicide, but after long inner turmoil he found peace of mind again and became a minister in Bedford.

Headed for heaven

Bunyan wanted nothing else than to preach the gospel and he did so, yet without obtaining the written permit that the government had decided to be necessary for preachers. He ended up in prison, where he spent twelve years from 1660 to 1672. In 1675 he was thrown back into jail, and there he started writing *The Pilgrim's Progress*. The book allegorically describes the travels of a Christian headed for heaven. As soon as the book came out in 1678 it became a bestseller, attracting

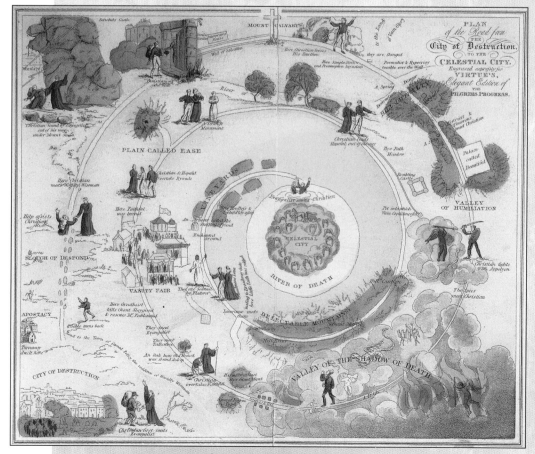

◆ **The pilgrim's route map, from the City of Destruction (bottom left) to the Celestial City, engraved for a later edition of *The Pilgrim's Progress*.**

a large working-class audience. It was not until the nineteenth century that the more educated learned to appreciate it as a book of spiritual comfort and literary quality. Bunyan had found the key to people's hearts in using the language of the King James version to write an entertaining and even thrilling story that could be read and understood by all kinds of people.

In 1688 Bunyan rode his horse through storm and rain on his way back from a successful meeting in which he reconciled a father and son. As a result of that ride he was taken ill and died soon after. His writings, however, live on today.

'The Shepherd Boy Sings in the Valley of Humiliation'

He that is down needs fear no fall,
  He that is low, no pride.
He that is humble ever shall
  Have God to be his guide.

I am content with what I have,
  Little be it or much:
And, Lord, contentment still I crave,
  Because thou savest such.

Fullness to such a burden is
  That go on pilgrimage:
Here little, and hereafter bliss,
  Is best from age to age.
(From The Pilgrim's Progress)

slavery and poverty. She founded schools, helped the gypsies, took care of the homeless, and distributed Bibles wherever she could. Her active compassion for the situation of female prisoners was ahead of its time. For twenty years she travelled through England, Scotland and Ireland to bring physical and spiritual help to all in person and this gave her the name 'the angel of the prisoners'. Her dedication to improve the rough lives of the many families along Britain's coast living in lighthouses was also remarkable. Her main intent was to bring the gospel of liberation to the oppressed. The Bible was her source, and from there she took the warmth and hope she passed on to so many in cold and dark places.

Jakob Boehme (1575–1624)

Many of the smaller Protestant movements that sprang up across Northern Europe during the seventeenth century were influenced by this remarkable man, at heart a Lutheran, whose combination of mysticism, scriptural interpretation and speculative theology proved extremely popular.

The son of a farmer, Jakob Boehme was born in Alt-Seidenberg, a small town in Silesia, Germany. After finishing his apprenticeship as a cobbler, he opened his own workshop in 1599. After a few years he sold his stores and became a grain salesman. In 1624 he died at the rather early age of forty-nine. Although without scholarly learning, he knew the writings of Martin Luther and Caspar Schwenckfeld. More than that, he was at home with scripture. As he afterwards confessed, it was in the year 1600 that he came to see what true knowledge was. While working in his shop he suddenly saw the light of the sun reflected in a tin vessel. At that moment he knew that there existed a constant division between light and dark, good and evil, God and sin, and that through true knowledge we can get to the light. This is how he explains it: 'God has given me that knowledge. Not I, as the I that is me knows this, but God knows it in me. Wisdom is his bride, and the children of

Christ are in Christ, in wisdom, also his bride.'

He started to write down his new insights in various books and pamphlets. The main question in his works is how an imperfect and sinful human being can enter a saving communion with the holy God. The answer is the way of knowledge, a mystical knowledge that leads to, and stems from, a mystical union of the soul and Christ.

> The Disciple said to his Master: Sir, how may I come to the Supersensual Life, so that I may see God, and hear God speak?
>
> The Master answered and said: Son, when thou canst throw thyself into That, where no Creature dwelleth, though it be but for a Moment, then thou hearest what God speaketh.
>
> Disciple: Is that where no Creature dwelleth near at hand; or is it afar off?
>
> Master: It is in thee. And if thou canst, my Son, for a while but cease from all thy thinking and willing, then thou shalt hear the unspeakable Words of God...
>
> Disciple: But wherewith shall I hear and see God, forasmuch as he is above Nature and Creature?
>
> Master: Son, when thou art quiet and silent, then art thou as God was before Nature and Creature; thou art that which God then was; thou art that whereof he made thy Nature and Creature: then thou hearest and seest even with that wherewith God himself saw and heard in thee, before ever thine own Willing or thine own Seeing began.[19]

Controversial but successful

In Boehme's day a gulf had arisen between the theologians and the people in the pew. The churchmen were so busy with their discussions that they did not notice the craving of the people for spiritual food; in addition there was a social rift between the elite office-bearers and the relatively uneducated and poor believers. Boehme was no theologian, but he had real spiritual depth and that made him widely read. But this also attracted criticism from Lutheran theologians who could not tolerate any thought not fitting their own theological systems. They criticized the fact that Boehme seemed to lose sight of the boundaries between God and humanity; however, they were not finding ways of allowing the biblical message to reach the hearts of their parishioners.

Boehme was hardly known during his life in Germany and, surprisingly, it was first in the Netherlands and then England that his translated works made him one of the most famous thinkers of the seventeenth century.

Romantic spirituality

The nineteenth century displays something of a combination of the three preceding centuries with regard to spirituality. Elements of the Reformation, Pietism and rationalism were mixed up and resulted in what can be labelled 'romantic spirituality'. This century reveals a world that is not too sure if it really needs redemption, since new human achievements made it seem possible for human beings themselves to build a perfect world. The authority of scripture was denied, or at least seriously attacked. And yet Christians did not want to let go of the biblical message. The story of how the biblical message was defended can best be told through the stories of three individuals: a theologian, a philosopher and a poet.

The theologian

In theology, this period was dominated by the influential and original thought of Friedrich Daniel Schleiermacher (1768–1834).

This son of an army chaplain grew up in the atmosphere of German Pietism and combined these roots with the rationalistic university climate of the day. In his book, *On Religion: Speeches to its Cultured Despisers*, he tried to make the Christian faith intelligible to the intellectuals of his day:

I ask, therefore, that you turn from everything usually reckoned religion, and fix your regard on the inward emotions and dispositions, as all utterances and acts of inspired men direct, despite your acquisitions, your culture and your prejudices. I hope for good success. At all events, till you have looked from this standpoint without discovering anything real, or having any change of opinion, or enlarging your contemptuous conception, the product of superficial observation, and are still able to hold in ridicule this reaching of the heart towards the Eternal, I will not confess that I have lost.[20]

To Schleiermacher, doctrines were the rational expression of religious affections. The problem was that he stressed subjectivity in religion so much that the resurrection, ascension and return of Christ became dispensable. However Schleiermacher's definition of religion as the 'consciousness of absolute dependence on God' has affected church and theology so intensely that he can rightly be called 'the church father of the nineteenth century'.

◆ *Faust and Wagner in Conversation in the Countryside,* by Eugène Delacroix (1798–1863).

The philosopher

The work of the Danish philosopher Søren Kierkegaard (1813–55) has been of comparable importance and influence. Melancholy by nature, Kierkegaard became depressed after he broke off his engagement to a girl for whom he thought himself unworthy. This event pervaded all of his works. Kierkegaard's message is that there is no objective truth; quite the opposite in fact – 'Subjectivity is truth.' There exists a permanent tension between God and humanity, time and eternity. Christian faith therefore is a paradoxical matter, as though two opposites are joined together. Human beings can only find God when they make an absurd and paradoxical leap of faith, regardless of reason. Kierkegaard complains that the self-sufficiency of the official church prevents it from making this bold venture of faith. These views have created a widely accepted spirituality that could be characterized as 'restless certainty'.

The poet

The literary exponent of this period is the German poet and novelist Johann Wolfgang von Goethe (1749–1832). His poems and plays document the Pietistic influence he experienced over a long period. 'One great confession' is his own characterization of his work. The contents of this confession are explicitly revealed in his famous *Faust*. The religion of the main character, Faust, is the pursuit of the highest and the noblest. Evil is simply the other side of good and can be overcome by one's own strength. Salvation, therefore, takes place every time one surmounts a barrier in the service of the gods named Art and Science. Goethe mastered the language in a way no one else has ever done; and he knew how to describe the innermost feelings and emotions of the human heart.

Stairway to heaven: the spirituality of prayer

In the Bible we find the story of Jacob's dream at Bethel (Genesis 28:10–17). In this dream he sees a ladder coming down from heaven. On this ladder angels are descending and ascending as a sign of the road that leads from God to us and from us to God. Through prayer, believers ascend that ladder into heaven. At all times the Christian church has seen and experienced prayer as the most intimate form of communion between God and humanity. Christians live in the steadfast faith that God has given prayer as a way to his heart and they are truly convinced that God attentively listens to each individual believer.

Though Christian theologians differ on many issues, at least they all have the practice of prayer in common. Prayer opens up the possibility of laying all emotions of faith, all ups and downs, all joys and griefs, all sorrows and blessings before God. The spirituality of prayer is located between the extremes of crying out to God and being silent before God, between the heights of praise and the depths of prostration. As to these extremes, prayer has through all ages remained the same. And yet, each period in church history has its own accents.

Prayer rules

The sixteenth-century reformers were convinced that it was useless and unscriptural to direct prayers to Mary and other deceased saints. At the same time they all renounced ritualized, seemingly thoughtless, prayer. Rethinking prayer became necessary. Calvin therefore called prayer a ladder on which believers could ascend to God from the midst of their anxieties. As a kind of manual he sums up four rules of prayer in his *Institutes*.[21] The first rule is that we come to God with reverence, being aware that we speak with the most Holy One. Secondly there must be a longing for prayer, mindful of the fact that we simply need prayer. The third rule is that we abandon all self-confidence and beg God for forgiveness. Finally, a prayer is only good when the one who prays fully trusts that God will hear the prayer.

Friedrich Schleiermacher, the eighteenth-century German theologian who drew attention to the experiential dimension of believing, reduced these rules to one line: 'Being pious and praying are in fact one and the same.'

Attitude

Protestantism has always stressed the prevalence of the inner attitude. It is not so much the physical position, but the spiritual attitude that counts in prayer. What this inner attitude has to be is best expressed in a book that for millions has become a companion to prayer, called *My Utmost for His Highest*. It is a collection of daily readings taken from sermons written by the Baptist preacher Oswald Chambers (1874–1917). His zeal to bring the gospel to new places took him to countries as diverse as Japan and Egypt. His many publications are characterized by a mystical spirit and a strong emphasis on practical, personal holiness. *My Utmost for His Highest* has gone through a multitude of reprints and has to the present day been a bestseller in prayer literature. It is the best example of the general Protestant practice of devotions: reading a book with daily devotions, which leads you into praying to God.

Personal prayer

Although Reformed liturgy demands ample opportunity for communal prayer during the worship service, much more emphasis is on personal prayer. From childhood, believers are not only taught standard prayers, but also encouraged to express their personal needs and thanks in prayer. This personal touch accounts for the fact that not too many prayers of famous Christians are known. Prayer is too private to be written down and made public. What is well known, however, is the fact that these Christians spent much time in prayer. Philipp Melanchthon arose at around 4 a.m. to start with prayer before daybreak, and his colleague Luther was of the opinion that the busier the day ahead, the more time one should spend in prayer.

Reformed thoughts on prayer

Kneel down or remain standing, join hands and direct your eyes to heaven and say or think as briefly as you can: O, heavenly Father, You, dear God, I am an unworthy, poor sinner, unworthy to lift up my eyes or hands to you. But, since you have commanded all of us to pray, and since you have promised to hear us and on top of that you have through your son Jesus Christ taught us in word and deed how to pray, I come to obey this commandment and trust in your gracious response and I pray in the name of my Lord Jesus Christ with all your holy Christians on this earth, Our Father, who art in heaven…

Martin Luther, *A Simple Way to Prayer* (1535)

When thou first openeth thine eyes in a morning, pray to God and give him thanks heartily. God then shall have his honour and thy heart shall be the better for it the whole day following. For we see in experience, that vessels keep long the taste of that liquor with which they were first seasoned. And when thou liest down, let that be the last also, for thou knowest not whether once fallen asleep, thou shalt ever rise again alive. Good therefore it is that thou shouldest give up thyself into the hands of God, whilst thou art awake.

William Perkins, *A Grain of Mustard Seed* (1592)

When you are brought face to face with a difficult situation and nothing happens externally, you can still know that freedom and release will be given because of your continued concentration on Jesus Christ. Your duty in service and ministry is to see that there is nothing between Jesus and yourself. Is there anything between you and Jesus even now? If there is, you must get through it, not by ignoring it as an

◆ *Jacob's Ladder*, **by William Blake (1757–1827).**

irritation, or by seeking to ignore it, but by facing it and getting through it into the presence of Jesus Christ. Then that very problem itself, and all that you have been through in connection with it, will glorify Jesus Christ in a way that you will never know until you see him face to face.

Oswald Chambers, *My Utmost for His Highest* (1937)

Literature and music

Are not poetry and spirituality twins? Is not a song the highest expression of spirituality? Is not a story or novel the best way to show how spirituality is an everyday item? Christian spirituality is not only a matter of theology, but just as much a matter of literature and music. While some of the writers, poets and composers intensely wanted to convey a message to their audience, most simply expressed their own spirituality, and in this way influenced the spiritual life of others. Many poems, novels and hymns display this remarkable combination of demonstration and influence.

Spirituality longs for expression; it cannot remain hidden. And in many cases words are not sufficient in themselves, but need to be completed by music.

Literature

If a Christian novel is to be defined as a book that builds up the faith through an entertaining story, *John Foxe's Book of Martyrs* (1559) is the first Protestant novel. It was first of all meant to encourage persecuted believers by telling them the stories of those who had suffered for Christ before them and who had been sustained in the faith. Yet the way in which Foxe wrote these stories made them even more dramatic and injected suspense and romance. The success of the book encouraged a spirituality that advocated obedience to God rather than human beings, even if it cost believers their lives.

A masterful example of doctrine put to verse is John Milton's (1608–74) *Paradise Lost*. This description of paradisal life and the way it ends for humanity articulates the Puritan principles of the power of sin and grace, the sovereignty of God and human stewardship:

They, looking back, all the eastern side beheld
Of Paradise, so late their happy seat,
Waved over by that flaming brand, the gate

◆ 'Now night her course began…', from *Paradise Lost*, engraved by Ligny (1882).

With dreadful faces thronged and fiery arms.
Some natural tears they dropped, but wiped
*   them soon;*
The world was all before them, where to
*   choose*
Their place of rest, and Providence their guide:
They hand in hand, with wandering steps
*   and slow,*
Through Eden took their solitary way.
('The Banishment')

A much more mystical spirituality can be read and seen in the works of William Blake (1757–1827). Blake rejected industrialism and rationalism and believed in the power of imagination. The results of his imagination can be seen in his impressive and somewhat eerie copperplates, filled with signs and symbols. The despair of his younger years was slowly replaced by a hope of salvation through mutual compassion and forgiveness. These verses, from *Songs of Innocence*, demonstrate the mystical dimension of Blake's work:

For Mercy, Pity, Peace and Love
Is God, our father dear,
And Mercy, Pity, Peace and Love
Is Man, his child and care

And all must love the human form,
In heathen, Turk or Jew;
Where Mercy, Love and Pity dwell
There God is dwelling too.
(**'The Divine Image'**)

Stressing the primacy of love in religion, Henry Drummond (1851–97) created for himself a place in the history of Christian spirituality with an essay on 1 Corinthians 13 in which the apostle Paul describes love as indispensable for the true believer. Drummond called the essay *The Greatest Thing in the World* because that is what he believed love to be. Love is the motor that will bring the world towards the kingdom of heaven. In this positive message Drummond combines Christian and non-Christian ideas in such a way that the orthodoxy of Drummond's teaching came to be questioned. His own words, however, seem to take away all suspicion:

The power to set the heart right, to renew the springs of action, comes from Christ. The sense of the infinite worth of the single soul, and the recoverableness of a man at his worst, are the gifts of Christ. The freedom from guilt, the forgiveness of sins, come from Christ's cross; the hope of immortality springs from Christ's grave. Personal conversion means for life a personal religion, a personal trust in God, a personal debt to Christ, a personal dedication to his cause.

Christ and the soul were also at the heart of the works of George Macdonald (1824–1905). This poet, novelist and preacher had a large family at home and (perhaps unsurprisingly) wrote with children particularly in mind. Therefore, apart from his many works for grown-ups, he also wrote children's books. Macdonald, who was a direct influence on C.S. Lewis and J.R.R. Tolkien, introduced his young readers into a fantasy world. Macdonald was convinced that all imaginative meaning comes from God and that fantasy is a powerful means of conveying God's thoughts to adults, as well as children.

Hymns

Whereas poetry remained initially largely reserved for the learned classes, hymns were for everyone. Hymns are able to reflect as well as influence the state of theology and the state of the soul. They are a means of expressing the most contradictory feelings of sorrow and gladness, hope and despair. Among Protestants it was that old biblical hymn book, the Psalms of David, that was held in highest esteem; from this fundamental hymnal, countless other hymns originated. From childhood, Protestants were taught to sing. In Calvin's Geneva it was the children who in church services taught their parents to sing. No wonder that the Protestant tradition brought forth a considerable number of songwriters.

A prime example of orthodoxy put to song is the work of the German Lutheran preacher Paul Gerhardt (c. 1607–76). Some 120 hymns were written and composed by him and they have influenced generations of believers, among them many who were not Lutheran. Gerhardt knew to combine Lutheran orthodox beliefs with a warm spirituality. Since four of his five children died in infancy, he certainly knew from experience the sorrow, trust and faith his hymns deal with.

The hymns of Isaac Watts (1674–1748) and Philip Doddridge (1702–51) were internationally appreciated. Watts, known as the father of the English hymn, was an independent minister in London, but had to quit most of his minsterial responsibilities when he fell seriously ill and became a near-invalid. He devoted himself to writing books and songs which resulted in an

◆ *A Village Choir*, by **Thomas Webster (1800–86).**

output of fifty-two theological works and 600 hymns. Watts was convinced that our songs are a human offering for God. Therefore songs should be composed with our own words and the Psalms should be modernized and Christianized. His hymns 'When I Survey the Wondrous Cross' and 'O God, Our Help in Ages Past' have found a solid place in many hymnals all over the world and in many different languages.

His friend Doddridge also transformed Puritan spirituality into song. Doddridge deserted the embattled position most Puritans had taken and aimed at the breadth of evangelical Christianity as he found it in Jonathan Edwards and the Great Awakening (see chapter 9, p. 283f). In his songs he called out for conversion to and praise of God. The joy of this attitude of faith is well expressed in the hymn, 'O Happy Day, That Fixed My Choice'.

The Collection of Hymns for the Use of the People Called Methodists (1780) consists mainly of songs written by Charles Wesley. In the foreword to this hymnal the work is described as 'a little body of experimental and practical divinity' which contains 'all the important truths of our most holy religion'. This hymn book became the mother of all official Methodist hymnals until the present day. In one case the song became more famous than the composer. It was John Newton (1725–1804) who gave Christianity the ever-popular classic 'Amazing Grace':

Amazing grace – how sweet the sound
  That saved a wretch like me!
I once was lost, but now am found,
  Was blind, but now I see.

'Twas grace that taught my heart to fear,
  And grace my fears relieved;
How precious did that grace appear
  The hour I first believed!

The great preachers

The spirituality of the missionaries and great preachers is quite the opposite of an inwardly directed spirituality, withdrawn from the world and its desires. William Carey (1761–1834) was mocked as the 'consecrated cobbler', a sneer at his trade before becoming a Baptist minister. Yet he emerged as the father of modern missions as he did not and could not restrain his passion to proclaim the gospel to the heathen. This urge – this enthusiasm – was not extinguished by the apathy in the churches, prompted by the thought that mission work should be the preserve of the apostles. Carey went to India where he preached, taught and translated, and all these activities contributed to the spiritual and physical well-being of thousands of people. His spirituality resulted in resistance to slavery and child- and widow-sacrifices. His life motto, 'Expect great things from God, undertake great things for God,' is the best expression of the trust in God and zeal for God that lived in Carey's heart. It is not so much his own spirituality as his influence in expanding Christian spirituality that makes Carey important.

What Carey was for India, David Livingstone (1813–73) was for Africa. Because of his travels he is mostly known as an explorer, but first of all he wanted to be a missionary. Having studied both theology and medicine, he was well equipped for this work. His attitude towards the Africans was unconventional for his time as he saw them as human beings, equal in dignity to Europeans: 'In Christ we see all other races as image-bearers of God and fellow-brothers.' The same applied to the Chinese, as James Hudson Taylor (1832–1905) discovered and taught: in order to reach the heart of the Chinese, you have to dress, live and talk like them. At the age of fifteen Taylor was converted and all he wanted thereafter was to work as a missionary in China. His wish was fulfilled and in spite of adversities he started and organized the China Inland Mission so successfully that at Taylor's death there were 828 missionaries.

Missionary work, through these and other apostolic men and women, has been the means through which Christian spirituality has become a worldwide religion.

Popular spirituality

Towards the end of the nineteenth century a new phenomenon appears: the mass meeting. It was the age of enthusiastic speakers who could enthrall a crowd with only words and gestures. Ministers and evangelists made use of these meetings to proclaim the gospel to those who otherwise would not come to church. One of them was the vocally powerful Charles Haddon Spurgeon (1834–92). Without a microphone he could speak to thousands in his London Tabernacle. Those present not only heard what he said, but through his enthusiasm and rhetoric Spurgeon also reached many hearts. Those who were not able to attend

◆ **Charles Haddon Spurgeon at the start of his preaching career.**

and those who lived after Spurgeon died studied his influential sermons and biblical studies. The message was clear: we can only be saved through faith in Jesus Christ. Spurgeon stressed the guilt and depravity of humanity, but did this in such a way that his compelling invitation to come to Christ was all the more attractive:

If you are all like me, you are far from being always alike. I am sometimes lifted up to the very heavens, and then I go down to the deeps; I am at one time bright with joy and confidence, and at another time dark as midnight with doubts and fears. Even Elijah, who was so brave, had his fainting fits. We are to be blamed for this, and yet the fact remains: our experience is as an

April day, when shower and sunshine take their turns. Amid our mournful changes we rejoice to hear the Lord's own voice, saying, 'Fear not: for I have redeemed thee.' Everything is not a changeful wave; there is a rock somewhere. Redemption is a fact accomplished.[22]

Practical preaching

As a young boy William Booth (1829–1912) was impressed by the sermons of the Wesleyan Methodists. At the age of fifteen he experienced his conversion to Christ and some years later he felt an urge to preach the gospel himself. He chose the slums of Nottingham as his pulpit and soon grew to be a well-known revivalist preacher, although he had not studied theology and was not ordained. He could not accept the church's apathy and the immorality of its members and his decision to break with the church lay at the root of his organization, which came to be called the Salvation Army. Booth wanted to combine piety and practice in such a way as to make them inseparable. Booth was convinced that spirituality suffers when people live in poverty and misery. The original aim of his Army was to save souls, but saving lives was a means to that aim.

General Booth was militant in his fight for a holy life and his battle against the use of alcohol. No wonder that a quarter of the handbook for the soldier in Booth's Army is devoted to sanctification and holiness. The military aspect of his thought is also evident in a strong belief in winning the battle. The triumphant sound of the Army's brass bands demonstrates a spirituality of enthusiasm and determination.

◆ 'Saved!'; a popular cutting or 'scrap' from the late 19th century showing the work of the Salvation Army.

Abraham Kuyper
(1837–1920)

The Dutch theologian and politician Abraham Kuyper certainly belongs to the category of 'great preachers'. Having retired from his office as a minister in 1874 in order to enter politics, he soon became Minister of the Interior in the Netherlands. Meanwhile he founded a fast-growing political party and a prestigious university, all of which made him deserve the nickname of 'Mighty Abraham'. His energy, as revealed in his activities and publications in various fields, is impressive. Kuyper became most famous for his public appearances and addresses on political, ecclesiastical and religious issues. The source of this power, however, was a deep personal piety. All of his activities found their source in the conviction that the sovereignty of Christ must find visible expression in every sphere of life. But, first of all, the human heart has to surrender to the kingship of Christ. Kuyper himself experienced his spiritual conversion through his pastoral work with the ordinary believers in the church.

As a student he had joined in a standing ovation for a professor who denied the resurrection of Christ, but later on he became a staunch opponent of modernism. He came to see that all his knowledge was useless if it was not rooted in his heart. His spirituality was characterized by a deep sense of sin and guilt and the awareness of our daily need of the grace of God. He stimulated Christians to social and political activities and yet he said, 'More is needed. There must be moments in our life that we exclude the world from our heart, so that we can – even for a short time – be completely alone with our God.'[23]

Methodism

Methodism was born out of a desire for true spirituality, and a widespread fear that the gospel of Christ was going to be suffocated by dead orthodoxy and a petrified liturgy. Leaders, notably John Wesley (1703–91) and George Whitefield (1714–70), tried to revive the Church of England and its people. The Church of England had, in their view, replaced the original message of sin and grace by instructions on how to become a decent citizen. John Wesley and his brother

Charles (1707–88) had studied at Oxford (see box, p. 198). While there they formed a group with fellow Christian students in order to encourage and help each other in scripture-reading, prayer and fasting. At first mockingly called the 'holy club', they were later named Methodists because of the fact that they strongly advocated bringing order into one's spiritual life and relating every aspect of life to faith in Jesus as Lord. Yet, there was also 'method' in their attitude towards conversion and religion. A brief but thorough experience of sin, guilt and grace should lead to a sudden, powerful conversion. In order to foster this experience in the hearts of people, Methodist preaching stressed the wrath of God and its consequences for those who were not willing to surrender to Christ.

Christian holiness

The early Methodists were convinced that conversion of the heart should be demonstrated by a conversion in lifestyle. Whitefield, willing to test the power of the gospel as well as the power of his preaching qualities, went to the mining district of Kingswood near Bristol, England. Would it be possible to radically change these miners, well known for their rough manners and loose living? After having derailed the preacher, first a few, and later hundreds, came to see, hear and believe. From that time on Methodist preaching spread through England and colonial America; it was widely popular among common folk (see chapter 9, p. 286), much less among the clerics. The successes of Whitefield, however, far outnumbered those of the Wesley brothers. As one hearer of a Whitefield sermon responded:

> I felt love to Christ in my Soul, and so much joy that the sweet offers of Christ as a husband to my Soul that the joy of my heart had almost made me to cry out among the people, that I was ready to strike hands at the Bargain. And after the sermon, meeting with a Lad of my acquaintance who I knew had been under

John and Charles Wesley

John Wesley (1703–91) was the Augustine of his age. Energetic, restless, an immensely effective communicator and teacher, he was also minutely interested in the inner workings of his own soul, and with recording every conceivable event in each day. It was this fascination with *method* and structure that gave his followers their name.

Wesley's sole aim was to promote 'so far as I am able, vital, practical religion'. He passionately opposed any thin, superficial kind of faith; the only kind of spirituality which meant anything to him was one that was *lived*. He and his brother Charles (1707–88) were two of nineteen children born to Susanna and Samuel Wesley (only nine survived from infancy). At Oxford, where the brothers were educated, they formed a group (the 'holy club') in 1729, consisting of a small number of devout lay Christians. In 1735 both sailed to Georgia as missionaries. On the way they encountered

some of the German Moravian Christians who were to exercise so great an influence on them later.

Conversion

It was Pentecost 1738 which marked the crucial conversion experience for both Charles and John. In the afternoon of Wednesday 24 May 1738, John went to St Paul's in London, where the anthem was a setting of Psalm 130 ('Out of the deep have I called unto thee, O Lord…'). Then

in the evening I went very unwillingly to a society in Aldersgate Street, where one was reading Luther's Preface to the Epistle to the Romans. About a quarter before nine, while he was describing the change which God works in the heart through faith in Christ, I felt my heart strangely warmed. I felt I did trust in Christ, Christ alone for salvation, and an assurance was given me that he had taken away *my* sins, even *mine*, and saved *me* from the law of sin and death.

After this, John travelled to Germany to meet the Moravian Christians again. He was deeply influenced by their intense piety, as well as by their enthusiastic singing (which soon became a hallmark of Methodist worship as well): Charles Wesley was to write some 6,000 hymns, which contain some of the finest expressions of Methodist spirituality. Here is an example of Charles's hymnody:

'Tis not a dead external sign
Which here my hopes require,
The living power of love Divine
In Jesus I desire.

I want the dear Redeemer's grace,
I seek the Crucified,
The Man that suffer'd in my place,
The God that groan'd and died.

Swift, as their rising Lord to find
The two disciples ran,
I seek the Saviour of mankind,
Nor shall I seek in vain.

Come, all who long His face to see
That did our burden bear,
Hasten to Calvary with me,
And we shall find him there.

It is worth noting in this hymn the movement from the individual to the corporate, the longing for a personal encounter with Christ, and the passionate hope that the Christ who was present at Calvary will also be present in the lives of all who turn to him. It was these characteristics that gave early Methodism its dynamic and infectious power.

◆ **Opposite: Illustration by A. Hunt (1885), showing John Wesley preaching on his father's grave at Epworth, England.**

Exercize, I just flew with my Arms about him, and said, such a minister has married my Soul to Christ.

Although Whitefield also emphasized pure, godly living, he did not agree with John Wesley, who believed that total sinlessness was obtainable in this life. This 'faith in holiness' did characterize the Wesleyan branch of Methodism, whose spirituality laid much emphasis on suppressing sin, self-examination and a strict lifestyle.

The wrath of God, explicitly described in Methodism, was preached in order to encourage a lifelong attitude of penance. Yet penitential practice was combined with joy over the active presence of the Spirit in the heart. This presence creates an enthusiastic and (according to Wesley) perfect love for God and neighbour.

Fellowship

Stressing the individual faith-experience of the believer included the calling to share that experience with other believers. The Methodist way is to organize small groups in which an intimate spiritual fellowship can take place through Bible study and prayer. Originally these groups started as a means to make up for the lack of nurture received in the official church. Fellowship with God was nurtured by multiplying the number of times at which the Lord's Supper was celebrated. At a time when the Church of England celebrated this sacrament four or five times a year, John Wesley partook in bread and wine every four or five days. For these occasions the Wesley brothers wrote a special collection of 'Hymns on the Lord's Supper'.

Methodism can also be said to have a catholic spirituality, in the sense of a firm emphasis on sacramental life and devotion. As long as doctrinal differences do not touch the essentials of the Christian faith, a communion of all Christian believers can be maintained and expanded. There is even a longing to omit differences in order to share spiritual fellowship. Wesley said, 'From the

first hour that I entered the kingdom, it was a sacred rule with me never to preach on any controverted point – at least, not in a controversial way.'

Conclusion

Looking over the history of the Protestant Reformation with all its movements, moments and personalities, a common thread is easy to detect. The message of unconditional grace is constantly heard and received, and it is this message that in all of these times brought forth a spirituality characterized by a deep and joyful relation of faith and trust between God and the believer. This spirituality resisted tendencies to become individualistic, but kept seeking its norm in God's Word, kept finding its home in the church, and kept its focus on a practical faith amid society. These basic elements make this spirituality both contemporary and adaptable. The times may change and churches may vary in many things, but the mutual love between God and humanity remains for ever decisive.

7

Catholic Saints and Reformers

(16th to 19th centuries)

Liz Carmichael

Timeline

The period from the sixteenth to the nineteenth century saw vast changes. The Western church split into Catholic and Protestant branches and the emerging European nations took one side or other, with tolerance only gradually growing. Modern science and sceptical rational thought came to the fore from the seventeenth century onwards, and social attitudes changed with the rise of democracy throughout the period. Women slowly began to take a much more active role in society. The church in the West was involved in, and deeply affected by, these political, intellectual and social developments as the modern world came to birth.

Europe remained the centre for new developments in Catholic spirituality. Our focus will fall first on Spain, then move to Italy, England and France.

'Counter-Reformation' spirituality in Spain

In the sixteenth and early seventeenth centuries the Roman Catholic Church responded to the challenge of the Reformation by an internal reform, known as the 'Counter-Reformation', which had to be grounded in the renewal of Catholic spiritual life.

This reawakening first began in Spain, a country then in its own political 'Golden Age', where the monarchs Ferdinand and Isabella had ensured an internal church reform some time earlier through Cardinal Ximenes, primate of Spain from 1495 to 1517. This Spanish renewal produced many notable spiritual writers, and bore its most famous fruit in the fervent active spirituality of Ignatius Loyola and the Carmelite contemplative reform led by Teresa of Avila and John of the Cross.

Ignatius Loyola
(c. 1491–1556)

Iñigo Loyola was a Spanish Basque nobleman brought up in courtly circles in Castile to become a young professional soldier full of dreams of chivalry and knightly valour. His life changed abruptly in 1521 when his right leg was wounded at the siege of Pamplona. He spent his convalescence reading the *Life of Christ* by Ludolf of Saxony (a compendium of the gospel stories with commentary by major spiritual writers – an aid to meditative prayer) and the Lives of the saints. Now he was fired with enthusiasm to emulate saints such as Francis and Dominic in heroic service of Christ. He decided to begin with a penitential pilgrimage to Jerusalem. In March 1522 he went to the shrine of Our Lady at Montserrat to confess all the sins of his life, taking three days to write them all down, then hung up his sword and dagger, gave away his fine clothes to a poor man and adopted pilgrim dress: a sackcloth tunic and staff.

Ignatius spent the next year living as a beggar in the small town of Manresa, getting used to his new lifestyle of poverty and prayer. He took with him a notebook into which he had copied passages from the *Life of Christ* and Lives of the saints, to which he added his own notes as he found methods of prayer and spiritual discernment that helped him. This was the origin of the *Spiritual Exercises*. Ignatius made extensive use of 'imaginative contemplation' which was then a popular way of praying: imagining a scene, usually from the gospels, and allowing oneself to enter into it. His own mystical experience was characterized by intuitive visions, with or without visual imagery.

In 1523 Ignatius arrived in Jerusalem intending to stay permanently, praying at the holy places and 'helping souls'. The Franciscan Provincial, in charge of Western pilgrims, thought otherwise and ordered him to leave. His visit lasted two weeks. As he returned to Spain he realized he needed to study in order to be of more use. So began his student years (1524–36) in Barcelona, Alcalá, Salamanca and Paris, during which he taught

◆ **Ignatius Loyola, by Peter Paul Rubens (1577–1640).**

catechism, conversed about 'spiritual things', such as vices and virtues, and began to guide others through his 'exercises'. A group formed around him in Spain but did not last, and several times he was denounced to the Inquisition and imprisoned. In 1534 in Paris he and six friends including Francis Xavier made a life vow of poverty and service to others, committing themselves to live and work in Jerusalem if possible and, if not, to offer their services to the pope for whatever task he might assign. War between Venice and the

Ignatian spirituality

Why is Ignatian spirituality popular?

Ignatian spirituality links the gospels with our own everyday experience, using methods that are easily learned. The 'exercises' can be done either in daily prayer times in ordinary life, or in retreat. Both individuals and groups can use Ignatius's methods of reflection and discernment. In recent years, lay people have been trained as directors, so many are now being helped to develop their prayer life in this way.

The Ignatian spiritual exercises

These exercises are an ordered programme of prayer and meditation, and Ignatius's book, *Spiritual Exercises*, is an instruction manual for people who guide others through them. In the first part, or 'week', the retreatant considers the purpose of life, God's call, and the seriousness of sin. The second 'week' opens with Christ's call to serve him as king and leads through the life of Jesus from the incarnation to Palm Sunday; the third 'week' concerns the passion and crucifixion; the fourth, the resurrection. The retreatant learns various ways of praying, of examining themselves and making decisions ('elections'). The whole experience leads to deeper Christian commitment. The exercises can be done intensively in retreat (over a few days or a month), or in ordinary life by praying an hour or more each day. They are offered to everyone as a way for 'the Creator to deal directly with the creature, and the creature directly with their Creator and Lord'.

An Ignatian gospel meditation or 'imaginative contemplation'

Here is the prayer on the nativity, from the *Spiritual Exercises*. Set aside a time, between twenty minutes and an hour, when you will not be interrupted; it is helpful to set an alarm to define the time. Be in a comfortable position, sitting or perhaps kneeling on a prayer stool. Offer the time to God and ask for the presence and guidance of the Holy Spirit. Read Luke 2:3–7 slowly once or twice. Now put your Bible aside and allow yourself to enter into the scene:

First see, in imagination, the road from Nazareth to Bethlehem. Consider its length, its breadth; whether level, or through valleys and over hills. Observe the place or cave where Christ is born; whether big or little; whether high or low; and how it is arranged. Now I ask for what I desire: I ask for an intimate knowledge of our Lord, who has become man for me, that I may love him more and follow him more closely.

Now I see the persons: Our Lady, Joseph, the maid, and the child Jesus after his birth. I will make myself a poor little unworthy servant, and as though present, look upon them, contemplate them, and serve them in their needs with all possible homage and reverence. Then I will reflect on myself so as to reap some fruit.

Next I consider, observe, and contemplate what the persons are saying, and then reflect on myself and draw some fruit from it.

Turks made Jerusalem impossible to reach, so after being ordained in Venice the group, now grown to ten, made for Rome. Ignatius had been praying to Mary to 'place him with her Son', in preparation for celebrating his first Mass, and in the church of La Storta near Rome he 'felt such a change in his soul, and saw so clearly that God the Father placed him with Christ his Son, that he would not dare to doubt that the Father had placed him with his Son'.[1] In 1540 the group was constituted as the Society of Jesus by the pope, with Ignatius as its first Superior-General. An excellent organizer, he spent the years until his death in 1556 writing the full *Constitutions* and

Next I see and consider what they are doing, for example, making the journey and labouring that our Lord might be born in extreme poverty, and that after many labours, after hunger, thirst, heat, and cold, after insults and outrages, he might die on the cross, and all this for me. Then I reflect and draw some spiritual fruit from what I have seen.

Finally I think over what I should say to our Lord, and I converse freely with him. According to the light that I have received, I will ask for grace to follow and imitate him more closely, who has just become man for me. I end with the 'Our Father'.[2]

Do not rush; you may want to take several prayer periods for this. It can be very helpful to discuss what happens with a spiritual director, who will be able to suggest further prayer. An individually guided retreat is a good way to deepen this way of praying.

Ignatius's method of discernment

As a 'contemplative in action', a phrase coined by one of Ignatius's closest followers, Jerome Nadal, Ignatius was also concerned with decision-making (making an 'election' as he put it), seeking to discern the leading of God's Spirit and distinguish it from 'the evil one'. He recommends a method of carefully evaluating the causes and effects of our feelings of 'consolation' and 'desolation'. While convalescing after the siege of Pamplona in 1521, he considered his future and noticed that thoughts of knightly romance satisfied him temporarily, but afterwards he felt dissatisfaction and emptiness; whereas his thoughts of emulating the saints caused lasting feelings of cheerfulness and satisfaction. He drew the general conclusion that worldly pleasures in themselves offer merely superficial and passing delight, or 'false consolation'; but lasting joy and peace which is 'true consolation' can be found in actions directed to the glory of God – and it is God's Spirit who leads us towards them. True consolation also shows its effect in an increase of faith, hope and love. Continuing to study his own and others' feelings, Ignatius noted that a person who is just beginning to be converted may well feel desolation on being drawn away from worldly pleasures towards spiritual things; but as they advance they will begin to feel the opposite. Ignatius taught a twice-daily exercise of examining how one has felt about the events of the morning or the afternoon, to increase awareness of how God is leading and our response.

A prayer attributed to Ignatius

Lord, teach me to be generous; teach me to serve you as you deserve, to give and not to count the cost, to fight and not to heed the wounds, to toil and not to seek for rest, to labour and not to seek reward, save that of knowing that I do your will. Amen.

supervising the work of the rapidly growing society. He was canonized in 1622.

The Society of Jesus ('Jesuits')

The Society (or Company) of Jesus that Ignatius founded was a new kind of religious order of well-trained and motivated priests, not confined to monasteries but available to work anywhere in the world. They were to pray wherever they happened to be: the world, and not the cloister, was their 'house'. In the *Constitutions* Ignatius urges them to 'find God in all things', through events, persons and the surroundings of their daily work and life.

◆ **Two Jesuits at the court of a Muslim prince in India;
illumination by Nar-Singh (c. 1605).**

The Jesuits spread quickly through Europe,
the Far East (especially through the missions
of Francis Xavier in India and Japan) and Latin
America, taking their preaching, spiritual
direction, works of mercy and education. Their
instant availability was underlined in the 'fourth
vow' of direct obedience to the pope, although
their independence of local ecclesiastical
authorities, and the political influence that their

The spirituality of Teresa of Avila

Teresa's *Interior Castle* or *The Mansions*

Teresa describes the human person as like a castle
or a great house with a moat around it and many
rooms inside, like the 'many mansions' in heaven.
This castle is made of diamond or crystal, and its
rooms are arranged in concentric circles. God dwells
in the central (seventh) rooms, so the light of God's
presence should fill the castle and shine out through
it – but the crystal is darkened by sin. The spiritual
life is a journey that begins outside the castle and
leads inwards, towards the innermost rooms where
God dwells. God calls us on this journey, and it is
accomplished through prayer. Its goal is the union of
our love and will with the will and love of God: then
the diamond that is our self can shine out in its full
beauty.

We enter the first rooms when we are converted
to Christ and begin to pray. We continue through the
second rooms, where it is easy to be discouraged, by
making efforts to follow Christ and avoid sin. Many
people succeed in reaching the third rooms, where
we are more committed but not yet deep and are in
danger of getting stuck as conventional churchgoers,
being Christians by our own efforts and neither
experiencing nor demonstrating the fullness of God's
love. The journey continues if we now allow God to
begin to take over in our life, giving ourselves to him.
The beginnings of the contemplative prayer of silence
and love mark the fourth rooms. In the fifth,
closeness to God increases and the fruit of this is a
visible growth in love for our neighbour. By now we
realize that following Christ means being with him
in suffering as well as joy; and in the sixth rooms
Teresa describes the desolation and pain, as well as
the unexpected joy and delight, that are likely to
accompany profound spiritual growth. Finally, in

◆ Teresa of Avila, by Juan de la Miseria (c. 1526–1616).

the seventh rooms, we arrive at peace and stability springing from deep mutual love between the self and God; a 'spiritual marriage' has taken place. The two aspects of Christian life, the contemplative Mary and the active Martha, are now united in an apostolic life in Christ that bears fruit in the world.

The *Interior Castle* is an invaluable guidebook, but, as Teresa points out, the stages are schematic and will not exactly match an individual's own experience. We may find things happening simultaneously or in a different order, and go backwards as well as forwards. The essential is to want to love and serve God above all else, and to allow God to lead us. A learned and experienced spiritual director can greatly help.

Teresa on friendship with God

Anyone who has not begun to pray, I beg, for love of the Lord, not to miss so great a blessing. There is no place here for fear, but only for desire. For, even if a person fails to make progress, or to strive after perfection, so that he may merit the consolations and favours given to the perfect by God, yet he will gradually gain a knowledge of the road to Heaven. And if he perseveres, I hope in the mercy of God, whom no one has ever taken for a friend without being rewarded; and mental (inner) prayer, in my view, is nothing but friendly intercourse, and frequent solitary converse, with him whom we know loves us.[3]

The Carmelites and Teresa's reform

The Carmelite Order began in the crusader period of the twelfth century as a group of hermits on Mount Carmel in the Holy Land just south of modern Haifa. They took their inspiration from the stories of Elijah's flight into the desert and his community of prophets. In the thirteenth century, moving to Europe, they became Carmelite Friars with a life of prayer, study and apostolic work. Enclosed convents for women were added in 1432, to pray for the friars and the church. The 'primitive Rule', with its fasting and continual prayer, was gradually relaxed until Teresa restored the original challenging lifestyle. The reformed Carmelites, both sisters and friars, call themselves 'Teresian', or 'Discalced', meaning they ceased wearing shoes, adopting sandals as a sign of poverty and simplicity.

work in education and spiritual direction gave them, sometimes led to severe tensions. Through giving the exercises, the Jesuits contributed to a widespread growth in retreats and personal spiritual direction.

Teresa of Avila
(1515–82)

Several Jesuit priests were important as friends and spiritual guides in the life of Teresa of Avila, the great reformer of the contemplative order of Carmelites. Doña Teresa de Ahumada, who became Mother Teresa of Jesus, was born in 1515 in Avila on the high plateau of central Spain. Her father came from a wealthy Jewish merchant family recently converted to Christianity; her mother from the minor nobility of Castile. Teresa was an adventurous child, who aged seven tried to run away to seek martyrdom in 'the land of the Moors', taking her elder brother Rodrigo; they were caught just outside Avila and taken home. Later, at her Augustinian convent school, the holiness of one of the nuns impressed her and she became a Carmelite nun at the Convent of the Incarnation in Avila in 1536.

Teresa began a long and confused period of growth, often torn between her inner impulse to serious prayer and the fairly easy life of the convent, where sisters had their own servants and entertained visitors. During an illness she stayed with her devout uncle Don Pedro and there found and read a book on contemplative prayer, the *Third Spiritual Alphabet* by Francisco Osuna; but it was only in 1554 that her own prayer life ceased to be a long dry struggle, based on the lengthy exercises in deliberate meditation that were then popular, and entered a new mystical contemplative stage. Her confessors and advisers frequently took a negative view of the experiences she recounted to them, telling her that her visions, locutions (words she heard spoken to her) and short trance-like states were from the devil or her imagination. She had a few good learned friends, such as the

Jesuit Balthasar Álvarez and the Franciscan Peter of Alcántara, who took her dedication to Christ seriously and helped her to understand her experiences in terms of growth in the love of God. Her writings are an unusually clear and helpful guide to the stages of spiritual growth, and to experiences that may sometimes consciously accompany it, but are not to be sought for themselves. She wrote an autobiographical Life in obedience to her confessors in 1562–65 which the Inquisition then confiscated. Believing that a serious prayer life needed a more dedicated lifestyle, Teresa founded the reformed Carmelite convent of St Joseph in Avila in 1565, and wrote the *Way of Perfection* (1565–66) on prayer and living in community for her nuns. It was for them that she wrote her mature and complete description of the spiritual journey, the *Interior Castle* or *Mansions*, in 1577.

Between 1567 and her death in 1582, as her *Book of the Foundations* tells, she founded fourteen more convents all over Spain. In 1567 she met a keen young Carmelite friar, the future John of the Cross, and persuaded him to begin the reform in the men's order. Teresa was canonized in 1622 and declared a Doctor (teacher) of the Church in 1970.

John of the Cross
(1542–91)

Teresa's younger friend and colleague was born in 1542 as Juan de Yepes, in a poor home in the little town of Fontiveros near Avila. He became one of Spain's greatest poets and an authority on contemplative prayer. He joined the Carmelite friars in 1563, studied at the University of Salamanca and was ordained. Then he met Teresa, with whom he worked from 1568 to reform the Carmelites, changing his name to John of the Cross. He spent a year in a tiny village house with one other friar, praying and evangelizing. Then began his career as teacher and spiritual director. From 1572 to 1577 he was chaplain to the Convent of the Incarnation in Avila, where Teresa had

◆ **John of the Cross was imprisoned for 9 months in 1577 at Toledo;** *View of Toledo,* **by El Greco (1541–1614), a contemporary.**

become prioress in 1571. Friars opposed to his reforms kidnapped him late in 1577 and imprisoned him in Toledo for nine months. He began the *Spiritual Canticle* in prison, and the imagery in his later poem *The Dark Night* probably owes something to the joy of his eventual night-time escape. The reformed ('Discalced') Carmelites became a separate order in 1580 and John continued to develop it, teaching at its college in Baeza, then as prior at Granada and Segovia. He also directed lay women and men. He died aged forty-nine, from septicaemia. He was canonized in 1627 and declared a Doctor of the Church in 1926.

Different kinds of prayer

Christian prayer can be broadly classified under three headings: vocal, meditative and contemplative prayer. The classical spiritual journey takes a person through vocal prayer (for example, saying the Lord's Prayer and participating in the liturgy) into meditation (inner prayer using the mind or imagination) and so on into contemplation (essentially the silent prayer of loving attentiveness, beyond thoughts and images). The ways of praying that Ignatius taught are mainly vocal and meditative, while Teresa and John move into the simplicity of contemplation. Meditative prayer involves actively thinking about, or imaging, scripture passages and scenes, or mysteries of the faith such as Christ's incarnation, passion and resurrection, in a way that arouses love, wonder and praise. It is the foundation for the loving prayer of the heart, silent contemplation.

Luis de Granada
(1504–88)

In the later sixteenth century one of the most widely read and influential books on meditation was Luis de Granada's *Libro de la Oración y Meditatión* ('Book of Prayer and Meditation') written in 1554 and translated into many languages. Luis was born in a poor family in Granada, became a Dominican and worked in Spain and Portugal. Teresa of Avila used and recommended his book, as did Francis de Sales.

Luis taught a six-point method, a clear outline of meditative prayer to help beginners learn how to do it: (1) *Preparation*: we come before God, casting all our sins into the depth of his mercy, recalling his awesome greatness and that we are here to pray so that we may receive his Spirit and fulfil his will. (2) *Reading of the subject*: we read a brief scripture passage, with the heart as well as the head, pausing as necessary. (3) *Meditation* may involve the imagination, picturing the scene in Christ's life, and/or the intellect, thinking about God's actions, his goodness and mercy; and here loving attentiveness is more important than understanding each detail. This leads to (4) *thanksgiving*, then (5) *offering* of ourselves, and (6) *petition* for others and ourselves. Luis had beginners specifically in mind, but a person used to prayer can also find his method helpful.

The spirituality of John of the Cross

The spiritual journey

The books of John of the Cross, the *Ascent of Mount Carmel*, *The Dark Night*, *Spiritual Canticle* and *Living Flame of Love*, take the form of commentaries on his mystical poems, so they begin from poetic symbolism, but are also systematic, practical and based on scriptural and theological scholarship. He makes extensive use of the love-poetry imagery from the Song of Songs.

John wrote for Christians who have already journeyed some way, at least as far as Teresa's third rooms, and have a real desire for God. His 'beginners' in contemplation are experienced in vocal and meditative prayer and have arrived at a point where these activities seem no longer to excite or satisfy them – and yet they long to know and love God better. John guides such people, who want to 'reach union with God quickly', as he says at the beginning of the *Ascent*. He prescribes a 'negative' way, a radical inner attitude of unpossessiveness and detachment from all created things whether earthly or spiritual, in order to be open to a direct relationship of love with God the Creator. The journey is both active and passive: sometimes we must act, sometimes allow God to act in us. John's spiritual path is a lover's journey at night, in darkness, up the slopes of Mount Carmel. 'Night' is a complex symbol: it means the exciting mystery, the bare faith, the pain and the detachment, that accompany the journey.

John's diagram of Mount Carmel shows a flat-topped mountain like the real Carmel (see diagram). The way to the summit is a single-minded desire for God that refuses to be delayed by any rival desire, whether for possession of worldly wealth or spiritual delights (mystical experiences, visions and so on). The goal is not the gifts but the Giver. Paradoxically, although the way is through desiring God only and renouncing desire for everything except God, it is precisely through union with God that we come to participate in God's loving

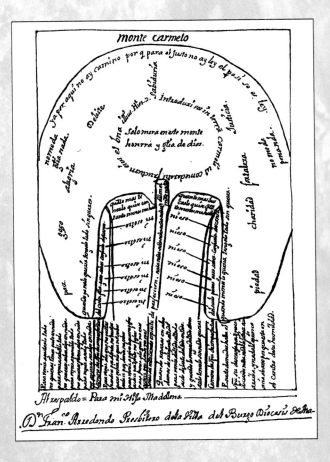

◆ **Sketch of Mount Carmel, by John of the Cross. The central path, of desiring nothing except God, leads directly to the summit, union in love with God.**

delight in all creation. The negative way, famously outlined on the diagram and in *Ascent* chapter 13, leads to positive fulfilment: 'To reach satisfaction in all, desire satisfaction in nothing… To come to possess all, desire the possession of nothing.' When the journey is as complete as is possible in this life, the result is the profound peace and joy that John celebrates in *Living Flame of Love*.

The 'dark night of the soul'

John of the Cross is often associated with this concept, which needs to be understood within his scheme of the spiritual journey. John talks about two 'active nights': the 'active night of sense' means our deliberate renunciation of possessive desire for the things of this world for their own sake; the 'active night of spirit' means the same detachment from possessive desire on the level of spiritual experiences. He also talks about two 'passive nights', and it is the second of these that is the true 'dark night of the soul'. The first 'passive night' is the 'passive night of sense' which is a state of restless dissatisfaction with this world and with meditative prayer, into which God may bring those whom he wants to move on into contemplation. The 'passive night of spirit' is the much deeper and more painful dispossession of spiritual consolation that God may later give to those he wants to draw even closer to himself; it is a stage through which a person may pass on the way to the joy of union with God in love, and is the 'dark night of the soul' in the proper sense. John describes an agony of depression and desolation, of feeling abandoned by God and yet longing for God, which may continue for months or years, and his description helps many Christians, at all stages of the spiritual life, to find meaning in deep experiences of pain and loss. They can be experiences of the cross, and lead on to unimaginable resurrection.

'The Living Flame of Love'

O living flame of love
that tenderly wounds my soul
in its deepest centre! Since
now you are not oppressive,
now consummate! if it be your will:
tear through the veil of this sweet encounter!

O sweet cautery,
O delightful wound!
O gentle hand! O delicate touch
that tastes of eternal life
and pays every debt!
In killing you changed death to life.

O lamps of fire!
In whose splendours
the deep caverns of feeling,
once obscure and blind,
now give forth, so rarely, so exquisitely,
both warmth and light to their Beloved.

How gently and lovingly
you wake in my heart,
where in secret you dwell alone;
and in your sweet breathing,
filled with good and glory,
how tenderly you swell my heart with love.[4]

What is 'mysticism'?

Christian mystics such as Teresa of Avila and John of the Cross follow a way of life that has the shape of the life, death and resurrection of Jesus Christ. He is the Way, so his life is the map, and, although the details of the journey differ for every individual, it will include self-dedication, the desire to love God above and through all things, willingness to suffer in the service of God's love, and openness to the surprising joys of new life in Christ. It is a transforming journey; as Paul writes, 'we are being changed into his likeness from one degree of glory to another' (2 Corinthians 3:18), and its goal is union in love with God.

The word 'mystic' is linked to the idea of hidden mystery, truth that is not capable of discovery by the intellect alone, but may be revealed to those who genuinely ask. 'Mystical theology' traditionally means either the knowledge of God imparted through contemplation, or the accumulated wisdom about living the contemplative life. The terms 'mystic' and 'mysticism', however, are often used to refer to many different phenomena, ranging from those in other religions who take a life of prayer seriously, to almost anything vaguely mysterious even if it is superficial and ephemeral. Mysticism sounds attractive, and so it should; but the path of Christian mystical life, while open to all and deeply joyful, is never superficial or easy.

Meditation versus contemplation

During the sixteenth century and later, disputes occasionally arose between advocates of methodical meditation as the only acceptable way of inner prayer, and those such as John of the Cross who believed that people who had a good grounding in faith and the love of God through meditative prayer should then be free to move on to the simpler prayer of the heart, or contemplation. Jesuits sometimes took one side, sometimes the other. Writers, such as Luis de Granada, whose main aim was to teach the art of prayer to beginners, go into great detail on such subjects as the passion where he presents an exhaustive list of points to consider, and it is easy to see why those who are attracted to wordless loving contemplation would find these long lists of 'considerations' very difficult to continue to use in prayer. Although contemplative and mystical prayer are firmly established and recognized within Christian tradition, church authorities are sometimes suspicious that contemplatives, like charismatics, are deluded or moving beyond their control, claiming an immediate personal source of divine inspiration apart from scripture and the church's teaching. Such suspicions led to persecution of groups of contemplative *alumbrados* (the 'enlightened' or 'illuminated') in sixteenth-century Spain and to the 'quietist' controversy at the end of the seventeenth century.

Renewal in Italy

Philip Neri (1515–95) and the Roman Oratory

Rome and the papal court lie at the spiritual centre of Roman Catholicism. It was to Rome that Ignatius and his friends came to offer their services to the pope, and to play a part in the spiritual renewal of Rome itself. In the early sixteenth century the city was in decline. It had been on the sidelines of the intellectual life of the

Italian Renaissance; it was reeling from the shock of the Reformation and, due to the status of the pope as a temporal prince, the city had been pillaged by the troops of the Emperor Charles V in 1527.

The charismatic Philip Neri has been called the 'apostle of Rome' for his role in its Counter-Reformation renewal. He arrived from Florence aged eighteen in 1533 and was a prayerful presence in Rome for the next sixty years. He worked as a tutor, studied theology for three years, then gave more time to prayer, often in the catacomb of San Sebastian. There at Pentecost in about 1544, as he stood praying for the gifts of the Holy Spirit he 'saw' a ball of fire descending and filling him; he felt overwhelmed with God's love and fell to the ground. From then on his prayer was accompanied by involuntary trembling (which he could control by an effort), heat and palpitations of the heart. He helped found the Confraternity of the Most Holy Trinity to assist poor pilgrims, worked in hospitals, and challenged the uncommitted and lapsed, asking, 'When shall we begin to do good?'

In 1551 he was ordained and began a ministry of confession and spiritual direction at the church of San Girolamo. Young laymen from business, court and professions came to him and he developed a programme of study and prayer every weekday afternoon. They met for a couple of hours for informal study of theology, Lives of the saints and church history (the talks were aimed at the heart, applying scripture to daily life, and were given by laymen as well as by Philip), and to sing the new worship songs, *laudi spirituali*; one had the chorus: *Jesus! Jesus! Everyone call on Jesus!* The group grew too large for Philip's room so they built an 'oratory' (a prayer room) above an aisle of the church. This was the original 'Oratory', and Philip saw its meetings as a pastoral and apostolic method, a way of Christian formation and evangelization which could be used anywhere.

In 1564 Philip had a few of his disciples ordained to minister at the Florentine church in Rome, San Giovanni dei Fiorentini. These priests lived a simple communal life under Philip's

◆ *The Virgin Mary Appearing to Philip Neri*, **by Carlo Maratta (1625–1713).**

supervision, providing confession, spiritual direction and a well-celebrated liturgy. They continued to help with the Oratory at San Girolamo. In 1575 this growing group of priests was constituted as the Congregation of the Oratory by Pope Gregory XIII, with S. Maria in Vallicella as their own church, and Philip was made provost – although he had not intended to found a new order. The Congregation spread to other cities. In Naples, oratory meetings for women were run for a time in a private house by Philip's eloquent disciple Tarugi.

This Congregation remains unusual: it is a loose federation of autonomous houses of priests and lay brothers, who take no vows but live according to a simple common rule under the authority of the diocesan bishop. The houses vary in how they interpret and live out the charism of their spiritual father.

Philip taught frequent confession and communion, and the use of short prayers such as 'O God make speed to save me, O Lord make haste to help me' and 'My Jesus, what can I do to fulfil your will?' He taught that humility is basic: it is necessary to recognize we are unworthy of the gift of prayer and throw ourselves entirely into the arms of the Lord, who will teach us how to pray. When healings and prophetic knowledge were attributed to Philip he insisted that God and the faith of others were responsible, and he deflected sentimental admiration with a puckish and eccentric sense of humour. He died in 1595 and was canonized in 1622 on the same day as Teresa of Avila, Ignatius Loyola and Francis Xavier.

Lorenzo Scupoli
(c. 1530–1610)

Lorenzo Scupoli provides another example of spiritual renewal in Italy. He was a member of the Theatines, a strict order of priests founded in Rome in 1524 by the future Pope Paul IV, then Bishop of Chieti (or 'Theate'). He worked in Venice and possibly met Francis de Sales who was studying law in nearby Padua. Certainly in 1590 a Theatine gave Francis a copy of Lorenzo's book *The Spiritual Combat*, published anonymously in 1589, and Francis tells us he carried it in his pocket as his constant companion. A few years later Mary Ward grew up in Yorkshire reading the first English translation.

The goal of the 'combat' is pure love of God for his own sake. The four weapons are distrust of self, trust in God, exercises to replace vices with virtues and prayer. Today we find 'contempt of self' a difficult notion, but its positive meaning is to overcome selfishness and to realize we need God's help:

> When anything occurs to thee to be done, any struggle with self to be undertaken, any victory over self to be attempted, before thou propose or resolve upon it, think upon thine own weakness; next, filled with mistrust of self, turn to the wisdom, the power, and the goodness of God, and in reliance on these... and with prayer, fight and labour.[5]

Lorenzo advises patiently working on one virtue at a time, making a concentrated and generous effort to become kind, or courageous, and so on. Vices can be tackled by practising the opposite virtue. Prayer is the most important weapon; it places in God's hand the sword with which he will fight for us. Meditation on the passion is central: 'The crucifix is the book I give you to read, from which you can derive the true portrait of all virtue.' We find an invincible weapon in holy communion, because there Christ himself enters the battle with us and for us.

Francis de Sales was involved in the French translation and still recommended this book to others even when he had written his own *Introduction to the Devout Life* (1609) which owes much to Lorenzo. There were several new English translations in the nineteenth century, both Catholic and Anglican.

English Roman Catholic spirituality

In England, the Reformation began in the 1530s under Henry VIII and was fully established under Elizabeth I (reigned 1558–1603). Roman Catholics were placed under obligation by the pope to overthrow the monarchy, so their activity went underground among families who secretly sheltered itinerant priests, and they contributed to developments in continental Europe through the exiled English Catholic base that was maintained at Douai in Flanders. Gradually restrictions on Catholics were relaxed, and by the time of Bishop Richard Challoner life became more normal, although even in the nineteenth century those such as Newman who became Catholic were regarded as having betrayed not only their tradition and friends, but their country too.

At the Reformation there were martyrs on both sides. Probably the best-known Catholic in public life who refused to accept the Reformation was Sir Thomas More (1478–1535). He was a devout humanist renaissance scholar and statesman. Son of a judge, he studied at Oxford and became a lawyer at Lincoln's Inn. While a lawyer he lodged at the nearby Carthusian monastery, the Charterhouse, apparently testing his vocation. He decided on marriage, and his home in Chelsea became a lively mini-college where his own children and others were educated in classical and Christian studies. Erasmus, his great friend, said he seemed 'born for friendship' and called him the *omnium horarium homo*, the 'man for all seasons'. His public career culminated in becoming Lord Chancellor, equivalent to a modern Prime Minister, under Henry VIII in 1529.

As a humanist scholar, More was a critic of political life and the medieval church. His *Utopia* (1516) was a satire that contrasted the property-grabbing lifestyle of his day with life in an ideal island state where there is no private property, everyone lives communally like the early Christians, and those who serve seek only a heavenly reward. He was, however, deeply committed to the continuity of church tradition, understanding it to spring from the decisions of general councils rather than from the pope alone. When Luther set up scripture as a greater authority than tradition, More pointed out that it was the church, from the apostles onwards, that had established the canon of scripture. Thus he became a defender of Catholicism, and in 1532, when Henry VIII began to detach England from the ecclesiastical authority of Rome, More resigned as Chancellor. He was imprisoned in the Tower in

1534 and executed, on probably perjured evidence, in 1535. He was remembered very differently by the Protestants he attacked (some were executed on his orders as Chancellor) and the Catholics he defended, but his integrity has won him general respect. In prison he wrote meditations, letters and prayers that show commitment to Christ and forgiveness of enemies. He was canonized in 1935. Here is one of his prayers:

> Almighty God, have mercy on *N* and *N*, and on all that bear me evil will, and would me harm, and their faults and mine together, by such easy, tender, merciful means, as thine infinite wisdom best can devise, vouchsafe to amend and redress, and make us saved souls in heaven together where we may ever live and love together with thee and thy blessed saints, O glorious Trinity, for the bitter passion of our sweet saviour Christ.[6]

◆ Frontispiece to *Utopia* by Thomas More; engraving by the 16th-century French school.

Forty Roman Catholic martyrs were executed at Tyburn (near Marble Arch, in London) in 1581. Among them was Edmund Campion (1540–81), a former Anglican deacon and fellow of St John's College, Oxford, who had become a Jesuit in Rome in 1573 and returned to England in 1580 to preach.

Two British contemplative priests, Benet of Canfield and Augustine Baker, lived and worked mainly across the Channel in France and Belgium. Benet will be discussed under French spirituality. The Benedictine Augustine Baker (1575–1641) was born David Baker, and was a lawyer in his home town of Abergavenny in Wales. He became Roman Catholic in 1603 and took the name Augustine on joining the Benedictines in 1605. After his noviciate and ordination in France he lived in England, secretly gathering documents useful for the history of the English Benedictines. From 1624 he was in Cambrai as spiritual director to the exiled English Benedictine nuns, and began to teach and write on contemplative prayer. He felt himself attracted to contemplation but struggled with it, giving up several times before settling into it for the last twenty years of his life. Despite having friends among the nuns, including Dame Gertrude More, a descendant of Thomas, whose Life he wrote, he attracted controversy and was moved after nine years to retirement at Douai, finally dying in London.

Baker knew the mystical tradition well, including the fourteenth-century English *Cloud of Unknowing* for which he wrote a preface and notes, and Hilton's *Ladder of Perfection*, as well as Carmelite and Flemish writers. He wrote many short treatises on contemplative life for private circulation, over forty of which were summarized and published after his death by Dom Serenus Cressy as *Sancta Sophia* ('Holy Wisdom').[7] This book shows him to be essentially orthodox but pedantic and idiosyncratic. He strongly rejected detailed methodical discursive meditation, except for beginners and in moderation. His way into acquired contemplation is through a 'constant and fervent exercise of recollections' (III.i.iv), i.e. the incessant and earnest repetition of short prayers from the heart: 'acts of remorse, fear, contrition etc. (which belong to the purgative way) and likewise acts of adoration, glorification, humiliation, resignation, and love (which belong to the illuminative and unitive ways)' (III.iii.ii).

This active contemplation could also take the form of deliberate interior silence. Such effortful 'imperfect contemplation' will lead into a state of 'perfect contemplation' which is still active but habitual, fed by short inspired prayers of aspiration now springing from the Holy Spirit within: 'My God, when shall I love thee alone? When shall I be united to thee… Let me be nothing, and be thou all, O my God' (III.iv.ii); and here prayer may become an experience of timeless, spaceless union with God who is all in all. Baker assumes there will be a desolate dark night for the advanced, before union is full. He reserves the term 'passive' contemplation for specific divine touches in ecstasies and inner visions.

Mary Ward
(1585–1645)

A very different contributor to Catholic spiritual life and to the role of women, was the English-woman Mary Ward, the first pioneer of active religious life for women under female leadership. She came from a Catholic family in Yorkshire, and as a teenager was sure of her vocation to religious life. Like Francis de Sales she found Scupoli's *Spiritual Combat* helpful (it was translated by John Gerard SJ in 1598). She briefly joined the Poor Clares at St Omer, and founded a convent of English Poor Clares there in 1608; but she was given a deep conviction that she was to found something quite different. She left the Clares and began an ascetic community life with a few friends, running a school at St Omer. Then the inspiration came to her that her Institute should take the form of an apostolic women's order with the same Rule as the Jesuits. At that time all women's orders had to be enclosed, so what she proposed was revolutionary and, to most, unthinkable. She and her companions persevered, drawing up a Rule, walking to Rome to seek the support of the pope, and founding houses in many cities in Germany. The Institute was suppressed in 1631, leaving only a house in Rome from which Mary eventually returned to

An English Catholic 'metaphysical' poet: Richard Crashaw (1613–49)

Richard Crashaw was a prayerful young man from a Puritan background who became a high Anglican at Cambridge. Like George Herbert, he was a close friend of Nicholas Ferrar and the community at Little Gidding. During the English Civil War he sided with the king, was forced to leave Cambridge, moved to France in 1646 and became Roman Catholic.

His last years were spent in Rome in the household of Cardinal Palotta; he died at Loreto aged thirty-six. He wrote religious and lyrical poems in English, Latin and Greek, and was strongly influenced by Spanish poetry: his poem 'The Flaming Heart' on Teresa of Avila owes much to a Spanish poem on the same subject. His collection *Steps to the Temple* was published in 1646, revised and enlarged in 1648; further poems appeared in *Carmen Deo Nostro* (1652).

'A Song of Divine Love'

Lord, when the sense of thy sweet grace
Sends up my soul to seek thy face,
Thy blessed eyes breed such desire,
I dy in love's delicious fire.
 O Love I am thy Sacrifice.
Be still triumphant, blessed eyes.
Still shine on me, fair suns! that I
Still may behold, though I still dy.

Though still I dy, I live again;
Still longing so to be still slain,
So gainful is such loss of breath,
I dy even in desire of death.
 Still live in me this loving strife
Of living Death and dying Life.
For while thou sweetly slayest me
Dead to my self, I live in Thee.

'Two went up to the temple to pray'

Two went to pray? O rather say
One went to brag, th'other to pray:

One stands up close and treads on high,
Where th'other dares not send his eye.

One nearer to God's Altar trod,
The other to the Altar's God.

England and died in York in 1645, but her inspiration bore fruit in the papal approval given to the Institute of the Blessed Virgin Mary in 1703 and in the whole host of active women's orders which followed.

Mary Ward several times addresses God as 'Parent of all parents' and 'Friend of all friends', and her letters express confidence and hope:

Be merry and doubt not our Master.

We must not only love our neighbour as ourself, but behave as if we do.

I never wonder at another's faults, I only wonder at God's mercy to me after many failings.

Real strength and courage consists in doing what one knows to be good in all circumstances in which we are placed, and in not letting ourselves be deterred from this good by any opposition.[8]

Richard Challoner (1691–1781): a Catholic bishop in England

Born into a Presbyterian family in Lewes, Sussex, Richard Challoner grew up in a Catholic household where his widowed mother worked. At the age of thirteen he decided to become Catholic. He was sent to the English College at Douai, and received ordination in 1716. After teaching philosophy and theology at Douai he worked in London from 1730, was consecrated assistant bishop to the Vicar Apostolic in London in 1741, and succeeded him in 1758. He carried out pastoral and charitable work, founded schools, translated the Bible and devotional works (Augustine's *Confessions*, Thomas à Kempis's *Imitation of Christ*, Francis de Sales's *Introduction to the Devout Life*), and wrote Lives of the English Catholic martyrs and the desert fathers. He produced two popular and long-lasting works of his own: *The Garden of the Soul* (1740), a complete manual on faith, life, personal prayer, services and the Mass, and *Meditations for Every Day of the Year* (1753), a set of 365 meditations forming a course on Christian life and tracking the readings for the Sundays and feasts of the church's year:

Consider first, how many years of your life are past and gone: how long it is since you first came to the knowledge of good and evil: and in what manner you have spent all this precious time, given you for no other end but that you might employ it in the love and service of your God…

Consider secondly, the present state and condition of your conscience. What is your life at present? How stand accounts between your soul and God? What would you think, if this day you were to be called to the bar of divine justice? Should you not earnestly desire a delay?…

Consider thirdly, that the mercy of God has borne with you for so many years past; and notwithstanding all the provocations of your repeated crimes, and perpetual ingratitude, has brought you now to the beginning of this new

year, out of a sincere desire, that now at least might begin a new life, and such a life as might secure to your souls that true life which never ends…

Conclude to begin from this very hour, to turn away from sin; and to dedicate yourselves hence-forward in good earnest to the love and service of your God. Alas! how few Christians seem to be truly in earnest in this greatest of all concerns, where their all is at stake for eternity.[9]

(January 2: 'On beginning a new life with the new year')

Roman Catholic converts from the Oxford movement

In the early part of the nineteenth century a group of Anglican priests and scholars in Oxford began a movement to renew the spiritual life and the authority of the Anglican Church by emphasizing its heritage from the early church in doctrine, sacraments and liturgy. Some of those who joined this movement later became Roman Catholic. They included the poet Gerard Manley Hopkins (see box, p. 220), but the most famous and influential was John Henry Newman.

John Henry Newman (1801–90)

Newman was a learned Anglican who became Catholic, taking with him a mind nurtured in scripture and patristic theology, able to contribute ideas to the Catholic world that were then ahead of their time. He was born into the Church of England, studied at Oxford and in 1828 became Vicar of its University Church, St Mary's. He joined Keble and Pusey in the Oxford movement to which he contributed through sermons and 'tracts' (pamphlets). In 1842 he and several followers began a semi-monastic life in Littlemore village. They became Roman Catholic in 1845 and joined the Oratory

He was never a bishop, but was made a Cardinal in 1879.

Some of Newman's many poems became well-known hymns. 'Lead, kindly Light' was written in Sicily in 1833, after recovering from a serious attack of typhoid. Two more come from *The Dream of Gerontius* (1865), an extended poem on the journey of an old man's soul through death into purgatory: 'Firmly I believe and truly' is Gerontius's statement of faith; and 'Praise to the Holiest in the height' is sung by the angels.

Newman's spirituality

At the age of fifteen Newman read a 'Calvinist' book on conversion and perseverance, and felt assured of his commitment to God; it confirmed 'my distrust of the reality of material phenomena... making me rest in the thought of two and two only absolute and luminous self-evident beings, myself and my Creator'. For Newman, the true spiritual world lay beyond that of the senses, and he found symbolism and ritual helpful to mediate the invisible reality. He chose celibacy because he did not wish to be oriented to this world; his relationship with God was of prime importance, his ordination as deacon 'my espousal'. Truth includes divine mystery, so faith cannot depend only on the power of human reasoning; therefore he opposed 'liberalism' which he defined as 'the mistake of subjecting to human judgment those revealed doctrines which are in their nature beyond and independent of it...' (*Apologia*, appendix). Aware of his intellectual power, he feared pride and its attendant sins of impatience and contempt – but his life was a continuing, prayerful search for truth, for integrity of thought, faith and action.

In 1856 Newman addressed the Birmingham Oratory on 'perfection', suggesting it is not a matter of doing extraordinary things but of doing ordinary things well: 'He, then, is perfect who does the work of the day perfectly, and we need not go beyond this to seek for perfection. You need not go out of the *round* of the day... If you ask me what you are to do in order to be perfect, I say, first –

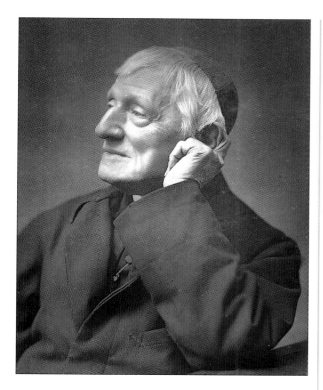

◆ **John Henry Newman, after becoming a cardinal in the Roman Catholic Church (1888).**

of St Philip Neri in Rome. They dreamed of a network of missionary oratories in English industrial cities; but foundations were only made in Birmingham under Newman and London under F.W. Faber, both in 1849. From 1854–58 Newman was rector of a new Catholic University in Dublin, then spent the rest of his life in Birmingham – a place he himself described as 'not a centre'! His thinking on the church, based on his patristic and scriptural scholarship, was to influence Catholic thought more in the twentieth century than the nineteenth: he has been regarded as a father of the thinking of Vatican II. He stood for the liberty of the individual Christian conscience (formed within the church), conciliarity and consultation; and he realized the need to engage with scientific and historical scholarship. He wrote his autobiography, *Apologia pro vita sua*, in 1864 to explain the integrity of his inner journey.

Three poets of the late nineteenth century

Spirituality may be strikingly expressed in art, as in the poetry of the following English Catholic poets who wrote towards the beginning of the twentieth century: Hopkins, Thompson and Meynell.

Gerard Manley Hopkins
(1844–89)

Gerard Manley Hopkins was from a high church Anglican family in Essex and became Roman Catholic in 1866 at Oxford. He wrote poetry from his schooldays, ceased after joining the Jesuits in 1868 and began again during his theological study at St Beuno's in north Wales, to express his feelings at the drowning of a group of nuns in the *Deutschland*'s shipwreck. Although aware of his unusual talent he did not try to publish poems in his lifetime except in the Jesuit journal the *Month* which, because of their innovative style and obscurity of expression, did not accept them. Only a close circle of friends, including Robert Bridges and Coventry Patmore, knew and encouraged his work. He understood priesthood in terms of sacrifice, on the pattern of Christ's self-emptying which rules out seeking personal glory. Ordained in 1877, he was moved through a number of teaching posts and curacies, filling in as need arose, and in 1844 became Professor of Greek at the Catholic

◆ Gerard Manley Hopkins, lithograph by the 19th-century English school.

University College, Dublin, a stressful and depressing task which prompted poems of desolation. He died there of typhoid in 1889. Robert Bridges published his collected poems in 1918.

His poetry uses varied rhythms and alliteration, and looks beneath the surface to see the world as sacramental: God's presence is the reality within the reality of all things. He is passionately sensitive to God's beauty and love, to human need and sin, and the despoiling of nature by human greed.

'God's Grandeur'

The world is charged with the grandeur of God.
  It will flame out, like shining from shook
    foil;
  It gathers to a greatness, like the ooze of oil
Crushed. Why do men now not reck his rod?
Generations have trod, have trod, have trod;
  And all is seared with trade; bleared, smeared
    with toil;
  And wears man's smudge and shares man's
    smell; the soil
Is bare now, nor can foot feel, being shod.

And for all this, nature is never spent;
  There lives the dearest freshness deep down
    things;
And though the last lights off the black West went
  Oh, morning, at the brown brink eastwards,
    springs –
Because the Holy Ghost over the bent
  World broods with warm breast and with ah!
    bright wings.

Francis Thompson
(1859–1907)

As a child, in a Catholic family in Lancashire, Francis Thompson read avidly and at sixteen knew he only wanted to be a poet – but he was deeply introverted and told no one. His father, a doctor, had sent him to the Ushaw seminary school, but being 'timid' and physically frail he was not recommended for ordination training. Sent on to medical school, he failed his exams and began to take opium. He left home in 1885 and lived as a down-and-out in London until 1888 when one of his poems was published in the Catholic magazine *Merry England*. His literary career then took off, assisted by the magazine's editor Wilfred Meynell and his poet wife Alice. Although subject to periods of depression he led a relatively stable life, writing, spending retreats with the Capuchin Franciscans at Crawley and Pantasaph, forming a few deep friendships, until dying of tuberculosis aged forty-eight. His poems are of rare ability and many reflect his relationship with Christ forged through suffering. Probably the most quoted is 'The Hound of Heaven': 'I fled him, down the nights and down the days…', with its varied repeated refrain: 'Naught shelters thee, who wilt not shelter Me', and its ending in encounter with the pursuing love of God: '"I am he whom thou seekest! Thou dravest love from thee, who dravest me."'

'The Kingdom of God (In No Strange Land)'

O world invisible, we view thee,
O world intangible, we touch thee,
O world unknowable, we know thee,
Incomprehensible, we clutch thee!

Does the fish soar to find the ocean,
The eagle plunge to find the air –
That we ask of the stars in motion
If they have rumour of thee there?

Not where the wheeling systems darken,
And our benumbed conceiving soars! –
The drift of pinions, would we hearken,
Beats at our own clay-shuttered doors.

The angels keep their ancient places; –
Turn but a stone, and start a wing!
'Tis ye, 'tis your estrangèd faces,
That miss the many-splendoured thing.

But (when so sad thou canst not sadder)
Cry; – and upon thy so sore loss
Shall shine the traffic of Jacob's ladder
Pitched between Heaven and Charing Cross.

Yea, in the night, my Soul, my daughter,
Cry; – clinging Heaven by the hems;
And lo, Christ walking on the water
Not of Gennesareth, but Thames!

▶

Alice Meynell (1847–1922)

Born Alice Thompson, to well-off parents, much of this poet's childhood was spent in Italy. She began taking Christian life seriously when confirmed as an Anglican at seventeen; and chose four years later to become Roman Catholic. Her first poems were published in 1875 and attracted the attention of Wilfrid Meynell, a Quaker become Catholic; they married in 1877 and formed a literary team. Wilfrid established the Catholic literary magazine *Merry England* in 1883. Alice published further collections of poems, many on religious themes, models of precise thought and compact expression. The Meynells befriended the destitute Francis Thompson, published his poems and supported him, making his poetic career possible.

◆ **Scripture reader in a night refuge in London (1872).**
   Francis Thompson was living in these conditions when
   'rescued' by Alice Meynell and her husband.

'Christ in the Universe'

With this ambiguous earth
His dealings have been told us. These abide:
The signal to a maid, the human birth,
The lesson, and the young man crucified.

But not a star of all
The innumerable host of stars has heard
How he administered this terrestrial ball.
Our races have kept their Lord's entrusted Word.

Of his earth-visiting feet
None knows the secret, cherished, perilous,
The terrible, shamefast, frightened, whispered,
      sweet,
Heart-shattering secret of his way with us.

No planet knows that this,
Our wayside planet, carrying land and wave,
Love and life multiplied, and pain and bliss,
Bears, as chief treasure, one forsaken grave.

Nor, in our little day,
May his devices with the heavens be guessed,
His pilgrimage to thread the Milky Way,
Or his bestowals there be manifest.

But, in the eternities,
Doubtless we shall compare together, hear
A million alien gospels, in what guise
He trod the Pleiades, the Lyre, the Bear.

Oh, be prepared, my soul!
To read the inconceivable, to scan
The million forms of God those stars unroll
When, in our turn, we show to them a Man.

Do not lie in bed beyond the due time of rising; give your first thoughts to God; make a good visit to the Blessed Sacrament; say the Angelus devoutly; eat and drink to God's glory; say the Rosary well; be recollected; keep out bad thoughts; make your evening meditation well; examine yourself daily; go to bed in good time, and you are already perfect.'[10]

Frederick William Faber (1814–63)

Born in Yorkshire, and an evangelical Anglican while at school, F.W. Faber moved into Newman's high church circle at Oxford. He was ordained in 1839, travelled on the continent and wrote about his encounters with the Roman Catholic Church. When appointed Rector of Elton in Cambridgeshire in 1843 he went to study pastoral methods in Rome, and after a brief but intensive ministry at Elton he and a group of followers became Catholics in 1845. They began an ascetic community near Birmingham with Faber, now 'Brother Wilfred', as its head. In 1848 he insisted on his group joining Newman's Oratory, and in 1849 was ordained and sent to head its new London house. His impulsiveness led to the independence of the London house and caused much conflict, while his enthusiasm and gift for preaching gave him pastoral success.

Faber wrote numerous hymns of which the most lasting have been 'My God, How Wonderful Thou Art' and 'There's a Wideness in God's Mercy'. He wrote or edited the Lives of a large number of saints, but his most popular books, based on his talks on the spiritual life, were *All for Jesus, or the Easy Ways of Divine Love* (1853) and *Growth in Holiness* (1854). Neither is profound or original, and they are partisan in their enthusiasm for topics such as purgatory and the centrality of devotion to Our Lady; but they are lively, easy to read, and grounded in scholarship and pastoral experience.

Baron Friedrich von Hügel (1852–1925): intellectual and ecumenist

Friedrich von Hügel was a unique character, a cosmopolitan European who chose to settle in London. His father was an Austrian Catholic diplomat, his mother a Scottish Presbyterian. He was born in Florence, lived in Brussels and settled in England in 1867. His education, from a succession of Catholic, Protestant, Quaker and Jewish tutors, awakened a lifelong interest in theology, philosophy, psychology, history and literature, and the relationships between these disciplines. In 1871 he was helped through a crisis of belief in Vienna by a Dutch Dominican, and later had the Abbé Huvelin as his spiritual director. His daily schedule included a simple rule of vocal and contemplative prayer, intercession and spiritual reading from the Bible, *The Imitation of Christ*, or Augustine's *Confessions*. He married in 1873, had three daughters, and lived in London from 1876 until his death, writing and engaging with a wide circle of Catholic, Anglican and other friends. He was a teacher to everyone, and ahead of his time in seeing the need for the Catholic Church to look beyond its borders and relate to other faith communities and the modern world.

Von Hügel's major book, *The Mystical Element in Religion as Studied in St Catherine of Genoa and her Friends*, was published in 1908 and established him as an authority on mystical theology. In it he distinguishes three fundamental strands in religion: the institutional-historical, intellectual-rational and mystical-intuitive (and emotional), all three being necessary and complementary while any one strand may predominate in the life of an individual or group. Many of his letters have been published, including those to his niece Gwendolen Greene on a wide variety of cultural and religious topics. He knew the Anglican mystic and writer Evelyn Underhill (see chapter 10, p. 327f), and from 1921 was her spiritual director. When he died he was working on a book on the central theme of his life, the objective reality of God:

God is a stupendously rich Reality – the alone boundlessly rich Reality. His outward action throughout the universe – his creation, sustenation and direction of the world at large – is immensely rich. Still deeper and more delicate is this richness and reality in God's incarnation and redemptive action. Yet his Being, his Interior Life, are in no wise exhausted by all this outward action, nor does this action occasion or articulate his character. We indeed, we little mortals – they too, the greatest of angels – we become our true selves, we articulate our spiritual characters, by apprehending, willing and serving God. But God is God, already apart from his occupation with us. These are the great facts which I believe to be specially revealed to us in the dogma of the Holy Trinity – facts of which we have an especial need in these our times… Our prayer will lack the deepest awe and widest expansion, if we do not find room within it for this fact concerning God. We will thus retain a strong sense that not even Jesus Christ and his redemption exhaust God.[11]

Catholic spirituality in France

As activity in sixteenth-century Spain waned, that in France rose. During the late sixteenth century France had been embroiled in a series of bloody religious wars between Catholic and Protestant ('Huguenot') factions. These were brought to an end under Henry of Navarre, a former Protestant who became Catholic in order to take the throne of France in 1593 and established religious tolerance by the Edict of Nantes in 1598. The way was now open for a renewal of Catholic life in France, which was marked by a flowering of spirituality and a reform of the clergy.

Until the revolution of 1789, Paris and the royal court were at the centre of French political, social

Francis de Sales (1567–1622)

Francis de Sales provides a homely welcome amid the austerities of French spirituality. His positive attitude to human nature has been called 'devout humanism'. He was born to a noble family in Savoy, an Alpine dukedom between France and Italy. He attended the Jesuit College of Clermont in Paris and studied law at Padua. During two brief crises of despair as a student he was greatly helped by Lorenzo Scupoli's *Spiritual Combat* which he was given in Padua; he translated it into French, and carried and read it throughout his life. Ordained in 1593, in 1602 he became Bishop of Geneva (but was based in Annecy, since Geneva was Calvinist). In the same year he met Madame Acarie and Pierre de Bérulle in Paris, read Teresa of Avila's autobiographical Life and helped get permission from Rome for the founding of Carmelite convents in France. In 1604 he met Jeanne de Chantal in Dijon, and began the relationship of spiritual direction and friendship that led to their foundation of the Visitation sisters in Annecy in 1610. In 1618 he met Vincent de Paul, put him in charge of the Visitation convents in Paris, and asked him to advise Jeanne.

Francis wrote two great spiritual books: *Introduction to the Devout Life* (1609) for lay people, and the contemplative *Treatise on the Love of God* (1616) for the Visitation sisters. After twenty years of constant activity, preaching, reforming, directing, founding, writing and administering, he died in 1622 and was canonized in 1665.

Introduction to the Devout Life

The *Introduction* was the first widely popular book of spirituality written specifically for lay people. Francis emphasizes God's love and goodness and his will to save everyone so that all are called to union with God; the real possibility of an interior life amid the world's busyness; and the centrality of the heart in the spiritual life: 'Since the heart is the centre of all our actions, as the heart is, so are they.'[12] The *Introduction* is a lively and practical course on Christian prayer and life, for all who want to take their baptism seriously and be committed to the love of God. It begins with conversion, teaches a method of meditative prayer, then considers the sacraments, the practice of virtue, meeting temptations and trials, and finally the deepening and renewal of commitment. Francis teaches recollection of the presence of God by short prayers throughout the day; and his method of meditation for longer periods of prayer became a classic. It is described below.

The 'Salesian' method of meditative prayer

The preparation consists in recalling that you are in the presence of God, asking God's assistance, and reading or recalling a scripture passage, a gospel scene or a truth of the faith. Second, consider this truth or scene, reflecting on its meaning for you in such a way as to stir up affection for God and desire for virtue. Third, take these feelings and transform them into very specific resolutions to change your behaviour and make it more Christlike. Conclude with thanksgiving, offering of yourself and your resolutions, petition for yourself and intercession for others. Finally, Francis famously suggests that when we have spent time in this sacred space of prayer, as if we had been wandering in a garden, we could reflect back on what we have experienced and select two or three points that have struck or pleased us: these will form a 'spiritual nosegay' that we can take with us to 'think frequently on them, and to smell them as it were, spiritually, for the rest of the day'.[13]

◆ **Francis de Sales; engraving by the 17th-century English school.**

A Treatise on the Love of God

Contemplation, Theotimus, is but a loving, artless, unremitting, mental preoccupation with the things of God... We set out on the path of prayer by reflecting on God's goodness in order to prompt our wills to love him; but once love is conceived in our hearts, we continue our reflections on that goodness so as to gratify our love – and only constant sight of what we love can appease it. It comes to this: when love is wedded to meditation, it gives birth to contemplation; we meditate to awaken love, we contemplate because we love... Once love has quickened us to the attentiveness of contemplation, that attentiveness gives rise to a greater, more fervent love, which is eventually crowned with perfection in the possession of what it loves.[14]

Jeanne de Chantal (1572–1641)

◆ Jeanne de Chantal; engraving after Restout.

The friend and co-worker of Francis de Sales was born Jeanne-Françoise Frémyot, the daughter of a Dijon lawyer. She married the Baron de Chantal, had six children (four survived infancy), and was widowed in 1601. She felt God was calling her, and asked Francis de Sales to become her spiritual director in 1604. A close friendship grew up although, in contrast to Francis's usual joyful experience of God's presence, Jeanne's way of prayer was often one of bare faith, a desert journey. Francis wanted to found a new order for women to make religious life accessible to those not suited to the severe exterior asceticism practised by the Poor Clares and Carmelites. In 1610 Jeanne and two others began a common life in Annecy, others quickly joining them.

Their aim was contemplative prayer, growth in love through interior renunciation of pride and selfishness, and some charitable visiting of the sick. But, according to the rules of the Council of Trent, women's orders always had to be enclosed: so in 1618 the order was cloistered, taking its name from the Visitation of the Virgin Mary to Elizabeth, and active work ceased except for the welcoming of visitors coming for retreats.

From 1618, Jeanne travelled to found new Visitation convents: when she died there were eighty-seven. Her letters are full of advice, practical and spiritual, to the heads of the new houses as well as to lay people and ecclesiastics. Vincent de Paul and Charles de Condren, who headed the French Oratory after Bérulle, were among her correspondents. She edited Francis's letters and talks for publication, and gave talks like his on simple contemplative prayer, teaching his method of meditation as the path towards it. She emphasized forgetfulness of self, humility, indifference (unpossessiveness, entrusting all circumstances and outcomes to God) and profound abandonment to God's will. She was canonized in 1767.

To a busy priest, full of projects and preoccupations, she wrote:

Without worrying about them, try to remain calm amid this warfare of distractions and be satisfied... to spend the appointed time of prayer quietly and peacefully, doing nothing in God's presence, content simply to be there without wishing either to feel his presence or make an act [of devotion], unless you can do so easily. Just sit there, in inner and outer tranquillity and reverence, convinced that this patience is a powerful prayer before God... To sum up, we must be as satisfied to be powerless, idle and still before God, and dried up and barren when he permits it, as to be full of life, enjoying his presence with ease and devotion. The whole matter of our union with God consists in being content either way.[15]

and religious life. In Paris at the turn of the century lived a remarkable woman, Madame Acarie (1566–1616), in whose house many of those who were to be influential in the renewal met one another. Born as Barbe Avrillot into a well-to-do Parisian family, she had wanted to join the Poor Clares but when she was married off to Pierre Acarie she not only ran a happy home with six children but made their Paris house a meeting place for people interested in Christian life and prayer: Pierre de Bérulle, Francis de Sales, Jesuits and reformed Franciscans (Capuchins). She was herself a mystical contemplative with a gift of spiritual discernment. Her spiritual director was Benet of Canfield. She did charitable work and helped reform or establish several religious communities. After reading the Life of Teresa in 1601 she founded the first French convents of the Discalced Carmelites, and after her husband's death she became a Carmelite for the last four years of her life as Sister Mary of the Incarnation. Only a few of her prayers and letters remain, but the influence of her life was considerable and three biographies were published between 1621 and 1666. She was beatified in 1791.

Benet of Canfield
(1562–1611)

Madame Acarie's spiritual director was an Englishman, born William Fitch in Little Canfield in Essex. He became Roman Catholic while studying law in London and joined the Franciscan Capuchin friars in Paris in 1587. By 1593, when he was ordained, he had already experienced a range of mystical phenomena and was regarded as an authority on contemplative life. He attempted a mission to England in 1599, was arrested and spent four years writing in prison, then returned to live in Paris.

Benet's major work was the *Rule of Perfection*, intended only for his directees and novices but published on the order of his superior in 1610. It structures the spiritual life around three aspects of God's will: beginners seek God's will in the exterior events of the world; the more advanced find it in inner inspirations and illumination; while the most advanced contemplate God's will directly without help of intellect or images. This third part shows the influence of *The Cloud of Unknowing*, Dionysius and the Flemish writers; it talks of the 'annihilation' (*anéantissement*) of the self before God, and thus helped to make the 'nothingness' of the self a key concept in seventeenth-century French spirituality. Benet wrote an English translation of parts one and two of his *Rule* (1608), and Augustine Baker later translated the third part. Benet's intention was in line with the genuine Christian mysticism he lived, in which the personality is not destroyed when God's love acts in the person; but his *Rule* was sufficiently open to misunderstanding that Francis de Sales preferred people not to read part three, and Benet fell into two centuries of obscurity when the whole work was condemned by the Roman Inquisition during the 'quietist' crisis in 1689.

Pierre de Bérulle
(1575–1629)

Bérulle began the movement of renewal and priestly reform in France which is known as the 'French school' of spirituality. Born an aristocrat, he was educated by the Jesuits, then at the Sorbonne, and ordained in 1599. With Madame Acarie in 1604 he founded 'Teresian' Carmelite convents in France; and in 1613 he established his own Oratory of Jesus Christ on a similar pattern to Philip Neri's Oratories. He moved in the circles of the royal court. In 1624 he went to Rome to negotiate Henrietta Maria's marriage to King Charles I, and was sent to England with her in 1625. He was made a cardinal in 1627 and died in 1629.

By his early twenties Bérulle had developed an austere spirituality of inner detachment and dependence on God's guidance, aiming at a stable inner state (*état*) of self-abnegation and devotion to God. His thinking centred on imitating Christ in his incarnation: 'The incarnation is the basis of our salvation, and I have pondered deeply on how great must have been the emptying [*anéantissement*, annihilation] of himself.' Christians must be similarly dispossessed of selfish love so that grace can transform them, and the way consists in participating in the inner and outer life of Jesus, in a mystical Christ-centredness, 'not seeking ourselves in Jesus but Jesus in Jesus'. Bérulle associated Mary closely with Jesus in the work of the incarnation; his own personal vow was to serve Jesus and Mary. His courtly context shows in his language of honouring and pleasing God. Bérulle taught the pursuit and practice of virtue until it becomes habitual; but his search for Christlike humility perhaps led him to an unbalanced emphasis on self-annihilation. His popularity as a spiritual writer was limited to seventeenth-century France, but he influenced the church more widely through the renewal of priestly training and devotion which he began and handed on to his followers Charles de Condren, Jean-Jacques Olier, John Eudes and Vincent de Paul.

The Oratory of Jesus Christ (the Bérullian or French Oratory)

In 1611 Bérulle and five other educated priests began a communal life in Paris, leading in 1613 to the founding of the 'Oratory of Jesus Christ'. Although partly influenced by the Roman Oratory, this new initiative was a centralized structure aimed specifically at the renewal of the priesthood through priestly holiness and the training of the clergy. Bérulle urged that priests focus on spiritual rather than material concerns: 'To govern a soul is to govern a world, and a world that has more secrets and diversities than the world we see.' The Oratory emphasized inner devotion to Jesus, in liturgy and daily life. Self-examination in the light of Jesus' life was to be done three times a day, and activities were to be accompanied by the prayer: 'I offer you these actions in honour of those you have done on earth... take from me all that may displease your love.' The liturgical year, from Advent to Ascension, was to be used to practise

and deepen this spirituality of adherence to Jesus Christ.

The French Oratory spread rapidly, mainly in France, growing by 1629 to 400 priests in sixty houses, with many more students. It peaked in the eighteenth century with eighty-four houses, declined, was suppressed by the atheist French revolutionary government in 1792, and revived on a much smaller scale in 1852.

Vincent de Paul (1581–1660): mission, welfare and the Sisters of Charity

In 1885, two centuries after his death, Vincent de Paul was made patron saint of works of charity. His spirituality is an active following of Christ: he taught that we can see and love Christ today in the faces of the poor, among whom Christ chose to become incarnate. He was born in a peasant family, was ordained and studied theology in Toulouse, became a protégé of Bérulle in Paris and knew Francis de Sales and Jeanne de Chantal. He joined the household of the General of the Galleys, Count de Gondi, and from 1619 to 1626 worked as chaplain of the galleys to improve the conditions of the convicts who rowed them. He preached missions in the rural areas, reviving the life of the church, and founded the Congregation of the Mission, called 'Lazarists' from their base at St Lazare in Paris, dedicated to preaching, catechizing, teaching prayer, and the training of priests. He involved lay men and women in confraternities for charitable work and founded the Sisters of Charity which was the first active uncloistered women's order. He trained Olier and Bossuet, among many others, as priests.

Many active religious orders and fraternities have taken their inspiration from 'Monsieur Vincent', including the widespread lay Society of St Vincent de Paul for charitable work, founded in 1833. The American Sisters of Charity were founded in 1809 by Mother Elizabeth Seton (1774–1821), who was born in New York in 1774

as an Anglican (Episcopalian), married and had four children and became Roman Catholic in 1805 after the death of her husband. The first sisters settled at Emmitsburg in Maryland, visiting the

◆ *Vincent de Paul and the Sisters of Charity* (c. 1729), painting attributed to Jean (Frère) Andre (1662–1753).

◆ **A representation of a Lazarist, of the order founded by Vincent de Paul.**

sick and teaching. After Mother Seton died in 1821 her foundation gave rise to six independent groups of Sisters of Charity in the USA, all taking their inspiration and rule from Vincent de Paul.

Jean-Jacques Olier (1608–57) and the 'Sulpician method' of meditative prayer

Olier was trained for ordination by Vincent de Paul, and later had as his spiritual director the French Oratorian Charles Condren, who was Bérulle's successor in the training of priests. He conducted missions all over France until becoming curé of St Sulpice in Paris with its large parish in

1642. There he too trained priests in prayer and pastoral skills, and wrote two small books on prayer for his parishioners: *A Christian Catechism for the Inner Life* and *Introduction to Christian Life and Virtues*.

His method of meditation is Christ-centred and is itself a summary of what Christian life is about: 'having our Lord before our eyes, in our heart, and in our hands… that is, to look *at* Jesus, unite oneself *with* Jesus and act *in* Jesus'. So we take a gospel passage or we recall a mystery such as the incarnation, passion or resurrection, and in meditating on it we first look at Jesus, we notice his attitude and we worship him, opening ourselves to the action of the Holy Spirit. Then we give ourselves to him in order to participate in what he is. Finally we ask that his will be done in us, and we make specific resolutions, imagining the situations in which we will act in the way we have resolved. The emphasis lies on opening ourselves so that Christ can transform and act in us.

Popular Catholic spirituality

Popular expressions of Catholic spirituality underwent change in the Counter-Reformation period. Medieval piety had centred on pilgrimages and the cults of local saints, on guilds and independent confraternities with their feast days and processions. These now gave way to more sober and centralized devotions, under closer clerical control. The devotion to the Sacred Heart was probably the most widely practised new popular form of spirituality. It owes its establishment partly to John Eudes but much more to Margaret Mary Alacoque (see box, p. 232).

Jansenism

Jansenism was an influential strand in French spirituality emerging in the mid-seventeenth century. It is named after Cornelius Jansen, theology professor at Louvain and Bishop of Ypres, whose book on Augustine's theology of the fall, grace and free will was published posthumously in 1640. He emphasized predestination, teaching that only a few among all Christians will be chosen or 'elect'. He taught that the elect are saved by the grace of Christ overcoming their free will and irresistibly drawing them back to God: thus they are saved both by faith and by the good works they inevitably do. Despite the emphasis on predestination, Jansenists did not assume they were saved. Their spirituality concentrated on the fallenness of humanity and the serious need for moral effort in cooperation with grace. They were scandalized by the 'casuistry' (special pleading, in particular moral cases) of the Jesuits, especially those influential as spiritual directors at the French court. The conflict was politicized and resulted in condemnation of aspects of Jansenism in a Papal Bull of 1642 and the suppression of its centre, the Convent of Port Royal in Paris. But Jansenism remained an influential strand of thought in France influencing Blaise Pascal and the Curé d'Ars (see boxes, pp. 236 and 240).

Brother Lawrence
(c. 1611–91)

During the Jansenist and enlightenment controversies that surrounded Pascal, another very different character was living and praying in Paris. Brother Lawrence of the Resurrection was born Nicholas Herman in a village in Lorraine. As a young soldier he was wounded in the leg, and decided to aim for the religious life. He tried to be a hermit under the direction of an uncle who was a Carmelite, then after a spell as a footman (at which he said he was clumsy) he eventually became a Discalced Carmelite lay brother in Paris, in charge of the priory kitchen. He became known as a friendly, attractive person of unusual spiritual depth. In 1666–67 he was interviewed about his spirituality by a priest, the Abbé Joseph de Beaufort. Soon after Brother Lawrence's death in 1691 Beaufort published the interviews, together with a short description of him and some of his

'spiritual maxims' and letters. Because of the 'quietist' controversy, into which his name was unfairly drawn, Brother Lawrence was hardly known in France although Fénelon quotes him; but from 1724 there were numerous English editions under the title *The Practice of the Presence of God*.

Brother Lawrence's way is one of continual prayer, practising the awareness of God's presence until the awareness becomes habitual.

> The time of action does not differ from that of prayer. I possess God as peacefully in the bustle of my kitchen, where sometimes several people are asking me for different things at the same time, as I do upon my knees before the Blessed Sacrament... This practice of the presence of God... must stem from the heart, from love rather than from the understanding and speech. In the way of God, thought counts for little. Love does everything and it is not needful to have great things to do... I turn my little omelette in the pan for the love of God. When it is finished, if I have nothing to do, I prostrate myself on the ground and worship my God, who gave me the grace to make it, after which I arise happier than a king... People look for ways of learning how to love God. They hope to attain it by I know not how many different practices... Is it not a shorter and more direct way to do everything for the love of God, to make use of all the tasks one's lot in life demands to show him that love, and to maintain his presence within by the communion of our heart with his? There is nothing complicated about it. One has only to turn to it honestly and simply.[16]

In his maxims, Brother Lawrence says this inner focus on God needs practice and perseverance, and it presupposes a serious conversion to purity of life. He suggests arrow prayers: 'God of love, I love you with all my heart,' or whatever words love suggests. As one becomes less distracted and more centred on God, faith, hope and love will grow. 'By the practice of God's presence and this inner gaze the soul becomes familiar with God in such

Devotion to the Sacred Heart

John Eudes (1601–80)

John Eudes was a member of the French Oratory, a priest with a strong sense of mission, aware of the social implications of the gospel. He was known for his work during plagues in 1627 and 1631, and conducted many missions. In 1641 he founded a women's order of Our Lady of Charity dedicated to the heart of Mary, to run refuges for 'fallen women', and in 1643 an association of priests to teach in seminaries, the Congregation of Jesus and Mary ('Eudists'), dedicated to the hearts of Jesus and Mary. He saw Mary's love as a sharing in the heart of Jesus, so that devotion to the hearts of Jesus and Mary could be regarded theologically as one single devotion, and he wrote prayers and offices for it. From 1672 the Eudists celebrated an annual feast of the Sacred Heart of Jesus on 20 October.

Margaret Mary Alacoque (1647–90)

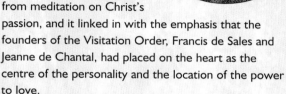

Margaret Mary Alacoque was an invalid during much of her childhood and entered the Visitation convent at Paray le Monial in Burgundy in 1671. Within the Visitation Order there was a strong tradition of devotion to the wounded heart of Jesus. This devotion had medieval roots, springing from meditation on Christ's passion, and it linked in with the emphasis that the founders of the Visitation Order, Francis de Sales and Jeanne de Chantal, had placed on the heart as the centre of the personality and the location of the power to love.

In Margaret Mary's case this strongly 'affective' devotion took specific visual form. She reported a series of visions of Christ, starting on the Feast of St John the Evangelist in December 1673. She felt allowed to 'rest on his heart with his beloved disciple' and that Christ had placed her heart in his own, giving it back to her 'as a flame of fire in the form of a heart' and naming her 'the beloved disciple of my sacred heart'. Later she saw Christ's heart as artists had already often depicted it, wounded and radiant, encircled by the crown of thorns with the cross above. On a third occasion she saw Christ with his five wounds, in glory that flowed from his heart which was visible in his opened breast, and

◆ **Above: Margaret Mary Alacoque.**

◆ **Left: John Eudes represented beneath an illustration of the Sacred Heart.**

reported that he asked that people spend a 'Holy Hour' on Thursday evenings before the Blessed Sacrament, keeping company with him in Gethsemane, and receive communion every first Friday of the month. In the 'great apparition' shortly after Corpus Christi in 1675, she said Christ asked her to establish a special annual Feast of the Sacred Heart. Communion on that day would be an act of reparation for the insults to Christ's love and to his Presence in the Eucharist.

At first the Visitation Order regarded the visions as delusions but, supported by a Jesuit priest, Claude de la Colombière, the devotion was accepted and spread. The first feast was in 1685 at Paray and it became a universal feast in the Roman Catholic Church in 1856. Margaret Mary was canonized in 1920.

Background to the devotion to the Sacred Heart

Imaginative meditation on scenes in the life of Christ was a popular way of prayer from the eleventh century onwards. When people imagined the crucifixion they focused on the wounds in Christ's hands, feet and side; and the wound in his side from which blood and water flowed led to his heart, the source of saving love: 'He who contemplates the passion of our Lord, and enters into his opened side, will find his most sacred heart. Blessed are the hearts of those who unite themselves in this way with the sweet and sacred heart of God.'[17] Symbolic pictures of the five wounds were circulated by Franciscans, among others, showing the wounded heart crowned with thorns and bearing a cross. As in the later hymn 'Rock of Ages', Christ's heart was a refuge and the source of salvation and joy.

Devotion to the Sacred Heart

The meaning behind the devotion to the Sacred Heart is a desire to live in close union with the love of Jesus. Margaret Mary enthused about its rewards and benefits, and encouraged people to wear a picture of Christ pointing to his heart with its flames of love, or to hang such a picture in their house. The devotion has its own prayers and litanies, the weekly 'Holy Hour' of prayer, and annual feast. The inner attitude is total consecration of one's self to the love of Jesus, as most strongly expressed in this prayer by Margaret Mary:

I give and consecrate to the Sacred Heart of Our Lord Jesus Christ, my self and my life, my actions, toils and sufferings, so that I may no longer employ any part of my being except to love, honour and glorify him. It is my unalterable will to belong wholly to him and do everything for his love, renouncing with my whole heart whatever might displease him. I take you then, O Sacred Heart, as the unique object of my love, the protector of my life, the assurance of my salvation, the remedy for my inconstancy, healer and atonement for all the faults of my life, and sure refuge at the hour of my death.

Be then, O Heart of goodness, my justification before God the Father, and turn away from me the shafts of his just anger. O Heart of love, I place all my trust in you, for I fear everything from my weakness, but hope everything from your kindness. Consume then everything in me that can displease or resist you. And let your pure love so imprint itself on my heart, above all else, that I may never be able to forget or be separated from you; so that, I beg you by all your mercies, my name may be inscribed in you, for I wish all my happiness to consist in living and dying as nothing less than your slave.[18]

fashion that it passes almost all its life in
continual acts of love, worship, contrition, trust,
acts of thankfulness, sacrifice, petition and all the
noblest virtues.'[19]

The quietist controversy

At the end of the seventeenth century
contemplative prayer came under the shadow
of the 'quietist' controversy. 'Quietism' meant
an exaggerated emphasis on passivity in prayer
together with a lack of the balancing active
elements of Christian life such as meditating
on Christ's life and practising virtues.

On the level of ecclesiastical politics the issue
was tied up with fear of seditious groups and
conspiracies. 'Spiritual' persons might consider
they had greater theological insight and spiritual
authority than the ecclesiastics, and in this regard
the fear of quietism in the late 1600s links back to
the suppression of *alumbrados* ('the illuminated')
in Spain in the 1500s, and earlier suppressions of
'spiritual' groups. In popular suspicion, 'quietism'
was linked to immorality on the assumption that
people who falsely believe they have attained
interior heights may consider themselves now
immune from sin and free to do whatever they like
in the exterior world.

The controversy burst around the Spanish priest
Miguel de Molinos in Rome in 1687, and a general
witch-hunt by the Inquisition followed: groups
practising contemplative prayer were broken up,
individuals and writings were condemned. It went
on to involve leading personalities in France:
Madame Guyon, Fénelon and Bossuet.

Miguel de Molinos (1628–96)
and the Papal Bull against 'quietism'

Miguel de Molinos settled in Rome in 1663,
worked as a spiritual director and wrote a popular
Spiritual Guide to contemplative prayer (the
prayer of silence, or in Spanish, *quietud*). In 1682
he was attacked both for his doctrine and alleged

◆ **The Spanish Inquisition was established in 1479 to deal
with insincere converts to the faith. It was much harsher
than the Papal Inquisition which dealt with heresy. This
anonymous engraving shows Spanish prisoners being
taken to the stake (1610).**

immorality (no details of the latter accusations
are known). He had based his teaching on major
writers, in particular John of the Cross, but he
seems to have confused active and passive
contemplation and perhaps gave inappropriate
advice to the less advanced. At first Pope Innocent
XI supported him but, under pressure of the
Inquisition, a Papal Bull of 1687 condemned
him and this text became the basic document
used against others accused of 'quietism' or
'Molinism'. Molinos recanted any errors he
might have made but was still imprisoned until
his death nine years later. His books continued

to be read in Protestant Pietist circles.

The Bull of 1687 is the nearest thing to a definition of 'quietism'. It is an undigested list of sixty-four points, giving a blanket objection to a mixture of teachings and attitudes, some of which would not necessarily be wrong in their correct context. Thus it condemns prayer that involves the negation of activity, of thinking or knowing, and all suggestion that knowledge can be secretly transmitted by God. It associates quietism with refusing to say vocal prayers of any kind (no thanksgivings, no reflection on one's faults, no thoughts about Christ, no actions such as the sign of the cross or saying the Our Father), with non-resistance to temptation, making no effort to practise virtues, rejection of mortification, claiming to be the unique way of salvation, and questioning the institutional church. This package of faults was used in hunts for 'quietists' in the succeeding years: anyone accused under one heading could be suspected of the rest and of probable insubordination and immorality.

This condemnation of 'quietism' had repercussions for true contemplative prayer and the genuine mystical tradition, placing it under suspicion in Roman Catholic circles for much of the eighteenth and nineteenth centuries.

Madame Guyon (1648–1717)

Madame Guyon was a teacher of contemplative prayer. She was born Jeanne Marie Bouvier de la Mothe, at Montargis in 1648. She had a patchy education in several convents, but read avidly and gained a thorough knowledge of the mystical tradition. After she had struggled to pray in conventional active meditative ways, her contemplative life began suddenly in 1668 when she had shared the dryness she felt with a priest who advised her: 'It is, Madame, because you seek outside what you have within. Accustom yourself to seek God in your heart and you will find him there.' She felt released into the joy of silent prayer of the heart, experiencing in this the presence of God. The rest of her life was marked

by her enthusiasm to teach what she had discovered.

She touched the lives of Catholics in France and Italy and, later, Protestant friends from Holland, Germany and England. The *Spiritual Torrents* (1682) likens the mystical journey with its joys and sufferings to a rushing mountain river. Her best-known work is the *Short and Easy Method of Prayer* (1685). She wrote a mystical commentary on the Song of Songs, other scripture commentaries, and a long autobiography that was published posthumously and later reissued in a severely edited translation by John Wesley.

She writes, in a traditional but enthusiastic way, of complete renunciation of self-centredness (annihilation, *anéantissement*), abandonment to the will of God, pure disinterested love of God and detachment from anxieties about what may or may not happen (*indifférence*). She had, and taught, a personal devotion to the Child Jesus.

Madame Guyon experienced many journeys and sufferings in her outer life. She was widowed at twenty-eight, left with three living children out of five, and vowed the rest of her life to piety and good works. She fell foul of intrigue at the French court, being attacked as a 'quietist' and becoming a pawn in the conflict of Bossuet, Bishop of Meaux, against her friend and disciple François Fénelon: she was twice imprisoned, spending 1698–1703 in the Bastille. Despite these controversies, her work was not directly censured by Rome and she died a fully committed Catholic. Evelyn Underhill aptly commented, 'that busy lady is, as a matter of fact, far from being the typical quietist'.[20]

François Fénelon (1651–1715)

Madame Guyon's friend François de Salignac de la Mothe Fénelon was born of an ancient aristocratic family, a brilliant student of philosophy and theology, ordained after training at Olier's Seminary of S. Sulpice in Paris. He worked in that parish, became superior of a community of women newly converted from Protestantism, wrote on the education of girls, became tutor to the grandson

Blaise Pascal (1623–62)

The seventeenth century saw the emergence of modern rationalist atheism. Pascal was a brilliant mathematician, a scientist and an inventor, who set out to write an *Apology for the Christian Religion* to commend Christian faith and life to his 'free-thinking' contemporaries. He died before completing it but his notes were published after his death, together with other ideas and jottings, in 1670 in the volume we know as his *Pensées* ('Thoughts').

Pascal's life, and his spiritual life, were full of drama and struggle. His father, a lawyer and mathematician, taught him that reason and faith have different objects. Pascal struggled to hold faith and reason together, through a strong belief in God's transcendence such that faith applies to truths beyond the reach of human reason. He believed profoundly in the human need for God: 'Wretchedness of man without God. Happiness of man with God' (*Pensée* 6). Faith is a matter of the heart, understood as the will, the centre of our being: 'The heart has its reasons, of which reason knows nothing... It is the heart which perceives God and not the reason' (423–24). He invites his reader to take the reasonable risk of wagering that God does exist and committing their life to Christ: if they win, they win eternity; if they lose, they still live a good life in this world (418). His Augustinian Jansenist convictions made him finally unable to see how to reconcile his fascination with scientific exploration, and the pride he took in it, with a life dedicated to God. Science seemed to him to be a distraction from what really mattered, so he gave it up and worked with the poor, establishing Paris's first public bus service.

Pascal had an intense experience of God's presence one evening in November 1654, and kept a brief record of it sewn into his clothing next to his heart. It is published as *Pensée* 913, 'The Memorial':

From about half past ten in the evening until half past midnight. Fire. 'God of Abraham, God of Isaac, God of Jacob,' not of philosophers and scholars. Certainty, certainty, heartfelt, joy, peace. God of Jesus Christ. God of Jesus Christ. My God and your God. 'Thy God shall be my God.' The world forgotten and everything except God.

He can only be found by the ways taught in the Gospels.

Greatness of the human soul.

'O righteous Father, the world had not known thee, but I have known thee.'

Joy, joy, joy, tears of joy...[21]

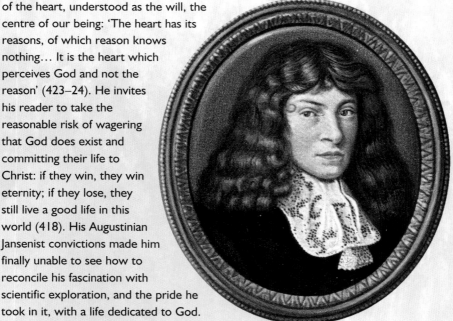

◆ **Miniature of Blaise Pascal, by Paul Prieur (active around 1670), in a German album.**

of Louis XIV, and by 1693 was elected to the Académie Française. He was sought after as a spiritual director. In 1695 he was exiled from court to become Archbishop of Cambrai, where he continued writing, but also concentrated on administrative, pastoral and charitable work in his diocese until his death in 1715.

He met Madame Guyon in 1688 and was attracted to her way of simple contemplative prayer. He believed in her as a genuinely spiritual person, although he was less impressed with her writings. He worked with her and stood by her when she was investigated as a 'quietist', an act of integrity that cost him the friendship of the influential and decidedly anti-mystical Bishop of Meaux, Jacques-Bénigne Bossuet, and his position at court, as well as a mild degree of censure from Rome. His *Explication des maximes des saints sur la vie intérieure* (1697) is a study of the Christian mystical tradition written in defence of his and Guyon's teaching.

Fénelon's spiritual teaching is found in his correspondence, some short books written in epistolary style, and his *Maximes*. His ideas are in line with the 'French school' and Francis de Sales, emphasizing renunciation of self-love and abandonment to God. His key themes are 'indifference' and 'pure' disinterested love of God. Indifference is the absolute conformity of the human and divine will, so that if it were possible a person would even accept damnation if God's love demanded it. It is exercised in everyday life by practising the presence of God (he quotes Brother Lawrence) and entrusting the outcome of all activities to God, without stopping working. It makes 'pure love' possible. Fénelon describes the theology of pure love with rigorous logic: God has made us and wants our happiness, but 'it is indeed for his glory that he wishes our happiness', so 'it is not our own interest in our blessedness which should make us desire his glory. It is on the contrary, the desire for his glory which should make us desire our blessedness, as one of the things which he is pleased to make part of his glory.'[22] Contemplative prayer is 'pure love', a singleness

of will focused on God, and one moves into it from discursive meditation, Fénelon thinks, as love becomes more disinterested.

Fénelon's activity as a director was often in the context of court life. He suggests there is no need to go looking for special ways of 'mortification': 'We will find enough to mortify ourselves by entertaining contrary to our taste the people we cannot get rid of, and by being tied down by all our real duties.'[23] Christian perfection simply 'asks us to be God's from the bottom of our hearts', and 'peace of conscience, liberty of heart, the sweetness of abandoning ourselves in the hands of God, the joy of always seeing the light grow in our hearts, finally, freedom from the fears and insatiable desires of the times, multiply a hundredfold the happiness which the true children of God possess in the midst of their crosses, if they are faithful.'[24]

Jacques-Bénigne Bossuet (1627–1704)

Bossuet, Bishop of Meaux, was an influential preacher and writer whose importance for the history of spirituality in France rests on his role in the 'quietist' controversy. He had been a brilliant pupil of the Jesuits in his home town of Dijon, took a doctorate in theology and became a preacher at court and tutor to the son of Louis XIV. He was not an ascetic, and regarded mystical experience as exceptional, but he took an interest in spiritual direction and the theology of the spiritual life. His spirituality centred on obedience to God's sovereignty and trust in his providence. He taught an 'admirative', adorational style of meditative prayer and wrote classic meditations on the gospels and the mysteries of Christ. He approved of Teresa of Avila, and was not entirely against contemplation, but in 1694 he began to lead the opposition to Madame Guyon's writings on contemplative prayer, condemning her for an unbalanced emphasis on passivity (absolute 'abandon' and self-annihilation) and insufficient emphasis on the need for meditation on Christ's humanity in the gospels. He attacked his former

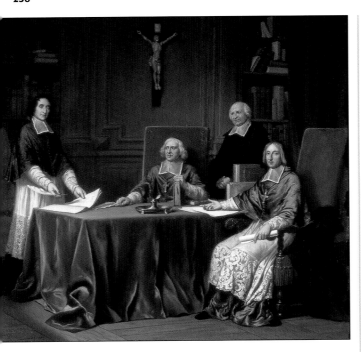

◆ *Signing the Agreement at the Conference of Issy between François Fénelon, Jacques Bossuet and Louis Antoine de Noailles, the Archbishop of Paris (1697); painting by the 17th-century French school.*

friend François Fénelon who stood by Madame Guyon. A chief result was that all contemplative prayer, both true and false, fell under suspicion in France for the next two centuries – although in 1741 De Caussade showed it was possible to use the references to orthodox mystical teaching in Bossuet's *Instruction on the Various States of Prayer*, which Bossuet had used against quietist errors, in a defence of genuine contemplative prayer.

Jean-Pierre de Caussade (1675–1751)

De Caussade comes at the close of this creative period in French spirituality. He was a Jesuit preacher and spiritual director who was sympathetic to contemplative prayer at the time when it had fallen under suspicion in France after the 'quietist' controversy. He joined the Jesuits in

Toulouse in 1693, taught there, then moved between several Jesuit houses preaching and conducting retreats. In 1729 he began to give spiritual direction to the Visitation sisters at Nancy, writing many letters in response to their questions and giving talks that were kept in notebooks by the sisters. In 1867, over 200 years after his death, some of these notes and letters were published by Father Henri Ramière as *L'Abandon à la Providence divine*, immediately gaining a wide readership and re-establishing 'abandonment' at the centre of French spirituality. Several editions of this book, and more letters, have since been published. De Caussade published one book himself, *Spiritual Instructions… On the Various States of Prayer According to the Doctrine of Bossuet, Bishop of Meaux* (1741). This was a strategically clever book, in the form of a dialogue with Bossuet (who was still regarded as an authority in France) using the orthodox teaching on mystical prayer which Bossuet quotes or implies in his book against quietism to show that he in fact supported *true* mysticism and contemplation.

De Caussade's teaching has roots in the mystical tradition, and in Ignatius Loyola and Francis de Sales. He is enjoyable to read and full of insight. He focuses on the idea of entrusting (abandoning) oneself to the providence of God as being for all Christians as well as, in more specific ways, for contemplatives. His 'abandonment' is not pure passivity: it involves attentiveness to God through the actual circumstances of life, and a responsive self-giving to be the instrument of God's loving will:

To discover God in the smallest and most ordinary things, as well as in the greatest, is to possess a rare and sublime faith. To find contentment in the present moment is to relish and adore the divine will in the succession of all the things to be done and suffered which make up the duty of the present moment. The pure of heart, simple souls, worship God in all the most adverse circumstances; their faith triumphs over everything.[25]

De Caussade, knowing its value from experience, follows the traditional division of the spiritual journey into an active phase and a later more passive contemplative phase:

> There is a time when the soul lives in God and there is also a time when God lives in the soul. What is appropriate to one of these conditions is inappropriate to the other. When God lives in souls, they must surrender themselves totally to him. Whereas when souls live in God, they must explore carefully and scrupulously every means they can find which may lead them to their union with him.[26]

Bernadette of Lourdes
(1844–79)

Bernadette Soubirous was the eldest child of a poor family in the small town of Lourdes, on the River Gave in the foothills of the Pyrenees. On 11 February 1858, aged fourteen, she went with two younger children to collect firewood beside the river. At a grotto above the bank she saw the apparition of a woman dressed in white, with a blue girdle. These appearances were repeated over the following weeks. The vision spoke to Bernadette in the local dialect asking her to tell the priests to build a church and come there in procession, and instructing her to pray for the conversion of sinners; she also told her to dig and uncover a spring below the grotto. Prompted by the parish priest, Bernadette asked the woman her name and reported that the answer was 'The Immaculate Conception'. This was four years after the proclamation by Pope Pius XI that Catholics should believe in the immaculate (sinless) conception of the Virgin Mary as an article of faith, which had been read out in the local church in 1855; but Bernadette said the phrase was new to her when the vision spoke it.

Bernadette's accounts of her visions are simple and clear; she comes over as an honest and balanced young person with no desire for drama or self-aggrandizement. The local bishop declared her visions authentic and the pilgrimage was established. Bernadette worked for eight years in the infirmary at Lourdes run by the Sisters of Charity and Christian Education, and in 1866 she joined that order and lived in its mother house in Nevers. Her own spirituality, in her letters and notebooks, shows a deep desire to give herself to God and pray for sinners. She was severely ill on several occasions and died after a painful illness at the age of thirty-five. She was canonized in 1933.

Elizabeth of the Trinity
(1880–1906)

Born near Bourges, Elizabeth Catez was an enthusiastic and balanced young person with an unusually deep prayer life. She made her own vow of celibacy at fourteen and entered the Carmelite convent at Dijon at twenty-one, dying after an illness at the age of twenty-six. Her gift was a felt awareness of God the Holy Trinity dwelling in the depth of her being. She summed up her spirituality in a prayer in 1904: 'O my God, Trinity whom I adore, help me to be oblivious of myself that I may be rooted in Thyself, changeless and calm as though my soul were in eternity...'[27] Reading Teresa of Avila and John of the Cross helped her to understand her own experiences, which included times of dryness in prayer. Typically, she spoke of God's indwelling as a foretaste of heaven: 'I already live the life of heaven for I bear it within me';[28] 'I live in the heaven of faith in the centre of my soul, and I try to please my Master by being, even here on earth, "a praise of his glory".'[29] She left letters and retreat notes, and to a sister shortly before she died she wrote:

> It seems to me that in heaven my mission will be to attract souls by helping them to go out of themselves in order to cling to God... and to keep them in the great interior silence which allows God to imprint himself upon them, to transform them into himself.[30]

Charles Péguy
(1873–1914)

As the twentieth century opened, France produced Charles Péguy, a poet and stimulating social philosopher, a pioneer of Christian socialism. He came from a poor Catholic family in Orleans, was an atheist for a time and had a civil marriage which meant being barred from the sacraments; but although he remained an ecclesiastical rebel he wrote out of a profound recovered faith.

Jean-Baptiste Marie Vianney, the Curé d'Ars (1786–1859)

Jean Vianney was a remarkable nineteenth-century priest. He came from a devout peasant family at Dardilly near Lyons and was born just before the French Revolution of 1789. In that social turmoil his education was disrupted and he saw the church persecuted by the atheist government. At nineteen he began to train for the priesthood in the nearby parish of Écully. He struggled with the obligatory Latin but after ten years (interrupted by two years of conscription during which he was separated from his regiment and lived as a deserter) he passed ordination exams in French with flying colours. He was curate for three years at Écully, where the Jansenist parish priest gave him a strong sense of God's transcendence, humanity's sinfulness, and the need for repentance and conversion. In 1818 he was posted to the village of Ars, to begin forty-one years of ministry there until he died aged seventy-three.

Jean Vianney understood that his priestly ministry consisted in reconciling people to God, and he rooted this ministry in his many hours of prayer in the church focusing on Christ present in the Blessed Sacrament. He first renewed the life of the village and parish, run down by the years of conflict, and founded a girls' school and orphanage, 'La Providence'. Then he preached missions at the invitation of neighbouring curés, and his reputation as a confessor gifted with unusual insight, and as a preacher who spoke simply from the heart, began to attract visitors to Ars. By 1830 a continual 'pilgrimage' was taking place, bringing 20,000 or more people in the course of each year. They waited in the prayerful atmosphere of the church for their turn for confession or a short interview. The Curé worked in the church from midnight to noon and again from 4 to 8 p.m., hearing confessions and assisting the troubled, giving a daily catechetical talk before noon and saying Mass. The stress was immense and he tried several times to leave or retire, longing for rest and retreat, but was always prevented by the people or his bishop.

The many stories and legends recorded about him include numerous accounts of his insight, his apparent ability to know details before being told and to foretell future events, and several stories of healings, which he attributed to the intercession of Philomena, a young Roman martyr to whom he had a devotion. There were

◆ Popular French print showing
Jean-Baptiste Marie Vianney.

Péguy's ideal society was a 'harmonious city' where justice reigns, where all are welcome and none excluded, in which the concept of eternal damnation has no place. The incarnation was central for him as the point where the sacred and the secular history of the world become closely

also stories of the miraculous increase of grain or flour at La Providence, and of his battles with the devil (some of which appear to be pious misunderstandings of his joking references to 'le grappin', the grappler, as he called him). Through all this, Jean Vianney remained simple and humble, and even fearful for his own salvation. He died having worked to the end, was canonized in 1925 and made patron saint of parish priests in 1928, although his ministry had extended far beyond his own parish.

When we are before the blessed Sacrament, instead of looking about us, let us shut our eyes and open our hearts; and the good God will open his. We will go to him, and he will come to us, the one to give, the other to receive. It will be like a breath passing from one to the other. What delight we find in forgetting ourselves that we may seek God!

It reminds me of the first time I came to Ars... Listen to this, my children: there was a man who never passed the church without entering it. In the morning when he went to work, and in the evening when he returned, he left his spade and his pickaxe at the door, and remained a long time in adoration before the blessed Sacrament. Oh! I used to like that!... I asked him once what he said to our Lord during the long visits he paid to him. Do you know what he answered? 'Oh, I don't say anything to him, Monsieur le Curé, I look at him and he looks at me...' How beautiful that is, my children, how beautiful that is![31]

entwined. He passionately criticized the church for identifying with the rich, instead of siding with the workers and 'the poor and the oppressed' in a communion of love like the early church. Socialism for him was about love and justice; he rejected orthodox Marxist ideas of 'scientific' social progress and class struggle. His motto was: 'The social revolution will be moral or nothing.' He ran a socialist bookshop near the Sorbonne, and a magazine, *Cahiers de la quinzaine*, in which he and his friends expounded their ideas. He was killed in 1914 in the First World War. His fiery and mystical vision found later expression in the development of worker priests, and ensured the centrality of communion and solidarity with the poor in French Christian socialism.

Charles de Foucauld (1858–1916) and the Little Brothers and Sisters of Jesus

Charles de Foucauld founded one of the most quietly influential new forms of religious life in the twentieth century. Born in Strasbourg, he was orphaned and inherited the title of viscount at the age of five. Headstrong and independent, he made a fervent first communion in 1872 but soon became an atheist. He trained at the military colleges of Saint-Cyr and Saumur, becoming a dashing and dissolute cavalry officer. In 1883–84 he made a dangerous solo expedition to survey Morocco disguised as a Jew, and was impressed by the religious fervour of the Muslims. Back in Paris he was influenced by his devout cousin Marie de Bondy, who introduced him to her own spiritual director, the famous Abbé Huvelin. Charles made confession to him and received communion. Later he wrote, 'As soon as I knew there was a God, I understood I could not do otherwise than to live only for him: my religious vocation dates from the same hour as my faith.'

He learned the life of prayer for three years with Abbé Huvelin and then, wishing like Jesus to 'take the lowest place', became a strict Cistercian

Thérèse of Lisieux (1873–97)

Thérèse Martin became the best-known Carmelite saint of the nineteenth century. She was the ninth child of a devout family, born in Alençon and growing up in Lisieux in northern France. Lively and outgoing as a small child, she became withdrawn after her mother's death when she was four. She was brought up by her father and two eldest sisters, Marie and Pauline. Five years later when Pauline entered the nearby Carmelite Convent, young Thérèse reacted by becoming tearful and unwell. At the same time she had only one desire for herself which was to enter the same convent, where Marie also went in 1885, and to become a saint. She remained in a painfully disturbed emotional state, still very much the baby of the family, until an event she experienced as a 'conversion' at Christmas 1886. Quite simply, she returned from Midnight Mass knowing that she would find her shoes, placed in the chimney-corner, filled with small presents. As she came in she overheard her father saying this was altogether too babyish and was the last time it must happen. It was a moment of sudden awakening to maturity. She was now fourteen, and was clear in a more adult way that her vocation was that of a Carmelite nun, not simply to follow her sisters but in order to pray, 'to save souls and especially to pray for priests', to forget herself, receive the love of the suffering Jesus and pass it on to others.

During the next year Thérèse went on a diocesan pilgrimage to Rome with another sister, Céline, who was to follow her into the convent. They met Pope Leo XIII and insisted on climbing down into the ruins of the Colosseum to kiss the ground on which the martyrs died. Meanwhile Thérèse requested permission to enter the convent early, which was granted in 1888 when she was still fifteen. She took final vows in 1890 as Thérèse of the Child Jesus and of the Holy Face. In 1893 she became novice mistress. In 1895 she began to write her spiritual autobiography at the request of her elder sister Pauline (Sister Agnes), then Mother Prioress. Her own title for it was *The Story of the Springtime of a Little White Flower*.

In April 1896 she began to cough blood, and died of tuberculosis in September 1897 at the age of twenty-four. Her last months were marked by physical and spiritual suffering, a 'dark tunnel' or 'night' which she accepted with the help of John of the Cross as an experience of sacrifice and purification. She remained convinced that God was working out a purpose in her: 'I feel my mission is soon to begin… to make others love God as I have loved him… to teach souls my little way… I will spend my heaven in doing good on earth.'

On her death the sisters followed the usual custom of sending a note about her life to other convents, but this time they sent the autobiography. It was soon circulating outside the convents, a first edition being printed in 1898, and became widely popular. Thérèse was canonized in 1925.

Thérèse's 'little way of spiritual childhood'

The childhood of Jesus had provided a strong image of self-emptying and trustfulness towards God in French spirituality since the time of Bérulle. Thérèse used this image and grounded it in verses from scripture that helped her to describe a short way to God for ordinary people. She says she had been looking for 'a lift by which I may be raised up to God, for I am too small to climb the steep stairway of perfection'. She came across these verses, which had been copied into a notebook by her sister Céline: 'Whoever is a little one, let him come to me' (Proverbs 9:4) and 'You shall be carried at the breasts and upon the knees: as one whom a mother caresses, so will I comfort you' (Isaiah 66:12–13). Thérèse was deeply struck: 'O Jesus! Your arms, then, are the lift which must raise me even to heaven. To reach heaven, I need not become great; on the contrary I must remain little, I must become even smaller than I am.' Shortly before her death Thérèse described this 'little way', which she wanted to teach, as 'the way of

Letter 143, to Céline

St Teresa says we must maintain love. *The wood* is
not within our reach when we are in darkness, in
aridities, but at least are we not obliged to throw
little pieces of straw on it? Jesus is really powerful
enough to keep the fire going by himself. However,
he is satisfied when he sees us put a little fuel on it.
This *attentiveness* pleases Jesus, and then he throws
on the fire a lot of wood. We do not see it, but
we do feel the *strength* of love's warmth. I have
experienced it: when I am *feeling* nothing, when I am
incapable of praying, of practising virtue, then is the
moment for seeking opportunities, *nothings*, which
please Jesus more than mastery of the world or even
martyrdom suffered with generosity. For example,
a smile, a friendly word when I would want to say
nothing, or put on a look of annoyance, etc., etc....[33]

spiritual childhood, the way of trust and absolute
surrender... there is only one thing to do here below –
to offer to our Lord the flowers of *little sacrifices* and
win him by our caresses'.[32]

Taken in an unsentimental way, this is a spirituality of
simplicity and openness before God, offering ourselves
as we truly are and experiencing the joy of being
accepted by God. It means accepting everything – joys
and sorrows, pleasures and pains – as expressions of
God's mercy and an occasion for thanks; and taking the
many opportunities that each day brings to renounce
selfish reactions and express Christlike love. It is not of
course as 'new' as Therese thought; it is in tune with
French spirituality since the seventeenth century.

Trappist monk at Akbès in Syria. There a further vocation unfolded. He conceived the idea of a new kind of religious order living a simple contemplative life of prayer and open hospitality among the people, as Jesus did, in his home at Nazareth. He began to write a Rule for the new community of 'Little Brothers', hoping that others would join him, and received permission to pursue this vocation. For four years, 1897–1900, he lived in retreat at Nazareth as domestic worker at a convent. After ordination in 1901 he built a hermitage at Béni-Abbès on the border of Morocco, and in 1905 moved to Tamanrasset deeper in Algeria. He lived an apostolate of 'kindness and friendship', welcoming all, 'good or bad, friend or enemy, Muslim or Christian'. Although no one then joined him, he did succeed in founding an association of lay people committed to a similar evangelical Christian lifestyle. In 1916 he was killed at Tamanrasset by robbers.

Brother Charles's writings consist of the Rule, letters and retreat notes. His vision was fully taken up by both women and men in 1933 when communities of Little Brothers and Little Sisters began to live the contemplative life in the world that he had pioneered, and to spread it round the globe. Years later the first Brothers at Taizé received their formation with the Little Brothers in the Algerian desert.

Conclusion

During the centuries we have surveyed, the Roman Catholic Church contributed much of lasting value to Christian spirituality: Ignatius with his vision of worldwide mission and his practical ways to link prayer and life, and the great Carmelite mystics with their understanding of the deep aspects of prayer; Francis de Sales who affirmed the possibilities of commitment and holiness for lay people; Brother Lawrence with his inner peace amid the bustle of the kitchen; Vincent de Paul exemplifying practical care for those in need; Pascal the intellectual who experienced God in a new age of scepticism; De Caussade with his

attentiveness to God in the present moment.

Mary Ward in the seventeenth century began the movement towards active participation by women in the practical work of the church, in which, by the end of our period, many thousands of women were engaged across the world. The nineteenth century threw up considerable diversity: the extraordinary insight and ministry of the Curé d'Ars; Newman with his reach into both the ancient and modern worlds; the childlike trust of Thérèse of Lisieux; the theological contemplation of Elizabeth of the Trinity; poets and people of action. Finally as the twentieth century begins we encounter new trends in Péguy's spirituality of political engagement for social justice, and the contemplative life lived amid ordinary people pioneered by Charles de Foucauld. We glimpse the beginnings of a rapprochement between divided Christian denominations in the ecumenical spirituality of Von Hügel. As yet, few of these riches had spread outside the Roman Catholic sphere; but in the following century an unprecedented sharing was to take place.

8

The Anglican Spirit

(16th to 19th centuries)

Gordon Mursell

Timeline

Anglicanism was born of a heady cocktail of politics, sex and religion mixed in the central decades of the sixteenth century. The English king, Henry VIII, wanted to divorce his wife and marry a new one: the pope would not let him. So, inch by inch, never entirely comprehending what he was doing (for his real interests lay elsewhere), Henry set up his own church, which later historians would call 'Anglican'; and he got his archbishop, Thomas Cranmer (1489–1556), to help him do it. From the start, then, politics and religion, the secular and the sacred, have intertwined inseparably in the Anglican tradition. One of its early martyrs, Hugh Latimer (c. 1485–1555), tells the story of a gentleman who inadvertently dropped the cover of the bowl when serving Henry VIII's father and predecessor with some refreshing liquor:

> The king, seeing his folly, saith, 'Sir, is this well done?' 'Yea, Sir,' said he, 'if your majesty take it well.' With this pretty answer the king was pacified.

And Latimer proceeds to take this as an unlikely but vivid analogy for how God 'takes well' our sins by imputing Christ's righteousness to us, a cornerstone of Reformed theology.[1] In other words, God looks at us, and instead of taking us as we are, he sees Christ taking our place, and accepts us.

Negatively, then, Anglicanism was exposed from birth to the infection of political spinelessness; positively, its true spiritual founders were able to chart a careful course between the extremes (as they saw it) of Roman dogma and contemporary continental Protestantism. Adrian Hastings, writing in 1986, acutely describes the nascent Church of England as 'intellectually one of the freest of Christian churches, [but] socially... one of the most subservient'.[2] And if Latimer's bold use of courtly banter to explain theological truth surprises us, it does at least underline the refusal of Anglicanism to separate the sacred from the secular: one of the most distinctive features of the new church's spirituality would prove to be its insistence on holding this world and the next together.

It must also be remembered that, if Anglicanism's birth took place in the midst of sixteenth-century English *realpolitik*, its conception happened much earlier. Like many before and after him, Cranmer sought to recover for the English church the original purity of the apostolic faith; early apologists for Anglicanism constantly defended its principles on the basis of scriptural and patristic precedent.

In secular terms, too, Henry VIII's church was conceived before it was born in the changing context of the early sixteenth century. The growth of royal power, the invention of printing and the rapid dissemination of continental Protestant ideas, the translation of scripture into the vernacular, the discovery of new and strange lands far from European shores – all these and many other factors helped to shape the new church and to give it colour and content. Furthermore, recent scholarship has established virtually beyond doubt that late-medieval English piety was in a far healthier state than was once thought: if the bulk of English people accepted the new church, it was not because they were weary of the old one, but because it was imposed upon them from above. Here, too, external and political factors were crucial: the early death of the Catholic queen Mary Tudor, followed by the long reign of her Protestant sister Elizabeth and the defeat of the Spanish Armada, ensured the Church of England's survival. It was a very strange birth for a major new spiritual tradition, though no more so than that of its ultimate founder at Bethlehem.

This is not to imply that the English laity passively acquiesced in the birth and growth of the Anglican way: by the early sixteenth century, lay people were more literate, confident and cosmopolitan than in any previous Christian era. Even so, the impact on them of Henry's brutal dissolution of the monasteries must have been considerable. When no fire from God came to devour the perpetrators of this shocking act of royal greed, something of the essence of the old

◆ *King Henry VIII*, by Hans Holbein (1465–1524). Henry's desire to marry Anne Boleyn in order to have an heir resulted in the split from the Roman Catholic Church and Henry's excommunication in 1533.

faith vanished with the monks: the old certainties, and the power they were believed to possess, were subverted. This had happened before, notably when John Wycliffe (c. 1330–84), an Oxford academic, questioned some of the central tenets of Catholic faith and order, encouraging many of the growing number of articulate and literate lay people of his day to do the same. What was different this time was that royal power was on the side of those doing the questioning; and the English gentry, in particular, were not slow to see the advantages of following their master's example.

The Book of Common Prayer

It was the peculiar genius of Thomas Cranmer to be able to conjure, from the curious mix of sex, politics and religion that marked the birth of Anglicanism, something of enduring spiritual power. The Book of Common Prayer had its origins in the medieval Catholic prayer books, whose variety and popularity attest to the growing appetites of a literate laity. The appearance of the first national prayer book in 1545 was an important precedent: with the centralization of royal power it soon became apparent that such books could be helpful means of disseminating the right religious beliefs and practices; and the successive versions which duly appeared under the Protestant Edward VI and the Catholic Mary Tudor reflect the vicissitudes of rapidly changing theological policy.

It was the 1549 book which first bore the title 'Book of Common Prayer', and the title is significant. This was, from the start, intended to be a prayer book for the entire English nation, and, although its character became more markedly Protestant when it was revised three years later (and again over a century later in 1662, after the restoration of the monarchy), it was this prayer book (in essence the work of Cranmer himself) which gave Anglican spirituality its distinctive character. What were the defining features of this spirituality?

A religion for all

First, Cranmer wanted to recover the original purity of the age of the apostles, and to make it accessible to all the people of England. Parishioners were to hear the scriptures read aloud in church twice every day, when the parish priest rang the bell and summoned them to join him for Morning and Evening Prayer:

> The Curate that ministereth in every Parish-Church or Chapel, being at home, and not being otherwise reasonably hindered, shall say [Morning and Evening Prayer] in the Parish-Church or Chapel where he ministereth, and shall cause a Bell to be tolled

thereunto a convenient time before he begin, that the people may come to hear God's Word, and to pray with him.

In a stroke of genius, Cranmer took the old sevenfold monastic rhythm of common prayer and reduced it to just two daily services (Matins and Evensong, soon to be accessibly renamed Morning Prayer and Evening Prayer), both of which were to be recited not just *for* the people but *by* them – and in their own language, not in the Latin of the old dispensation:

> The Service in this Church of England these many years hath been read in Latin to the people, which they understand not; so that they have heard with their ears only, and their heart, spirit, and mind, have not been edified thereby.

This kind of daily common prayer was recorded in the Acts of the Apostles as the practice of the first Christians; Cranmer was determined to restore it. The question of how far he succeeded is immensely difficult to answer, but there is substantial evidence to suggest that, in the century and a half after his death, the prayer book did indeed furnish the basic pattern of daily prayer and Sunday worship for the vast majority of the English people.

Spirituality for everyday life

Secondly, this was to be a genuinely lay spirituality, not a complex monastic or priestly operation duly watered down for simpler tastes. The prayers and thanksgivings in the prayer book are for a rich variety of secular needs: for rain, a good harvest, peace, for those at sea. The yearly calendar, much simplified from that of medieval Catholicism, retains popular English saints such as Crispin, the patron saint of shoemakers, on whose feast day the battle of Agincourt had been fought in

◆ **Portrait of Thomas Cranmer (1546) by Gerlach Flicke (fl. 1547–58).**

1415. The sober 'service of commination' seeks further to integrate religion with everyday life by setting clear moral standards, and denouncing those who curse their parents, lead the blind astray, 'smite their neighbours secretly' or drink too much; and the introduction to the confession in the eucharistic rite encourages only those who live in love and charity with their neighbours to draw near.

A local religion

And in these our doings we condemn no other Nations, nor prescribe any thing but to our own people only. For we think it convenient that every country should use such ceremonies as they shall think best to the setting forth of God's honour and glory, and to the reducing of the people to a most perfect and godly living, without error or superstition…

Thirdly, the Book of Common Prayer is nothing if not English, not only in its (arguably over-reverential) approach to the English monarchy and hostility to foreigners, but also in its use of the rhythms and richness of the English language in what (by happy chance) was to be that language's golden age. We should not be too critical of the former: Cranmer was writing at a time when England was highly vulnerable to threats from overseas, and his xenophobia is no worse than that of the Psalmist centuries earlier. And the latter is ample compensation: the well-sprung rhythms of even the simplest lines ('O Lord, open *thou* our *lips*'), and the wonderfully memorable quality of Cranmer's collects and Coverdale's psalms, bequeathed to the Anglican tradition a range of texts which could be stored in the heart, and recalled at will. And that inheritance was extended further when James I (1566–1625) commissioned a new translation of the entire Bible which still bears his name. In the best Protestant fashion, Cranmer made the Word primary, and helped to foster a spiritual tradition in which God's word to us, and ours to him, encountering one another in Jesus, the Word made flesh, were given ultimate reverence.

Praying in church

Finally, the prayer book made an important contribution to what might be called an evolving spirituality of buildings. Where the late-medieval church sought to express God's *presence*, its Protestant equivalent sought to express God's *truth*: reverence for the sacrament was replaced in Puritan and Lutheran buildings with reverence for the pulpit. Cranmer could be said to have caught more exactly than either of these traditions the creative tension inherent in the Bible's approach to religious buildings: God promises Solomon ▶

that he will dwell in the king's fine new temple, but only for as long as his people live according to his teaching (see 2 Chronicles 6–7). As we have seen, the people were encouraged to come to church twice each day to pray with their priest; and it is in the church that the clergy are to be instructed in their faith. In the official homilies issued in 1547 for use in Anglican churches, it is made clear that the church building is still a holy place, a place where Christ is to be found:

> If we lack Jesus Christ, that is to say, the saviour of our souls and bodies, we shall not find him in the market-place, or in the guildhall, much less in the ale-house or tavern, amongst good fellows (as they call them), so soon as we shall find him in the temple, the Lord's house, amongst the teachers and preachers of his word, where indeed he is to be found.[3]

For the church 'is the house of prayer, not the house of talking, of walking, of brawling, or minstrelsy, of hawks, or dogs'.[4]

Christ is not restricted to the church; but he is present there, for as long as his teaching governs and animates the lives of his people. And it is just this synthesis of scripture and daily life, of prayer and morality, which the prayer book was designed to uphold.

◆ **Frontispiece of the Book of Common Prayer (1549).**

Richard Hooker
(1553–1600)

Cranmer's legacy (see box, p. 248) might well have proved short-lived had it not been for the work of Richard Hooker, a country parson whose *Laws of Ecclesiastical Polity* helped to give depth and direction to the evolving Anglican spirit. Hooker scorned both Roman dogma and Protestant fundamentalism, espousing a theology rooted in scripture, tradition and human reason, for all three find expression in the law of God. For Hooker, that law, as it is expressed in scripture, is a luminous and living treasure of divine truth. That truth must be appropriated by each Christian inwardly; but it is not just an inward principle. It is, as the apostle Paul said, the glory of God in the face of Christ; and it is by our *participation* in the life of Christ, who adopts us for his own and calls us into his church, that we experience what it means to be forgiven and saved. So Hooker said that

> the participation of Christ importeth, besides the presence of Christ's Person, and besides the mystical copulation thereof with the parts and members of his whole church, a true actual influence of grace whereby the life which we live according to godliness is his.[5]

In the Eucharist, Christ is really present; but his presence is not restricted to the consecrated bread and wine. Rather 'the real presence of Christ's most blessed body and blood is not... to be sought for in the sacrament, but in the worthy receiver of the sacrament';[6] and that real presence is thus to be carried out into the world at large. Hooker defends the Anglican view of the church as very much more than an invisible company of elect believers: it exists to sanctify the whole life of the nation, and to call everyone to experience for themselves the divine glory in the living presence of Christ in their midst, so that (as Cranmer put it) 'we may evermore dwell in him, and he in us'. This is the rationale for the Anglican tradition of cathedral liturgy, at once inclusive and stately, thoughtful and sensuous, in which human beings are caught up into the life and glory of the living God.

Lancelot Andrewes
(1556–1626)

The theological foundations provided by Richard Hooker for the fledgling Church of England were further strengthened by the life and work of Lancelot Andrewes, successively Bishop of Chichester, Ely and Winchester. Andrewes was an able scholar and diplomat who forged a number of links with continental Protestantism, and wrote a number of ferocious attacks on Roman Catholic teaching at the bidding of James I (who himself played an important role in fostering the Anglican spirit by commissioning the Authorized Version of the Bible).

Andrewes sought, like Hooker, to set the Church of England on the firm foundation of apostolic and patristic teaching. He set the incarnation at the centre of his spirituality: he believed that the reason we speak of the Word becoming 'flesh' rather than 'man' is to emphasize the fact that God embraced the lowest part of humanity, thereby assuring us that he also embraced the highest. The whole of creation is thus the arena of God's redeeming and sanctifying love. And our role is no dull passivity, as Andrewes emphasized in relation to Mary:

> To conceive is more than to receive. It is so to receive as we yield somewhat of our own also. A vessel is not said to conceive the liquor that is put into it. Why? because it yieldeth nothing from itself. The blessed Virgin did, and therefore is because she did. She did both give and take. Give of her own substance whereof his body was framed; and take or receive power from the Holy Spirit...[7]

By taking part in the drama of our redemption as Mary did, we become far more than *followers* of Jesus: we become, as Hooker also said, *participants* in his own life: 'To become like to him we worship is the pitch of all religion.' The work of grace, and the action of the Holy Spirit, alone can make this possible:

> It is not in the power of nature to elevate and lift itself up to conceive hope of being partakers of the blessedness of the life to come, to be made 'partakers of the Divine Nature', and of the heavenly substance; if men hope for any such thing, it is the Spirit of God that raiseth them up to it.[8]

We are called by Jesus to be perfect; and the grace he bestows on us not only takes away our sins but endues our souls with 'inherent virtues', so that we can 'proceed from one degree of perfection to another all our life time, even till the time of our death, which is the beginning and accomplishment of our perfection'. We become partakers of the divine nature, and 'after a sort gods', as Andrewes vividly expresses the classical Christian doctrine of deification.[9]

Andrewes has, then, a lofty and positive view of human nature; and he loves to celebrate the compassion and generosity of God:

> There is in God that faithfulness that is in a mother towards her children, for as a woman cannot but pity her own child and 'the son of her womb', so the Lord 'will not forget' his own people.[10]

But Andrewes is also acutely aware of human sin, and of the need for a sustained and mature life of prayer if we are to lay ourselves open to the life-giving grace of God. 'When we come to pray,' he wrote, 'the whole man must be occupied, and all the members of the body employed in the service of God.'[11] And it is characteristic of him to insist that here too human beings have a vital part to play: prayer without some endeavour to achieve what we ask for is useless: 'As we know we shall have our part in heaven, so we must begin our heaven here on earth; and this shall be done if we add our endeavour to those things which we pray for at the hands of God.'[12] It is not enough to 'sit still, and hear a Sermon and two Anthems, and be saved'.[13] But we never pray alone; and when our own prayer is weak and lacking in fervour, those deficiencies are made up for by those who pray for us:

> Albeit we pray but faintly and have not that supply of fervency that is required in prayer, yet we have comfort that ever when we most faint in prayer there are of God's saints that pray for us with all instancy, by which it comes to pass that being all but one body their prayers tend to our good as well as their own… so that the weakness of one member is supplied by the fervent and earnest prayer of the other.[14]

His own personal prayers, or *Preces privatae*, are a careful compilation of devotions designed to draw the whole of life into prayer:

> In war there is a note of charge: fitted to action;
> > of recall: whereby stragglers are called back.
> So the human mind, like as in the morning it must be awakened, so at eventide as it were by a note of recall it must be called back to itself and its Captain.[15]

Nothing is left to chance or spontaneous impulse: it is the finest example of ordered, thoughtful, structured Anglican piety, and one of the brightest flowers of the Anglican spirit.

The seventeenth century: lay spirituality

The seventeenth century was at once a period of seismic disruption and extraordinary creativity in English national life; and it witnessed some of the severest challenges, as well as some of the greatest enhancements, to the Anglican spirit. It also witnessed the spread of Anglicanism beyond England. Two fundamental theological traditions exerted broadly equal influence on the young Church of England: the Reformed tradition of Calvin, stressing God's absolute control over all that happened and the ultimate fate of human beings, and the more Catholic tradition associated with the Dutchman Arminius (hence Arminianism), who attached more importance to the part played by human beings in the work of salvation. It used to be thought that the reigns of James I and Charles I (1625–49) saw the dominance of the Arminian (later to be called 'high church') party in the church, while the ensuing Commonwealth (1649–60) witnessed the triumph of the Calvinists (or 'Puritans', a term used, initially as an insult, to refer to those who sought to uphold the purity of a Christianity founded on scripture alone). But this is simplistic: Calvinist influence on the Church of England was powerful well before Oliver Cromwell presided over King Charles's decapitation. What can confidently be affirmed is that the Book of Common Prayer, revised in 1661–62 after the restoration of the monarchy, became something of a benchmark for all that was distinctively Anglican, a careful synthesis of Calvinist and Arminian, Protestant and Catholic, of a distinctively English hue. It also seems genuinely to have played a vital role in nourishing the spiritual lives of countless English people, sanctifying the rhythms and healing the wounds of daily life.

Yet the Book of Common Prayer alone was not enough to satisfy the spiritual needs of so turbulent and uncertain an age. Numerous books and pamphlets were published with the aim of providing spiritual and moral guidance for everyday life. One of the most popular of these, *The Whole Duty of Man* (1657), provided a range of prayers and encouraged those who could not read to learn them by heart. It also contained extensive directions for holy living, covering every aspect of human life from Sunday worship and family prayers to the dangers of excessive drinking and gambling. Women kept journals (where literacy and leisure time allowed), embroidered biblical scenes, and meditated or sang psalms as they worked. For many people, life remained arduous and unpredictable; and their prayers were likely to be primarily concerned with survival, with protection from epidemics or bad harvests or untimely death. Some people hedged their spiritual bets: bishops' visitation records from the seventeenth century often include questions put to churchwardens such as 'whether have you any conjurers, charmers, calcours, witches, or fortune-tellers, who are they, and who do resort unto them

◆ *An Eyewitness Representation of the Execution of King Charles I of England (1649), by Weesop (fl. 1641–49).*

for counsell?'[16] And some took their evident puzzlement at the sheer unfairness of life to God in their prayers: thus Ralph Josselin, a diarist and parish priest, wrote this in his diary for 22 August 1680:

> A good weeke. I made a good progresse in my harvest blessed bee god; this morning my dogs kild a lambe, and a sheep dead: often on sabbath mornings I have thes losses lord lett me see why.[17]

John Donne
(1572–1631)

One of the most significant figures in the Anglican tradition of the seventeenth century began his life as a Roman Catholic. The circumstances surrounding his conversion to the Church of England remain uncertain; though it is noteworthy that, in a highly polemical age, Donne never lost his concern for the union of all Christians. He was a man of exceptional learning combined with a persistent tendency to melancholy, which was at least in part caused by the early death of his wife. He became Dean of St Paul's Cathedral in London in 1621. His written works reflect the influence of Augustine and Calvin among others; and his literary style is one of the glories of English literature and the Anglican spirit.

Donne had a positive view of the created universe. He followed Aquinas in describing the world as the *theatrum* where we sit and see God:

◆ John Donne, from the frontispiece to *Eighty Sermons Preached by Donne*, published in 1640 and engraved by Mattaus Merian the Younger (1621–87).

There is not so poore a creature but may be thy glasse to see God in… all things that are, are equally removed from being nothing; and whatsoever hath any beeing, is by that very beeing, a glasse in which we see God, who is the roote, and the fountaine of all beeing.[18]

He had a gregarious, almost donnish, view of society as rooted in the life of the trinity, which he once described as a 'holy and whole college'.[19] 'Be not apt', he wrote in a sermon, 'to think heaven is an Ermitage, or a Monastery, or the way to heaven a sullen melancholy; Heaven, and the way to it, is a Communion of Saints, in a holy cheerfulnesse.'[20] Each Christian forms a church in miniature, and each is dependent on others. And it is this stress on our fundamental spiritual unity that finds expression in one of his most famous utterances: 'No man is an island' (see box, p. 255).

Donne had an acutely realistic view of human nature: 'There are but two things necessary to us to know, how ill we are, and how good we may be.'[21] He believed that human beings are created good, but that at the very moment of our birth we inherit the taint of Adam's sin and thus become prey to all the evils the world contains. This is the human paradox: the fact that 'my soul is capable of God, as soon as it is capable of sin; and though sin doe not get the start of God, God does not get the start of sin either'.[22] The means by which we are called and saved is above all else through the free and undeservable grace of God; but this does not mean we are passive recipients of our fate. Donne went beyond Calvinist orthodoxy in asking, 'How long shall we make this bad use, of this true doctrine, that, because we cannot doe *enough*, for our salvation, therefore we will doe *nothing*?'[23]

The first step to faith is 'to wonder, to stand,

and consider with a holy admiration, the waies and proceedings of God with man'.[24] But coupled with our wonder at what God has done for us in becoming human we must wonder at our pervasive sinfulness: hence the importance of contrition in Donne's spirituality, not just once but as a vital element in our personal spiritual lives. For repeated sins create 'a spunginesse in the soul, an aptnesse to receive any liquor, to embrace any sin, that is offered to it'.[25] And by becoming penitent, by beginning to glimpse the power and reach of God's love, we begin to be changed into the people God created us to be. And this in turn demands of us a generous and inclusive love of neighbour:

> A man is thy Neighbor, by his Humanity, not by his Divinity; by his Nature, not by his Religion; a Virginian is thy Neighbor, as well as a Londoner; and all men are in every good mans Diocess, and Parish.[26]

Donne's sense of the reality of tragedy and evil in the world gives to much of his work a hint of melancholy, though even in suffering he insists that God does not and will not desert us. Indeed there is a higher kind of joy which we experience precisely in suffering:

> This... is not a collaterall joy, that stands by us in the tribulation, and sustaines us, but it is a fundamentall joy, a radicall joy, a viscerall, a gremiall joy, that arises out of the bosome and wombe and bowels of the tribulation it selfe. It is not that I rejoyce, though I be afflicted, but I rejoyce because I am afflicted; It is not because I shall not sink in my calamity, and be buried in that valley, but because my calamity raises me, and makes my valley a hill, and gives me an eminency, and brings God and me nearer to one another, then without that calamity I should have been [because I am counted worthy to suffer for Christ's sake].[27]

He is clear that 'there is no joy in the suffering itself', nor is it to be overvalued: rather it is only when I acknowledge that all my sufferings can be directed to God's glory that I can, so to speak, own my own sufferings and find joy through them.[28]

'No man is an island'

The church is Catholic, universal, so are all her actions; all that she does belongs to all. When she baptizes a child, that action concerns me; for that child is thereby connected to that head which is my head too, and ingrafted into that body whereof I am a member. And when she buries a man, that action concerns me: all mankind is of one author, and is one volume; when one man dies, one chapter is not torn out of the book, but translated into a better language: and every chapter must be so translated; God employs several translators; some pieces are translated by age, some by sickness, some by war, some by justice; but God's hand is in every translation, and his hand shall bind up all our scattered leaves again, for that library when every book shall lie open to one another... No man is an island, entire of itself; every man is a piece of the continent, a part of the main. If a clod be washed away by the sea, Europe is the less, as well as if a promontory were, as well as if a manor of thy friend's or of thine own were; any man's death diminishes me, because I am involved in mankind, and therefore never send to know for whom the bell tolls; it tolls for thee.[29]

To do this requires resources beyond my own: hence the crucial importance of the church in Donne's view of the spiritual life. 'I can build a Church in my bosome,' he wrote. 'I can serve God in my heart, and never cloath my prayer in words... But yet, I finde the highest exaltations, and the noblest elevations of my devotions, when I give thanks in the great Congregation... for so, me thinks, I come nearer and nearer to the Communion of Saints in Heaven.'[30] He described the whole world as 'God's Exchequer', the arena of his gracious self-giving; but the church is God's 'Court of Requests, there he receives our petitions, there we receive his answers'.[31]

The use of secular language is characteristic, and has led to Donne being accused of conceiving of God as a kind of superior courtly monarch, to be approached in an attitude of grovelling submission. But this is unfair: Donne took from Calvin the fundamental principle that we can pray, and pray *boldly*, precisely because we have been accepted by God as his own. 'When thou art established in favour,' he wrote, 'thou maist make any suit.'[32] We may remain God's courtiers, but only because we are God's children first. And, preaching on the passage in Genesis where Abraham intercedes with God for the people of Sodom, Donne comments that

The words of man, in the mouth of a faithfull man, of Abraham, are a Canon against God himselfe, and batter down all his severe and heavy purposes for Judgements. Yet, this comes not, God knows, out of the weight or force of our words, but out of the easinesse of God. God puts himself into the way of a shot, he meets a weak prayer, and is graciously pleased to be wounded by that: God sets up a light, that we direct the shot upon him, he enlightens us with a knowledge, how, and when, and what to pray for; yea, God charges, and discharges the Canon himselfe upon himselfe.[33]

It is this same God who drew Donne from sadness and despair to become one of the greatest figures in the Anglican tradition. And he was convinced that what God had begun to do in this world would be consummated in the next. Here he is, in marvellously witty form, preaching on the life of heaven, where

I the same body, and the same soul, shall be recompact again, and be identically, numerically, individually the same man. The same integrity of body, and soul, and the same integrity in the Organs of my body, and in the faculties of my soul too; I shall be all there, my body, and my soul, and all my body, and all my soul. I am not all here, I am here now preaching upon this text, and I am at home in my Library considering whether S. Gregory, or S. Hierome, have said best of this text, before. I am here speaking to you, and yet I consider by the way, in the same instant, what it is likely you will say to one another, when I have done. You are not all here neither; you are here, now, hearing me, and yet you are thinking that you have heard a better Sermon somewhere else...[34]

The Anglican spirit in the later seventeenth century

The execution of Charles I in 1649 was a traumatic event for those who devoutly believed royalty to be divinely ordained: if kings were no longer sacred, then what was? And the ensuing Commonwealth saw an eruption of radical and Puritan movements and ideas, most of which proved short-lived. For the restoration of the monarchy in 1660 saw the rapid reinstatement of Anglican clergy and the reissue, in 1662, of the Book of Common Prayer. All those who could not accept bishops and the prayer book were obliged to leave the Church of England, becoming part of what came to be called 'Dissent'. Thereafter the Church of England would be, whether it liked it or not, only one part of

This is a day of good Tydings. 2 Kings. 7.9.

And he brought forth the Kings fon, put the Crowne upon him, and gaue him the teftimony, and they made him King. and anoynted, him and they clapt their hands, & faid, God fave y King 2K:11.12.

◆ **The return of Charles II; illustration from a prayer book (c. 1660).**

English Christianity. And the post-1660 church inhabited a world sharply different from that of Hooker and Donne. Some of the old certainties had gone for ever. New insights in science were giving rise to fresh questions about religious truth. It was not only kings whose existence and authority could no longer be taken for granted. There was, as a result, something of a turning inwards in English spirituality in the second half of the seventeenth century, both within and outside the established church: a renewed vitality, but of a very different temper – a love of poetry and beauty; a new interest in the created order, and in what kind of God could be seen at work within it; and a new longing for heaven.

Thomas Traherne
(1637–74)

One example of this new tone in spirituality was Thomas Traherne. Like Herbert, he was a country priest; and much of his written work remained unknown until the first decade of the twentieth century. It is suffused with a profound sense of wonder at the beauty of creation; but always as a signpost towards the far greater beauty of its Creator. There is a Franciscan-style sense of gratitude in Traherne's lovely poem 'The Salutation': how could I conceivably be worthy of so wonderful a world, a world which is mine precisely to the extent to which I do not seek to possess it?

> From Dust I rise,
> And out of Nothing now awake,
> These Brighter Regions which salute mine Eys,
>   A Gift from GOD I take.
> The Earth, the Seas, the Light, the Day,
>   the Skies,
> The Sun and Stars are mine; if those I prize...
>
>   A Stranger here
>   Strange Things doth meet, Strange Glories
>   See;
> Strange Treasures lodg'd in this fair World
>   appear,
>   Strange all, and New to me.
> But that they mine should be, who nothing
>   was,
> That Strangest is of all, yet brought to pass.

('The Salutation', verses 5 and 7)

Traherne writes in a different tradition from Herbert: his spirituality is indebted more to Plato than to Calvin, though he like Herbert is profoundly influenced by Augustine. But perhaps most attractive of all is his reverence for the childlike as perhaps the single most vital attribute for any authentic Christian spirituality: 'God in our Childhood with us walks', he wrote ('The Approach', verse 2); and in his poem 'The Return' (verse 1) he prays thus:

George Herbert (1593–1633)

◆ *George Herbert at Bemerton* (1860), **by William Dyce** (1806–64).

If John Donne was the greatest preacher of the Anglican tradition, George Herbert could be justly called its greatest poet. Educated at Westminster School and Cambridge, he served briefly in the English Parliament before becoming a priest and, in 1630, rector of two villages near Salisbury, where he died three years later aged only thirty-nine. Herbert has often been seen as a high-churchman, thanks in part to Izaak Walton's portrayal of him written decades after his death. In reality he was deeply indebted to Calvin's theology, as well as to the Bible in general and the Psalms in particular: their imagery, and their vivid interweaving of lament and celebration, profoundly influenced his poetry. In Herbert's spirituality, theology and earthy human life are inseparable:

Pitch thy behaviour low, thy projects high;
So shalt thou humble and magnanimous be:
Sink not in spirit: who aimeth at the sky,
Shoots higher much then he that means a tree.
  A grain of glory mixt with humblenesse
  Cures both a fever and lethargicknesse.
('Perirrhanterium' II.331–36)

Like many great Protestant writers on the spiritual life, Herbert is deeply interested in the interior life, and in the way we experience God's saving work within us. Poems such as 'The Glance' articulate this with exquisite delicacy.

The emphasis in this poem on God contemplating the furthermost depths of our sinfulness and estrangement and redeeming it through his grace is powerful; so too is the reference to God's second 'glance', at the end of time, in the last stanza ('When thou shalt look us out of pain'). It is worth noting too the movement within the poem from the lonely individual of the first verse to the corporate Christian family of the third: 'What wonders shall *we* feel.' But most important of all is the profound and vivid description, not unlike that of Augustine's *Confessions*, of God's unimaginable free gift of life and wholeness to those who know how little they deserve it.

This is not to say that Herbert regards life after having been 'saved' or justified as a bed of roses. In a poem entitled 'The Temper (1)', he explores the range of experiences, some good and some terrible, which the soul undergoes; and this leads him to complain bitterly to God for 'stretching' him too far (the use of the fearful word 'rack' is particularly telling):

> O rack me not to such a vast extent;
>   Those distances belong to thee:
> The world's too little for thy tent,
>   A grave too big for me.

> Wilt thou meet arms with man, that thou
>   dost stretch
>   A crumme of dust from heav'n to hell?
> Will great God measure with a wretch?
>   Shall he thy stature spell?

He continues by asking God for shelter:

> O let me, when thy roof my soul hath hid
>   O let me roost and nestle there:
> Then of a sinner thou art rid,
>   And I of hope and fear.

But finally he submits himself to God's will in a superb conclusion:

> Yet take thy way; for sure thy way is best:
>   Stretch or contract me, thy poore debter:
> This is but tuning of my breast,
>   To make the musick better.

> Whether I flie with angels, fall with dust,
>   Thy hands made both, and I am there:
> Thy power and love, my love and trust
>   Make one place ev'ry where.

The Glance

> When first thy sweet and gracious eye
> Vouchsaf'd ev'n in the midst of youth and night
> To look upon me, who before did lie
>   Weltring in sinne;
>   I felt a sugred strange delight,
> Passing all cordials made by any art,
> Bedew, embalme, and overrunne my heart,
>   And take it in.

> Since that time many a bitter storm
> My soul hath felt, ev'n able to destroy,
> Had the malicious and ill-meaning harm
>   His swing and sway:
>   But still thy sweet originall joy,
> Sprung from thine eye, did work within
>   my soul,
> And surging griefs, when they grew bold,
>   controll,
>   And got the day.

> If thy first glance so powerfull be,
> A mirth but open'd and seal'd up again;
> What wonders shall we feel, when we shall see
>   Thy full-ey'd love!
>   When thou shalt look us out of pain,
> And one aspect of thine spend in delight
> More then a thousand sunnes disburse in light,
>   In heav'n above.

To Infancy, O Lord, again I com,
That I my Manhood may improv:
My early Tutor is the Womb;
I still my Cradle lov.
'Tis strange that I should Wisest be,
When least I could an Error see.

Anglican spirituality in Scotland

Notable spiritual writing in the Anglican tradition was not restricted to England as the seventeenth century progressed. The Scottish Episcopal Church underwent traumatic confrontations with the Presbyterians during the century; but it still produced some outstanding figures, of whom the pre-eminent was Robert Leighton (1611–84), Archbishop of Glasgow and someone who was to exert a profound influence on Samuel Taylor Coleridge. Leighton wrote a number of scholarly texts, including a fine *Exposition of the Lord's Prayer*. And he seems to have sought to learn lessons from the painful turmoil that had afflicted his church and country in a profound sermon he wrote, 'The Christian's Course in the Church's Calamity'. It concludes with a moving exhortation for Christians who are troubled or suffering to wait upon God with a 'pious obstinacy that will not yield to the greatest opposition, nor give over so long as there is any possibility of prevailing'. And he concludes:

> And this is the purest acting of faith, when there is nothing of sense to support it, and yet it holds out, and, as Abraham did, against hope believes in hope. When the soul is at the hardest pinch, Faith will say, I will lie at the footstool of the Throne of Grace until I be thrown from it. I will not away from it. I will wait on till the last moment.[35]

Jeremy Taylor
(1613–67)

One of the many Anglican clergy who had clung to their belief in the monarchy and the established church, and who as a result had been expelled from their livings during the Commonwealth, was Jeremy Taylor, one of the greatest prose writers of his generation. He spent the Civil War as a chaplain attached to the king's household, and in 1645 was captured by parliamentary troops. At the restoration in 1660 his fortunes were transformed: he was appointed Bishop of Down and Connor in Ireland, where he died seven years later. Taylor had a wonderfully inventive and enquiring mind; but his thought was undergirded by a strong pastoral spirituality, and a deep longing to provide spiritual resources to sustain those many devout Anglicans who, like he, had suffered both physically and spiritually during the political upheavals of their day. His work remains of enduring value for Christians living in an age of uncertainty and change.

Taylor knew that it was lay Christians, not clergy, who were the seedbed of the church, and sought in all that he wrote to offer them guidance and support. 'Marriage', he wrote, 'is the seminary of the church.'[36] And he was a shrewd judge of character: 'men love sin only because it is forbidden.'[37] He knew very well that people would gain little from their religious beliefs if they put little into them:

> It is so little we spend in religion and so very much upon ourselves, so little to the poor and so without measure to make ourselves sick, that we seem to be in love with our own mischief, and so passionate for necessity and want, that we strive all the ways we can to make ourselves need more than nature intended.[38]

The remedy was also the title of Taylor's most famous book: holy living. But Taylor did not see this in a narrowly churchy way. The work of the Holy Spirit in us transforms our potential: we become sons and daughters of God by adoption, 'capable of a new state... enabled to do new and greater actions in order to higher ends; we have new affections, new understandings, new wills'.[39] The trouble is that we misdirect this divinely given potential towards inappropriate ends: instead of devoting ourselves to 'religious walking with God', we spend our time on worldly civilities, unsuitable company, or overeating.[40] Fortunately for us, God has enabled us to make the necessities of nature into parts of our religious duty, and thereby 'he, by adopting them into religion, may turn our nature into grace, and accept our natural actions as actions of religion'.[41]

But how do we do this? Taylor suggests three basic principles; and the first is care of our time. 'Idleness', he writes, 'is the greatest prodigality in the world.'[42] This is not to say that we must be busy all the time: rather it is to seek a right prioritizing in life, setting our religious obligations first:

> not like the patriarch [of Constantinople], who ran from the altar in St Sophia to his stable, in all his pontificals, and in the midst of his office, to see a colt newly fallen from his beloved and much-valued mare Phorbante.[43]

Instead we must 'redeem the time'; at the end of each day we should 'examine the actions of the past day with a particular scrutiny'[44] and we must 'suppose every day to be a day of business' (even though there must be time for recreation and rest); 'for your whole life is a race, and a battle; a merchandise, and a journey'.[45] We must examine our desires as part of our preparation for receiving Holy Communion: great and noble desires will disturb and unsettle us until we respond to them as we should.[46]

The second key ingredient of holy living is purity of intention – doing all that we do for the glory of God. It is quite possible to be religious for all the wrong reasons:

> If a man visits his sick friend, and watches at his pillow for charity's sake, and because of his old affection, we approve it; but if he does it in

hope of legacy, he is a vulture, and only watches for the carcase.[47]

People who are eager to engage in business activities, but engage in their duties to God and neighbour 'slowly, flatly, and without appetite' can tell for themselves that their hearts are 'not right with God'.[48] We must want what God wants; we must seek in all we do to accomplish God's will; and in so doing we shall discover our own deepest fulfilment.

Taylor's third ingredient for holy living is the practice of the presence of God. We may do this anywhere, for God is everywhere, in the beauty of creation as much as in the lives of our neighbours:

> God is wholly in every place, included in no place; not bound with cords except those of love... we may imagine God to be as the air and

◆ **Engraving of Jeremy Taylor.**

the sea, and we all enclosed in his circle,
wrapped up in the lap of his infinite nature;
or as infants in the wombs of their pregnant
mothers: and we can no more be removed from
the presence of God, than from our own being.[49]

Taylor's world-view is frequently pessimistic: he
is acutely sensitive to the terrible and seemingly
random sorrows that afflict humanity; and this
leads him to offer wise guidance on seeking to live
this life in the light and anticipation of the next
(see his *Holy Dying*). But this does not mean we
should be craven, or gloomy, as Christians:

> He that means to please God by his faith, must
> have his faith begotten in him by the Spirit of
> God and proper arguments of religion; he must
> profess it without fear, he must dare to die
> for it, and resolve to live according to its
> institution; he must grow more confident and
> more holy, have fewer doubtings and more
> virtues, he must be resolute and constant.[50]

Prayer is hard work; and we must persevere in it
in the face of disappointment. Taylor's reflections
here are a vigorous antidote to much twentieth-
century consumerist assumption that everything
must happen instantly:

> He that prays to recover a family from an
> hereditary curse, or to reverse a sentence of
> God, to cancel a decree of heaven gone out
> against his friend; he that would heal the sick
> with his prayer, or with his devotion prevail
> against an army, must not expect such great
> effects upon a morning or evening collect.[51]

We must keep at it, and work hard. But in the
end the spiritual life is not just drudgery: it is
what God does in and through us, and it is, or will
be, suffused with joy: 'our duty to God should be
hugely pleasing, and we should rejoice in it'.[52]
Taylor quotes the Roman philosopher Seneca on
the spiritual life: 'There is no science or art in the
world so hard as to live and die well: the professors
of other arts are vulgar and many.'[53] Few Anglican

writers have combined scholarship, wit, pastoral
shrewdness and a deep sense of compassion so
completely as Jeremy Taylor did; and few, if any,
wrote so well.

The Anglican spirit in the eighteenth century

England in the eighteenth
century was socially
more settled
than in the
seventeenth,
but spiritually
no less
troubled.
Overseas
colonies
were founded,
some of which
(in North
America)
became
independent;
at home, increasing
numbers of people
came to live in towns

◆ **Engraving of Joseph Butler.**

and cities with the impact of industrialization
and the expanding economy. It was an age of
expansion, of enlarging horizons, and unsettling
dilemmas: philosophers, scientists and historians
such as David Hume and Edward Gibbon
increasingly questioned the nature or even
the possibility of religious belief. It was also the
heyday of English Dissent; spiritual figures such
as John Wesley and Isaac Watts dominated the
religious landscape. Yet the Church of England was
not lacking in vitality and inventiveness, though
it was itself divided between 'high church', 'low
church' and Evangelical groupings. Among its

most impressive theologians was Joseph Butler (1692–1752), whose *Analogy of Religion* was to have an enduring influence because it endeavoured to show that Christian belief was thoroughly compatible with both reason and science. For Butler, so rich and varied a creation must have had an intelligent Creator; and this approach encouraged many eighteenth-century Anglicans to give a greater value to the created order than most of their predecessors had done. The poet Christopher Smart reflected on the theme of beauty in this exquisite hymn for a young girl:

Christ, keep me from the self-survey
   Of beauties all thine own;
If there is beauty let me pray,
   And praise the Lord alone.

Pray – that I may the fiend withstand,
   Where'er his serpents be:
Praise – that the Lord's almighty hand
   Is manifest in me.

It is not so – my features are
   Much meaner than the rest;
A glow-worm cannot be a star,
   And I am plain at best.

Then come, my love, thy grace impart,
   Great Saviour of mankind;
O come, and purify my heart,
   And beautify my mind.

Then will I thy carnations nurse,
   And cherish every rose;
And empty to the poor my purse,
   Till grace to glory grows.
(from *Hymns for the Amusement of Children*, no. 11)

William Law (1686–1761)

Not all Anglican writers were so positive: William Law, whose *Serious Call to a Devout and Holy Life* (1729) was to attain the status of a spiritual classic, took a far more introspective view of spirituality. A prominent eighteenth-century English Anglican, he represents something of a reaction against contemporary interest in science and exploration; and where Butler embraced that interest, Law raised the drawbridge and effectively withdrew to a rigorous and interior view of the spiritual life. His later work, profoundly influenced by the esoteric German theologian Jakob Boehme, was marred by a speculative and relentlessly otherworldly tone. Even so, he insisted on seeing Christian faith as affecting every aspect of a person's life; and there is a heartwarming ecumenism and compassion in much of his writing.

Law sought to respond to the challenges of an increasingly secular society with an integrated but introspective Christian faith. In his attack on the theatre (which was immensely popular in eighteenth-century London), he wrote to an imaginary opponent, Jucunda:

> You are for a Religion that consists in Modes and Forms of Worship, that is tied to *Times* and *Places*, that only takes up a little of your time on *Sundays*, and leaves you all the Week to do as you please. But all this, *Jucunda*, is nothing. The Scripture has not said in vain, *He that is in Christ is a new Creature*. All the Law and the Gospel are in vain to you: all Sacraments, Devotions, Doctrines, and Ordinances, are to no purpose, unless they make you this *new Creature* in all the Actions of your Life.[54]

What really interested Law was the nature of Christianity as an agent for real interior change, not for mere superficial improvement in etiquette (another eighteenth-century preoccupation):

> Christianity is not a *School*, for the teaching of moral Virtue, the polishing of our Manners, or forming us to live a Life of this World with Decency and Gentility. It is deeper and more divine in its Designs, and has much nobler Ends than these, it implies an *entire Change* of Life, a Dedication of ourselves, our Souls and Bodies unto God, in the strictest and highest Sense of the Words.[55]

For Law, the mainspring of this change is a recovery of the biblical virtue of childlikeness:

> One peculiar Condition of Infants is this, that they have everything to learn... It is in this Sense, that we are chiefly to become as Infants, to be as though that we had everything to learn... to pretend to no Wisdom of our own, but be ready to pursue that Happiness which God in Christ proposes to us, and to accept it with such Simplicity of Mind, as Children, that have nothing of our own to oppose to it.[56]

And he offers all Christians, of every age, a searching question to answer:

> I cannot see why every *Gentleman*, *Merchant*, or *Soldier*, should not put these questions seriously to himself: *What is the best thing for me to intend and drive at in all my actions? How shall I do to make the most of human life? What ways shall I wish that I had taken, when I am leaving the world?*[57]

Samuel Johnson (1709–84)

Perhaps the single most famous Englishman of the eighteenth century was also one of the greatest Anglicans of any age: Samuel Johnson, whose erudition and wit were balanced by a profound spirituality and a pervasive melancholy induced in large part by the early death of his dear wife Tetty. Johnson's piety was never self-regarding or pompous; and even when depression clouded his spiritual horizons he never lost a sense of playfulness. In January 1764 he visited a friend in Lincolnshire, and, while walking at the top of a very steep hill, suddenly made an extraordinary decision, as his friend later recalled:

> Poor, dear Dr Johnson, when he came to this spot, turned to look down the hill, and said he was determined 'to take a roll down'. When we understood what he meant to do, we endeavoured to dissuade him; but he was

◆ *Portrait of Dr Samuel Johnson* (c. 1783), by John Opie (1761–1807).

resolute, saying, he had not had a roll for a long time; and taking out of his lesser pockets whatever might be in them – keys, pencil, purse, or pen-knife – and laying himself parallel with the edge of the hill, he actually descended, turning himself over and over till he came to the bottom.[58]

The centre of Johnson's spiritual life was an unflinchingly honest concern for the truth; and it was his steadfast refusal to avoid confronting that truth, however unwelcome it might be, which gave his piety its strength and resilience. When his wife died in 1752, he wrote this prayer:

> Forgive me, O merciful Lord, all my sins, and enable me to begin and perfect that reformation which I promised her, and to persevere in that resolution, which she

implored thee to continue, in the purposes which I recorded in thy sight, when she lay dead before me, in obedience to thy laws, and faith in thy word. And now, O Lord, release me from my sorrow…[59]

His intellectual integrity caused him uncertainty as to whether or not he should pray for those who had died; so, a year after Tetty's death, he wrote in his diary: 'I kept this day as the anniversary of my Tetty's death with prayer & tears in the morning. In the evening I prayed for her conditionally if it were lawful.' Yet sorrow was not the only ingredient in his spirituality, as we have seen; both wit and sadness were anchored in his lifelong determination to live without illusion. In 1758 he wrote to his Lincolnshire friend, criticizing him gently for lamenting the death in action of an English general:

The only reason why we lament a soldier's death is that we think he might have lived longer, yet this cause of grief is common to many other kinds of death which are not so passionately bewailed. The truth is that every death is violent which is the effect of accident, every death which is not gradually brought on by the miseries of age, or when life is extinguished for any other reason [than] that it is burnt out… Let us endeavour to see things as they are, and then enquire whether we ought to complain. Whether to see life as it is will give us much consolation I know not, but the consolation which is drawn from truth, if any there be, is solid and durable; that which may be derived from error must be like its original, fallacious and fugitive.[60]

Johnson believed that we pray *in order to* discover trust in God, rather than as a result of a trust already experienced:

Trust in God… is to be obtained only by repentance, obedience, and supplication, not by nourishing in our hearts a confused idea of the goodness of God, or a firm persuasion that we are in a state of grace; by which some have been deceived.[61]

It was precisely in this determination to refuse all false comforts and seek only a spirituality that honestly confronted the ambiguities and sorrows of human life that Johnson's importance lies.

The Evangelicals in the eighteenth and nineteenth centuries

Butler's rational theology and Johnson's thoughtful piety were two possible reactions to the growing challenge represented by secular and scientific thought. Another was a determined attempt to recover the fullness of the gospel by setting revelation above reason, and the supernatural above the scientific. The Evangelical movement, as it came to be known, was deeply influenced by the Protestant Reformers, the Puritans, the European Pietists, and of course by the founders of Methodism. It gradually came to form a major ingredient in Anglicanism; and its impact was by no means only an inward one. Evangelicals such as William Wilberforce played a crucial role in achieving the abolition of slavery in England, and in influencing government policy at the highest levels during the eighteenth and nineteenth centuries. The movement as a whole helped Anglicanism to recover its nerve at a time when the spiritual initiative might otherwise have gone altogether to Dissenters and Roman Catholics. Three figures in particular represent the finest flowering of English Anglican Evangelicalism: William Cowper, John Newton (see box, p. 269) and Charles Simeon.

Women spiritual writers in the eighteenth century

The eighteenth century saw significant improvements in the education of women, though this was at least in part intended to enable them to serve their husbands better. Even so, it had the effect of producing many able and highly intelligent women who in turn challenged many accepted traditions and assumptions.

Sarah Trimmer (1741–1810)

Sarah Trimmer was actively engaged in social reform, and wrote religious books designed to improve both children's and adults' understanding of Christianity. She denounced the sufferings of the poor and in the process espoused a spirituality worthy of the Old Testament prophets:

> It really is a scandal to the nation, to see such numbers of the common people in extreme indigence, while the plenty and riches of the land, enable the higher ranks to indulge in all the conveniencies and luxuries of life. Every Parish is a large family, and it behoves the heads of it to see that each individual in it has food and raiment, or the means of procuring them at least; and that provision is made for their instruction in such things as concern their temporal and spiritual interests.[62]

She believed that true holiness was rooted in a happy family life, and that husbands had a particular responsibility in ensuring that every member of the household joined together in daily common prayer.[63] And, like many others, she strongly encouraged a proper observance of the Christian sabbath: it is neglect of this that leads to 'domestic evil'.[64]

Hannah More (1745–1833)

Hannah More was the daughter of a schoolmaster and one of the most influential figures in the movement to improve the religious education of children. Like Sarah Trimmer, she was deeply committed to social reform and the moral and spiritual lives of her contemporaries; and her works were immensely popular. Her book *Practical Piety* (1811) is rooted in her conviction that all healthy religion is based on an internal principle:

> Genuine religion demands not merely an external profession of our allegiance to God, but an inward devotedness of ourselves to his service. It is not a recognition, but a dedication. It puts the Christian into a new state of things, a new condition of being… The happiness of a Christian does not consist in mere feelings which may deceive, nor in frames which can only be occasional; but in a settled, calm conviction that God and eternal things have the predominance in his heart.[65]

She defines 'practical Christianity' as 'the actual operation of Christian principles… It is "exercising ourselves unto godliness".'[66] Among the principles thus to be practised is forgiveness, which she describes as 'the economy of the heart'.[67] Above all, she wants to encourage a piety rooted in the specific willingness to live a moral and compassionate life: 'It is by our conformity to Christ, that we must prove ourselves Christians,' says a character in

◆ **Engraving of Hannah More, by E. Scriven.**

one of her edifying stories (*Stories for Persons in the Middle Ranks*). She had no interest in a distant or speculative spirituality that was of no earthly use; and, in another of her stories, the intelligent but ineffectual philosopher Mr Fantom is criticized by Mr Trueman:

'Well, Mr Fantom, you are a wonderful man to keep up such a stock of benevolence at so small an expense. To love mankind so dearly, and yet avoid all opportunities of doing them good; to have such a noble zeal for the millions, and to feel so little compassion for the units; to long to free empires and enlighten kingdoms, and yet deny instruction to your own village, and comfort to your own family. Surely none but a philosopher could indulge so much philanthropy and so much frugality at the same time.'[68]

More was no radical; and she was fully at ease in the established church of her day. But she was far in advance of many of her contemporaries in condemning any kind of religious intolerance because it hindered a growth in true piety:

Every man who is sincerely in earnest to advance the interests of religion, will have acquired such a degree of candour, as to become indifferent by whom good is done, or who has the reputation of doing it, provided it be actually done.[69]

And she conceived of such piety as rooted in a prayer at once direct, honest and passionate. For her, prayer is

the application of want to him who only can relieve it; the voice of sin to him who alone can pardon it. It is the urgency of poverty, the prostration of humility, the fervency of penitence, the confidence of trust. It is not eloquence, but earnestness, not the definition of helplessness, but the feeling of it; not figures of speech, but compunction of soul. It is the 'Lord, save us, we perish' of drowning Peter; the cry of faith to the ear of mercy.[70]

◆ **A family saying grace before a meal:**
Grace Before Meat, **by Sir David Wilkie
(1785–1841).**

William Cowper (1731–1800)

William Cowper began his adult life as a lawyer, but serious psychiatric illness as well as a profound religious conversion led him to spend much of his time writing poetry. Cowper's hymns and poems are gentle and reflective, but reflect a pervasive Evangelical faith rooted in his own personal conviction that God was in control of all that happened, however grim life might sometimes be:

Judge not the Lord by feeble sense,
But trust him for his Grace;
Behind a frowning Providence,
He hides a Smiling face.
('Light Shining Out of Darkness')

This conviction did not prevent him from suffering anguish over the question of whether God had saved him or not. One of his hymns explores this dilemma with searching honesty:

The LORD will happiness divine
*   On contrite hearts bestow:*
Then tell me, gracious GOD, is mine
*   A contrite heart, or no?…*

I sometimes think myself inclin'd
*   To love thee, if I could;*
But often feel another mind,
*   Averse to all that's good.*

My best desires are faint and few,
*   I fain would strive for more;*
But when I cry, 'My strength renew,'
*   Seem weaker than before.*

Thy saints are comforted I know
*   And love thy house of pray'r;*
I therefore go where others go,
*   But find no comfort there.*

◆ **Slum scene, Drury Lane, London.** Cowper was passionate about social justice and poverty in urban England.

John Newton (1725–1807)

John Newton had an extraordinary life, and his own autobiographical *Authentic Narrative* describes it with vigour and passion in the manner of his Puritan forebears. After years as a merchant sailor, slave trader and surveyor, he was converted through the preaching of George Whitefield, and was eventually ordained in 1764: he became incumbent of Olney, in Hertfordshire, where he offered hospitality and support to Cowper. In 1779 he became parish priest of a city church in London, where he had an outstanding ministry as an advocate of the abolition of the slave trade. Newton's spirituality is strongly biblical in imagery and content, and the fruit of his own personal prayer life and experience. Some of his hymns (notably 'Amazing Grace') have become established classics in the Christian church.

Newton was convinced that religious faith was itself a gift from God, and in no way the result of rational assent, 'such as we give to a proposition in Euclid',[71] he remarked scornfully. But he does stress that the life of faith is often a hard struggle (see below). The crucial point for him is that faith is indeed a *life*, transforming the whole person and demanding of us a radical unselfing: 'As grace prevails,' he wrote in a letter, 'self is renounced.'[72] And the results are self-evident:

> grace, like the salt in the cruse,
> When cast in the spring of the soul,
> A wonderful change will produce,
> Diffusing new life through the whole...

Even though faith is ultimately God's free gift, we can prepare ourselves to receive it by turning away from sin and praying: 'For this waiting upon God [the would-be Christian] has a moral ability; and if he persevere thus in seeking, the promise is sure, that he shall not seek in vain.'[73] Christ comes to us, makes us his own by adopting us as his children, whereupon, 'we are united to him in whom all the fullness of the Godhead

substantially dwells, and all the riches of divine wisdom, power, and love, are treasured up'.[74]

And this union with Christ is no private or exclusive privilege: on the contrary, the life of the true Christian 'is divided between serving his country in public, and wrestling for it in private'[75] – a vision that Newton himself sought to make his own. Such a life will transform others as well as oneself; and it demands of us all we have to give:

> When my prayers are a burden and task,
> No wonder I little receive;
> O Lord, make me willing to ask,
> Since Thou art so ready to give...

Prayer in despair

Notwithstanding all my complaints, it is still true that Jesus died and rose again, that he ever liveth to make intercession, and is able to save to the uttermost. But, on the other hand, to think of that joy of heart in which some of his people live, and to compare it with that apparent deadness and want of spirituality which I feel, this makes me mourn. However, I think there is a scriptural distinction between faith and feeling, grace and comfort; they are not inseparable, and perhaps when together, the degree of the one is not often the just measure of the other. But though I pray that I may be ever longing and panting for the light of his countenance, yet I would be so far satisfied, as to believe the Lord has wise and merciful reasons for keeping me so short of the comforts which he has taught me to desire and value more than the light of the sun.[76]

O make this heart rejoice, or ach;
Decide this doubt for me;
And if it be not broken, break,
And heal it, if it be.

Despite his uncertainties, and the terrible
legacy of his own repeated mental breakdowns,
Cowper's spirituality remained firmly optimistic.
Like many Evangelicals, he showed relatively
little interest in the created order, but he was
passionately concerned with social justice,
especially with the increasing immorality and
poverty in England's cities, and with the evils of
the slave trade. Above all, he wanted his fellow
Christians never to take for granted the blessings
they had received:

Have you no words? ah, think again,
Words flow apace when you complain;
And fill your fellow-creature's ear
With the sad tale of all your care.

Were half the breath thus vainly spent,
To heav'n in supplication sent;
Your cheerful song would oft'ner be,
'Hear what the LORD has done for me!'
('Exhortation to Prayer' verses 5–6)

Charles Simeon (1759–1836)

Charles Simeon was one of the outstanding
Evangelicals of his day, and, as a central figure in
the University of Cambridge for the whole of his
adult life, he exerted an enormous influence on
the students who flocked to hear him preach. Like
Newton, he too was deeply concerned with social
justice, and was instrumental in founding the
Church Missionary Society in 1799.

Simeon emphasized the importance of
recognizing our own sinfulness, as inheritors of
the sin of Adam and Eve, if in turn we can be open
to receive the free gift of God's salvation. He
follows classical Christian teaching in arguing that
we are created in God's image, an image which is
both intellectual and moral,[77] and, although that

◆ **Opposite:** *The Christening* (1863), by Emma Brownlow
(1832–1905).

image has been defaced by sin, it imparts to us a
longing which God alone can satisfy: 'The true
Christian will affix no limits to his exertions; he
will set no bounds to his heavenly desires.'[78] Hence,
like Newton, he sees the spiritual life of those who
have been set free through Christ as something
that transforms them totally: 'It is not to preach a
scanty morality that we are called; but to publish
the glad tidings of a full and free salvation.'[79] Note
the emphasis on fullness: Evangelicals countered
the inexorable rise of secularism and scepticism by
a full-blooded restatement of biblical Christianity
in all its unbridled power; and for Simeon there
was literally no limit to what the Christian could
become, 'no measure of holiness with which we
should be satisfied'.[80]

And the means by which we experience
this transforming power is by being born again.
Simeon manages to be entirely loyal to Anglican
teaching on the propriety of infant baptism while
distinguishing it from the new birth: baptism is a
change of *state*, 'for by it we become entitled to all
the blessings of the new covenant. But it is not a
change of *nature*.'[81] After all, as Simeon goes on to
say, Simon Magus was baptized but did not change
(Acts 8:9–24). It is by being born again in Christ
that we are transformed in our innermost nature.
Then, and only then, Christianity becomes not an
outward formalism, but an all-embracing source of
delight: 'Religion is, indeed, a source of joy.'[82]

The Oxford movement

If Evangelicalism represented one reaction against
the tides of secularism and apathy, another was
represented by a movement that had its origins
among a group of academies at the University
of Oxford in the early years of the nineteenth
century. The Oxford movement, as it came to be

called, was not, however, simply a reaction against secularism in general: rather it was an attempt, no less all-embracing than that of the Evangelicals, to recover an authentic and full-blooded Christianity in order to prevent England from becoming a moral and spiritual vacuum. But whereas the Evangelicals sought guidance from the Bible alone, the Anglo-Catholics or Tractarians (as they came to be called) sought it from the teaching of the early Christian centuries, and above all from the great patristic theologians whose inheritance they believed (like Hooker and Andrewes) to be crucial to the Anglican spirit.

The Oxford movement was centred upon three scholarly priests: John Henry Newman (1801–90), Edward Bouverie Pusey (1800–82) and John Keble (1792–1866). Newman's resignation from the incumbency of the University Church at Oxford in 1843, and his subsequent reception into the Roman Catholic Church, left the movement leaderless, for neither Pusey nor Keble were charismatic leaders. But their combination of solid theology, powerful preaching and wise spiritual guidance bequeathed an enduring legacy that not only restored a distinctively Catholic dimension to the Anglican spirit, but also generated a new concern with social justice at a time when the burgeoning industrial cities were posing an enormous challenge to church and society alike.

In 1840 Pusey set down in a letter what he took to be the central principles of the new movement: an emphasis on the two sacraments of baptism and the Eucharist, as well as on episcopacy; a 'high estimate of the visible church' (by contrast to the Evangelical emphasis on the individual's relationship with God); 'regard for the visible part of devotion, such as the decoration of the house of God, which acts insensibly on the mind'; 'reverence for and deference to the Ancient Church... instead of the Reformers, as the ultimate expounder of the meaning of our Church'; and 'the necessity of continued repentance of past sins'. These principles affected every aspect of the spirituality of the Oxford movement.

For Pusey, infant baptism 'engrafts us onto the true vine', while the main purpose of the Eucharist 'is the support and enlargement of life' – and not just any life, but the life of Christ himself in us. The perfection for which Paul speaks of all of creation groaning (Romans 8:22) is the perfection of union with Christ through the mystery of the incarnation and the Eucharist. And by regular participation in the Eucharist we experience 'a union with God so close; that we cannot mostly, I suppose, imagine to ourselves, how we could daily thus be in Heaven, and in our daily business here below'.[83] Furthermore, frequent communion brings about a real change in the worshipper, making us more conscious of God's living presence and more inclined to live a holy life.

The Tractarians' emphasis on the importance of

◆ **Edward Bouverie Pusey caricatured in *Vanity Fair* (1875), by Carlo Pelligrini.**

the visible church led to a recovery of ritual and ceremonial, and colourful, ordered liturgy; but it also gave Anglo-Catholic spirituality a strongly corporate tone not always present in Evangelicalism. For Keble, the church is 'our Mother',[84] and he and his fellow Tractarians devoted much effort to stressing the separateness of the church from the state. The Oxford movement gave a powerful stimulus to church-building, and many of the new or restored churches represent, in their flamboyant and neo-medieval Gothic grandeur, an unapologetic challenge to the modern world, the soaring spires reaching above the factory chimneys and designed to bring hope and sustenance to the mushrooming slums.

The Oxford movement was also deeply concerned with interior transformation, and the Tractarians sought to offer wisdom and guidance for the spiritual life. Conscience played a major role in their teaching, as did careful and regular self-examination: 'The remembrance of a life well spent, and a heart carefully guarded and kept pure, is the greatest possible help in our devotions to God.'[85] Like the Evangelicals, the Tractarians stressed the importance of an integrated spirituality, a pattern of religious life which united head and heart, mind and body, the will and the emotions. But where the Evangelicals tended to stress the importance of *obedience* to Christ, Tractarians tended to stress *union* with him. For Pusey, the inner life of God as trinity is in itself intimate union, and at our baptisms 'we had, though knowing it not, the first seed of spiritual life imparted to us. This union is increased whenever we pray to God, for we call him into himself...'[86]

Prayer is 'calling God into himself', for God already dwells within us in virtue of our sharing his own life in the Eucharist. It is an entering

into the light of Eternal Brightness, to be kindled with the glow of everlasting Love, to enter, a bidden guest, into the unseen glory of the Divine Presence, and there, face to Face, to ask him who is more ready to give than we to ask.[87]

◆ **Interior of the Divinity School, Oxford, illustration from the *History of Oxford* (1813), engraved by F.C. Lewis (1779–1856).**

Prayer is thus always more than simply asking for things. It is praise and adoration, and a simple delighting in someone's presence, as another prominent Tractarian, Henry Liddon, put it:

> When we seek the company of our friends, we do not seek it simply with the view of getting something from them; it is a pleasure to be with them, to be talking to them at all, or about anything... So it is with the soul, when dealing with the Friend of friends – with God.[88]

This emphasis on friendship with God is one of the many attractive features of Tractarian spirituality. Another is its emphasis on the presence of God in creation – supremely in the Eucharist, but also, as a result of the incarnation, in the world all around us. Pusey stressed that creation is stained through human misuse of it – a strikingly modern insight; but 'all nature, having suffered together, shall be restored together'; for 'things animate and inanimate, as being the works of God... bear in themselves some likeness to their Maker, and traces of his Hands'.[89] The influence of the Romantic movement on the Tractarians is perceptible here, and some of Keble's poetry reflects the spirit of Coleridge and Wordsworth.

More generally, the concern of its members to recover the integrity of the patristic age inevitably gave the Oxford movement an academic tone which limited its accessibility. But its influence on Anglican worship, and the stimulus it gave to the work of priests and people in some of the poorest areas of Great Britain, were both immense. And the renewal of the monastic life in the country during the nineteenth century was another of the movement's major achievements; many of the new orders, such as the Community of the Resurrection at Mirfield in Yorkshire, or the Society of St John the Evangelist at Oxford itself, went on to exert an immense influence in church and society, in England and across the world, in the twentieth century.

Conclusion

The beginning of the twentieth century saw an Anglicanism vastly different from the fledgling Church of England conceived by Cranmer and Henry VIII. No longer, even in England, could the church enjoy so privileged a relationship with the state (though Anglican leaders, such as Janani Luwum of Uganda, would still suffer for their faith in the years ahead). No longer could Anglicanism be assumed to be the only, or even the dominant, spiritual tradition in increasingly pluralistic societies. Yet there were important continuities; and these helped to equip Anglicanism to face the uncertainties of the twentieth century with hope. The Anglican spirit was still, as it had always been, one which refused to separate the sacred from the secular, the head from the heart, the individual from the community, the Protestant from the Catholic, the word from the sacrament. The weaknesses of so comprehensive an approach are well known: it has been justly pointed out that some of the greatest religious figures in the centuries we have just explored (John Bunyan, John Wesley, John Henry Newman) rejected the Anglican tradition precisely because they felt it to be too greatly wedded to the spirit and structures of the age, rather than to the transforming truths of the Christian gospel. But the Anglican spirit – eirenic, thoughtful, integrated, rooted in scripture

and tradition – gave depth and nourishment and vision to countless Christians across the world through some of the most turbulent centuries in Christian history. It was not the first, and would not be the last, occasion on which a creature born in the unlikeliest conditions of selfishness and partisan greed could blossom into unimaginably fruitful life. And that in itself is no small testimony to its spiritual character and power.

9

The Protestant Tradition in America

(17th to 19th centuries)

Stephen R. Graham

Timeline

1600	1588–1649	John Winthrop
	c. 1603–83	Roger Williams
	c. 1612–72	Anne Bradstreet
	1630s	**Puritan migration from England**
	1631–1705	Michael Wigglesworth
	1644–1718	William Penn
1700	c. 1645–1729	Edward Taylor
	1703–58	Jonathan Edwards
	1714–70	George Whitefield
	1718–47	David Brainerd
	1720–72	John Woolman
	1730–60	**The Great Awakening**
	1736–84	Ann Lee
	1743–1826	Thomas Jefferson
	1745–1816	Francis Asbury
	1748–84	Henry Alline
	1760–1831	Richard Allen
	1776	**Declaration of Independence from Britain**
	1780–1842	William Ellery Channing
	1792–1875	Charles G. Finney
	1797–1878	Charles Hodge
1800	c. 1797–1883	Sojourner Truth
	1800–30	**The Second Great Awakening**
	1802–76	Horace Bushnell
	1803–82	Ralph Waldo Emerson
	1803–86	John Williamson Nevin
	1805–44	Joseph Smith
	1807–74	Phoebe Palmer
	1809–65	Abraham Lincoln
	1811–96	Harriet Beecher Stowe
	1813–87	Henry Ward Beecher
	1819–93	Philip Schaff
	1819–1910	Julia Ward Howe
	1820–1915	Fanny J. Crosby
	1830–86	Emily Dickinson
	1832–1911	Hannah Whitall Smith
	1837–99	Dwight L. Moody
1850	1839–98	Frances Willard
	1861–65	**The American Civil War**
	1861–1918	Walter Rauschenbusch
	1865	**Abolition of slavery (13th Amendment)**
	1870–1922	William J. Seymour
	1890–1920	**The Third Great Awakening**
	1906–1909	**Height of the Azusa Street Revival**

The great church historian of the nineteenth century, Philip Schaff, once described Christianity in America as a 'motley sampler' of all church history. Everything remotely Christian that was to be found in the old world, every church and sect, had appeared in the New World. In addition, he said, these Americans were an innovative group and they had invented movements and sects that their European forebears had not even imagined. Any dreamer, Schaff lamented,

who has, or fancies that he has, some inward experience and a ready tongue, may persuade himself that he is called to be a reformer; and so proceed at once, in his spiritual vanity and pride, to a revolutionary rupture with the historical life of the church, to which he holds himself immeasurably superior. He builds himself of a night accordingly a new chapel, in which now for the first time since the age of the apostles a pure congregation is to be formed; baptizes his followers with his own name… and with all this, though utterly unprepared to understand a single book, is not ashamed to appeal continually to the scriptures, as having been sealed entirely, or in large part, to the understanding of eighteen centuries… till now at last God has been pleased to kindle the true light in an obscure corner of the New World![1]

The same could be said of experimentation in spirituality. American Christians drew on the riches of the Christian past. Like Europeans, they read Thomas à Kempis and Augustine. Some of them discovered Julian of Norwich and Teresa of Avila. What they did with those resources, however, frequently took novel forms. Their new place, with its wide open spaces and bounty, their new neighbours representing ultimately every people from around the globe, their optimism, individualism, social mobility, and especially their new political philosophy – which shaped their understanding of civil and church government – caused them to discard much of the past and seek ever new forms for spirituality.

A helpful typology for categorizing – always a dangerous endeavour, especially when speaking of spirituality – is that of Geoffrey Wainwright, based on the now classic models of 'Christ and Culture' developed by H. Richard Niebuhr.[2] Each type has been present throughout the church's history; four of them have emerged in nuanced forms within the American context.

Christ against culture

According to this model, the world to come and this world are in irresolvable conflict. Those who pursue this type of spirituality seek distance from the world and its systems. Martyrdom is the most extreme example of this type and the dominant

◆ *Across the Continent*, one of a series of 19th-century American lithographs by Nathaniel Currier and James Ives.

image of Christ is the suffering servant whose own opposition to the world's systems led to his death. This counter-cultural form of spirituality appeared in radical reform groups like the Mennonites and Hutterites, in outcast minorities like some Baptist groups or the Quakers, and in more recent groups like the early Pentecostals.

The Christ of culture

When the church aligns itself closely with its host culture in an attempt to ensure relevance, or, worse, out of indifference to its prophetic calling, it fits the model of 'the Christ of culture'. In complete contrast to the Christ-against-culture model, the spirituality of the age dominates the church to the point that it becomes difficult to tell the difference. Nearly every form of spirituality faces the danger of drifting into cultural conformity, and even while rejecting one cultural stream, may actually embrace another. For example, the holiness spirituality of Phoebe Palmer and Hannah Whitall Smith shunned the 'worldliness' that they believed characterized so many within and outside the church, but it remained unconsciously captive to a form of comfortable, middle-class, respectable Christianity that fitted very easily within the culture of mid-nineteenth-century American society.

Christ and culture in paradox

This type of spirituality 'strikes the apocalyptic note of conflict' between a prophetic Christianity and its host cultures.[3] Not as negative as Christ against culture, this model is guided by hope, but is realistic about the challenges of an evil world. The prime example of this type of spirituality is that of the African-American slaves who lived in hope of exodus and equality, but for most that dream was deferred to the next world.

Christ the transformer of culture

Many of the spiritualities profiled in this chapter fit best within this category, because the activist character of the great majority of American institutions and people makes the idea of transformation of society a leading image. The Puritans, with their vision of a 'city on a hill', the post-millennial revivalists in the eighteenth and nineteenth centuries, and late-nineteenth and early-twentieth-century social gospel reformers, all believed that their mission was to create a new society on earth.

American Christians have always moved between the poles of the interior spirituality of the heart and the outward spirituality of action. The balance has tended to move in the direction of the latter. Contemplation has largely given way to activity.

Having said that, though, it is important to re-emphasize the thoroughgoing pluralism of the American spiritual landscape. Within every type, there are many variations, and for every rule there are scores of exceptions. And this is only within the 'Protestant' camp, saying nothing about Catholic and Orthodox bodies, or the myriad spiritualities outside the Christian orbit. What follows, then, includes only a selection of the Protestant stream of American spirituality.

Puritans in colonial America

Puritanism represents a type of Protestant spirituality that adapted many of the forms of an earlier Catholic spirituality while altering its language. Puritans and other Protestants spoke of 'religious experience' and 'sanctification' rather than mysticism and spiritual direction, but the paths were often similar. The Puritans believed, however, that spirituality developed best within normal family life and the ordinary routines of work, worship and the home. Puritan saints were not persons of extraordinary gifts living separated from the world and engaged in mystic contemplation, but ordinary believers who took their Christian lives with proper seriousness. This shift to spirituality within ordinary life was one of the most important contributions of Puritanism to the development of a distinctively 'American' spirituality.

◆ **Opposite: John Winthrop aboard the *Arabella*.**

The spirituality of the Holy Commonwealth

This emphasis on 'ordinary' saints is evident in the life and writings of John Winthrop (1588–1649), first governor of the Massachusetts Bay Colony. Elected in 1629 before the company set sail to the New World, Winthrop would serve the new colony for the greater part of the next twenty years until his death. He shared the Puritan vision to make private and public piety one, to nurture lives that would contribute to the Holy Commonwealth they intended to establish in America and make it conform to God's design. Sailing across the Atlantic Ocean on the *Arabella*, Winthrop encouraged the company, in the words of the Old Testament prophet Micah, 'to do justly, to love

mercy, to walk humbly with our God'. His sermon, 'A Model of Christian Charity', insisted that theirs must be a community bound together by love:

> We must love brotherly without dissimulation; we must love one another with a pure heart fervently. We must bear one another's burthens. We must not look only on our own things, but also on the things of our brethren, neither must we think that the Lord will bear with such failings at our hands as he doth from those among whom we have lived.[4]

Winthrop believed that the Puritans had been given a special commission by God based on God's covenant agreement with them. Their commonwealth would be like a 'city upon a hill' which others would use as a model for what society could be on earth.

Winthrop's vision was threatened, however, by internal strife, much of it generated by a similarly devout Puritan, who would be regarded as a saint only by later generations. Roger Williams (c. 1603–83) came to Massachusetts in 1631 and almost immediately found himself at odds with the leadership of the colony and church. Williams's desire for purity led him to seek a clean separation from what he regarded as the 'tyrannical church order in England'. Williams castigated the congregations in Massachusetts for their ties to the corrupt Church of England, their state coercion in religious matters, and for stealing land from the Indians. The Massachusetts authorities banned Williams in 1635, and after a time he purchased land from the Indians for a new settlement, Providence, which ultimately led to a new colony, Rhode Island. From the beginning, this new colony became a haven for religious dissenters, having as its foundation complete religious liberty.

Williams's spirituality is most clearly revealed in a book of reflections on the spiritual life he wrote as a letter to his wife after her recovery from serious illness. His chapter 'Helps to Preserve Spiritual Health and Cheerfulness' captures many of the dominant themes in Puritan spirituality.[5]

In silent night when rest I took,
For sorrow neer I did not look,
I waken'd was with thundring nois
And Piteous shreiks of dreadfull voice.
That fearfull sound of fire and fire,
Let no man know is my Desire.

I, starting up, the light did spye,
And to my God my heart did cry
To strengthen me in my distresse
And not to leave me succourlesse.
Then coming out beheld a space,
The flame consume my dwelling place.

And, when I could no longer look,
I blest his Name that gave and took,
That layd my goods now in the dust:
Yea so it was, and so 'twas just.
It was his own: it was not mine;
Far be it that I should repine...

Then streight I gin my heart to chide,
And didst thy wealth on earth abide?
Didst fix thy hope on mouldring dust,
The arm of flesh didst make thy trust?
Raise up thy thoughts above the skye
That dunghill mists away may flie.

Thou hast an house on high erect
Fram'd by that mighty Architect,
With glory richly furnished,
Stands permanent tho' this bee fled.
It's purchased, and paid for too
By him who hath enough to doe.

A Prise so vast as is unknown,
Yet, by his Gift, is made thine own.
Ther's wealth enough, I need no more;
Farewell my Pelf, farewell my Store.
The world no longer let me Love,
My hope and Treasure lyes Above.[6]

The chapter is shaped around seven 'helps':

(1) Self-examination [is] a means of spiritual preservation.
(2) Prayer with Fasting is an undoubted means of Christian Health and Cheerfulness.
(3) Avoid cold societies and places destitute of Christ Jesus.
(4) God's children must watch against feeding too much on worldly comforts.
(5) Meditate upon the joys that are to come.
(6) Bitter and untoothsome things may be of a blessed and wholesome use.
(7) The meditation of death.

Any Puritan could have affirmed these – though few would have identified Puritan congregations as 'cold societies' as Williams might have. Williams reminded his wife (and readers since) that, 'This is our seedtime, of which every minute is precious, and that as our sowing is, so shall be our eternal harvest.'[7]

Anne Bradstreet
(c. 1612–72)

Perhaps the finest exemplar of Puritan spirituality growing out of the regular cycles of life in the household is Anne Bradstreet. Born in Northampton, England, Anne married Simon Bradstreet in 1628 and the couple joined Winthrop and the others on board the *Arabella* in 1630 for the journey to the New World. In the midst of a busy home life, Anne found time to write poetry, risking the disapproval of most of her neighbours:

I am obnoxious to each carping tongue
Who says my hand a needle better fits.

Charles E. Hambrick-Stowe has noted Bradstreet's similarities to Teresa of Avila. Both women describe a pilgrimage of faith that included a wayward youth, serious illness that shook them out of spiritual lethargy, the influence of spiritual

◆ **The Sea Monster and the Beast with the Lamb's Horns,**
from a series of woodcuts by Albrecht Dürer (1471–1528).

writers, and times of spiritual dryness followed
by spiritual renewal. The key difference between
them, though, illustrates a fundamental difference
between Catholic and Puritan spirituality: Teresa
took religious vows, while Anne nurtured a
household.

Bradstreet's spirituality was shaped by loss:
loss of health, loss of children to adulthood and
grandchildren to death, and loss of her home to
fire. She wrestled with the mystery of the God
who gives all good things, but who also chastises
through afflictions and loss.

This tension is revealed with power and
poignancy in her poem written on the occasion
of the burning of her home in 1666 (see box,
opposite). Puritans frequently saw spiritual
significance in the details of life and the date
of the disaster was no exception. Revelation 13
described the satanic beast of the last days
whose sign was 666, and who 'maketh fire come
down from heaven on the earth in the sight of
men'.

Bradstreet's reflections are representative
of many mainstream Puritan views.

Edward Taylor
(c. 1645–1729)

A good example of Puritan spiritual introspection
was Puritan pastor Edward Taylor. Taylor immigrated
to New England in 1668, studied at Harvard, and
served as pastor in Westfield, Connecticut, from
1671 until his retirement in 1725.

Like mystics in the Catholic tradition, and like
a number of other Puritans, Taylor drew on the
Song of Songs for images to express his desire for
intimacy with Christ. He regularly used images
from marriage to describe the Christian's spiritual
union with the Saviour. Most revealing of his
personal spirituality is the series of meditations

he wrote over a period of forty-three years, as
preparation on Saturday evenings for preaching
and celebration of Holy Communion on Sunday,
called *Preparatory Meditations*:

Stupendious Love! All Saints Astonishment!
Bright Angells are black Motes in this Suns
Light...

My Soule had Caught an Ague, and like Hell
Her thirst did burn: she to each spring
did fly,

But this bright blazing Love did spring a Well
   Of Aqua-Vitae in the Deity,
   Which on the top of Heav'ns high Hill
      out burst
   And down came running thence t'allay
      my thirst.

But how it came, amazeth all Communion.
   Gods onely son doth hug Humanity,
   Into his very person. By which Union
   His Humane Veans its golden gutters ly.

And rather than my Soule should dy by thirst,
   These Golden Pipes, to give me drink, did
burst...

Nay, though I make no pay for this Red Wine,
And scarce do say I thank-ye-for't; strange
      thing!
Yet were thy silver skies my Beer bowle fine
I finde my Lord, would fill it to the brim.
Then make my life, Lord, to thy praise proceed
For thy rich blood, which is my Drink-Indeed.[8]

Quaker spirituality in America

From its beginnings in the 1640s under George Fox, Quaker spirituality has represented what has been called a 'religious democracy' of the Spirit. Fox and his Society of Friends affirmed the reality of direct communion with the Holy Spirit because of the 'inner light' in all human beings. Radically egalitarian, because the Spirit is in all people and can speak to and through all people, Quakers rejected many of the structures and hierarchies that characterized the societies in which they lived. Their form of worship emphasized the communal nature of the body of Christ and the community became both the context for the voice of the Spirit, and the crucible in which impulses of the Spirit were tested.

Quaker spirituality was guided by the practice of sensitizing oneself to the voice of the Spirit, called by some 'the tendering of the indwelling Christ', and the growing ability to yield oneself to that voice.

John Woolman (1720–72)

The most striking example of Quaker spirituality in the colonial period is certainly John Woolman. Nurtured in the Quaker tradition by pious parents, Woolman developed unusual sensitivity of conscience and profound awareness of the 'inner light' at an early age. Like many Quakers, among whom the practice was encouraged, Woolman recorded his experiences and thoughts in a journal where he collected many remarkable stories and 'operations of divine love' in his life. The *Journal* tells us that as a small boy he thoughtlessly threw stones at a mother robin, killing her. With horror he realized that her young would die of starvation without her to feed them, and he resolved to kill them quickly to minimize their suffering. Recalled and recorded at age thirty-six, the event obviously left a deep scar on the boy's psyche and taught him a vivid lesson of the value of life and of all God's creatures.

Woolman recorded the typical youth of 'much wild grapes' and 'backslidings', but he was 'delivered' by a serious illness, from which he feared he would not recover:

Then did darkness, horror, and amazement with full force seize me, even when my pain and distress of body were very great... I had not confidence to lift up my cries to God, whom I had thus offended; but in a deep sense of my great folly I was humbled before him. At length that word which is as a fire and a hammer broke and dissolved my rebellious heart; my cries were put up in contrition; and in the multitude of his mercies I found inward relief, and a close engagement that if he was pleased to restore my health I might walk humbly before him.[9]

David Brainerd (1718–47) and Jonathan Edwards (1703–58)

David Brainerd is best known for his work as a missionary to Native Americans in New York, Pennsylvania and New Jersey. His legacy to Puritan spirituality, however, is his *Journal* written in 1746, then edited and published by Jonathan Edwards in 1749. For Edwards, despite his youth, Brainerd provided a paradigm of saintliness and an illustration of the criteria for holiness that Edwards had set down in his *Treatise Concerning Religious Affections* in 1746. Brainerd had experienced a dramatic conversion in 1739 and went to Yale to study for the ministry. While there, his zeal led him to the unfortunate statement that one of the instructors showed no more evidence of the work of grace in his life than a chair. Following his dismissal from the school, he nonetheless was licensed to preach and began his career as a missionary. Edwards noted Brainerd's tendency to

An event that would shape much of his later life and message took place after Woolman had accepted a position as clerk and bookkeeper in a shop. One of his duties was to write basic legal documents for customers, and he was caught up short when one Quaker customer asked him to write a bill of sale for a slave. Woolman recalled that

> I gave way, and wrote it; but at the executing of it I was so afflicted in my mind, that I said before my master and the Friend that I believed slave-keeping to be a practice inconsistent with the Christian religion.[10]

Eventually, Woolman would refuse to write such documents and when writing wills, would write the rest of the document, but refuse to have anything to do with the transfer of slaves. As he began his ministry of travelling to visit Quakers in other areas, he adopted the practice of witness against slavery by providing funds to pay slaves for serving him. Eventually the example and writings of this 'quiet revolutionary' helped move the Quakers to be the first religious group in America to outlaw slavery among their membership.

Continuing his work for justice for African-Americans and Native Americans, Woolman eventually developed an understanding of the source of injustice, seeing it as

◆ **Quaker emigrants leaving London for America are seen off by Charles II in the Royal Barge off the Tower of London (1673), by C.S. Reinhart.**

the product of the insatiable human desire for luxury which caused those with many possessions to want more, with the consequence that the poor were unable to acquire what they needed for survival.

melancholy and discouragement, but believed that his spiritual maturity provided a model for serious Christians. The young missionary struggled with illness, all the while wrestling with 'spiritual pride', and chastising himself for his 'spiritual pollution' and 'childish follies', calling himself no better than 'a very good Pharisee'.

The criteria by which Edwards measured Brainerd's spirituality also reflect Edwards's own spiritual pilgrimage. Son and grandson of pastors, Edwards attended Yale and, upon graduation, became assistant to his grandfather, Solomon Stoddard, pastor of the congregation at Northampton, Massachusetts. In 1729, on Stoddard's death, Edwards became pastor at Northampton. One of the key leaders in the Great Awakening of the 1740s, Edwards regularly called for spiritual renewal in the congregation. His demand for strict admission requirements to church membership led to his dismissal from Northampton in 1750.

As one of America's greatest theological and philosophical minds and a profoundly spiritual man, Edwards not only led within the Awakening, but also provided theological categories for evaluating its effects. The *Treatise Concerning Religious Affections* is Edwards's effort to distinguish between true manifestations of spirituality and mere emotionalism. Edwards's heartfelt, yet intellectually grounded, spirituality blended heart and head with a skill and insight that would not be matched by many American Christians.

Spirituality of renewal and revival

A form of American Christianity that would come to dominate the conceptions of many and which would be a source of controversy for generations was revivalism. Revivalists and others who sought renewal within the church reshaped the conception of what it meant to become and remain Christian – as they moved within the streams of democratization (in both politics and religion), individualism, focus on conversion and concern for personal piety. Historians from the time of Philip Schaff, who wrote in the last half of the nineteenth century, have described an 'American' style of Christianity that came to dominate the thinking of many. Americans sought to distance themselves from their European pasts. Their focus was on the present and the future as they constructed their new order for the ages. Along with their focus on the present and the future was a strong pragmatism that superseded the theoretical: 'Does it work?' came to be the dominant question rather than 'What are the ideas behind it?' This pragmatism served a growing marketplace model of church and society. To paraphrase Alexis de Tocqueville, where you expected to find a priest you found a politician – or a salesperson. In the free marketplace of ideas, sellers of religious 'commodities' competed with other sellers of ideas and with each other for consumers. The revivalists and advocates of church renewal developed many new ways of presenting the gospel message to attract followers.

George Whitefield (1714–70)

The first great shaper of the revival tradition was George Whitefield. Born in Gloucester, England, Whitefield studied at Oxford and became a colleague of John and Charles Wesley in their 'Holy Club'. In 1737, Whitefield was ordained a preaching deacon in the Church of England, but almost immediately established his lifelong pattern of being an irritant to the church hierarchy by his novel practices. Concerned that common, working people were not being reached with the gospel, Whitefield began preaching in the open fields, eventually attracting John Wesley, 'to be more vile', as Wesley put it, and join Whitefield in the practice.

This novelty was but a foretaste of things to come, and Whitefield's real fame came later when he toured the American colonies in 1740 as an itinerant evangelist – the 'Grand Itinerant' – leading what came to be known as the Great Awakening. Hearers noted his powerful voice and dramatic delivery that made every sermon an event not to be missed. Like Edwards, Whitefield affirmed the importance of the religious affections. Unlike Edwards, however, the itinerant believed that the human will was less guided by intellect than by the emotions.

The result was a new spirituality of conversion shaped by a market society, a form that has exerted tremendous influence on American

understandings of the Christian faith ever since. The Great Awakening, under the leadership of George Whitefield and others, dramatically and permanently changed the shape of a significant part of American Protestant Christianity.

Henry Alline (1748–84)

In Canada, Henry Alline, the 'George Whitefield' of the Canadian Maritime Provinces, promoted revival during the late 1770s. Born in Newport, Rhode

The 'enlightened' spirituality of Thomas Jefferson (1743–1826)

As the new nation was in the process of formation, the ideas of the Enlightenment exerted a tremendous influence on many of those who shaped its political and social structures. The greatest exemplar of what can be called an 'enlightened spirituality' was Thomas Jefferson. Affirming fully the Enlightenment's assertions about human progress, ability and freedom, Jefferson was a prime architect of many American traditions, including the separation of church and state, and complete religious liberty. According to Jefferson, Christianity had become something that Christ himself would not recognize due to its intolerance, superstition and irrational dogmas. The problem was not what Christ actually taught, but what Christians had done with his teachings. Get rid of the 'rags' of dogma and superstition, Jefferson argued, and Christianity is the religion above all others 'most friendly to liberty, science and the freest expansions of the human mind'.[11]

The Life and Morals of Jesus of Nazareth

The most extraordinary of Jefferson's contributions to conversation about religion and spirituality was his book called *The Life and Morals of Jesus of Nazareth*. He described its genesis to a friend:

> I have made a wee little book which I call the philosophy of Jesus. It is the paradigm of his doctrines, made by cutting the texts out of the book and arranging them on the pages of a blank book, in a certain order of time and subject. A more beautiful or precious morsel of ethics I have never seen. It is a document in proof that I am a real Christian, that is to say, a disciple of the doctrines of Jesus.[12]

The volume omitted any reference to Jesus' supernatural powers; these were superstitions best relegated to the wastebasket, according to Jefferson. Clearly unorthodox, but reflecting fully the stream of Enlightenment thinking that influenced many of the nation's founders, Jefferson's is a prime example of a spirituality that has been prevalent in the new nation alongside more traditionally Christian versions.

Island, Alline experienced a crisis conversion in 1775 which became the focal event in his life and led him to urge others to experience similar transformations. Alline's preaching was like that of Whitefield, characterized by 'a burning drive to preach to the unconverted, the exaltation of the New Birth, the cultivation of a distinct language of religious emotion, and an expectation that holiness of life would flow from the experience of conversion'.[13]

Like Whitefield in many respects, including spreading what some called 'the Whitefieldian sound', Alline differed sharply in his theology of salvation, viewing the Calvinism taught by others in Nova Scotia as 'a pernicious heresy'.[14]

Alline recorded his spiritual wrestlings over a period of years with lows and highs in his *Journal*:

Thus the poor awakened soul in his distress is seeking and roving here and there, and every scheme he can contrive to find peace, rest and happiness fails him, and can find nothing beneficial to his poor, starving wandering soul, until he finds the Lord Jesus Christ… Thus I was wandering night and day in this distressed state, loaded with guilt and darkness, and a stranger to one moment's solid rest or true happiness…

My whole soul, that was a few minutes ago groaning under mountains of death, wading through storms of sorrow, racked with distressing fears, and crying to an unknown God for help, was now filled with immortal love, soaring on the wings of faith, freed from the chains of death and darkness.[15]

Frontier spirituality

At the turn of the nineteenth century on the American western frontier (at that time east of the Mississippi River), camp-meeting revivals emerged as a phenomenon that in many ways captured the essence of revivalistic Christianity. Graphically portrayed in the souls and bodies of converts, the battle between good and evil, between the cause of Christ and the works of the devil, played out with remarkable manifestations. Simultaneously, revivals had broken out in New England at Yale

◆ **Camp meeting in Tennessee (1850).**

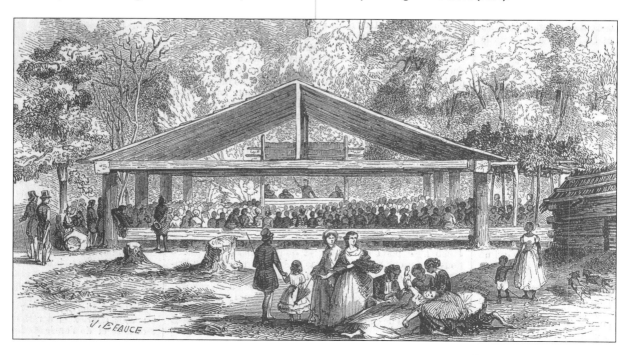

College and congregations throughout the region, but the frontier revivals were something quite different. In contrast to the cultured, respectable people of the older settlements of the east, people of the western frontier lived life on the edge. According to historian Bernard A. Weisberger,

> The frontiersman was different. He lived, worked, and died hard. It was natural that he should convert hard; that he should cry aloud in wrestling with his guilt; and that he should leap and twist and shout in rejoicing over his forgiveness.[16]

According to circuit-riding preacher Peter Cartwright, who was perfectly willing to evangelize through preaching *and* fighting, if necessary, frontier ministers needed to be of sturdy stock as well. 'I have seen so many of these educated preachers,' Cartwright disdainfully noted, 'who forcibly reminded me of lettuce growing under the shade of a peach tree... that I turn away sick and faint... The illiterate Methodist preachers actually set the world on fire... while they were lighting their matches!'[17]

In their urgency to save souls, the frontier denominations – Presbyterians, Methodists and Baptists – for the moment dropped their competitive guard and cooperated in gatherings that became regional spectacles. Literally thousands of people gathered over many days in the wilderness for preaching, singing, Holy Communion, conversion and dramatic examples of God's power. The granddaddy of them all was held at Cane Ridge, Kentucky, in 1801. Barton Stone, an eyewitness, recalled some of the graphic manifestations:

> The bodily agitations or exercises, attending the excitement in the beginning of this century, were various, and called by various names... The falling exercise was very common among all classes... The subject of this exercise would, generally, with a piercing scream, fall like a log on the floor, earth, or mud, and appear as dead...

Stone went on to describe the 'jerks', the 'dancing exercise', the 'barking exercise', and laughing, running and singing exercises.[18] Eventually, camp meetings were tempered somewhat and became known as primarily a Methodist institution.

Charles G. Finney
(1792–1875)

Second only to George Whitefield as a shaper of revivalism was Charles G. Finney. Born in Connecticut, his family moved to upstate New York, to an area that would come to be known as the 'burned-over district' because of the regular sweep of revival fires through the land. Never very committed to Christianity as a young man, and scornful of dry, manuscript preaching, Finney's interest was piqued through reading the Bible as a source for English law during his apprenticeship in a law office. As he wrestled with the state of his soul, Finney decided that the issue must be settled once and for all, without delay. He experienced a dramatic conversion and received 'a mighty baptism of the Holy Ghost' that became his pattern for the experience of all converts in his revivals. No longer would he be consumed with legal matters, but now he had a 'retainer from the Lord Jesus Christ to plead his cause'.[19]

In the true creative spirit of American revivalism, Finney developed a whole set of 'new measures' for bringing souls into the kingdom. Despite harsh criticism, he vigorously defended practices such as praying for individuals by name within public meetings, organizing and leading 'protracted meetings' over weeks and even months, use of an 'anxious bench' where repenting sinners could come for encouragement and instruction, failing to secure cooperation of a town's ministers, and the use of women in 'promiscuous' meetings – that is, meetings including both men and women.

Finney also sparked controversy with his

doctrine of 'Christian perfection'. According to the revivalist, holiness consists primarily in the perfection of the will and is available to every Christian after conversion. In his *Lectures to Professing Christians*, published in 1837, Finney gave his understanding of the doctrine:

Christian perfection is perfect obedience to the law of God. The law of God requires perfect, disinterested, impartial benevolence – love to God and love to our neighbour. It requires that we be motivated by the same feeling, and act on the same principles upon which God acts. It

Fanny Crosby (1820–1915)

Less known than the famous revivalists of the era, though arguably no less influential, was the prolific hymn-writer Fanny J. Crosby. As an infant, Fanny suffered from an eye irritation which a quack doctor mistreated, leaving her completely blind. She developed an extraordinary memory, and as a girl of eight or nine, Fanny memorized the books of Genesis, Exodus, Leviticus and Numbers, as well as the four gospels. Fanny also loved to sing and memorize hymns, particularly those of Charles Wesley and Isaac Watts. Crosby studied at the New York Institution for the Blind and became an instructor there. In an era when people expected events to be memorialized in verse, Fanny became a master at writing occasional poems. As one friend put it, 'she seemed to exude verse', writing for every event in her life and the lives of her friends.

Crosby experienced a dramatic deepening of her faith in 1850 during revivals in New York. As a penitent, she went forward to the altar three times, but recalls that little happened until she heard the fifth verse of Watts's hymn 'Alas and Did My Saviour Bleed': 'Here, Lord, I give myself away. 'Tis all that I can do.' The 'November experience', as she would call it, flooded her soul 'with celestial light'. 'For the first time,' she said, 'I realized that I had been trying to hold the world in one hand and the Lord in the other.'[20]

Gospel hymns

In 1864, Fanny believed that God had given her a new purpose and direction in her life: the writing of hymns. She embarked on a period of enormous productivity during which she would write literally hundreds of hymn texts, many of which remain widely used, including 'Pass Me Not, O Gentle Saviour', 'Rescue the Perishing', 'Praise Him! Praise Him!', 'Jesus Keep Me Near the Cross', 'Blessed Assurance', 'Draw Me Nearer', 'All the Way My Saviour Leads Me', 'To God Be the Glory' and 'Tell Me the Story of Jesus'.

Her hymns were popularized by revivalist singers, most notably Ira D. Sankey, with whom Crosby worked from their first meeting in 1876 during the Moody-Sankey revival in New York, until his death in 1908.

Crosby often received inspiration for her hymns during meditative states that she called 'the valley of silence'. During those times, she believed that she entered special, mystical communion with the Holy Spirit. She crafted her texts to be simple and rooted in the common experiences of ordinary people. She was unconcerned for formal theological categories or distinctions, even stating that she 'had never thought much about theology'. Her concern was more to engage the heart and soul than the mind, and to bring people to fellowship with Jesus the friend and close companion. Her hymns accomplished all of those things and remain sources of inspiration for Christians around the world.

◆ The great Chicago fire (1871) destroyed Moody's home and church, and left only one house standing on the North Side; painting by C. Graham in the *Chicago Tribune*.

requires us to leave self out of the question as uniformly as he does, to be as much separated from selfishness as he is – in a word, to be in our measure as perfect as God is.[21]

Christians must ardently desire and seek perfection and at the same time get involved in the work of bringing Christ's millennial kingdom to reality on earth. There was little time for the quiet, deep spiritual life of contemplation. Finney's spirituality 'demanded constant, frenzied activity for God'.[22]

Dwight L. Moody
(1837–99)

Another major shaper of revival spirituality and practice was Dwight L. Moody. Born in Northfield, Massachusetts, Moody inherited both the strength of character and tender-heartedness of his mother, Betsey Holton Moody. Widowed, with a house full of small children, Betsey determined that she would keep the family together, and through strength of will did it. Dwight was converted through Sunday school, and admitted to church membership even though the examining committee lamented his woeful lack of knowledge of the Bible. Moody became a successful salesman in Chicago, but turned his back on his success to become a salesman for Christ. He established a thriving Sunday school, which became the Illinois Street Church, renamed Moody Church after his death.

The great Chicago fire of 1871 destroyed Moody's home, the Illinois Street Church and the

The African-American experience

In his excellent book, *Slave Religion: The Invisible Institution*, Albert Raboteau describes the spirituality formed by African-Americans from their roots in Africa, through their experience of slavery in the United States. Theirs was a spirituality born through suffering, dislocation and dehumanizing conditions, and adapted to a religion new to them. As James Cone notes, the worship life of African-American congregations is 'dictated by an *historical* and *theological* necessity that is related to the dialectic of oppression and liberation'. He continues, 'A black congregation may be Methodist, Baptist, or even Catholic, but always with a difference.' Since 'black worship was born in slavery', its cadences resound with themes of liberation, freedom, security and the value of all people.

Raboteau notes that slaves drew on their African heritage with its understanding of a 'high' God and many lesser spirits and gods, its veneration of the spirits of ancestors, and the centrality of magic, ritual, music and dance, and created them within the Christian context to achieve a new form of faith and spirituality.

A spirituality of hope

Remarkably, the slaves adopted the faith of their oppressors, albeit with significant changes and differences of emphasis. Owners sought to evangelize their slaves and employed evangelists for plantation missions. Often, though, they heard a truncated 'gospel'. A former slave, Lucretia Alexander, recalled,

> The preacher came and... He'd just say, 'Serve your masters... Don't steal your master's meat. Do whatsomever your master tells you to do.' Same old thing all the time. My father would have church in dwelling houses and they had to whisper... That would be when they would want a real meetin' with some real preachin'.[23]

Such 'real meetin's' were usually outlawed and slaves caught participating in them subjected to severe punishment. Yet they flourished, and the themes of deliverance – especially as found in the book of Exodus – God's provision for his people, and their value as God's children, became central in slave worship.

One significant difference between the self-understanding of the slaves and that of the European-Americans was related to the image of God's 'new Israel'. The Puritans frequently used that image as a way to understand their place in God's plan. They were God's people, chosen to settle in the American 'promised land' and bound to God by a covenant. In sharp contrast, the slaves viewed the oppressing European-Americans as Egyptians, out of whose bondage they waited, like Israel, to be delivered. Their spirituality was powerfully shaped by this self-understanding as God's chosen, but suffering people. This difference from the dominant view of America as God's chosen 'new Israel' has allowed the black church to critique the tendency of Americans, including American Christians, to triumphalism. Rather than being the religion of the powerful and the wealthy, African-American spirituality has insisted that 'Christianity requires identification with the poor and the oppressed.'[24]

Slaves took the image of Jesus as the suffering servant (Isaiah 53:1–3) as a powerful type of their own experience. Jesus is companion, friend, fellow sufferer, of humble birth, mistreated; in all ways able to identify with their plight.

A spirituality of suffering

Slaves came to understand that suffering is redemptive. More than most Christians in the United States, particularly more than their masters, the slaves' faith was rooted in the basic paradoxes of Christianity: in weakness Christ is strong, in loss there is gain, and in suffering there is redemption. The slaves trusted in the Lord when there appeared to be no way out of their plight.

Even illiteracy could not dampen the slaves' fervour for their new faith, shared with other 'people of the book'. The Bible was at the heart of slave spirituality and the narratives of scripture became established in their oral traditions, passed down from generation to generation. One former slave recalled her favourite preacher, who, though illiterate, 'sure could read out of his hand'. He would 'hold out his hand and make like he was readin' and preach de purtiest preachin' you ever heard'.[25] Preaching with passion, worshipping with fervour, singing songs that would come 'a-gushing up from the heart', the slaves understood that this world was not 'home' and that their trials would not plague them for ever.

The spirituals

The slaves developed their own musical form, blending African rhythms with Christian themes. The 'spirituals' are perhaps the finest example of slave spirituality, with their expression of joy, hope and freedom in the midst of suffering and oppression. According to James Cone, in *The Spirituals and the Blues*,

> the basic idea of the spirituals is that slavery contradicts God; it is a denial of his will. To be enslaved is to be declared nobody, and that form of existence contradicts God's creation of people to be his children.[26]

The image of the exodus appears in many of the spirituals. For example, 'Go Down Moses':

When Israel was in Egypt's land,
Let my people go;
Oppressed so hard they could not stand,
Let my people go;
Go down Moses, 'way down in Egypt's land;
Tell ole Pharaoh,
Let my people go.

Other spirituals served both as songs of final deliverance and signals for escape, often through the underground railroad to freedom in the north. For example, 'Steal away, steal away, steal away to Jesus. I ain't got long to stay here,' was sometimes used as a signal to 'steal away' to the north.

The legacy of slave spirituality continued to shape the African-American community after emancipation. Their struggles certainly did not end with a constitutional amendment, nor even with the civil rights legislation of the twentieth century, and the spirituality born within the slave context continues to be one of the most powerful and deeply Christian types in the American religious context.

Sojourner Truth
(c. 1797–1883)

◆ **Sojourner Truth.**

Reflecting the same passionate spirituality of liberation and social justice was Isabella Baumfree. Born a slave to a Dutch master in Ulster County, New York, Isabella was separated from her family and sold twice before she was twelve years old. She was finally emancipated by her master in 1827. After casting about in various menial jobs, Isabella had a vision in which God told her to 'travel up an' down the land showin' the people their sins an' bein' a sign unto them'.[27] The new name God gave her as an affirmation of her mission was Sojourner Truth. She gained notoriety in the north as an itinerant preacher, abolitionist, advocate for the poor, and promoter of women's rights.

new YMCA building for which he had raised funds. More importantly, though, it destroyed Moody's confidence in his calling and drove him to a spiritual crisis. Broken and weeping before God, Moody felt an overpowering sense of God's love. He rededicated his life to preaching and reaching the lost.

The turning point in Moody's career as a revivalist came in Great Britain where he led evangelistic campaigns from 1873 to 1875. Moody returned home to the United States as a hero, with invitations to hold meetings in most major cities.

Moody did not have time for formal theological wrestling or distinctions: 'If I see a man tumble into the river and going to drown, it would do no good for me to sit down and bow my head and indulge in deep thought and reasoning how he came to get in there. The great question would be how he was to be got out!'[28]

Moody's was an activistic spirituality, like that of Charles Finney, in harmony with the progress-oriented busyness of American society. The Holy Spirit baptizes a person with power, Moody believed, and that power was for service to the kingdom of God.

In one sermon, Moody described the lamentable condition of most Christians: 'I do not think that I slander the church when I say nine-tenths of the church members today are without power.' God was ready to give people 'power and baptism', and then 'this whole community will feel the power'.[29]

The solitary spirituality of Emily Dickinson (1830–86)

Little known or appreciated during her lifetime because of her refusal to allow her works to be published, Emily Dickinson is now recognized as one of America's greatest poets, and, according to Roger Lundin, 'one of the major religious thinkers of her age'.[30] Her writings frequently wrestle with theological and spiritual issues that grew out of Dickinson's inner world as she increasingly constricted her physical world. As Lundin puts it, 'She pushed to the limit the Protestant tendency to shift the centre of God's activity from the world outside the self to the spiritual world within it.'

Emily was born to Edward and Emily Norcross Dickinson in 1830 at Amherst, Massachusetts. In 1847–48, as a student at Mount Holyoke Female Seminary in nearby South Hadley, Emily wrestled with the expectation that all students would express their Christian commitment, but she remained one of the few girls who refused to give public witness to faith. She also resisted conversion during a revival in Amherst in 1850. Through her schooling and religious training at home and church, she became very familiar with the Bible and the hymns of Isaac Watts, both of which would provide language and rhythms for her poetry.

The peak of her productivity came in 1862 when she wrote more than 350 poems. After 1865, she never left Amherst

◆ Emily Dickinson, painted by an unnamed artist.

Alternative spiritualities

Along with a remarkable variety of spiritual styles that fit, more or less, into the outlines of orthodoxy, America has provided space and refuge for many alternative forms.

An early developer of an alternative spiritual community was Ann Lee (1736–84). Born in Manchester, England, in 1758 Lee joined a group of millennialists led by Quakers. Lee married, but through the deaths of her four infants, she became convinced that God had condemned her for 'concupiscence'. She began proclaiming celibacy as the way to salvation and adopted a simple, communal lifestyle. She and her followers developed a worship form in which the power of the Holy Spirit would descend upon them, causing them to dance, shout and shake under the Spirit's power. In 1770, while in jail, possibly for Shaker 'sabbath disturbing', Lee had a vision of her unique union with Christ. She journeyed to America in 1774 and gathered around her a community who revered her for her prophetic powers, healings, and ecstatic singing and praying. After Lee died in 1784 from injuries sustained during an attack on the Shakers by angry neighbours during one of their missionary ventures, there arose among her followers the belief that 'Mother Ann' was the second coming of Christ in female form. The Shakers believed that

and hardly ever left her father's house. Yearning for outward security while she explored the inner depths of her soul, she grappled with the question of the existence of God:

Those – dying then,
Knew where they went –
They went to God's Right Hand –
That Hand is amputated now
And God cannot be found –

The abdication of Belief
Makes the Behavior small –[31]

She described her relationship with God as like the 'Mouse / O'erpowered by the Cat.' Yet, while God the Father remained inaccessible and terrifying, God the Son was there as a trustworthy friend. The human Jesus had been crucified and knew the reality of human suffering. Here was one who had experienced the human dilemma. Even Jesus, however, left some questions. The subject of one poem is dying and cries out,

And 'Jesus'! Where is Jesus gone?
They said that Jesus – always came –
Perhaps he doesn't know the House – .[32]

From 1874, when her father died, to her own death in 1886, Dickinson lost most of the people who were important in her life, including family and close friends and correspondents. Her sense of loss is painfully present in her poetry as hope is once again shattered by the realities of life and death.

they had recaptured the spiritual vitality and communal lifestyle of the early Christians.

Founder of one of the most vibrant and numerically significant new religious movements of the modern world, Joseph Smith (1805–44) gathered a following around an ideology and spirituality that were strikingly unorthodox. Born near Sharon, Vermont, Smith's parents were religious dissenters, not attached to any denomination. The family moved to Palmyra, New York, in 1816. As a young man Joseph prayed for God to lead him to the right denomination. Instead, Joseph received a visitation from God the Father and Jesus Christ, both in human form, who commissioned him to restore the true church on earth, the Church of Jesus Christ of Latter-day Saints. Directed to discover a set of golden plates, buried at a secret location, Smith translated them into the *Book of Mormon*, published in 1830. Local hostility against what were perceived as bizarre and dangerous social, political and theological teachings of the group forced Smith and his followers to move, first to Kirkland, Ohio, in 1832, and then to Nauvoo, Illinois, in 1838. Desiring to silence opposition, Smith and his brother Hyrum destroyed the printing press of a newspaper that had been critical of their practices. The brothers were arrested and, a few days later, a mob stormed the jail and murdered both men. Smith had a vision of America as the new land of promise with the Latter-day Saints in authority. Theirs was a spirituality of social and political control as they sought to establish their version of the kingdom of God on earth.

A form of spirituality that developed within American Protestantism and stepped outside mainstream understandings of orthodoxy was Transcendentalism. The Transcendentalists emphasized the supremacy of the spiritual over the material, and defended intuition as a reliable guide to truth. They affirmed self-expression, the worth of common people, the equality of races and sexes, and the interdependence of the natural world and its human inhabitants.

Ralph Waldo Emerson (1803–82) rejected his former Unitarianism because of what he called its 'corpse-cold rationalism', and sought spiritual vitality in nature. His 'Divinity School Address' of 1838 at Harvard set the stage for re-evaluation and rejection of traditional beliefs about Jesus and foundational doctrines of the Christian faith such as the incarnation and the trinity. Emerson's ideas influenced many, both outside and within traditional Christianity, including noted preacher Henry Ward Beecher.

Essayist and philosopher Henry David Thoreau (1817–62) emphasized the dignity and worth of all human beings and insisted that all people should live in harmony with the natural world. For a time he lived out his rejection of materialism, governmental control, and the American ideals of progress and power in a cabin at Walden Pond on Emerson's property.

Spirituality and the American Civil War

The American Civil War (1861–65) was a political, military, economic and social event of cataclysmic proportions. The case can also be made that it was the central spiritual crisis in American history. For generations, Americans had assumed their privileged place in God's plan and many had seen themselves as God's chosen people. A growing minority argued that the evil institution of slavery stood in the way of fulfilling God's plan of righteousness for the nation. Quaker John Woolman had worked tirelessly among the Friends prior to the American Revolution to eliminate slavery among them. By the middle decades of the nineteenth century, a growing abolitionist movement, led by prophets such as William Lloyd Garrison and Frederick Douglass, called for the immediate abolition of slavery. Determined to defend their rights and the political influence of their section, apologists such as Senator John Calhoun of South Carolina defended the 'peculiar

◆ **'The Death of Uncle Tom', from *Uncle Tom's Cabin*, by Harriet Beecher Stowe, engraved by Charles Bour (1814–81).**

institution' on the basis of social theory, economics and the Bible. Pastors entered both sides of the debate, throwing their spiritual weight behind each region's moral crusade.

With the appearance of Harriet Beecher Stowe's novel, *Uncle Tom's Cabin* (1852), opponents began to take their positions behind sharply drawn battle lines and compromise became an increasingly remote possibility. Harriet (1811–96), was the daughter of well-known pastor and teacher Lyman Beecher, and the sister of Henry Ward Beecher, who was becoming one of America's most noted preachers. Stowe's novel drew on her experience of visiting a slave-run plantation in Kentucky. First appearing in serial form in the *National Era*, an anti-slavery newspaper, *Uncle Tom's Cabin* energized many to work against slavery. This selection from the chapter called 'The Martyr' graphically portrays the slave, Uncle Tom, as a Christ figure as he refuses to disclose the hiding

place of two escaping slaves and is beaten to death:

'Speak!' thundered Legree, striking him furiously. 'Do you know anything?'

'I know, Mas'r; but I can't tell anything. *I can die!*'…

Tom looked up… 'Mas'r, if you was sick, or in trouble, or dying, and I could save ye, I'd *give* ye my heart's blood; and, if taking every drop of blood in this poor old body would save your precious soul, I'd give it freely, as the Lord gave his for me. O, Mas'r don't bring this great sin on your soul! It will hurt you more than 't will me! Do the worst you can, my troubles'll be

The complex spirituality of Abraham Lincoln (1809–65)

To say that Abraham Lincoln was a man of profound spirituality is to pronounce a truism. But what exactly was the character of that spirituality? Scholars have argued the point since Lincoln became a public figure as a candidate for the Illinois state legislature in 1832. Even Lincoln's closest friends and associates remained puzzled by his religious commitments – or lack of commitments. Yet, more than any president before or since, Lincoln wrestled in deep and profound ways with the inscrutable ways of providence as he struggled to make sense of the carnage of the American Civil War.

As a young man, Lincoln had read and appreciated the works of sceptics Thomas Paine and Voltaire, and in 1846 found it politically necessary to reject charges that he was 'an open scoffer at Christianity'. He was also profoundly shaped by his personal reading of the Bible. Lincoln was self-taught, having only a few months of formal schooling, and like many others in ante-bellum America, he found the Bible an available and useful textbook. His spirituality was shaped by the American pattern, especially pronounced on the frontier where Lincoln grew up, of reading the Bible without much regard for the traditions of Christian theology or ecclesiastical distinctions.

◆ **President Lincoln's wartime visit to the camps of Antietam (October 1862).**

Spirituality shaped by war

The most significant developments in Lincoln's spirituality came during his presidency in the crucible of the Civil War. As he grew to understand the tasks and responsibilities before him, he matured in spiritual depth and insight. He drew on his knowledge of the Bible to help him grapple with God's purposes through the disappointments of defeat and the ever-lengthening casualty lists, both north and south. He sought in the pages of the Bible insights into the social and political problems faced by the nation.

Lincoln's speeches and writings are filled with imagery drawn from the Bible and theological insights from its pages. In 1858, giving his most important speech yet, Lincoln chose the biblical metaphor of a house divided against itself to illustrate the dangers of attempting to exist as a nation, 'half slave and half free'.

Lincoln's most profound theological statement, which gives evidence of his deepening spirituality, is to be found in his second inaugural address. It was becoming ever clearer that the war was near its end and that the Union cause would triumph. In contrast to those on either side of the conflict who sought to place blame on the other, or those who wanted to celebrate northern victory, Lincoln noted that God's designs were beyond those of either side. He also recognized God's judgment on the nation as a whole, for its complicity in the evil of slavery.

Lincoln's second inaugural address (4 March 1865)

Neither party expected for the war, the magnitude, or the duration, which it has already attained. Neither anticipated that the *cause* of the conflict might cease with, or even before, the conflict itself should cease. Each looked for an easier triumph, and a result less fundamental and astounding. Both read the same Bible, and pray to the same God; and each invokes his aid against the other. It may seem strange that any men should dare to ask a just God's assistance in wringing their bread from the sweat of other men's faces; but let us judge not that we be not judged. The prayers of both could not be answered; that of neither has been answered fully. The almighty has his own purposes. 'Woe to the world because of offences! For it must needs be that offences come; but woe to that man by whom the offence cometh!' If we shall suppose that American Slavery is one of those offences which, in the providence of God, must needs come, but which, having continued through his appointed time, he now wills to remove, and that he gives to both north and south, this terrible war, as the woe due to those by whom the offence came, shall we discern therein any departure from those divine attributes which the believers in a living God always ascribe to him? Fondly do we hope – fervently do we pray – that this mighty scourge of war may speedily pass away. Yet, if God wills that it continue, until all the wealth piled by the bond-man's two hundred and fifty years of unrequited toil shall be sunk, and until every drop of blood drawn with the lash, shall be paid by another drawn with the sword, as was said three thousand years ago, so still it must be said 'the judgments of the Lord, are true and righteous altogether'.

With malice toward none; with charity for all; with firmness in the right, as God gives us to see the right, let us strive on to finish the work we are in; to bind up the nation's wounds; to care for him who shall have borne the battle, and for his widow, and his orphan – to do all which may achieve and cherish a just, and a lasting peace, among ourselves, and with all nations.[33]

over soon; but, if ye don't repent, yours won't *never* end!'...

Tom opened his eyes, and looked upon his master. 'Ye poor miserable critter!' he said, 'there ain't no more ye can do! I forgive ye, with all my soul!' and he fainted entirely away.[34]

Churches split along the fault lines in the nation, with Presbyterians, Methodists and Baptists forming northern and southern branches in response to political and social differences. Both eventually viewed the cause of their 'nation' as God's cause against the forces of infidelity. Southerners viewed the north as a haven for money-grubbing Yankees, free-thinking immigrants, and moral decay in the growing cities. Northerners looked south and saw an aristocratic system that defended the degrading evil of slavery, and flew in the face of democratic and Christian ideals.

Ministers on both sides regularly preached about God's favour for their cause and the impending defeat of the forces of unrighteousness.

One of the most powerful examples of blending patriotic and religious themes that reflected patterns of thinking on both sides of the conflict was Julia Ward Howe's 'Battle Hymn of the Republic'. After visiting a Union army camp, Howe (1819–1910) composed her poem, first published in *Atlantic Monthly* in 1862, which was then set to the tune of a tribute to an executed abolitionist, 'John Brown's Body'. The final stanza reveals Howe's understanding of the essential spirituality of the cause: 'As Christ died to make men holy, let us die to make men free.'

◆ Civil War: *The Battle of Spotsylvania* (10–12 May 1864), by E. Packbauer in Elson's *Civil War*.

Spirituality in the armies

Both armies experienced revivals as preachers offered comfort and called for repentance from soldiers whose time on earth might be short. Estimates range from 100,000 to 200,000 total conversions in both armies. Soldiers' diaries and letters reflect a strong sense of God's providence within the conflict that allowed them to view the deaths of their friends, and perhaps their own deaths, as within God's will. They knew that a better life awaited them and that the terrors of death need not mean final separation from loved ones.

The following accounts, the first from a northern soldier and the second from a southerner, represent views held by the great majority of the common soldiers:

> *Camp near Warrenton, Va., Sept. 6th 1863* – We are having considerable religious interest in our Regiment, and I pray God that it may continue. Soldiers are not the worst men in the world, but they are very careless in regard to matters of religion.[35]

A Confederate soldier reflected on the death of a soldier friend:

> He was one of God's noblemen, indeed – none braver, none more generous. God alone controls our destinies, and surely he who watched over us and took care of us in those dark and bloody days, will not forsake us now. God alone fits and prepares for us the things that are in store for us. There is none so wise as to foresee the future or foretell the end. God sometimes seems afar off, but he will never leave or forsake anyone who puts his trust in him.[36]

In their piety, the soldiers often reflected the devotion of their commanders. Northern generals such as George MacLellan, Oliver O. Howard and Joshua Chamberlain were known for their faith.

According to biographer Stephen Sears, MacLellan experienced conversion while serving as general-in-chief of the northern armies. Howard, known by his soldiers as 'Old Prayer Book' because of his piety, blamed the northern defeat at the first Battle of Bull Run (Manassas) on the fact that the northern army attacked on the sabbath. Chamberlain struggled to understand God's role in the war. 'Was it God's command we heard, or his forgiveness we must forever implore?'

Southern generals were even more conspicuous for their religious devotion. General Leonidas Polk graduated from West Point and later became Episcopal Bishop of Louisiana. Southerners admired Robert E. Lee not only for his skill on the battlefield, but also for his godly character. One of the most famous portraits of Lee shows him in his Confederate uniform with a child on his knee, together reading the Bible.

Easily the most idiosyncratic of all the generals, as well as one of the most fervent in his faith, was Thomas J. 'Stonewall' Jackson. Described as one who 'lives by the New Testament and fights by the Old', Stonewall was a staunch Calvinist Presbyterian who saw himself and his army as the instruments of God to bring judgment and vengeance on God's enemies. A tender husband and father, and at one time a Sunday school teacher for slaves, Jackson could be utterly ruthless in discipline with his own men and a cold, calculating killer of the enemy. He was another of those who believed that battle should be avoided on the sabbath, although his soldiers came to suspect that he initiated conflict on Sunday, thinking that Stonewall believed God especially favoured the southern army on that day.

People on the home front were also shaped spiritually by the war. Most homes experienced the loss of family members, friends or acquaintances. The 'empty chair' became a reality for many, with its attendant spiritual questions. Americans in the 1860s lived with a simple and profound faith in their leaders and in their God. Southerners developed a spirituality of the 'lost cause' to help explain and come to terms with their defeat.

Holiness spirituality

Growing out of the Methodist Church, and in particular its camp meetings and revivals, the 'Holiness movement' emerged in the mid-nineteenth century. For decades there had been disagreement and controversy over the doctrine of sanctification; in particular, whether it could be experienced instantaneously as the gift of perfect love, or whether it involved a lifelong struggle against sinfulness. The movement championed the cause of the work of the Holy Spirit in bringing an immediate deliverance from sin. Called the 'Mother of the Holiness movement', Phoebe Palmer (1807–74) developed and popularized a theology that included an emphasis on total surrender to God, bringing full cleansing from sin. Her ideas were distinctive, but Thomas Oden observes that 'Phoebe Palmer's spirituality… is deeply grounded in classical Christianity, not on the fanatic, idiosyncratic fringe of centreless enthusiasm. She deserves to be counted among the most penetrating spiritual writers of the American tradition.'[37] In particular, Palmer drew upon the writings of the Methodist tradition, especially those of the Wesleys (John, Charles and Susanna), and John and Mary Fletcher.

Palmer's spiritual breakthrough came as a result of the tragic loss of three children, two of whom died of natural causes, while the third was burned to death in her crib. Palmer believed that the tragedies had been intended as a sign that she had loved the children more than she loved God. She determined to surrender herself totally to God; as she put it, to 'lay all on the altar'. She spoke of 26 July 1837 as her 'Day of Days' when she received sanctifying grace by surrendering herself wholly to God.

Leaders and members from a variety of churches adopted her themes of 'holiness', 'entire devotion' and 'entire consecration'. According to Oden, 'It would be difficult to identify any Protestant denomination of mid-nineteenth-century America or Britain that did not feel her

◆ **Hannah Whitall Smith.**

influence.'[38] Oden notes that Palmer provides the important link between Methodist and Pentecostal spirituality.

Despite the mystical sound of Palmer's understanding of sanctification, she believed that mystical experience or feeling had little to do with sanctification. She insisted that understanding and accepting God's promise of sanctification was enough. One must believe what God has said, lay claim to it, and give witness to the reality in one's life.

Similar to Phoebe Palmer in ideas and influence was Hannah Whitall Smith (1832–1911). Raised in a Quaker home, Hannah struggled with religious doubts as a young woman. She and her husband,

Robert Pearsall Smith, were converted in 1858 at a prayer-meeting revival. Hannah experienced spiritual rebirth in 1867 and she and Robert became popular speakers at holiness meetings in the United States and England. In 1875, Hannah published *The Christian's Secret of a Happy Life* which rapidly became a popular devotional guide. As the title indicates, Smith's understanding of the faith has little of the dark self-examination of the Puritans. Instead, she reflects the spiritual optimism of her time: 'She took the gloom from the gospel… and made life an unending joy.'[39] Smith recalled, 'For the first time I saw, as in a flash, that the religion of Christ ought to be, and was meant to be, to its possessors, not something to make them miserable, but something to make them happy.'[40]

Mainstream nineteenth-century spiritualities

Normally known for their steadfastness and conservatism in affirming and teaching Calvinism, proponents of nineteenth-century 'Princeton theology' were also concerned with spirituality. Most representative and important in that stream of theology and spirituality in America was Charles Hodge (1797–1878). Hodge combined an unwavering concern for objective truth, as revealed in the Bible, with recognition of the importance of the subjectivity of lived religious experience. Ever the controversialist, Hodge did battle with numerous trends in American religion, including revivalism and its emphasis on emotion and excitement. Hodge's emphasis on religious orthodoxy reduced the distinction between religious belief and religious life. His preface to *The Way of Life*, written as a basic statement of the Christian faith for the

American Sunday School Union, reveals his sense of the close relationship between truth and the life of piety:

> It is one of the clearest principles of divine revelation, that holiness is the fruit of truth; and it is one of the plainest inferences from that principle, that the exhibition of the truth is the best means of promoting holiness.[41]

Horace Bushnell (1802–76)

For Horace Bushnell, pastor, writer, and teacher, the ultimate goal of the Christian faith was 'to evoke or encourage growth in the life of the spirit'.[42] He viewed the Christian faith as dynamic and lively, and only properly 'symbolized by imaginative metaphor'.[43] The contrast with Hodge and the Princeton theologians could hardly be sharper, and the two theologians mark out clearly the battle lines within American Protestant theology during the last half of the nineteenth century.

Called the 'American Schleiermacher' because of his focus on religious experience as the beginning point of the Christian faith, in 1848 Bushnell experienced a new understanding of the gospel that would change his life. He told his wife that he had 'seen the gospel of the New Testament from a fresh perspective'. The gospel was not 'something to be reasoned out', but was 'an inspiration, – a revelation from the mind of God himself'.[44] The theologian should seek to preserve religious mystery through poetry and imagery, and not assume that the purpose of theology was to explain the mysteries of God. Bushnell yearned for the occasions when he attained what he described as a mystical union with God.

He argued that communion between the Holy Spirit and the human spirit is not due to an act of reason or will, but by virtue of the mystery of the indwelling Christ. The centre of spirituality and attention should not be the self, but God. As Bushnell described it in his book, *The Spirit in Man*,

The sublime reality is that the divine has made a junction with our nature, and Christ has begun to be formed within us – only begun. Henceforth the great object and aim of the Christian life is to have what is begun completed. Whether we speak now of growth, of sanctification, of complete renovation, or redemption, everything is included in this, the having Christ formed within us.[45]

The Mercersberg theologians

Another mainstream option developed in the mid- to late nineteenth century that tried to bridge sectarian and theological division was that of John Williamson Nevin (1803–86) and Philip Schaff (1819–93) at the tiny, German Reformed Mercersberg Seminary in Pennsylvania.

The Mercersburg theologians developed a form of liturgical spirituality that was churchly, sacramental and historical, all in direct opposition to the dominant trends in American Christianity. Like Hodge, Nevin and Schaff opposed the excess emotionalism and theological looseness of the revivalists. Yet they affirmed an ecumenical and developmental model of the church that Hodge found distasteful and dangerous. According to the Mercersburg theologians, the truest form of Christianity was an evangelical-catholic church that affirmed the riches of the Christian tradition *and* the reform and renewal movements in the church's history. Against the tendency within many American denominations towards what was called 'free' or 'non-liturgical' worship, Schaff argued for the revised German Reformed liturgy on which both he and Nevin had laboured, saying that the liturgy was designed 'as a sacred bond of union between the different ages of Christ's church'. The revisers desired 'a truly *scriptural, historical, evangelical catholic*, and *artistic* liturgy for the *people* as well as the ministry'.[46]

The social gospel movement

Emerging within late-nineteenth-century American assumptions about progress and optimism about the future was a form of spirituality that examined the underside of American society and found those left out of the prosperity. The social gospel movement never achieved dominance or even prominence within American Protestantism. In their hope for the future, the proponents of social change probably never anticipated such for their prophetic and critical movement. Yet they plunged forward with vigour.

The best-known and most influential leader in the social gospel movement was Walter Rauschenbusch (1861–1918). Despite the growing rift between the revivalists' emphasis on personal conversion and the focus of religious liberals on social concerns, Rauschenbusch kept the two firmly joined. He was convinced that social changes would only be lasting if they were nourished by 'deep wells of personal religious life'.[47] He drew on many spiritual classics of the Christian tradition, including Augustine's *Confessions*, Thomas à Kempis's *Imitation of Christ*, John Bunyan's *Pilgrim's Progress* and Richard Baxter's *The Saints' Rest*.

For Rauschenbusch, the Holy Spirit was the source of the church's power to fight social injustices:

We must open our minds to the Spirit of Jesus in its primitive, uncorrupted, and still unexhausted power. That Spirit is the fountain of youth for the church. As a human organization it grows old and decrepit like every other human organization. But again and again it has been rejuvenated by a new baptism in that Spirit.[48]

Rauschenbusch's favourite book was his *Prayers for the Social Awakening* written in 1910. He was surprised by the book's popularity, but it remains remarkably relevant and powerful.

Rauschenbusch's prayer for the kingdom of God

O Christ, thou hast bidden us pray for the coming of thy Father's kingdom, in which his righteous will shall be done on earth. We have treasured thy words, but we have forgotten their meaning, and thy great hope has grown dim in thy church. We bless thee for the inspired souls of all ages who saw afar the shining city of God, and by faith left the profit of the present to follow their vision. We rejoice that today the hope of these lonely hearts is becoming the clear faith of millions. Help us, O Lord, in the courage of faith to seize what has now come so near, that the glad day of God may dawn at last. As we have mastered nature that we might gain wealth, help us now to master the social relations of mankind that we may gain justice and a world of brothers. For what shall it profit our nation if it gain numbers and riches, and lose the sense of the living God and the joy of human brotherhood?

Make us determined to live by truth and not by lies, to found our common life on the eternal foundations of righteousness and love, and no longer to prop the tottering house of wrong by legalized cruelty and force. Help us to make the welfare of all the supreme law of our land, that so our commonwealth may be built strong and secure on the love of all its citizens. Cast down the throne of Mammon who ever grinds the life of men, and set up thy throne, O Christ, for thou didst die that men might live. Show thy erring children at last the way from the City of Destruction to the City of Love, and fulfil the longings of the prophets of humanity. Our Master, once more we make thy faith our prayer: 'Thy kingdom come! Thy will be done on earth!'[49]

◆ **Men at a mission soup kitchen in the Bowery, New York (1908), receiving free coffee.**

The vibrant spirituality of Pentecostalism

The Christian tradition has always affirmed the surprising, unexpected work of the Holy Spirit bringing renewal. No movement in the twentieth century was more surprising or ultimately more influential than Pentecostalism. At the end of the nineteenth century numerous Christian leaders focused on the Holy Spirit, and those in the Holiness movement, for example, had begun to use the language of the 'baptism of the Holy Spirit,' the 'power of the Holy Spirit', and the 'Pentecostal' blessing. With the beginning of the new century, increasing numbers identified 'speaking in tongues' as the infallible sign of the baptism of the Spirit. Many argued that the 'latter-day' outpouring of the Spirit had begun and that the second coming of Christ could not be far away. Perhaps the most important figure in the early Pentecostal movement was William J. Seymour (1870–1922). Born in Centerville, Louisiana, the son of former slaves, Seymour represents wonderfully the beginnings of Pentecostalism among society's outcasts. Largely people outside the structures of power, wealth, education and influence, the early Pentecostals developed a spirituality that enabled them to believe they were at the heart of God's plan for the end of time. Seymour led the Azusa Street Revival in Los Angeles, a three-year, non-stop outpouring of the Holy Spirit, according to its participants. Its opponents, who were numerous and vocal, tended to view it as a disgusting display of excess emotionalism and overactive imaginations.

Such opposition only convinced those involved in the revival that they were right – after all, had not Jesus predicted opposition against his true followers? Reports from Azusa Street spread throughout the world and spiritual pilgrims came to witness (and perhaps experience) for themselves the power of the Spirit. Reports spread that language experts verified speaking in tongues, which some believed was the gift of a foreign language for missionary service. Articles named doctors who recognized divine healing. Participants claimed the exorcism of demons, and other manifestations of God's power, including a visible aura of the Spirit surrounding the Azusa Street building. Witnesses took what they had seen and experienced back to their homes and Pentecostalism literally became a worldwide movement.

Conclusion

In many ways, Pentecostalism offers a perfect conclusion to this survey of Protestant spirituality from the seventeenth through the nineteenth centuries in North America. The vitality of Pentecostal spirituality signalled one more powerful manifestation of Americans' interest in spirituality that has ebbed and flowed through the generations. Americans have fully explored a bewildering variety of spiritual styles and have experienced and experimented with many paths of the Christian life. From the Puritan emphasis on the Christian commonwealth made up of 'visible saints', to the revivalists' emphasis on individual conversion; from the African-American alternative vision of America and spirituality of suffering, to the Holiness movement's goal of entire sanctification, American Christians have yearned for closeness with God and harmony with one another, and have explored a multitude of ways to achieve their goals.

With a style that is predominantly activist rather than contemplative, and usually moving towards individualism rather than community, American Protestantism has offered a wonderful array of examples of the way Christianity interacts with culture and a fascinating laboratory of varieties of interaction between spirituality and society.

10

Spiritualities of the Twentieth Century

Bradley P. Holt

Timeline

1900	*Carmina Gadelica* published
1906	Azusa Street Revival, Los Angeles; Origins of Pentecostal movement
1908	First Week of Prayer for Christian Unity
1910	World Mission Conference, Edinburgh
1911	Evelyn Underhill's *Mysticism*
1913–15	William Wade Harris's mission to the Ivory Coast
1914–18	First World War
1917	Russian Revolution
1917	Virgin Mary apparition in Fatima, Portugal
1930s	Great Depression
1930s	Origins of East African Revival
1930s	Origins of the Iona community, Scotland
1930s	Origin of Alcoholics Anonymous
1930s	'Confessing Church' in Hitler's Germany
1932–67	Karl Barth's *Church Dogmatics*
1939–45	Second World War
1940s	Origins of Taizé community, France
1940s	Origins of Cursillo movement, Spain
1945	Dietrich Bonhoeffer executed
1945	Atomic bomb dropped on Hiroshima
1946	Mother Teresa called to found the Missionaries of Charity, India
1948	World Council of Churches
1948	State of Israel
1949	Billy Graham Crusade, Los Angeles
1950s–60s	Civil Rights Movement, USA
1950s–60s	Origins of charismatic renewal, USA
1957	Teilhard de Chardin's *The Divine Milieu*
1959	Election of Pope John XXIII
1962	Carl Jung's *Memories, Dreams, Reflections*
1962–65	Vatican Council II, Italy
1968	Thomas Merton electrocuted, Thailand
1968	Martin Luther King assassinated
1968	Mary Daly's *Beyond God the Father*
1978	Election of Pope John Paul II
1978	M. Scott Peck's *The Road Less Travelled*
1980	Assasination of Archbishop Oscar Romero
1981	Virgin Mary apparition in Medugorje, Croatia
1984	Desmond Tutu awarded Nobel Peace Prize
1989	Fall of the Berlin Wall
1990s	Era of the Internet
1990	Release of Nelson Mandela signals the end of apartheid in South Africa
1991	Soviet Union dissolved
1994	'Toronto blessing'
1994	Matthew Fox expelled from Dominicans

Timeline margin markers: 1910, 1930, 1940, 1950, 1970, 1990

A complete account of all Christian spirituality in the twentieth century is impossible to write, because most of the experience and the teaching of Christians is never written down. There are teachers of spirituality, especially in the two-thirds world, whose names we will never know. This study is largely dependent on printed materials in English. Even though English appears to be well on the way towards becoming the dominant language of international communication, there are vast amounts of Christian spiritual literature which have not been translated into English. Further, this account gives pride of place to those who are authors and are well known. The reader should remember that the complete story of Christian spirituality includes not only authors who are privileged to have their books sold in large numbers, but also ordinary Christians, including those who are suffering from poverty, discrimination or non-literacy.[1] The major criteria for selection here are that writers and movements are influential, representative and/or distinctive. It has been a painful task to reduce the number of writers and movements to the space allowed in this chapter.

Twentieth-century background: a few highlights

Christian spirituality is not a static, eternal 'given', but a dynamic, developing tradition, as the previous chapters of this book have illustrated. Spiritual writings and movements in the twentieth century also show the ways in which this tradition interacts with its context, responding to the events of the world and the various cultures in which Christians live, and influencing the course of these cultures. If the collaboration of church, state and society began with Constantine about the year

AD 300, it appears to many observers that this era came to an end in the twentieth century.

Yet it needs to be remembered that there are indeed elements of Christian spirituality which do not change over the centuries. 'Jesus Christ is the same yesterday, today, and for ever' (Hebrews 13:8). Christians are reading the same Bible, baptizing members, sharing in the meal of bread and wine, and expressing the same fruit of the Spirit which those of previous centuries have done. It is the interaction of the continuous elements of Christianity with the discontinuous which gives us a story to tell about spirituality.

What are the decisive events and ideas which influenced and were influenced by Christian spirituality in the twentieth century?

International developments

The great global events of the century include international influenza epidemics, the First World War, the Great Depression, the Second World War, the Cold War and the collapse of the Soviet Union. The end of the century seems fraught with ecological fears, ethnic conflicts, racism, torture and 'ethnic cleansing'.

All of these have chastened our optimism about human progress and caused us to question our destiny as a human race. At the beginning of the twentieth century the mood in Europe and the United States was optimistic; nations were confident that new technology and political developments would result in a new world of prosperity and peace. Before the century was over, we were much more dubious about the uses of technology, and nation states were threatened by ethnic tensions.

Yet there were hopeful signs in the century as well. The end of apartheid in South Africa and the removal of the Berlin Wall were wondrous events. Advances in technology meant much better means of communication and travel. Child and maternal mortality rates declined drastically, so more of us are living to the full span of human life. We visited the moon, are building a space station, and may

◆ **In July 1969 the first astronauts landed on the moon. Their photos of earth from space changed our consciousness of the beauty and fragility of our planet. Profound spiritual implications of this are still emerging.**

soon travel to Mars. We are understanding the basic building blocks of life and learning how to adapt DNA for useful purposes. We can write and edit and communicate by computers which often frustrate us but increase our capacities.

There have also been selective gains in literacy, human rights, women's rights, freedom of information and the acceptance of multicultural populations in Europe and the United States. The world religions are moving towards a better understanding of one another, after a century of growth. Those prognosticators who at the start of the century expected the fall of religion by its end were very wrong. Most of the major religions are stronger now in population or in commitment than they were in 1900 (see box, p. 308). Many observers noted an increasing hunger for spiritual sustenance in the Western world as the century came to an end.

Christian globalization, churches and theology

Building on the 'Great Century' of Christian missions (the nineteenth), the twentieth century saw the maturing of Christian communities throughout the world. Starting from its bases in Europe and North America, Christianity has spread in the last several centuries to all the continents of the world. The long middle ages of its concentration in Europe came to an end and it began to reclaim the universal character of its earliest centuries. The era of European colonization and missionary outreach in North America, South America, Africa, Asia and Australasia was darkened by the injustices of colonialism, genocide of native peoples and cultural imperialism. But it laid the foundation for the self-governing Christian communities in virtually every nation, who now contribute to one another their spirituality, music, personnel and funds. The missionaries of the late twentieth century came from all continents and went to all continents. The ease of travel meant that ordinary Christians, not just professional church workers, visited one another, and learned from one another. The sense that Christians must all be culturally European was being replaced by a Christian multiculturalism which rejoices in the differing gifts among different Christian communities.

The major theological movements in the century included liberalism, fundamentalism, neo-Reformation theology, existentialism, quests for the historical Jesus, biblical theology, secular theology and the death of God, liberation theology, black theology, dialogue with other religions, process theology, feminist theology, post-liberal theology, and a good deal of confusion. These theological movements influenced the writing of spirituality, as Christian spirituality is closely related to theology, its intellectual cousin. What one believes to be true, in a dialogue between the faith and the world of ideas, will inevitably affect what one experiences, for our world-view gives us both possibilities and blinkers.

One of the major developments in the century was the use of the term 'spirituality', first by Roman Catholics and later by Protestants in its current usage. At the end of the century it was possible to have an interdenominational, even an inter-religious conversation about spirituality and to have common understandings of its meaning. Earlier the concept was only partially available, in such terms as asceticism, mysticism, devotion or piety. The writing of a book like this one is only possible after the developments of the twentieth century.

Cultural developments from Victorianism to postmodernism

As the nineteenth century was the culmination of efforts to end slavery, an institution that had existed for thousands of years, the twentieth century may be remembered for its progress in regarding women as fully human. Indeed, just as there are pockets of slavery still existing, and racism still persists, so also the worldwide picture of women's rights is far from ideal. Yet the recognition of women's ability to vote and to lead, to have full standing before the law and to make decisions, has advanced dramatically in the twentieth century in most areas of the world. Amid the many cultural developments we shall discuss, this is one which arguably may be the most significant for human society and for Christian spirituality in the long run.

The century began with great confidence in Europe. The technological advances of the nineteenth century, the colonization of much of the non-European world, and the diplomatic balance of power all led to pride in human accomplishments and sanguine hope for the future of the new century. It was an era of confidence in the human being, seen as little less than God in the dominant liberal theologies in Protestantism.

If the previous cultural period could be called Victorian after the long, stable reign of Queen

Victoria, the new epoch was called modernism. It rebelled against the idealism, historicism, optimism and ethical emphasis of the previous period. Influenced by Freud, it insisted on the open discussion of sex, in contrast to the 'prudery' and 'hypocrisy' of the previous era. Modernism was not so much concerned about the rightness or wrongness of an action as its aesthetic component: did it delight or engage one's sense of pleasure? It insisted that historicism – understanding a subject by means of recounting its history – was flawed. (Think of those interminable Victorian novels!) Rather, one needed only an incisive moment observed with intensity, to understand the essence of a subject.

In the arts, some of the representative figures were Van Gogh, Matisse, Munch, Klimt, Braque and Picasso. One of the leading lights of the Modernist movement was a Christian poet, T.S. Eliot. Philosophically, the different schools of Wittgenstein, Heidegger and James reacted against the nineteenth-century idealism of Hegel. A new physics was created by Einstein, Rutherford, the Curies, Heisenberg and Bohr. Prominent in the development of modernism were the new social sciences, especially psychology and sociology, but also new developments in anthropology and economics.

If modernism can be used as a general description of Euro-American culture in the first four decades of the twentieth century, the following period is influenced by existentialism. The reactions of sensitive people to the brutalities of the two world wars was a radical individualism, often understood in bleakly immediate terms. If the classical philosopher seeking objectivity, claimed, 'Since all men are mortal and Socrates is a man, therefore Socrates was mortal,' the existentialist forced the reader to respond to the human dilemma by saying, 'You are going to die!' This basic perspective was already articulated by

◆ Stained-glass window from the interior of the
Chapelle de Rosaire, Vence, France, by Henri Matisse
(1869–1954).

the nineteenth-century Christian gadfly of
Denmark, Søren Kierkegaard. Thus there were
existentialists in the twentieth century who were
also Christian (such as Marcel and Tillich), but the
movement as a whole was atheist, led by Sartre,
Heidegger and others.

Marxism-Leninism and Nazism

The extremes of left and right which rose so
powerfully in the century produced martyrs and
strains in the Christian community. Millions were
killed by the Soviets and millions by the fascists.
These two blocs were the enemies of Christianity,
but the fascists were less blatantly so to begin with,
and used the churches to forward their cause. The
Bolsheviks were militantly atheist from the start.
Christian writing emerged from both empires
which would focus the minds of Christians in
other settings. The writings of Bonhoeffer and
Solzhenitsyn forced comfortable Westerners to
consider their Christianity as something to suffer for.

Postmodernism

The term 'postmodernism' was being used
increasingly in the late twentieth century to
indicate deep cultural changes, but the meaning
of the term is ambiguous. It refers to the fact
that a new cultural era has dawned, but no one is
completely sure of its character yet, and therefore
it is called 'after modernism'. But which modernism
is referred to? One option is the twentieth-century
movement profiled above which rejected the culture
of nineteenth-century Victorianism. The meaning
would then be the rejection of the ideals and style
of that twentieth-century movement. But a wider
understanding of 'modern' leads to a different
conclusion. Here it is pointed out that 'modern'
can refer all the way back to the Enlightenment of
the eighteenth century, and the scientific theories
and confident cultural norms which we have been
using in the West ever since. In that case, the term
'postmodernism' has a much wider historical sweep,

and a more radical rejection of beliefs and
assumptions on which the modern nation states and
churches have developed. Norman Cantor assesses
the movement in this way:

> The culture of Postmodernism is reminiscent
> of the baroque era of the seventeenth century...
> Both periods display astounding capability
> in detailed technique, in the mastery of
> technology, whether it be the technology
> of science or art and language. Yet these
> capabilities are accompanied in both periods
> by the same redundancy and sterility of ideas.[2]

Geographical survey
Global Christianity: intercontinental developments

The 'centre of gravity' of the Christian community
gradually moved south in the twentieth century.
This means that the numbers of Christians in the
tropics and southern hemisphere have gradually
outnumbered those in the north Atlantic region.
Africa is the continent with the most dramatic
growth of Christianity, but the population growth
in Latin America and Asia has also contributed to
the global growth. According to David Barrett, the
population of the world in 1900 was about 1.6
billion, but it is over 6 billion at the start of the
twenty-first century. The percentage of Christians
is about the same, about one third of humankind,
but it is a much larger Christian community
numerically.[3]

Ecumenical spirituality

The movement for Christian unity known as
ecumenism did not begin in the twentieth century.
Ever since there have been divisions in the

Taizé

A very special expression of ecumenical spirituality is the community of Taizé in France. Founded by Roger Schutz and Max Thurien during the Second World War, it is a semi-monastic order with members from both Catholic and Protestant traditions. Since the 1950s large numbers of young people from all over the world have come to stay for a week or more at the community. Since the 1960s the youth of Eastern Europe have been especially numerous. The Orthodox tradition has visibly made its contribution to life at Taizé, from the onion tower on the main chapel to the use of icons within.

The Taizé community has drawn thousands of young people to its own site in France by its openness to raising questions and by its seriousness about helping the poor. But the community has reached out beyond its locale in Burgundy in a variety of ways. The brothers live in slums throughout the world. There is also an annual meeting drawing upwards of 100,000 young people to various European cities. It has been a common occurrence for cathedrals to be packed with young people at services led by Brother Roger. Many non-Orthodox believers join in kissing a large cross-shaped icon lying in the middle of the church floor, as a prayer of solidarity with Russian Christians. Brother Roger has also written a number of books. But perhaps the most pervasive influence of Taizé has been in its music, which is sung all over the world. Because visitors speak many different languages, the music has developed in simple, short, repetitive chants, often in Latin, which is not the language of anyone present. The ease of learning this music has made it accessible to people everywhere.

◆ **Church of the Reconciliation at Taizé.**

churches there have been those who have prayed for their reunion. For example, Philipp Melanchthon, the young associate of Luther, tried hard to reconcile Lutherans with others. But in the last century ecumenism has developed not only major institutions, but also widespread themes for prayer among denominations.

What is of special interest to us here is a movement of prayer for Christian unity. A week specially devoted to this cause was started in 1908, then approved by Pope Pius X in 1909. At that time many Protestants understood Roman Catholic ecumenism to mean that Protestants should 'come home' to Rome. But Abbé Paul Couturier (1881–1953), who was experienced in building understanding between French Catholics and Reformed churches, was able to convince Protestants to adopt the same week, 18–25

January, for the purpose of prayer for unity. Since 1966 the Vatican and the World Council have planned and promoted the week together.

Orthodox, Catholics and Protestants in the present century have learned to pray together on many levels at meetings, conferences and retreats. Many believe that it is only prayer which has kept the movement going in spite of many obstacles. As yet there has been little approved sharing of Holy Communion, but a great deal of intercommunion has taken place informally.

Pentecostal and charismatic spirituality

Pentecostalism was consciously founded as a re-enactment of primitive Christianity as seen in the Acts of the Apostles. The experience of the earliest church seemed such a contrast to what was observed in twentieth-century churches. What was new in Pentecostalism was the identification of John Wesley's 'second blessing' with the biblical 'baptism in/with the Holy Spirit' (see Luke 3:16;

Acts 1:5). Furthermore, the outward sign of the baptism was speaking in tongues followed by the 'spiritual gifts' listed by Paul in 1 Corinthians 12, among them prophecy, speaking in tongues and healing.

The pivotal moment in the development of a new style of Christian spirituality was in a store-front church on Azusa Street in Los Angeles in 1906. At that time a black evangelist, William Seymour (1870–1922), introduced both black and white seekers to 'baptism with the Holy Spirit' and speaking in tongues. The movement spread with lightning speed, and grew quickly in North and South America, gained a foothold in Europe, and influenced emerging indigenous churches in Africa. Today many believe that Pentecostal denominations are the fastest-growing group in Christianity.

Earliest Pentecostalism was multiracial, but,

◆ **The storefront church on Azusa Street, Los Angeles (c. 1906).**

as the movement spread and solidified into denominations, black and white generally organized separately. They were despised and rejected by the established churches because they were mostly poor, uneducated people. Pentecostalists charged that the churches had lost the power of the Holy Spirit. Over the decades Pentecostalism became more moderate as its members gained in affluence, just as Wesley's followers had. They began to found colleges and build handsome churches. The more extreme emotional outbursts in services, which had led to their nickname, 'Holy Rollers', were not so frequent.

Finally, they came to recognize genuine spiritual gifts in members of the so-called mainstream denominations. In the 1960s and 70s large numbers of Protestants and Catholics, and even a few Orthodox Christians, were led by the neo-Pentecostal or charismatic movement to the same experiences as 'classical' Pentecostalism. Unlike the people affected in the first few decades of this century, these charismatics remained in their historic denominations instead of starting new ones. They did not necessarily accept the fundamentalism and the proscriptions of the original Pentecostals. But they did begin to take evangelism, healing and praise very seriously. The movement had its greatest success, surprisingly, among Roman Catholics. The hierarchy saw to it that priestly guidance was given to an essentially lay movement, which began in universities. Cardinal Suenens and Pope Paul VI blessed the movement.

What is Pentecostal or charismatic spirituality? It focuses on the love of God seen to be present and active. The practice of speaking in tongues is experienced as an assurance of God's love. 'Letting go' to allow the Spirit to guide the sounds from the mouth is a form of surrender to God. Answers to prayers for healing of physical or emotional problems likewise underline the presence and power of God. The Holy Spirit, brought into prominence in this movement, nevertheless takes second place to Christ as the saviour and friend of the worshipper. The group is the locus for hearing the word of God both through scripture and 'prophecy'. Prophecies are often cast in the

form of the biblical prophets, 'My people, hear my voice...' It is understood that God is actively communicating with the group, in these spontaneous messages, which are subject to the norms of scripture and the judgment of the leadership. In this way the movement is similar to the Quaker form of worship.

A few charismatics took dramatic steps to help the poor as the result of their spiritual renewal. But as a whole the movement did not make care for the poor or advocacy for the oppressed a major theme. The prophecies rarely had the authentic challenge for justice found in the Hebrew prophets, but instead focused on inner assurance of God's love or challenges to religious duties within the group. Thus the movement came in some instances to meet the real need of Christians for an emotional and experiential faith, but it did not challenge their social or political involvement. The movement definitely led to ecumenical exchanges between surprising partners, notably the Pentecostals and Roman Catholics. But in some places it was divisive of congregations.

In 1994 a new chapter of the charismatic renewal began at the Airport Vineyard Church in Toronto, Canada. The Vineyard is a network of charismatic churches not connected to any historic denomination. The phenomena experienced there have become known as the 'Toronto blessing'.[4] Dramatic and controversial effects of a revival there included holy laughter, falling and barking, in the context of healings, speaking in tongues and evangelical preaching. This phenomenon quickly spread to Britain, especially to Holy Trinity Church in Brompton, London, which became one of the major centres for this revival in Britain.

Intercontinental Roman Catholic spirituality

Devotion to the Blessed Virgin Mary
In *Mary Through the Centuries* Jaroslav Pelikan demonstrates the continuity and the varieties of devotion to the mother of Jesus.[5] She has been

pictured more than any other woman. Among her titles are the Second Eve, the *Theotokos*, the *mater Dolorosa*, the Mediatrix and the Queen of Heaven. Pelikan points out that Marian doctrine in the Roman Catholic Church is a prime example of spirituality leading theology, not vice versa, for it has been popular devotion which has run ahead of official dogma and led the popes eventually to make pronouncements about the Blessed Mother, notably her immaculate conception (1854) and her assumption to heaven (1950).

Previous devotions to her may be found in other chapters of this book, but here we wish to focus on twentieth-century developments. One of these has been pilgrimage to sites of apparitions of the Virgin. Mary appeared to Juan Diego in Guadeloupe, Mexico, in 1531 and to Bernadette Soubiroux at Lourdes, France, in 1858. The striking fact is that these sites of previous apparitions became thriving pilgrimage sites in the twentieth century.[6] In these places the devotion to Mary herself, and not just

the occasional healing, is at centre stage.

New apparitions appeared in the twentieth century, among them to Lucia, Francisco and Jacinta at Fatima, Portugal, in 1917 and to six young people in Medugorje, Croatia, in 1981. They are international pilgrimage sites for people from all continents.

The Cursillo and Marriage Encounter movements

Among the international Catholic developments are the Cursillo movement and its offspring. Cursillo means 'little course' in Spanish. It was developed in the late 1940s in Spain during a time of considerable political pressure on the church and the need for renewal. The Cursillo is a carefully planned weekend, followed by small group meetings afterwards. It seeks to convert

◆ A scene from Lourdes in 1985.

Vatican II (1962–65)

When Pope John XXIII called for a new universal gathering of Catholic bishops, he was consciously opening the windows to let some fresh air into the musty library of Catholic thought. The council was the first for almost a hundred years, preceded by Vatican I in 1870. Vatican II was the culmination of a number of reform movements which had begun earlier in the century, but now came to fruition as official policy of the church. Among these were movements for biblical, liturgical and ecumenical changes. Each of these had implications for spirituality.

The renewal of biblical studies changed the whole frame of reference for theological thinking. Now the Bible was not only to be studied at greater depth in seminaries and cited more frequently in official documents, but was to be used by lay people in their private devotion. The church approved of Bibles with few or no notes, including the Revised Standard Version. Further, the faithful were encouraged to read the Bible. The Roman Catholic charismatic renewal took full advantage of this message, with its followers discovering the freshness of scripture study.

The liturgical movement emphasized the communal nature of the Mass, leading to the most dramatic changes for centuries. The priest used the language of the people, faced them during the Mass, preached from the Bible, offered wine as well as bread, and, most importantly, expected everyone to partake, not just observe. People were enjoined to participate in the liturgy and to receive the elements of the communion, not just to adore them from afar.

Music for the whole congregation was introduced, in contrast to the silent or low Mass of pre-Vatican II days, or even the high Mass, when the choir did most of the singing. The effect on spirituality was to lead people to recognize themselves as part of a community, and not just individuals before God. Teaching did not emphasize rosary use, but an increase in actual reception of the Eucharist.

The ecumenical movement meant that Catholics gave greater recognition to their non-Catholic Christian friends ('separated brethren') and to other religions around the world. This new openness was amazing to non-Catholics, who had before found Catholics unbending in their assurance that theirs was the only proper form of Christianity. The result for spirituality has been that Catholics, Protestants and Orthodox believers have a much more open flow of discussion about the Christian life than previously. The reforms of the council brought Catholics somewhat closer to Protestant practice, with regard to scripture, hymn-singing and communion with both elements. The effect has been to allow Catholic spirituality to receive insights from others, and for the others to learn from Catholics.

The reforms following Vatican II were not all put into effect with the same alacrity in all places, and the spirit of reform has not been uniformly continued by the popes since John. But there is no doubt that the council was one of the major events of the century for Christian spirituality in general, and for Roman Catholics in particular.

the retreatant to a conscious and deliberate discipleship to Jesus Christ. The Cursillo has spread not only to many other countries but also to other denominations in the course of time.

The Marriage Encounter movement models its weekends very much on those of the Cursillo. This movement attempts to strengthen good

marriages by introducing couples to a method of communication during the weekend, and then encourage further meetings in the follow-up. Like Cursillo, the Marriage Encounter movement is both international and multi-denominational. For recent developments, each of these movements has a large website.

Africa

As we turn now to many of the continents of the world, it is evident that the Western world, the so-called first world, needs the two-thirds world, or so-called 'third world', in order to develop an authentic and vital spirituality.[7] Whereas the numbers of Christians in Europe and North America show little increase, in other continents Christianity is growing rapidly, and mission societies are being founded to evangelize other countries, including the West. The very vitality of these Christians is a refreshment to the tired churches in secularized, affluent countries. *Christianity Rediscovered*[8] tells of the power of a simple gospel among the Masai in East Africa. Such rediscoveries are also needed in countries where Christianity has long been present.

Among the important spiritual writers of the century are many who served as cross-cultural missionaries. These people experienced both the commitment to the Christian gospel and the cultural wrenching which sometimes produced deep insights into the nature of the Christian life and its contacts with cultures and religions not typical of their homelands. Only the contact with their culture produced the insights that they wrote for the rest of the world. Most of these missionaries came from the North Atlantic region, but increasingly the two-thirds world is sending missionaries too.

On no continent did the Christian faith spread more rapidly in the twentieth century than in Africa. The foundations for this growth were laid in the nineteenth century, but it is only when Africans evangelize Africans that significant numbers have appeared. Most African Christians live in the presence of African traditional religions and of Islam. Their spirituality is often not bookish, although Christianity in Africa has been accused of constituting 'schoolroom religion'. African Christian spirituality is difficult to write about because it has not produced a great volume of literature by well-known writers. But it is a deep and lively spirituality for all who have the privilege of meeting it.[9]

◆ **A Pentecostal church service in Zaire.**

There are basically three types of Christians in Africa: those from ancient churches of the early centuries (such as the Coptic and Ethiopian Orthodox churches); denominations founded by missionaries from the West; and those from indigenous churches founded by Africans. It is difficult to generalize, as each type has tremendous diversity. The early fervour of the first converts has had to be renewed over the generations, for example by the East African Revival, as described by Max Warren, General Secretary of the Church Missionary Society. We do not know of any great writers of books from this movement, but it was a significant international, interdenominational force from the 1930s for several decades. It was characterized by a deep sense of repentance for sin and a new commitment to Christ.

Many of the indigenous churches were founded in the early decades of the twentieth century, some of questionable orthodoxy, many of a Pentecostal stripe without outside influence. Dreams and visions played an important role in their founding, as did healing. The Kimbanguist Church of Congo (Zaire) is an example, founded by Simon Kimbangu (1889–1951). The church was forced underground for decades by the Belgian authorities, but came into the open in the 1960s, and attained a membership of five million.

William Wade Harris (c. 1860–1929)

The Prophet Harris was a Liberian who claimed that he was called while in prison by the angel Gabriel. Upon his release, he no longer wore European clothing, and set out on a long evangelistic trek, walking from Liberia along the coast of Ivory Coast to Gold Coast (now Ghana) and then returning. These trips took place in the years 1913–15. He preached conversion to the God who sent Jesus among a population who had not responded to missionary appeals. Harris's approach was distinctive, in that it did not include European culture, it was accompanied by powerful sign-events, and, most important, included immediate baptism. Ivorians had feared the wrath of traditional gods if they left them for this new God who Harris claimed loved them. But Harris assured them that if they were baptized, his God would protect them. In other words, Harris recognized the power of the traditional gods, unlike the European missionaries, but claimed that Jesus' God was more powerful. His message was convincing, and more and more people responded, until on his return journey thousands came to hear him. It has been estimated that 100,000 people became Christian during his brief ministry. Harris was not concerned about denominations. He told his converts to go to the Catholic or Methodist churches where they were available, or to build a church, choose twelve elders and wait for further instruction, where they were not. After his journey, Harris returned to Liberia and was not notably successful thereafter.

Like Simon Kimbangu in Congo, Joseph Babalola and Garrick Braide in Nigeria, and countless others in East and South Africa, Harris was laying the foundation for a non-European Christian spirituality in Africa. The indigenous churches, sometimes called independent churches, were a major development in twentieth-century African spirituality. Many Africans were drawn to the teachings of Jesus and the promise of eternal life, but could not stomach the European culture and leadership of earlier churches. Almost all of the founders were trained in European-founded churches, including Harris, but all broke away to start their own churches.

It is important to emphasize the diversity of these churches. Some are close to the mission-founded churches, except with African leadership. Others place their founder in a special place which rivals that of Jesus Christ. A few allow polygamy. But the vast majority of them are Bible-based, with a spirituality which emphasizes healing, fecundity, visions, dreams, and overpowering evil spiritual forces. These 'Zionist' churches are not intending to combine African and Christian religion; they strongly oppose traditional healing and worship practices. But they are more culturally African than the mission-founded churches just because, like the Bible, they have not been influenced by the Enlightenment of eighteenth-century Europe.

South Africa, which suffered most of the century under racial divisions, half of it under official apartheid, has also produced some of the continent's most passionate peace and justice spiritualities. Among its writers have been Alan Paton, John de Gruchy and Desmond Tutu (see box, p. 318).

Alan Paton (1903–88)

Alan Paton made no claims to be a theologian. After service in the prisons of South Africa, Paton became a novelist. He was extraordinary, as an English South African, to learn both Zulu and Afrikaans languages, and to be able to identify with both Africans and Afrikaners in such a way that his novels display extraordinary compassion for both. His *Cry, the Beloved Country* was one of the first prophetic calls to the world about the issue of apartheid in South Africa. His later novels, especially *Ah, But Your Land is Beautiful* continued to throw a compassionate light on the people caught in this racist system.

Desmond Tutu (1931–)

The most well known of the Christian opponents of apartheid is Desmond Tutu, former Archbishop of Johannesburg and winner of the Nobel Peace Prize. He is the author of a number of short books containing sermons and meditations, appealing for both justice and reconciliation. Among his titles are *Crying in the Wilderness*, *Hammering Swords into Plowshares*, *Hope and Suffering* and *The Rainbow People of God*.

Tutu is known not only for leading marches and conducting mass funerals for the victims of apartheid, but also for his spiritual leadership. He is a person of prayer, rising very early each morning to spend an hour or more with God. He has edited an eclectic collection of prayers from his continent, *The African Prayer Book*, which includes some of his own compositions.

Tutu's daughter Naomi has collected some of his words from speeches which give the flavour of the man. Here are some samples:

An authentic Christian spirituality is utterly subversive to any system that would treat a man or woman as anything less than a child of God. It has nothing to do with ideology or politics. Every praying Christian, every person who has an encounter with God, must have a passionate concern for his or her brother and sister, his or her neighbour. To treat any one of these as if he were less than the child of God is to deny the validity of one's spiritual experience.[10]

All I am saying is that the Bible and our faith and its tradition declare unequivocally that for an authentic Christian existence the absolute priority must be spirituality. A church that does not pray is quite useless. Christians who do not pray are of no earthly worth. We must be marked by a heightened God-consciousness. Then all kinds of things will happen.[11]

Let me warn the government again. You are not God. You may be powerful, but you are mortal. Beware when you take on the church of God. Emperor Nero, Hitler, Amin, and many others have tried it and ended ignominiously. Get rid of apartheid…[12]

◆ Archbishop Desmond
Tutu with Nelson
Mandela.

Instrument of Thy Peace is a series of meditations on a famous prayer by Francis of Assisi. It is an activist book, in the sense that it urges the reader, whether in despair or hope, to go out and help someone. Helping another brings one out of self-absorption. Paton certainly did his part to reconcile the estranged groups in South Africa, but he also lived with criticism for his stands from both left and right.

Give us courage, O Lord, to stand up and be counted, to stand up for those who cannot stand up for themselves, to stand up for ourselves when it is needful to do so... Let us have no other god before thee, whether nation or party or church. Let us seek no other peace but the peace which is thine, and make us its instruments, opening our eyes and our ears and our hearts, so that we should know always what work of peace we may do for thee.[13]

Asia

No one who has read Kosuke Koyama's (1929–) whirlwind theological tour of Asia can assume that Asia is a homogenous unit. His *Waterbuffalo Theology* hints at the very different situations in Singapore, Thailand, China, Hong Kong, India, the Philippines, Indonesia, Burma, Vietnam, Japan and Taiwan. In the situation of northern Thailand where he is writing, he speaks of a 'monsoon orientation' as 'cyclical cosmic regularity and its saving dependability without hurry and without argument'.[14] How different from the spirit of the industrialized countries, including his own homeland, Japan! This difference is indicated in the meditations he titles *Three Mile an Hour God*.[15] Koyama is intensely aware of the cultural differences within Asia as well as those between Asia and the West. His conversational style, freehand drawings and witty remarks show a down-to-earth spirituality.

Koyama calls for quite a different direction in spirituality from the Latin American and African sources. This is not a spirituality of social justice or of contextualization, but a spirituality of the cross. In his *No Handle on the Cross* Koyama rejects human attempts to control God or to reduce the offensiveness of the Christian message by taking the spotlight away from the cross of Jesus. Koyama is very sensitive to the presence of idolatry of various kinds, and writes about it in *Mount Fuji and Mount Sinai*.[16]

William Johnston (1925–) has written extensively about Christianity and Zen Buddhism. He sees strong connections between the spirituality of *The Cloud of Unknowing* and other apophatic Christian texts and Zen. He has been writing and living in Japan over a long career, demonstrating the compatibility of these two major streams of spirituality.

An American missionary in the Philippines, Frank C. Laubach (1884–1970) came to be known as the Apostle of Literacy. His method, called 'Each One Teach One', is said to have led to 100 million new readers. He was also the author of fifty-six books. The most widely known of these is *Letters by a Modern Mystic*. The letters were written from 3 January 1930 to 2 January 1932. His spiritual method bears comparison to that of Brother Lawrence.

In India, Christianity has been present since the earliest centuries. In the early part of the twentieth century a remarkable Sikh, Sadhu Sundar Singh (1889–c. 1929), came to the attention of Westerners. Converted by a vision of the risen Christ, Singh had been expelled from his household and travelled within India before he made a tour which included Britain and the United States in the early 1920s. He returned to India and mysteriously disappeared, climbing into the Himalayas. His life was full of adventure and danger, a witness to the surprising grace of God which reaches out beyond missionaries to the person of God's choice.

India provoked in Christian missionaries a profound engagement between Christian and Hindu spiritualities.

A British missionary to south India, first motivated by the Keswick movement, Amy Carmichael (1867–1951) wrote prolifically.

Toyohiko Kagawa (1880–1960)

Toyohiko Kagawa was a poet, novelist and preacher who lived in the slums of Kobe, Japan, in order to minister to the poor. On the very first day he was forced to share his tiny hut with a man with a skin disease, and others. Kagawa studied at Princeton Seminary from 1915 to 1917. He later moved to Tokyo, housing between fifteen and thirty strangers in his home each night. He organized labour and peasants' unions and was arrested by the Japanese government in the 1940s for peace propaganda. The Second World War seemed to destroy all his work.

Kagawa's spirituality was known and admired internationally. It was characterized by evangelism, social concern and poetry:

> 'He cannot save himself' –
> Long ago
> The crowds
> Reviled a Man
> Who came
> To save them.
> And I,
> Who fain would follow him,
> Am spent.
> For I can see
> No hope
> For the slums…
>
> But oh,
> The pity, the pity!
> My people
> Must stay
> In the city;
> So this six-foot shack
> That shelters me
> Is the only place
> Where I want to be.[17]

Carmichael saw the Christian mission in India as a vast spiritual battle. She was an advocate for women, and especially children who had been given to temples by their parents and were mistreated and neglected there. In contrast, A.J. Appasamy wrote a contextualized Christian spirituality drawing on traditional Hindu sources.

Bede Griffiths (1906–93)

Bede Griffiths began his journey in Britain and finished after many travels in India. At Oxford he was not popular for supporting a miners' strike in 1926:

> By that time I was disillusioned with all of civilization, not just what I was and lived through. I think T.S. Eliot's 'Wasteland' and 'The Hollow Men' brought out the sense that civilization was collapsing. That made us turn to poetry, to art, to music, to another world altogether.[18]

In his third year, C.S. Lewis became his tutor:

> Of course, he was a big influence on my becoming a Christian. We were almost contemporary with that. We began to discover the Christian background of English literature… That's how we grew. I owe a tremendous amount to his influence in my becoming a Christian – actually, I believe it was mutual. We shared with each other.[19]

As he grew in Christian life, after a period in the Anglican Church, he became a Roman Catholic, professed as a Benedictine monk in 1936, took the name Bede, and was ordained a priest in 1940. For the next fifteen years he was a Benedictine in the UK. At this time he wrote an autobiography.[20]

But his whole life took a change in direction when he decided to go to India in 1955. After visiting and working in a number of communities and founding an ashram, in 1958 he joined Christians of the west Syrian rite in Kerala. Finally,

◆ **Bede Griffiths during a visit to London in 1991.**

feminine is the intuitive, the sensitive, and also the sensual mind – in a sense, the whole bodily life. Christianity tends to put this down; India has accepted it totally. In India it is all integrated: the sensual and the spiritual. I still go on discovering that other half all the time.[21]

Bede Griffiths founded the Society for the Renewal of Contemplative Life in California in September 1992. He said, 'Contemplation is the awakening to the presence of God in the human heart and in the universe which is around us. Contemplation is knowledge by love.'[22] He died in his ashram in May 1993, surrounded by faithful devotees.

Anthony de Mello (1931–87)

We turn now to a Jesuit in India, whose teachings and stories have become favourites with many around the world:

> What attracted so many to his person and his ideas was precisely that he challenged everyone to question, to explore, to get out of prefabricated patterns of thought and behaviour, away from stereotypes, and to dare to be one's true self – in fine, to seek an ever-greater authenticity.[23]

De Mello went through various phases of teaching. At first he was a gifted promoter of the Ignatian spiritual exercises. But then he developed two different approaches to spirituality, each called a *sadhana*. The first was influenced by a popular book of the time, *I'm OK, You're OK*, but the second reversed his judgment. 'I am whatever I am, and I feel whatever I feel, and it's fine. I need not be OK in order to be OK if you follow me; I may not be OK, and that is perfectly OK with me.'[24]

One of De Mello's accomplishments was introducing the Jesus Prayer (see chapter 1, p. 57) to the Indian Catholic Church, which he learned himself from *The Way of a Pilgrim*.[25] He contributed out of the store of Christianity,

not satisfied, he came to Shantivanam (in Tamil Nadu) in 1968 with two other monks.

Looking back on his experience of so many years, he reflects on some of the early themes of his life, and exhorts those of us in the West:

> I feel that India gave me the other half of my soul. My life in England, first of all, was dominated by the intellect, by the rational mind. I went from school to college and I passed exams in Latin and Greek, and so on. I was always searching to get beyond the mind... But whereas that was something rare in England, in India it was the norm – the natural order of society... I think I can say that I was discovering the feminine because the masculine mind dominates in Europe and was dominating my mind. The

Mother Teresa of Calcutta (1910–97)

By blood and origin I am all Albanian. My citizenship is Indian. I am a Catholic nun. As to my calling, I belong to the whole world. As to my heart, I belong entirely to the heart of Jesus.[26]

One of the most widely known Christians of the twentieth century was born in a small country among a people only ten per cent Christian. Agnes Gonxha Bojaxhiu was born Albanian, but later became a citizen of India. While being sent for rest to Darjeeling, she experienced the 'call within a call' to found the Missionaries of Charity, in September 1946:

And when that happens the only thing to do is to say 'Yes'. The message was quite clear – I was to give up all and follow Jesus into the slums – to serve him in the poorest of the poor. I knew it was his will and that I had to follow him. There was no doubt that it was to be his work. I was to leave the convent and work with the poor, living among them. It was an order. I knew where I belonged but I did not know how to get there.[27]

She planned an order with a fourth vow: 'Wholehearted free service to the poorest of the poor.' She led a retreat on 'I thirst', two words which are now inscribed in every Missionaries of Charity chapel: it means the thirst of Jesus and God for us, and ours for him.

Teresa was not a writer of books, but many of her speeches and shorter writings have been compiled into devotional books.

The greatest disease in the West today is not TB or leprosy; it is being unwanted, unloved and uncared for. We can cure physical diseases with medicine, but the only cure for loneliness, despair and hopelessness is love. There are many in the world who are dying for a piece of bread but there are many more dying for a little love. The poverty in the

◆ **Mother Teresa, photographed in 1987.**

West is a different kind of poverty – it is not only a poverty of loneliness but also of spirituality. There's a hunger for love, as there is a hunger for God.[28]

Teresa died on Friday, 5 September 1997. Her body was carried through the streets of Calcutta on the same gun carriage that had carried the bodies of Mahatma Ghandi and Jawaharlal Nehru.

in this case Orthodox Christianity, and he borrowed from Indian wisdom, especially in his stories. He believed in spiritual growth by story. Here is one of his favourite stories, an excellent one for affluent Christians:

> A monk in his travels found once a precious stone and kept it. One day he met a traveller, and when he opened his bag to share his provisions with him, the traveller saw the jewel and asked the monk to give it to him. The monk did so readily. The traveller departed overjoyed with the unexpected gift of the precious stone that was enough to give him wealth and security for the rest of his life. However, a few days later he came back in search of the monk, found him, gave him back the stone and entreated him: 'Now give me something much more precious than this stone, valuable as it is. Give me that which enabled you to give it to me.'[29]

E. Stanley Jones (1884–1973)

A major evangelical spiritual writer, one of the most prominent Methodist leaders of the century, spent most of his life in mission work in Asia. By 1968 his twenty-four books had sold over 3.5 million copies, of which *Abundant Living* accounted for almost one million. Other titles include *Christian Maturity*, *Victory Through Surrender*, *The Christ of the American Road*, *Christ at the Round Table*, *The Divine Yes*, *The Christ of the Indian Road* and *Growing Spiritually*. He gained prominence partly by his personal friendships with many important people, including Gandhi (about whom he wrote a book), Nehru, MacArthur, Kagawa, Tshombe, Syngman Rhee, Martin Luther King, John Foster Dulles, the Chiang Kai-sheks, Franklin Roosevelt and Martin Niemoller.

In his spiritual autobiography, *A Song of Ascents*, Jones writes that he was converted in Memorial Methodist Church in Baltimore at the age of seventeen. After a year of victory, he found

himself wavering, wrestling the 'unconverted subconscious'. His thoughts about this issue show him to be in dialogue with twentieth-century psychological currents, and very much influenced by a devotional classic, *The Christian's Secret of a Happy Life*, published in 1875 by Hannah Whitall Smith:

> The subconscious is like the submerged portion of an iceberg, one tenth above and nine tenths below. Freud says we are determined by lower drives in the subconscious. We think we consciously determine our conduct, but these basic drives in the subconscious actually determine us. These basic drives can be roughly described as self, sex, and the herd. These drives come down through a long racial history; hence they have bents, bents towards evil... In conversion a new life is introduced into the conscious mind as we consciously accept Christ as Saviour and Lord. A new love and a new loyalty flood the conscious mind.[30]

Jones thought that the subconscious could be the friend, not the enemy of the Christian life, once it was surrendered to the Holy Spirit. He wrote that out of this revival experience came his call to the mission field. He went to India in 1907, to Lucknow, centre of the Methodist mission. After debilitating illness he was made well, in body, mind and spirit. This experience gave him a sense of adequacy, and loosened his grip on his old theology and on Western culture:

> I needed no longer to try to defend Western civilization or Western forms of Christianity. Western civilization is only partially Christianized. The best things in Western civilization are rooted in the Christian faith... We say to the East: 'Take from our civilization anything good and beautiful you may find there if it appeals to you. But keep what is good in your own. We are not out to replace the cultures of the East with Western culture. The only thing we have to give is Christ, a gift to us, so a gift to you. If you can build up around

Christ a better culture and civilization than we have been able to do, we will sit at your feet. We mean that.' Cultures are imperfect and changeable – Christ is perfect and changeless.[31]

Latin America

Roman Catholic Christianity came to Latin America with the conquistadors and since then has spread, at least nominally, to the vast majority of the population. In many countries the ordinary people did not understand the faith and it became an overlay on their previous beliefs. Furthermore the church came to be a bastion of support for the European populations which held and still hold the land and economic power. In some countries two per cent of the people own ninety per cent of the land. The question of social justice was muffled by the cultural captivity of the hierarchy.

But in the mid-twentieth century 'base Christian communities' were started which involved the poor in Bible-based group meetings which enlivened faith and called into question the economic order (see box, opposite). The *camposinos* or peasants learned to read and to think critically about their lives. This grass-roots movement gave birth to a new kind of theology: liberation theology.

Among the first leaders to become well known was Bishop Helder Câmara (1909–) of Brazil, author of *A Thousand Reasons for Living* and many other books. His passion for the poor met with criticism from the Vatican, but inspired many others across the continent.

Europe

Rediscovering and reinterpreting the Christian tradition

Probably no century has had such a wide array of spiritual texts available to study and emulate as the twentieth. New texts have been discovered, and old ones translated into modern languages, especially English. This rediscovery has been the

Liberation theology

What is liberation theology?

Liberation theology was adopted by professional theologians eventually, and is now well known throughout the world. It advocates a new way of doing theology, from the perspective of the poor, from the 'bottom up'. It employs Marxist analysis to reveal the injustice and conflict in the human situation, then the Christian gospel to promise hope for liberation from oppression in the historical future. This theology has been criticized from conservative Catholic and Protestant perspectives on a number of accounts. To some it tends towards a secular theology of social and economic revolution without any transcendent or specifically spiritual content.

Gustavo Gutierrez (1928–)

Gustavo Gutierrez in *We Drink from Our Own Wells* describes a liberation spirituality which must give the critics pause. His book is valuable in many ways. On the basis of the Latin American poor, he finds traditional Catholic spirituality falls short on two counts: it is geared to a minority, namely the religious orders, and is too individualist and interior; what is needed is a spirituality for all the people which includes practical action for liberation on a communal level. Drawing on the Bible and on selected figures from the history of European spirituality, Gutierrez calls for a holistic view of the Christian life, consisting of a trinitarian 'encounter with the Lord, walking in the Spirit, and a journey to the Father'.

For Protestants, one of the attractive features of the book is the seriousness with which Gutierrez takes the Bible. In the course of his discussion he also deals at length with Paul's understanding of flesh, spirit and body. He shows that Paul is not following Neoplatonist denigration of the body, but is using the term 'flesh' in a different sense. This section would be helpful in many books on spirituality, and it is unfortunate that these findings of critical word study were not available centuries earlier.

The special marks of liberation spirituality as set forth in this book are conversion (the necessary break with the past which occurs again and again), gratuitousness (the free, unearned grace of God), joy in suffering and martyrdom (which come in the struggle for liberation), spiritual childhood (which he sees as necessary for a commitment to the poor) and community (as the proper context for solitude).

The problematic elements of liberation theology hardly appear in Gutierrez's book. There is nothing of Marxist analysis here. It is clear that spirituality is for personal and communal relationship to God, and not simply for political revolution. Gutierrez is known as a theologian who lives simply among the people, practising what he advocates in his writing. Similar in tone is Jon Sobrino's *Spirituality of Liberation*.[32] This book is a fresh and serious challenge to others in their own settings to rethink spirituality on biblical, liberationist lines.

The spirituality of 'base community'

One of the main vehicles for liberation theology is the 'base community', in which poor *camposinos* gather to discuss the Bible. We have a remarkable document of such discussion in Ernesto Cardenal's *The Gospel in Solentiname*, which recounts several texts and the comments on it by the people and by their priest, Cardenal. Here is a sample of comments about the Christmas story in Luke 2:

Pedro Rafael Gutierrez spoke again: 'I think that in this earthquake the ones who are suffering most are the rich, and I'm going to tell you why: *Acahualinca* has never had any water, any electricity, any milk, any rice, any beans. Now this Christmas the rest of them don't have any either. But the poor have been

without food and electricity for a long time. All their Christmases have been like this. The radio talks about people going out into the street without shoes or clothes, and how the hell long have the poor people gone without shoes and clothes?'

'They've been like that since the birth of Jesus...'

Felix spoke again: 'I'm going to tell you one thing. Listen to me, Pedro. The rich never suffer. The government puts a five per cent tax on business. And are they the ones who pay it? It's the poor...'

'He came to share the lot of the poor. And Joseph and Mary were turned away from the inn because they were poor. If they'd been rich they'd have been welcomed in.'

'God wanted his son to be born in a pigsty, in a stable... He wanted his son to belong to the poor class, right? If God had wanted him to be born to a rich lady, that lady would have had a room reserved at that hotel. Especially arriving in her condition.'

'I see in this the humility of God. Because it was his son, and his mother had him just like any dog. ▶

◆ A base-community meeting in Pich, Mexico.

And Jesus came to free the world from these injustices (which still exist). And he came so that we could be united and struggle against these injustices... With today's gospel, it seems to me that no poor person should feel looked down upon. It seems to me that it's clear that a poor person is more important than a rich one. Christ is with us poor people. I think we're worth more. To God. To the rich we aren't worth a thing, good only to work for them... Jesus was rejected in Bethlehem because he was poor, and he goes on being rejected in the world for the same reason. Because when you come down to it the poor person is always rejected. In our system, that is.'[33]

The world's attention to liberation thought was heightened by the assassination of Archbishop Oscar Romero in 1980, and other religious martyrs from the United States and other countries.

The challenge of liberation spirituality is two-fold. Is our spirituality so individualized and psychologized that it excludes issues of justice? Are we prepared to share power with groups which have been disempowered, either within our own societies or in the two-thirds world?

The opposition of Pope John Paul II reduced the impact of liberation theology in Latin America late in the century. The pope has, however, called for criticism of economic injustices related to capitalism and the globalization of the world economy. The questions raised by liberation theology will continue.

◆ Archbishop Oscar Romero (1917–80) in the cathedral of San Salvador (1979).

work of hundreds and thousands of scholars in different fields of study, whom we will not attempt to name in this chapter. Instead we will focus on two individuals and one revival movement.

An independent lay theologian, philosopher and scholar of the spiritual life, Friedrich von Hügel (1852–1925), was the author of large tomes and intimate letters. He was influential in England, but surprisingly not among Roman Catholics. Born in Florence, Von Hügel lived most of his life in London, England. His mother was a Scottish convert to the Roman Catholic Church, and he was a devout Catholic all his life.

Perhaps his greatest contribution was defining three elements of religious life: institutional, intellectual and mystical. He asserted that these three needed to be kept in balance. As spiritual director to Evelyn Underhill, this concept was put into practical advice. His writings include *The Mystical Element of Religion as Studied in Saint Catherine of Genoa and her Friends* (2 vols, 1908), *Eternal Life* (1912), *Essays and Addresses on the Philosophy of Religion* (1921, 1926) and *The Reality of God* (1931).

Evelyn Underhill (1875–1941)

Evelyn Underhill's external life was very quiet; her dramas were internal, spiritual ones. She journeyed from agnosticism via Neoplatonism and mysticism to Anglicanism and, finally, pacifism. Although baptized and confirmed Anglican, in 1907 she intended to become a Roman Catholic, until Vatican condemnations of modernism repelled her. Underhill was, after all, a graduate of King's College, London, and would not give up her intellectual freedom. She later became a practising Anglican and indeed a prominent voice in that communion. She was the first woman to be a lecturer in religion at Oxford and the first to give spiritual retreats. She was highly honoured in her lifetime as a writer, scholar and retreat leader. In her spare time, she was a competent bookbinder and sailor, and she loved cats.

Her main contribution was not something

original, but rather a cogent call for attention to the mystics of the past. She did not claim to be a mystic, only an interpreter, who refreshingly brought to life the Christian tradition for present-day needs. In this she was one of the most significant of twentieth-century English writers. The Archbishop of Canterbury, Michael Ramsey, himself an important spiritual writer, said that she was crucial in maintaining focus on the spiritual life in the Anglican Church between the world wars.[34]

The First World War was a great challenge to Underhill's views. She defended mysticism in articles and books, especially *The Life of the Spirit in the Life of Today*, but emotionally for a time she said she 'fell apart' during the war. After it was over, she was changed: no longer a Neoplatonist, she saw the importance of institutional religion. In the summer of 1922 she wrote to a respected friend whom she had known mostly by publications and by letters before this: Baron Friedrich von Hügel. He influenced her as a spiritual director until his death in 1925. He convinced her to recognize the historical nature of Christianity, to move out of her intellectual world and into the world of the poor, and to relate to God through Jesus Christ. She had been a mystical, intellectual, Neoplatonic, theocentric author; now she became an Anglican Christian visitor to the poor, retreat leader, spiritual director and author. After attending a retreat at Pleshey, north-east of London, she became a retreat leader there herself from 1924 until her health failed in the late 1930s. Her writing took on a different style, more accessible and vivid for the ordinary reader. She wrote *The Mystics of the Church* in 1925 from a very different perspective than her more famous *Mysticism* (1911). Here she showed the historical background of the mystics, their variety, and most important, their relation to the church, which had been completely missing in the earlier book.

Underhill insisted throughout her writing career that life in the Spirit meant practical engagement with the world. But she criticized that tendency in the church, present throughout the twentieth century, to identify the Christian gospel with social action. Getting straight the relation between prayer and daily life was a key concern of hers:

A shallow religiousness, the tendency to be content with a bright, ethical piety wrongly called practical Christianity, a nice brightly varnished this-worldly faith, seems to me to be one of the ruling defects of institutional religion at the present time. We are drifting towards a religion which consciously or unconsciously keeps its eye on humanity rather than on Deity, which lays all the stress on service, and hardly any stress on awe and this is the type of religion, which in practice does not wear well.[35]

She gave up all her speaking engagements in 1935 in order to write a major book, *Worship*, published in 1936. This was not so much about individuals, as *Mysticism* had been, but rather about communities of faith. She became very much interested in Russian Orthodoxy and attended Orthodox services regularly. Her book shows appreciation for worship in all the denominational traditions of Christianity, and comments on Judaism as well.

Other European scholars who helped recapture the classics include Hilda Graef (1907–) and David Knowles (1896–1974). There have been many excellent French writers, and Jean Leclercq's *The Love and Learning and the Desire for God: A Study of Monastic Culture* is well known. Finally Louis Bouyer (1913–) was among the first to write an extensive history of spirituality published in English. His three volumes led the way for many later attempts to assess the tradition as a whole.

Celtic revival

Among the Irish, Welsh, Scottish and English, perhaps no early Christian spirituality has gained so much present-day interest and devotion as the Celtic tradition. A.M. Allchin sees connections between the spirituality of Patrick and of later Welsh spirituality, as expressed in the hymnody of William Williams Pantycelin (1717–91) and in contemporary Welsh poetry.

Columba made the island of Iona a mission station, and it may have witnessed the creation of one of the world's most beautiful manuscripts: the *Book of Kells*. Today Iona is the home of an ecumenical Christian community founded by George MacLeod in the 1930s which emphasizes Christian living in one's calling, including prayer, meditation and social service. Many are the pilgrims who have travelled to Iona for retreats in the restored abbey, amid Celtic crosses which pre-date the Viking era. Newer communities have been formed on the Holy Island, Lindisfarne, on the north-east coast of England.

One of the sources of our knowledge of this spirituality is a collection of prayers published by Alexander Carmichael in 1900 called the *Carmina Gadelica*.

European theologians and writers

In this section we will consider spiritual writings by people who are primarily known as theologians and church leaders. They are often known for their contributions to Christian theology, but they have written directly about spirituality as well. There are many others who might be considered here. For example, each of the following has published at least one book about spirituality amid writing careers which largely dealt with other topics: William Temple (1881–1944), John Baillie (1886–1960), Wolfhart Pannenberg (1928–), Jurgen Moltmann (1926–), John Macquarrie (1919–), Austin Farrer (1904–68), David Martin Lloyd-Jones (1899–1981), Edward Schillebeeckx (1914–) and Francis Schaeffer (1912–84).

Karl Barth (1886–1968)

Karl Barth was arguably the greatest Protestant theologian of the twentieth century. His *Church Dogmatics* was certainly among the longest treatments of theology in history: even incomplete it is over 9,000 pages!

The implications of his views for Christian spirituality include emphases on the Bible, on Jesus Christ, the life of prayer, and engagement with the social order. As one of the founders of the 'Confessing Church' in Germany during the 1930s, Barth opposed the Nazi influence in the churches. Even though he later criticized the Confessing Church for not being bold enough, he led it to affirm in the 'Barmen Declaration' that only Jesus is Lord of the church, not Hitler.

In *Prayer* Barth meditates on the meaning of prayer by expounding the Lord's Prayer with the guidance of Calvin and Luther. During his discourse, Barth frequently breaks into prayer himself, addressing God in the middle of the lecture:

> To be a Christian and to pray are one and the same thing; it is a matter that cannot be left to our caprice. It is a need, a kind of breathing necessary to life.[36]

Dietrich Bonhoeffer (1906–45)

One of Barth's colleagues in the 'Confessing Church' has also come to be regarded as a theologian of long-lasting significance. He first became widely known for his provocative commentary on the Sermon on the Mount, *The Cost of Discipleship* (1937). Like Kierkegaard almost a century earlier, he castigated his own Lutheran tradition for preaching 'cheap grace', an easy, uninvolved Christianity. The whole nation, he said, has been baptized with little sense of the meaning of being Jesus' disciple.

Later Bonhoeffer became known as a martyr, after his execution by the Nazis five days before the Americans liberated his prison. He had been arrested for his role in plotting the assassination of Hitler. He had successfully emigrated to New York, but felt he had to return to Germany to fight Hitler. While he was there he taught at a secret seminary, in Finkenwalde, where he gave spiritual direction to the students and wrote *Life Together* (1938), which describes the basis of Christian community. It also describes his advice for reading

scripture and meditation. His perspective is astringent for idealists:

> On innumerable occasions a whole Christian community has been shattered because it has lived on the basis of a wishful image... But God's grace quickly frustrates all such dreams. A great disillusionment with others, with Christians in general, and, if we are fortunate, with ourselves, is bound to overwhelm us as surely as God desires to lead us to an understanding of genuine Christian community. By sheer grace God will not permit us to live in a dream world even for a few weeks and to abandon ourselves to those blissful experiences

◆ **Dietrich Bonhoeffer photographed before his imprisonment at Flossenberg by the Nazis.**

Pierre Teilhard de Chardin (1881–1955)

More than any other spiritual writer of the twentieth century, Teilhard focuses our attention on the creation, and thereby the relation of science and religion. Although most of his writing was done in the first half of the century, he did not become known until the second half, after his death. The reason was the censorship of the Roman Catholic Church and his superiors in the Jesuit order. For most of his life he was forbidden to publish and was virtually exiled from his native France. He chose to live in northern China, where he engaged in geological and palaeontological work.

Teilhard came from a large family, but lived to experience the deaths of almost all his siblings. He also observed gory wounds and psychological trauma as a stretcher bearer in the First World War. Yet his teachings were consistently optimistic, not seeming to take human pain and sin seriously. It was at the point of original sin that he got into trouble with his superiors in 1924, and agreed not to publish his ideas. The books later published include *Mass on the World*, *The Phenomenon of Man*, *The Divine Milieu*, *The Heart of Matter* and *Hymn of the Universe*.

The themes of these books are seen in an early poem:

◆ **Pierre Teilhard de Chardin, by Caroline Cowell (1993).**

'Hymn to Matter' (1919)

I bless you, matter, and you I acclaim: not as the pontiffs of science or the moralizing preachers depict you, debased, disfigured – a mass of brute forces and base appetites – but as you reveal yourself to me today, In your totality and your true nature...

You who batter us and then dress our wounds, you who resist us and yield to us, you who wreck and build, you who shackle and liberate, the sap of our souls, the hand of God, the flesh of Christ; it is you, matter, that I bless.

I acclaim you as the divine milieu, charged with creative power, as the ocean stirred by the Spirit, as the clay molded and infused with the life by the incarnate Word...

Raise me up then, matter, to those heights, through struggle and separation and death; raise me up until, at long last, it becomes possible for me in perfect chastity to embrace the universe.[37]

Teilhard's spirituality

The Divine Milieu: An Essay for the Interior Life was written in 1927 but not published until 1957. He addresses the book to waverers who stand on the threshold of the church:

> These pages put forward no more than a practical attitude – or, more exactly perhaps, a way of teaching how to see... If you are able to focus your soul's eyes so as to perceive this magnificence... your one thought will be to exclaim: 'Greater still, Lord, let your universe be greater still, so that I may hold you and be held by you by a ceaselessly widened and intensified contact![38]

In his autobiographical book *The Heart of Matter*, some of the implications for spirituality of his grand vision are expressed in his 'Prayer to the Ever-Greater Christ'.

> Lord of consistence and union, you whose *distinguishing mark* and *essence* is the power indefinitely to grow greater, without distortion or loss of continuity, to the measure of the mysterious Matter whose Heart you fill and all whose movements you ultimately control – Lord of my childhood and Lord of my last days – God, complete in relation to yourself and yet, for us, continually being born – God, Who, because you offer yourself to our worship as 'evolver' and 'evolving', are henceforth the only being that can satisfy us – sweep away at last the clouds that still hide you – the clouds of hostile prejudice and those, too, of false creeds. / Let your universal Presence spring forth in a blaze that is at once Diaphany and Fire. / O ever-greater Christ![39]

Teilhard's influence

Teilhard was very much discussed at the time of Vatican II. He brought a fresh vision about the nature of the world, focused on the central image of fire and the dynamic of evolutionary change. It was highly speculative, but he was attuned to the issues of the interior life which are connected to his theories.

In the 1990s his vision of a geosphere growing to a biosphere, in turn developing into a noosphere led to renewed interest in his theory as applied to the internet. As some people saw the interconnection between people revolutionized by the new technology, the noosphere provided a concept to explain the wonder of a new step in human evolution.

and exalted moods that sweep over us like a wave of rapture. For God is not a God of emotionalism, but the God of truth.[40]

Some have come to know Bonhoeffer exclusively through *Letters and Papers from Prison*, published after his death by his friend Eberhard Bethge. The letters introduced phrases much used in 1960s' theology: 'religionless Christianity', 'secular holiness', and 'man come of age'. He was critical of 'religion' as a replacement for the living God, and decried the 'God of the gaps', a God who was only used to explain what science did not yet explain. Bonhoeffer will surely be one of the theologians and spiritual writers who is remembered long beyond his own century.

Simone Weil (1909–43)

Simone Weil is known for courageous acts during the Second World War, as she refused to sleep on a bed and to eat plenty while others lacked lodging and food. Raised in an agnostic Jewish family, Weil came to believe in Jesus, but was never baptized. She admired George Herbert's poem 'Love', and memorized the Lord's Prayer in Greek, reciting both frequently. She also learned Sanskrit to read the *Bhagavadgita*. Her writings include *Waiting for God*, *The Need for Roots*, *Gravity and Grace* and *First and Last Notebooks*. She left France in 1942 and died in Ashford, Kent.

Karl Rahner (1904–84)

Rahner is among the greatest of twentieth-century theologians. He is also among the most prolific; it is said that he has over 4,000 written works to his name! But he is also an important spiritual writer.[41]

Like Teilhard, Rahner was a Jesuit, and like him he found the older strict theology of his teachers oppressive. Rahner managed to master the medieval tradition so thoroughly that when he showed his 'progressive' side, none of his detractors could better him in the use of the traditional sources. He was very influential at

Vatican II, but he came close to the same fate as Teilhard: he was to be silenced, but a special petition to Pope John XXIII led to the order not being enforced.

Rahner had a distinguished academic career. After earning his doctorate in 1936 he taught at Innsbruck, Vienna, Munich and Münster. He was invited to lecture at many of the major universities of the world. 'On Prayer' was delivered in bombed-out Munich in 1946. Later it sold over 100,000 copies in Germany.

Here are some samples from Rahner's writings:

Laugh. For this laughter is an acknowledgment that you are a human being, an acknowledgment that is itself the beginning of an acknowledgment of God. For how else is a person to acknowledge God except through

◆ **Dr Karl Rahner, photographed in 1968.**

admitting in his life and by means of his life that he himself is not God but a creature that has his times – a time to weep and a time to laugh, and the one is not the other. A praising of God is what laughter is, because it lets a human being be human.[42]

Our love of God and our prayer have one difficulty in common. They will succeed only if we lose the very thought of what they are doing in the thought of him for whom we are doing it. To be concerned mainly with the correct way to love or the correct way to pray, entails almost inevitable failure in the realization of either activity.[43]

Hans Urs von Balthasar (1905–88)

This eminent and immensely learned Swiss theologian was born at Lucerne and joined the Jesuit Order in 1929. Although he left the Jesuits to set up his own order with his close friend Adrienne von Speyr in 1950, he remained a devout Catholic throughout his life. He was nominated a cardinal shortly before his death, indicative of his more conservative outlook.

Balthasar's massive output includes the immense study of theological aesthetics which in English translation is entitled *The Glory of the Lord* (German *Herrlichkeit*). In it he sought to recover the full splendour of Catholic theology by seeking to restore the importance of the divine beauty as an integral part of Christian belief and spirituality: a beauty that is supremely displayed in the unconditional self-giving of God on the cross. In that work and in his *Mysterium Paschale*, a profound exploration of the meaning of Good Friday and Easter, Balthasar lays particular stress on the importance of Christ's descent into hell, as representing God's willingness to go to the furthest possible extremes in order to ensure that no dimension of human experience, not even death, was cut off from his love. Balthasar's influence since his death has been considerable, despite the demanding intellectual nature of his work.

John Main (1926–82)

John Main entered the Benedictine Order after other careers in the British Foreign Service and teaching law at Trinity College, Dublin. He later founded the Benedictine Priory of Montreal. From there his followers, notably Lawrence Freeman, started the World Community for Christian Meditation.

His approach to spirituality centres on meditation using a mantra. His suggested word for repetition in meditation is the Aramaic *Maranatha*, meaning 'Come Lord. Come Lord Jesus.' His teaching is very simple, and he urges on his disciples the need for childlike simplicity.

As one meditates for half an hour each morning and evening, one will enter a silence. Then, after a lengthy period, the silences will grow longer. These are the times when we may be experiencing the very heart of God.

John Main led group meditation many times in Montreal, using music, humour and teaching to aid the process. He would sit by a stereo with relaxing music, then turn it off and give a brief instruction. The instructions of the last year of his life are collected in *Moment of Christ: The Path of Meditation*.[44] He also published *The Heart of Creation*, *Word into Silence* and *Word Made Flesh*.

Jean Vanier (1928–)

Jean Vanier is known primarily as the founder of l'Arche, which began in 1964. It is now an international network of communities for the mentally handicapped. It was in such a community that Henri Nouwen spent his last years, serving as a priest. Vanier brings a refreshing emphasis on community in a society and spiritualities devoted to the individual. His own repute is such that he was invited to give a major address to the gathering of the Anglican bishops of the world at Lambeth in 1998.

Almost everything I say here is the result of my own experience of life in l'Arche, the community in which I have been living for nearly twenty-five years… L'Arche is special, in the sense that we are trying to live in community with people who are mentally handicapped. Certainly we want to help them grow and reach the greatest independence possible. But before 'doing for them', we want to 'be with them'. The particular suffering of the person who is mentally handicapped, as of all marginal people, is a feeling of being excluded, worthless and unloved. It is through everyday life in community and the love that must be incarnate in this, that handicapped people can begin to discover that they have a value, that they are loved and so are lovable.[45]

Archbishops and popes

Arthur Michael Ramsey (1904–88)

Ramsey, Archbishop of Canterbury from 1961 to 1974, was very much engaged in the turbulent times of the 1960s and 70s. He had been a theological professor, advocating biblical theology. As archbishop, however, he called attention to the need for spiritual life among the clergy, and wrote on spiritual issues. Among his titles are *The Gospel and the Catholic Church* (1936), *The Glory of God and the Transfiguration of Christ* (1949), *God, Christ and the World* (1969), *The Christian Priest Today* (1972) and *Be Still and Know: A Study in the Life of Prayer* (1982).

In *Sacred and Secular: A Study in the Otherworldly and This-worldly Aspects of Christianity*, he wrote in the midst of 'secular theology' and the arguments over Bishop John Robinson's *Honest to God*. In a chapter on mysticism he writes,

How are contemplation and action to be blended together? Both belong to the life of the Christian community in the world. Because the Christian community has the duality of this-worldliness and otherworldliness, there are inevitably within the Christian family those who are called specifically to contemplative lives and those who are called more specifically to lives of energetic service of their fellows. But both belong to the totality of Christianity in the world.[46]

He was known for insisting that any Christian was capable of contemplative prayer:

The contemplation of God with the ground of the soul is, as these old writers insisted, accessible to any man, woman or child who is ready to try to be obedient and humble and to want God very much. Has it not been a mistake in the last few centuries in the West to regard meditation as a norm for all Christians and contemplative prayer as reserved only for advanced souls?[47]

Ramsey's concern for specifically Anglican spirituality emerges from his historical writing:

There is the Anglican sensitivity to the significance of spirituality, the life of prayer, for theology… Anglicanism can draw upon something larger than itself, to correct and deepen passing tendencies which might become trivial and hollow.[48]

John XXIII (Angelo Roncalli) (1881–1963)

Among those who have written on spirituality in the Roman Catholic tradition, none has had a more influential position than the popes, two of whom stand out at the end of this century. John XXIII was, perhaps, the most popular pope of the twentieth century. A fat man who was not ashamed of his body, he exuded good will to all.

It is a remarkable fact that Angelo Roncalli, Vatican diplomat in Turkey and France, and later patriarch of Venice, always preferred common people: 'This morning I must receive cardinals, princes and important representatives of the government. But in the afternoon I want to spend a few minutes with some ordinary people who have no other title save their dignity as human beings and children of God.'[49] The son of a peasant family, he never forgot his origins and never apologized for them.

John XXIII is remembered for calling Vatican II, which began in 1962 (see box, p. 315). Through the council, John permitted refreshing voices and

◆ **Pope John XXIII visiting prisoners at Rome's largest jail in 1958.**

movements which had not been allowed to surface to become officially recognized in the Roman Catholic Church. 'The Council?' he said as he moved towards the window and made a gesture as if to open it. 'I expect a little fresh air from it... We must shake off the imperial dust that has accumulated on the throne of St Peter since Constantine.'[50]

> We are here on earth not to guard a museum, but to cultivate a garden flourishing with life and promised to a glorious future... The representatives of the church do not want to take refuge on an island or lock themselves up in a fortress. This would be tantamount to neglecting immense multitudes, many of whom, without being Christians, nevertheless have an idea of God.[51]

Angelo Roncalli kept a journal from the age of fourteen. It has been edited and now appears as a large volume which includes his early principles and rules for his spiritual life, as well as his reflections until the year before his death.[52] The jolly old man who came to be loved with such deep affection as pope was the product of long serious hours of self-examination and prayer.

John Paul II (Karol Jozef Wojtyla) (1920–)

John Paul II had the longest papacy in the century, marking its twentieth anniversary in 1998. Although a participant in Vatican II, his policies have taken the church in a very different direction from those of John XXIII. He is perhaps best known for his world travels, the attempt to assassinate him in 1981, and his conservative views on sexual matters. His election in 1978 surprised many.

As a young man, Karol Wojtyla was an actor, a poet, a mountain climber, a priest who focused on young people, and most of all a philosopher. All of this was in the context of Communist Poland, which meant that the struggle there has shaped his thinking ever after. He was also influenced by the mystical tradition as indicated by this reminiscence:

> Before entering the seminary, I met a layman named Jan Tyranowski, who was a true mystic. This man, who I consider a saint, introduced me to the great Spanish mystics and in particular to St John of the Cross. Even before entering the underground seminary, I read the works of that mystic, especially his poetry. In order to read it in the original, I studied Spanish. That was a very important stage in my life.[53]

He rose quickly through the ranks of the hierarchy, showing great personal integrity and intellectual skill. After he became pope he worked hard to overthrow the communist rule of Poland first, then of Eastern Europe, and his influence on the dramatic events of the late 1980s and early 90s may not be known for a long time. He retained his interest in young people and they were attracted to him.

The pope's conservatism can been seen in

warnings about theology and ethics, but also in spirituality:

> For this reason it is not inappropriate *to caution* those Christians who enthusiastically *welcome certain ideas originating in the religious traditions of the Far East* – for example,

◆ **People making a pilgrimage to the Virgin Mary at Fatima, Portugal.**

techniques and methods of meditation and ascetical practice. In some quarters these have become fashionable, and are accepted rather uncritically. First one should know one's own spiritual heritage well and consider whether it is right to set it aside lightly... A separate issue is the *return of ancient Gnostic ideas under the*

guise of the so-called New Age... [Gnosticism is] in distinct, but not declared, conflict with all that is essentially Christian.[54] (original italics)

The pope revived Marian devotion, which had declined after Vatican II:

> Thanks to St Louis of Montfort, I came to understand that true *devotion to the Mother of God is actually Christocentric, indeed it is very profoundly rooted in the mystery of the blessed trinity*, and the mysteries of the incarnation and redemption. And so, I rediscovered Marian piety, this time with a deeper understanding.[55] (original italics)

There is a connection between the pope's philosophy and his spirituality. The centre of that philosophy is an insistence on the importance of personhood:

> The word *person* has great significance... In reflection on mankind, Christianity and the gospel have always brought us back (and always will) from the numerical aspect to the person, to that concrete, human self, one and irreplaceable, which is found in a unique relationship with God.[56]

Orthodoxy in the West

The twentieth century has seen a number of developments which have brought Orthodox believers to the attention of the West. There has been a growing appreciation of Orthodox spirituality, due in part to a growing literature in English. The 'diaspora' of Russian believers after the revolution of 1917 resulted in a few Russian church leaders becoming very influential in the UK. Anthony Bloom (see box, p. 337) and Nicolas Zernov became well known to Anglican and Catholic leaders. Both participated in the Fellowship of St Alban and St Sergius. They influenced, among others, Canon A.M. Allchin, a prolific spiritual writer, and Archbishop A.M. Ramsey.

Anthony Bloom (1914–)

Although he was born in Lausanne, Switzerland, Anthony Bloom, son of a Russian diplomat, lived in Russia and Persia as a child. He says he was aggressively anti-church until the age of fifteen. Then, after hearing a priest speak, he ran home to read the gospel to disprove what he had heard:

> While I was reading the beginning of St Mark's gospel, before I reached the third chapter, I suddenly became aware that on the other side of my desk there was a presence. And the certainty was so strong that it was Christ standing there that it has never left me. This was the real turning point... History I had to believe, the resurrection I knew for a fact. I did not discover, as you see, the gospel beginning with its first message of the annunciation, and it did not unfold for me as a story which one can believe or disbelieve. It began as an event that left all problems of disbelief behind because it was a direct and personal experience.[57]

Later he became a doctor of medicine at the University of Paris. He served as an officer in the Second World War, then in the French resistance. He took monastic vows in 1943 while still practising as a surgeon, then in 1948 was ordained to the Orthodox priesthood. In 1949 Bloom came to England as Orthodox chaplain to the Fellowship of St Alban and St Sergius, a newly formed group which sought closer understanding between Anglicans and Orthodox. After he was advanced to bishop in 1958, he was soon made Archbishop of the Russian Church in Britain and Ireland, exarch to the patriarch of Moscow in Western Europe, and finally metropolitan of Sourozh. He is best known for his classic *School for Prayer*, first published in 1970. Here are some selections from a book which some count as among the best of the twentieth century on prayer:

The day when God is absent, when he is silent – that is the beginning of prayer. Not when we have a lot to say, but when we say to God, 'I can't live without you, why are you so cruel, so silent?' This knowledge that we must find or die – that makes us break through to the place where we are in the Presence. If we listen to what our hearts know of love and longing and are never afraid of despair, we find that victory is always there on the other side of it.[58]

Only if we stand completely open before the unknown, can the unknown reveal itself, himself, as he chooses to reveal himself to us as we are today. So, with this open-heartedness and open-mindedness, we must stand before God without trying to give him a shape or to imprison him in concepts and images, and we must knock at a door...

Where? The gospel tells us that the kingdom of God is within us first of all. If we cannot find the kingdom of God within us, if we cannot meet God within, in the very depth of ourselves, our chances of meeting him outside ourselves are very remote. When Gagarin came back from space and made his remarkable statement that he never saw God in Heaven, one of our priests in Moscow remarked, 'If you have not seen him on earth, you will never see him in Heaven.'[59]

Labyrinth

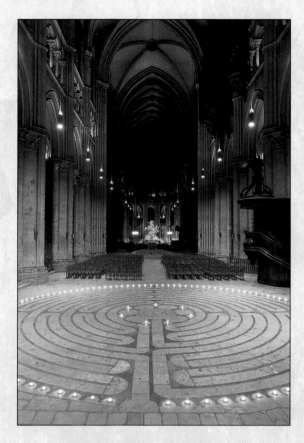

Built into the floor of Chartres Cathedral, France, there is a stone design which was originally used for meditative walking, but is now usually covered with chairs. This forgotten feature has been revived in Grace Episcopal Cathedral in San Francisco. With the leadership of Lauren Artress, not only has the cathedral itself built two labyrinths, but a centre for promoting their use internationally gives advice on how to build and teach about them.[60]

The spiritual practice involved is meditative walking. The labyrinth is not a maze, which confuses the searcher, but rather a very clear path from the periphery to the centre and back out again. Accompanied by music, a group of people can walk the labyrinth, meeting one another on the way, or one can walk in solitary. It is a practical way of using the body in meditation. The walk assumes added significance when considered as a metaphor for the journey of life. The walk inwards becomes a journey of purification, meditation in the centre is compared to illumination, and the journey outwards becomes union, a return to service in the world for the walking meditator who is refreshed and healed.

◆ **The labyrinth in Chartres Cathedral, illuminated by candles.**

North America

Recovering the traditions

In America, as in Europe, a number of writers have contributed to the discovery of classics of Christian spirituality. Among these have been A.W. Tozer (1897–1963), Douglas Steere (1901–), Bernhard Christensen (1901–84), E. Glen Hinson (1931–) and Lawrence Cunningham (1935–). But in addition to these 'generalists' are those who have focused on one particular tradition.

Among these we have revivals of the Benedictine tradition, the labyrinth (see box, above), and centring prayer.

Benedictine spirituality

The Rule of Benedict attracted late-twentieth-century writers. Like Esther de Waal in Britain, the American Joan Chittister, OSB, wrote a commentary, *The Rule of Benedict: Insights for the Ages*, in addition to other helpful spiritual writings. But the best-known advocate of the

Benedictine way in America is a third woman.

In 1993 a fresh voice spoke from Lemmon, South Dakota, a place which few Americans had heard of before reading Kathleen Norris's *Dakota: A Spiritual Geography*.[61] Here was a New York writer who moved to the Great Plains and rediscovered Christian faith. The book suggested that place was important to spirituality, and spent a good deal of time describing the climate, landscape and people of the plains. But it also described how this lapsed Presbyterian was renewed, especially by Benedictine monks! Kathleen Norris saw the unity of Christian faith and made an adult choice to adopt it as her own. She made her own observation of the present situation in the United States:

> The human need for religion did not disappear between the seventeenth century and the present day. If anything, its suppression as a respected form of emotional and intellectual engagement has resulted in a dramatic eruption of religion's shadow side, an America that is not a secular society, as some claim, but a land of myriad vague spiritualities, mostly individual and even secular in that they disdain the conventionally religious, anything related to church-going and other traditional practices of the Christian faith.[62]

In *Amazing Grace: A Vocabulary of Faith*, Norris deals with common religious terms in her usual frank manner, inviting the many people who consider themselves 'spiritual' but not 'religious' to reconsider the Christian church.

Centring prayer

Basil Pennington (1931–) and Thomas Keating (1917–) are two American monks who have written extensively on centring prayer.[63] This term is meant to describe an apophatic type of meditation, without images. Thus its main antecedents in the tradition are *The Cloud of Unknowing* and the writings of John of the Cross. Thomas Keating, a Cistercian who lives at St Benedict's Monastery at

Snowmass, Colorado, is a founder of Contemplative Outreach.

Through books and conferences, these men are teaching people how to centre themselves by quietly being in the presence of God, without petition; it is a difficult mental discipline to be free of thoughts, simply present to God. They teach the use of a special word of one's own choice, not as a mantra but as a homing device: when thoughts go astray, one comes back to God's presence by reminding oneself with this special word. This approach may be compared with those taught by John Main and Morton Kelsey.

Roman Catholic American writers and theologians

Dorothy Day (1897–1980)

Some of the most outstanding Christians have been adult converts to the faith. Dorothy Day dramatically changed her life when she was convinced of the truth, but she also took with her valuable convictions and skills from her past.

A Communist journalist living with her common-law husband in New York, she conceived a child, and at her birth insisted on baptizing her. This led to a sharp break with her lover, and her going full steam into the Roman Catholic Church. She was confused about what to do for a time, but then, as an answer to prayer, Peter Maurin appeared. He became her teacher, and she his disciple. He instructed her reading and gave her a vision of identification with the poor and opposition to war. This led to their founding first a newspaper, *The Catholic Worker*, and then a series of hospitality houses all over the country.

Dorothy Day's spirituality was a peace and justice commitment which was not comfortable for middle-class Catholics, nor for their priests and bishops. As a later social protester, Daniel Berrigan, wrote,

> Dorothy had written about, defended, explained, the following: cotton pickers, *braceros*, prisoners and ex-prisoners, families of every

Thomas Merton (1915–68)

Thomas Merton, arguably the greatest Catholic spiritual writer of the century, was a man of three continents. His boyhood and early manhood were lived in Europe, most of his adulthood in North America, and his last weeks and death were in Asia.

The child of a father from New Zealand and a mother from the United States, 'Tom' was born in Prades, a small city near the Pyrenees Mountains in southern France. He grew up first in French schools, then in English ones, culminating in a short time at Cambridge University.

Merton the monk

After he studied English literature at Columbia University, Thomas Merton made the decisive step of being baptized in a small Roman Catholic church in New York. Despairing of a world rapidly moving towards the Second World War, he gave himself to one of the strictest, most separate orders, the Trappists, whose Gethsemani Monastery in Kentucky he had visited on a retreat. Entering the monastery on 10 December 1941, he felt happy and at peace.

The abbot asked him to write about a number of saints; seeing his extraordinary gifts, he also asked him, against his will, to write an autobiography. The resulting book, *The Seven Storey Mountain*, became a bestseller in 1948, and thus made Merton known not only in the United States, but also around the world. The book seemed a twentieth-century version of Augustine's *Confessions*: the story of a worldly young man who radically changed direction, leaving the world behind to devote himself to God.

The Seven Storey Mountain had given him a national audience during the 1950s, but his perspective on the world changed in that decade. Perhaps it was sudden, as he described the awakening which occurred in Louisville, when he was sent there on business:

In Louisville, at the corner of Fourth and Walnut, in the centre of the shopping district, I was suddenly overwhelmed with the realization that I loved all those people, that they were mine and I theirs, that we could not be alien to one another even though we were total strangers. It was like waking from a dream of separateness, of spurious self-isolation in a special world, the world of renunciation and supposed holiness. The whole illusion of a separate holy existence is a dream…

This sense of liberation from an illusory difference was such a relief and such a joy to me that I almost laughed out loud. And I suppose my happiness could have taken form in these words: 'Thank God, thank God that I *am* like other men, that I am only a man among others.' To think that for sixteen or seventeen years I have been taking seriously this pure illusion that is implicit in so much of our monastic thinking![64]

His view of the world and its relation to the monastery changed so radically that he was no longer pleased to be known as the author of *The Seven Storey Mountain*. The book expressed a spirituality that he no longer believed. He saw now that as a monk, he was still in the world: he had not escaped it. And he saw his responsibility in that world to be wider than prayer for it:

The spiritual life is not a life of quiet withdrawal, a hothouse growth of artificial ascetic practices beyond the reach of people living ordinary lives. It is in the ordinary duties and labours of life that the Christian can and should develop his spiritual union with God… Christian holiness in our age means more than ever the awareness of our common responsibility to cooperate with the mysterious designs of God for the human race. This awareness will be illusory unless it is enlightened by divine grace, strengthened by generous effort, and sought in collaboration not only with the authorities of the church but with all men of good will who are working for the temporal and spiritual good of the human race.[65]

Merton the activist

As a participant in the world, Merton felt called to express his views, which went against the grain of American society. For the rest of his life, he was a prolific writer. He published about forty books of poetry, essays, inspirational books, and hundreds of journals and articles. The journals reveal a searching and wide-ranging intellect, with profound and sometimes humorous and wry insights into life. They do not tell us much about the intimate life Merton shared with God, but they reveal an eye for the ironies of life.

The articles address the major social issues of the day, and this was a new chapter in Merton's development. He came out for the civil rights movement, against the cold war, against nuclear weapons, and eventually against the Vietnam War. All of these were at one time lonely and unpopular stands, and the Catholic Church felt betrayed by its 'poster boy'. The censors attempted to shut him up, but he circulated mimeographed articles to a wide circle of friends.

As a monk, he was first professed as member of the order, then ordained a priest, and then served as novice master, teaching new monks, some of them attracted to the order by his own writings. Later he was the spiritual director of many in the monastery. He gradually desired to become a hermit within the order, and eventually obtained permission from his abbot to live alone in a small house on monastery grounds while still participating in the daily regimen of prayers seven times daily.

Merton in Asia

The third continent, Asia, engaged his attention from the 1950s. He began to study Zen Buddhism, Taoism, and Hinduism. He found a deep fellowship with the monks of these traditions, in their rejection of the values of much of Western society, the goals of wealth, power and pleasure. Merton's one and only long trip from the monastery was his last. He was able to visit India, Ceylon (now Sri Lanka) and Thailand on this journey. Near Bangkok, he was accidentally killed by an electric fan. He died twenty-seven years to the day after his entry into the monastery. After his death on 10 December 1968, many more of his writings were published, and his masterful spiritual authorship has continued to become better known.

◆ **Thomas Merton with the Dalai Lama at Dharamsala, India, in November 1968, shortly before his death.**

condition, the unemployed, priests and nuns, scholars, native Americans, monks, alcoholics, addicts, slum folks, auto workers, coal miners. Among others. She stood with them.[66]

Day wrote,

But the final word is love. At times it has been, in the words of Father Zossima, a harsh and dreadful thing, and our very faith in love has been tried through fire.

We cannot love God unless we love each other, and to love we must know each other. We know him in the breaking of bread, and we are not alone any more. Heaven is a banquet and life is a banquet, too, even with a crust, where there is companionship.

We have all known the long loneliness and we have learned that the only solution is love and that love comes with community.[67]

Protestant American writers and theologians

We begin our survey of Protestant writers in America with the following Quakers. The tradition of the Friends has many threads, but the intense waiting in Quaker worship has nourished both an inwardness of the Spirit and a social activism which many admire.

Rufus Jones (1863–1948), professor of philosophy at Haverford College, wrote some fifty-six books, most of them about spirituality or Quaker history. He wrote *Pathways to the Reality of God*, *Studies in Mystical Religion*, *A Boy's Religion from Memory*, *Finding the Trail of Life*, and many others. Jones was influenced by William James's *Varieties of Religious Experience*.

Thomas R. Kelly (1893–1941) is said to be 'the outstanding Quaker devotional writer of the twentieth century'.[68] He taught philosophy at Earlham and Haverford Colleges. Friends collected his writings after his death as *A Testament of Devotion*. It was so popular that it went through twenty printings.

Douglas V. Steere (1901–), also a Professor of Philosophy at Haverford, wrote *On Beginning from Within*, *Prayer and Worship*, *Dimensions of Prayer*, and *Doors into Life*, as well as translating Kierkegaard's *Purity of Heart is to Will One Thing* and introducing the writings of Friedrich von Hügel to Americans. He writes:

The individualism and pride and possessiveness that often creep into private prayer are dissolved away as we meet together in worship. The inward Christ makes the individual worshipper feel all afresh that he is just one ordinary sheep in God's vast fold, and often sweeps his heart with an overwhelming sense of creatureliness.[69]

Richard J. Foster (1928–)

Foster first became well known through his *Celebration of Discipline* (1978).[70] In it he describes twelve spiritual disciplines, divided into three types: the inward, outward and corporate disciplines. The opening chapter, on spiritual disciplines as a door to liberation, sets forth the need for disciplines as well as a theology concerning their role. While Foster believes that only by God's grace do we live the Christian life, he also asserts that the disciplines are needed to receive that grace in the continuous fashion necessary for the Christian journey:

Picture a long, narrow ridge with a sheer drop-off on either side. The chasm to the right is the way of moral bankruptcy through human strivings for righteousness. Historically this has been called the heresy of moralism. The chasm to the left is moral bankruptcy through the absence of human strivings. This has been called the heresy of antinomianism. On the ridge there is a path, the disciplines of the spiritual life. This path leads to the inner transformation and healing for which we seek... We must always remember that the path does not produce the change; it only places us where the change can occur. This is the path of disciplined grace.[71]

One of the values of this bestseller is its clear demonstration that the disciplines include the community and the world. Spirituality is intended to work itself out in daily life among others.

His first book was followed by many others. *The Challenge of the Disciplined Life* (originally *Money, Sex, and Power*) and *Freedom of Simplicity* carry on the theme of the disciplines, while *Prayer: Finding the Heart's True Home* and *Prayers from the Heart* focus on the central discipline of all.

In addition to these original works, Foster introduced many people to the classical writers in Christian spirituality through his co-edited book, *Devotional Classics: Selected Readings for Individuals and Groups* and his own *Streams of Living Water*.[72] This survey of the different Christian traditions of spirituality invites the reader to an appreciation of six different streams: the contemplative, holiness, charismatic, social justice, evangelical and incarnational. It will be noticed that these streams come from a variety of denominations: Catholic, Protestant and Orthodox.

Foster founded an organization called Renovaré which promotes teaching about the spiritual life in local congregations. His name will be remembered not only as a best-selling author, but also as the founder of an institution which focuses on ordinary people in Christian parish churches.

◆ **Martin Luther King shown in the jail cell in Jefferson County Courthouse Birmingham, Alabama (1967), from which he wrote *Letter from a Birmingham Jail*.**

Martin Luther King (1929–68)

Martin Luther King is the best known of African-Americans throughout the world. It is no accident that the civil rights leader was also a Baptist preacher. His vision of the mountain the night before his death testifies to spiritual roots which sustained his quest for justice through militant non-violence. His *Letter from a Birmingham Jail*, explaining why he chose to break the law for the sake of justice, and *Strength to Love*, indicating the spiritual basis for a long-term struggle, both testify to a spirituality which was expressed in his public actions.

The African-American population is overwhelmingly Christian, and has been nourished down through the centuries by a spirituality of endurance, liberation and celebration. African-Americans have suffered unspeakably from slavery and discrimination. Those sufferings have produced a community drawn together in worship which reaches the heart. James Cone, who earlier wrote hard-hitting books of black liberation theology, has turned in recent years to an analysis of the spirituality of the black church. He sees in the music and preaching of the Christian community the core of values which has sustained African-Americans.

Howard Thurman (1899–1981)

At the end of the century, Howard Thurman became better known than he ever was during his lifetime. His writings have been rediscovered by those who did not know him in person. He combines a deep sense of the importance of spirituality with his experience of discrimination as an African-American. First came *Jesus and the Disinherited* (1949), then *Meditations of the Heart* (1953) and *The Inward Journey* (1961). His autobiography, *With Head and Heart*, was published in 1979.

His 1935 trip to India, Burma and Ceylon was decisive for his spiritual experience and thought. In India he climbed to see Mount Kinchinjunga at sunrise:

More than forty years have passed since that morning. It remains for me a transcendent

Billy Graham (1918–)

One does not think of Billy Graham immediately as a spiritual writer; he is first and foremost an evangelist. But when one stops to think that more people have heard him speak in person than any other individual, and that he has influenced the spiritual practice of millions of Christians, not only in person but by television, radio, magazines, newspapers *and* spiritual books, then it is clear that Graham is a major figure in the history of Christian spirituality in our century. His is a Southern Baptist spirituality focused on the Bible and conversion.

The turning point in Graham's career was his 1949 Los Angeles campaign in a big tent. He did not arouse much attention until William Randolf Hearst sent reporters. It is still a mystery why Hearst did. The campaign was planned for three weeks but continued for seven, with 11,000 at the closing

service. In all there were over 400 Billy Graham Crusades.

Graham has written twenty-three books, including *Peace with God* (1953), *The Secret of Happiness* (1955), *World Aflame* (1965), *Angels: God's Secret Agents* (1975), *The Holy Spirit* (1978), *Approaching Hoofbeats* (1983), *A Biblical Standard of Evangelists* (1984) and *Storm Warning* (1992). The books reflect Graham's simple, straightforward style, his emphasis on eschatology and his appeal for faith. He was the founder of two major magazines: *Christianity Today*, which gives news and comment for evangelicals, and *Decision*, for supporters of his evangelistic association.

The crusades were deep exercises in prayer for those planning far in advance and for those present when Graham issued the invitation to come forward to 'receive Christ as your personal saviour'.[73]

Billy Graham's personal spiritual practice was focused on the Bible and prayer:

As for prayer, 'I have learned, I believe, to "pray without ceasing". I find myself constantly in prayer and fellowship with God, even while I am talking to other people or doing other things.' Sometimes this prayer is an unexpressed longing that an individual should come to Christ or find Christ's answer to a problem. It may be a flash thought, barely expressed as a prayer, when reading a newspaper or watching television news.[74]

◆ Billy Graham preaching at a crusade in St Paul, Minnesota (July 1973), to an audience of 21,000.

moment of sheer glory and beatitude, when time, space and circumstance evaporated and when my naked spirit looked into the depths of what is forbidden for anyone to see. I would never, ever be the same again.[75]

When he moved to San Francisco in 1945, he came deliberately to found a multiracial church, something he had never seen in America. His dream became the Church for the Fellowship of All Peoples. It was deliberately open to 'all denominations, nationalities, races, and cultures'. At Boston University, Thurman developed a course in Spiritual Disciplines and Resources. It was said that Martin Luther King carried Thurman's *Jesus and the Disinherited* in his briefcase.

Other prominent American Protestant writers

Another Southern Baptist who is widely influential, but may not come to mind immediately as a spiritual writer, is Jimmy Carter (1924–), the former president of the United States. In addition to building houses for Habitat for Humanity, leading diplomatic efforts to reconcile enemies and helping Africans to overcome widespread illnesses, Carter has been writing books: *Living Faith, Sources of Strength: Meditations on Scripture for a Living Faith* and *The Virtues of Aging*.

More radical is Jim Wallis, founder of *Sojourners* magazine, who calls evangelicals to political commitments far from the conservative 'Christian Coalition'. Wallis expects discipleship to include action with and for the poor.

There are many preachers and writers from Protestant traditions other than the Baptist who have been significant. Among those from a more liberal persuasion, Harry Emerson Fosdick (1878–1969) and Paul Tillich (1886–1965) wrote and preached on prayer.

More recently, two American Lutherans, among many, should be mentioned. Walter Wangerin, Jr, author of *Whole Prayer: Speaking and Listening to God*, is more widely known for his narrative abilities. He put these to work in his novelization

of the whole Bible, *The Book of God*, and in numerous other writings. Martin Marty (1928–) is arguably the best-known scholar of religion in America. He teaches at the University of Chicago and has appeared frequently in television documentaries. Beyond his scholarly writing (more than forty books), however, his pastoral heart has expressed itself in a number of spiritual writings. *A Cry of Absence: Reflections for the Winter of the Heart* uses the pain of his own griefs to minister to the reader, while *The Promise of Winter: Quickening the Spirit on Ordinary Days and in Fallow Seasons* is accompanied by photographs taken by his son Micah.[76]

Eugene H. Peterson (1932–) is a spiritual writer of the Presbyterian persuasion, until recently James M. Houston Professor of Spiritual Theology at Regent College, Vancouver. He was pastor for twenty-nine years at Christ Our King Presbyterian Church in Bel Air, Maryland. His spiritual writings include *Earth and Altar: The Community of Prayer in a Self-Bound Society, A Long Obedience in the Same Direction, Travelling Light, Take and Read: Spiritual Reading* and *The Contemplative Pastor.*

His *Subversive Spirituality* (1994) is a collection of shorter pieces which illustrate his main themes. Peterson's writing is often directly connected to the Bible. For example he writes on 'Saint Mark: The Basic Text for Christian Spirituality' and on 'Jeremiah as an Ascetical Theologian':

> Spirituality is always in danger of self-absorption, of becoming so intrigued with matters of soul that God is treated as a mere accessory to my experience. This requires much vigilance. Spiritual theology is, among other things, the exercise of this vigilance. Spiritual theology is the discipline and art of training us into a full and mature participation in Jesus' story while at the same time preventing us from taking over the story.[77]

Peterson is not afraid to speak boldly and controversially from his biblical posture. For example, he writes,

First overwhelmed and then considerably angered by the shopkeeper mentality of so many pastor colleagues, I felt the need to establish God-attentiveness and God-responsiveness in my own life and repudiate religious marketing entirely... My conviction is that the pastor must refuse to be shaped by the culture, whether secular or ecclesiastical, and insist on becoming a person of prayer in the community of worship. This is our assigned task; anything less or other is malpractice.[78]

An influential Episcopal writer is Alan Jones, Dean of Grace Cathedral in San Francisco. His titles include *Soul Making: The Desert Way of Spirituality*, *Exploring Spiritual Direction*, *Journey into Christ*, *Living in the Spirit*, and *Passion for Pilgrimage*.

Selected themes

Certain developments in twentieth-century Christian spirituality call for further comment. Among these is the emergence of spirituality as an academic discipline, from which this book has drawn. The actual life experience of spirituality is, of course, as old as humankind, and Christian spirituality emerged in the first century. After that time, monks, bishops and professors included spirituality in their theological writings as a matter of course. In the modern period, however, theology, like other fields, became specialized, and the concerns about spirituality were often left out or marginalized. In the late twentieth century, numbers of professors from seminaries, universities and colleges have woven together the different disciplines, including theology, biblical studies, history, literature, psychology, sociology, gender studies, and others, into a field of study called spirituality. The field is still very young, and not universally recognized. But there are doctoral programmes in the field in the United States, a Society for the Study of Christian Spirituality at Berkeley, California, and Oxford University has for

the first time a reader in the history of Christian spirituality, Benedicta Ward.

Among other themes which might be pursued, this chapter will conclude with reflections on the encounter with other religions; psychology, healing, spiritual direction and recovery; women's, men's, gay/lesbian and ecological spiritualities; and the media of spirituality.

Encounter with other religions

We speak today of the world as a global village, of a global neighbourhood. These phrases point to the new ease of transportation and communication in the twentieth century. Christians are now aware of the other major faiths in the world, perhaps as never before. These religions are no longer distant, but the faiths of our neighbours in the Western world as well as our global neighbours. The question this raises for Christian theology is the uniqueness of Christianity and its traditional claim to have the sole message of salvation for humankind. The questions raised for spirituality are about spiritual practice for Christians. To what degree ought Christians in Asia, Africa or the West adopt or adapt practices from other faiths? Are such practices helpful or hurtful? One can see a spectrum of opinion on these issues as Christians seek to contextualize the practice of their faith in different cultures.

Indigenous religions raise this question on different continents in different forms. For example, what should African and Asian Christians do concerning honouring their ancestors? Is it appropriate for North Americans of European descent to participate in sweat lodges and vision quests? How should Europeans respond to the revival of pre-Christian religions, including Celtic and goddess spiritualities? If North American Natives (Indians) lived in harmony with nature, can the new dwellers learn from their attitudes and practices? *Black Elk Speaks* is one of the classic books about Native American (Indian) spirituality.[79] Black Elk was a holy man who wanted to save the traditions of his people, the Oglala Sioux. Bulaji Idowu, Andrew Walls and John V. Taylor have all called for greater recognition of the wisdom of African traditions.

Judaism has become a major dialogue partner with Christians in the wake of the Holocaust. The horror of genocide by the Germans under Hitler has had its full impact only late in the century. Some Christians have come to think that this is a defining event for Christianity, and that all theology and spirituality should be changed from now on. The Holocaust was not initiated by Christians, but a vast number of Christians were complicit with it, either by ignoring the evidence or by serving as dutiful administrators of the horror.

A number of Jewish writers have been influential among Christians in this century, among them Martin Buber (1878–1965), Abraham Heschel (1907–72), both from very conservative Jewish backgrounds, and Elie Wiesel (1928–) perhaps the most well known of the Holocaust survivors. There is a revival of Jewish spirituality at the end of the century, and some Christians are finding its writings stimulating.

Christian-Jewish dialogues since Vatican Council II, and local dialogues between churches and synagogues are hopeful signs of reconciliation between the two communities.

Islam was the second largest religion at the close of the twentieth century, and claimed to be the fastest growing. Like Christianity, Islam is a global religion with people from every continent. Its most widely known American convert, Malcolm X (1925–65), after a period with the black Muslims, learned to know all Muslims as his brothers and sisters by joining the *haj* (pilgrimage) and praying with light-skinned believers.

Appreciating Islam is a challenge for Christians because of the long history of hostility between them and because of the present-day radical fundamentalists who have attacked people in the Middle East and the West with bombs, hijackings and guns. But the perception of Muslims as terrorists is an error. Surprising discoveries occur

◆ **Pope John Paul II welcomed by Muslim clerics in February 2000 at Cairo, accompanied by Sheikh Tantawi.**

when faithful Muslims and Christians enter into dialogue. Both may find similar criticisms of Western secular culture. Both honour a book and similar founders, including Abraham, the father of Judaism, Christianity and Islam.

Some Christians have found inspiration in the Islamic writings of the Sufis, especially the Persian sage, Rumi (1207–73).

Hinduism and Buddhism are major faiths whose spirituality has impressed Westerners deeply in this century. The conceptual differences between East and West are very deep, but many have jumped over this chasm to join the two, in different ways. Christian yoga and Christian Zen are practised by increasing numbers in the West. Among the leaders in this development have been Bede Griffiths, Thomas Merton and William Johnston.

Among those from the Buddhist tradition who are highly regarded and read by Christians are the Dalai Lama (1935–) from Tibet and Thich Nhat Hanh (1926–) from Vietnam.

Christians have differing and very strong feelings about the way to encounter people of other traditions. For some, recognizing any non-Christian practice as valuable is tantamount to abandoning the saving value of the Christian gospel. For others, Christians have too long been triumphalist, colonialist and arrogant, refusing to recognize the activity of God outside the Christian church. The questions raised for Christian spirituality are complex and need answering in specific cases with the wisdom of the Holy Spirit.

Psychology, healing, spiritual direction and recovery

Spirituality and psychology

The twentieth century is distinctive for the development of the new fields of psychology and psychoanalysis. By the end of the century, the general public thought in psychological terms and listened respectfully to the results of psychological research. Since spirituality has to do with the human person, even the soul (psyche), its interests clearly overlap with psychology. Early in the century there was a great rift between the two, which still has not been fully overcome. Psychologists and psychoanalysts were frequently opposed to religion as unscientific, neurotic and harmful to human well-being in general. Christians were mistrustful of therapists. Today the situation has improved a great deal. Psychologists are perhaps less defensive about their discipline as a science, and Christians have seen the value of psychological concepts and therapies.

The Myers–Briggs type indicator is now widely known, based on the work of Jung. It is one basis for understanding the variety of spiritualities within Christianity. *Prayer and Temperament*[80] draws out the implications of the four and the sixteen different personality types to show the prayer which is most natural to them. These types are associated with each of the four gospels and with major spiritual traditions, such as Ignatian, Augustinian, Franciscan and Thomistic spiritualities. The general point is that each person is different, and that churches should not expect all their members to appreciate the same types of spiritual disciplines or manners of prayer.

An alternative way of typing people, frequently used by spiritual directors also, is the enneagram.

◆ Jung spent many years researching mandalas as part of his belief in the collective unconscious. This 19th-century mandala shows the period between death and reincarnation.

This is a type indicator which has nine different roles which people tend to play. Again, it is a manner of understanding oneself and how one might differ from others in order better to find one's spiritual path and to serve others in the community.

The mythological context of the collective unconscious is what stimulated Joseph Campbell (1904–87) to write his many studies of world mythology. He came to the attention of many viewers in the United States when he made a series of television programmes, *The Power of Myth*, hosted by Bill Moyers. His views have become very influential among spiritual seekers, though they cannot be identified as Christian spirituality. His is a meta-religious view in which all religions are ultimately the same.

Karl G. Jung (1875–1961)

Among those who worked in this field, the most influential for Christian spirituality was Karl Jung. The son of a minister, Jung was born and spent most of his life in Switzerland. In 1909 his doctoral dissertation was titled 'On the Psychology and Pathology of So-Called Occult Phenomena'. This reflected a long interest in spiritual realities outside as well as within Christianity.

This was a sharp contrast to the inventor of psychoanalysis, Sigmund Freud. Whereas Freud dismissed religion in *The Future of an Illusion*, Jung welcomed it, even in its belief in life beyond the grave:

> I therefore consider that all religions with a supramundane goal are eminently reasonable from the point of view of psychic hygiene… From the standpoint of psychotherapy it would therefore be desirable to think of death as only a transition, as part of a life process whose extent and duration are beyond our knowledge.[81]

Among Jung's understandings of the human being which have influenced spiritual writers are the unconscious and the collective unconscious

with its archetypes, the stages of life, the masculine and feminine sides of the personality, the 'shadow', and the main factors in personality types used by the Myers–Briggs type indicator. Concerning the collective unconscious, he writes:

> Summing up, I would like to emphasize that we must distinguish three psychic levels: (1) consciousness, (2) the personal unconscious, and (3) the collective unconscious… The collective unconscious… is not individual but common to all men, and perhaps even to all animals, and is the true basis of the individual psyche… The collective unconscious – so far as we can say anything about it at all – appears to consist of mythological motifs or primordial images, for which reason the myths of all nations are its real exponents. In fact, the whole of mythology could be taken as a sort of projection of the collective unconscious.[82]

Morton Kelsey (1917–)

Morton Kelsey, an Episcopalian priest and former professor at Notre Dame University, is a major American spiritual writer who explicitly states his debt to psychology, and especially to Karl Jung. When writing on meditation, Kelsey voices his frustration that other writers have not seen the value of the psychologists:

> I found next to nothing written about prayer and meditation that took into account the discoveries about the human soul made by depth psychology in the ninety-five years of activity. Freud, Adler, Jung, Maslow, Carl Rogers and Rollo May might as well not have existed for all the importance they seem to have for most writers on prayer.
>
> Yet the masters of the devotional life and the depth psychologists need each other. They have each discovered something of the reality of the human soul, and each discipline has something important to say to the other. There is a burning need to see meditation in this new light.[83]

M. Scott Peck (1936–)

Scott Peck grew up in New York City, the child of well-to-do parents. He attended private schools, Harvard University and Columbia Medical School. He trained to be a psychiatrist, but then something surprising happened.

In 1978 Peck wrote *The Road Less Travelled: A New Psychology of Love, Traditional Values and Spiritual Growth*. It climbed to the bestseller list and remained there for years, finally reaching five million copies in print. Here was a psychotherapist who became a Christian during the writing of this bestseller, writing about spiritual growth in a society assumed to be thoroughly secular! He later described his own spiritual change in this way:

My faith is overtly Christian. Lily, with her gift for secrecy, is much less open about it; she is what I have come to call a closet Christian. In either case our faith did not come easily to us. As a child I was lukewarmly exposed to Christianity. Lily was exposed to it with a vengeance. Neither of us bought it at the time. Only after we had passed the midpoint of our lives did it begin to make sense to us, and then it was not a straw that we grasped in desperation. Rather it was an understanding that we were reluctantly dragged to by years of accumulated experience.[84]

If the book is about spirituality and psychology, there is no doubt that the psychology predominates. Some Christians will wince at some of his statements. But Peck was able to write about sin, grace and responsibility in a way that both Christians and sceptics could appreciate. Major sections of the book were titled 'Discipline', 'Love', 'Growth and Religion' and 'Grace'. The authority of his profession, his skill at telling stories of real people, and the fresh approach to old subjects like sin and love, led to the success of this book. Here are some samples:

I define love thus: the will to extend one's self for the purpose of nurturing one's own or another's spiritual growth.[85]

The path to sainthood goes through adulthood. There are no quick and easy shortcuts. Ego boundaries must be hardened before they can be softened. An identity must be established before it can be transcended. One must find oneself before one can lose it.[86]

When his first book was such a dramatic success, Peck quit the practice of psychotherapy and took on a new career and a new perspective: he gradually became a full-time writer and no longer focused on individual lives, but the building of community. In *The Different Drum: Community-making and Peace* (1987), he wrote, 'In and through community lies the salvation of the world.'[87]

Kelsey's manner of meditating uses images, which is different from centring prayer. Kelsey is quite clear that not everyone will find his own method most helpful. He notes that his wife uses centring prayer, which appealed more to her.

Morton Kelsey has written over forty books, many of them on subjects which others do not dare to touch. His writings on dreams are one of the few treatments of the subject from a Christian and Jungian point of view. He also writes about speaking in tongues, a subject ripe for dialogue between psychologists and charismatics. A personal favourite, however, is *Healing and Christianity*, which gives a brief history of Christian involvement in both physical and emotional healing.

Thomas Moore (1940–)

Another psychotherapist with a Christian background is Thomas Moore, a former monk. His *Care of the Soul: A Guide for Cultivating Depth and Sacredness in Everyday Life* and following books, *The Soul of Sex: Cultivating Life as an Act of Love, The Re-enchantment of Everyday Life, Soul Mates: Honouring the Mysteries of Love and Relationship,* as well as television appearances and conferences, have pointed to the need for a depth dimension in modern life. His choice of the term 'soul' has been so influential that dozens of new titles appeared thereafter with 'soul' prominently displayed. Moore does not mean spirituality exactly by this term, but clearly they are closely related. He invites the reader to take time for nourishment. Moore's approach is not explicitly Christian, and thus appeals to Americans who shy away from religion. Scott Peck has been much more open about his Christian faith and his problems with the churches than Moore.

Pastoral care and spiritual direction

The study of psychology has also influenced two very different approaches to personal ministry in the church. Pastoral care developed most completely in the United States, but is now part of theological curricula all over the world. Such care has not always had spiritual concern at its centre. After a long period of dominance by psychological objectives, the concerns of spirituality are becoming more evident. Another of the great spiritual writers of the century, Henri Nouwen, was trained in pastoral care in the United States, then, by his writing, helped to transform the field.

Henri Nouwen (1932–96)

Henri Nouwen was born to a pious family in Nijkerk, in the Netherlands. He was an energetic child who played being the priest from the age of six. Nouwen had a stable Roman Catholic home and felt an early calling to the priesthood. His education continued in both theology and

psychology, partly in the Netherlands and partly in the United States. Perhaps it was his fourth book, *The Wounded Healer,* a book about pastoral care, which first made him well known, but his second book, published in the same year (1972) in the United States, was an introduction to Thomas Merton, with the subtitle *Contemplative Critic.*

Three of his spiritual journals describe major periods of ministry: *Genesee Diary* concerns his monastic sabbatical at Genesee Abbey, Rochester, New York; *Gracias!* his Latin-American encounter with the poor and with Gustavo Gutierrez; and *The Way to Daybreak* his identification of the mentally handicapped as the poor whom he finally felt called to serve. He died in the autumn of 1996, after writing approximately forty books on the spiritual life.

There are two major changes I would point out in Nouwen's spiritual journey. He first became socially engaged in 1965 when he marched with Martin Luther King in Selma, Alabama. And in the mid-1970s he changed the way he wrote. He no longer tried to describe spiritual principles or practices in the abstract, but wrote about them in the context of his own experience. Much of his success as a writer is due to his ability to name common feelings and experiences in a very open and honest fashion. The intellectual brilliance of Merton the poet can be off-putting, in spite of his gregariousness and good humour; the frankness of Nouwen the counsellor invites identification with another wounded, stumbling human being:

> There is within you a lamb and a lion. Spiritual maturity is the ability to let lamb and lion lie down together. Your lion is your adult, aggressive self. It is your initiative-taking and decision-making self. But there is also your fearful, vulnerable lamb, the part of you that needs affection, support, affirmation, and nurturing.
>
> When you heed only your lion, you will find yourself overextended and exhausted. When you take notice only of your lamb you will easily become a victim of your need for other people's attention. The art of spiritual living is to fully

claim both your lion and your lamb. Then you can act assertively without denying your own needs. And you can ask for affection and care without betraying your talent to offer leadership.[88]

Spiritual direction

Spiritual direction has become an established practice not only in Roman Catholic circles but also in Anglican and Protestant ones. Among the writers who have added greatly to this field are Kenneth Leech (1939–), Gerald May (1898–) and Tilden Edwards (1935–).

Kenneth Leech is an Anglican priest who serves not in a comfortable suburb or university, but in East London, an area much in need of Christian ministry. The first of his trilogy is one of the basic books about spiritual direction: *Soul Friend*. His second, *True Prayer*, focuses on that most basic of the Christian disciplines. Finally, *Experiencing God: Theology as Spirituality* addresses the issues about God, the subject and object of the spiritual life:

There is indeed considerable evidence not of God's death, but rather of his absence and of the continued, and at times frenzied, quest for his presence by many people…

Of the upsurge in interest in spirituality there can be little doubt. The urgent need is for spiritual discrimination and discernment between the phoney and the authentic, between the false gods and the true God. What is certainly clear is that the uncritical espousal of the total secularization of the West, widely held in the 1960s, is wrong.[89]

Tilden Edwards and Gerald May teach at one of the newer schools for training spiritual directors, the Shalem Institute, Washington, DC. Edwards is known as the author of *Living Simply Through the Day: Spiritual Survival in a Complex Age*, *Living in the Presence: Spiritual Exercises to Open Your Life to the Awareness of God* and especially *Spiritual Friend*, his description of spiritual direction. May is

the author of *Care of Mind/Care of Spirit*, *Will and Spirit* and *Addiction and Grace*. Catholic training centres have been present for a long time, but Protestant centres are younger, and only now developing their potential.

Little has been written for the clergy who are interested in developing a programme of spiritual disciplines and spiritual direction in their parishes, but John Ackerman's *Spiritual Awakening: A Guide to Spiritual Life in Congregations* gives very practical advice.[90]

Positive thinking and self-esteem

One of the more controversial movements in American spirituality has been the 'positive thinking' school of thought first named by Dr Norman Vincent Peale. As pastor of an influential New York congregation, he wrote a number of books to promote the idea that our thoughts need to be positive if we are to be able to accomplish our goals. Later he was a founder of *Guideposts* magazine.

Part of the criticism of this school of thought is due to the similar approach taken in much 'success'-oriented literature available on the bookstands. It does not seem to be distinctly Christian, and its main focus may directly contradict the idea of grace and focus on the commercial and material rewards that so many seek who are not yet spiritually awakened. But the Christian promoters of this idea have had success themselves in reaching and influencing the American population.

Robert H. Schuller (1926–)

Schuller is known for his television programme, *The Hour of Power*, and for his congregation, the 'Crystal Cathedral', in Garden Grove, California. He is a minister of the Reformed Church in America, and has demonstrated his ability to communicate with the Californian culture. He is the author of many books and is acquainted with celebrities.

◆ **Crystal Cathedral, the glass-enclosed studio of TV evangelist Robert Schuller, in Garden Grove, California (1987).**

He prefers the term 'possibility thinking' to 'positive thinking'. His focus is on what the psychologists have called self-esteem: 'Self-esteem then, or "pride in being a human being", is the single greatest need facing the human race today.'[91]

Schuller believes that a new Reformation is needed in the way the church thinks, or it will fall by the wayside:

For decades now we have watched the church in western Europe and in America decline in power, membership and influence. I believe that this decline is the result of our placing theocentric communications above the meeting of the deeper emotional and spiritual needs of humanity...

I call upon the church to make a commitment to remodel itself until it becomes the best thing that has ever happened to the human race. The church becomes the best friend for all people

when we proclaim the gospel of Faith – Hope – and Love which truly stimulates and sustains human self-esteem.[92]

Chicken Soup

In the last decade of the twentieth century a popular series of anthologies ran to over fifteen million copies. Very much like inspirational stories told in the *Reader's Digest* or *Guideposts*, the contents are narratives of inspiring deeds, often by ordinary people. The first of these volumes was *Chicken Soup for the Soul: 101 Stories to Open the Heart & Rekindle the Spirit*.

Following the tremendous success of the first volume, more than fifteen others have appeared,

Recovery from addictions

A dialogue between twelve-step programmes and Christian spirituality is underway. Alcoholics Anonymous was founded in the United States in the 1930s by two men, 'Bill W. and Dr Bob' – William Wilson (1895–1971) and Robert Smith (1879–1950) – who were deeply influenced by the Oxford Group, later known as Moral Rearmament.[93] A thorough discussion of the influences which shaped AA indicates both Christian and secular movements.[94] They and other alcoholics were often repelled by the churches and conventional Christianity, but they deeply believed in the message of the gospel. They developed groups for alcoholics which accepted all people, unlike most churches.

Over the years, the original twelve steps have been supplemented by literature incorporating basic attitudes, prayer and meditation. One of the most widely used texts in the spirituality of AA is the 'Serenity Prayer' which is the first part of a longer prayer composed by theologian Reinhold Niebuhr:

God grant me the grace to accept with serenity
the things I cannot change,
courage to change the things I can,
and wisdom to know the difference,
living one day at a time,
enjoying one moment at a time;
accepting hardship as the pathway to peace,
taking as you did this sinful world as it is,
*   not as I would have it;*
trusting that you will make all things right,
*   if I surrender to your will;*
that I may be reasonably happy in this life,
and supremely happy with you forever
*   in the next. Amen.*[95]

In recent decades this literature has increasingly caught the attention of Christian spiritual directors and pastors. In the future there may be more possibility of cooperation between the churches and AA.

One of the elements in this interest is the insight about the ubiquitous nature of addiction.[96] That is, what AA pioneered for one kind of addiction is relevant for others, and not only the obvious ones like drugs, gambling and overeating. Compulsive behaviours are not necessarily a conscious choice; they relate to Paul's lament in Romans, 'I do not do the thing I want, but the very thing I do not want is what I do' (Romans 7:19).

The twelve steps are a programme which includes several features of earlier spirituality, such as a soul friend, daily examen, restitution, surrender to God and sharing your belief with others. It focuses on the discovery and overcoming of irrational, harmful habits which have at their root the insistence that 'I am God.' The root of addiction is seen to be spiritual, and healing begins by surrender to grace, the gift of God.

The combination of the twelve steps, the regular group meetings and the personal mentor provide a powerful programme for spiritual change, one that may be of great potential value for all church members.

including *Chicken Soup for the Christian Soul*. The Chicken Soup series is popular spirituality aimed at Americans who want something short and uplifting. The sales of this series and its expansion to television indicates Americans' desire for success and self-esteem as much as it does their hunger for the spirit.

Healing in the charismatic tradition and beyond

Virtually all Christians pray for healing at some point. The impetus for such prayer in the twentieth century has come from a number of sources, but perhaps none as widespread as the charismatic renewal. The antecedent influence for many in the United States was Agnes Sanford (1897–1976), born in China of missionary parents, the wife of an Episcopal clergyman, and with him the founder of 'Schools of Pastoral Care'. Her first writings, including her *Healing Light*, preceded the charismatic renewal, but she influenced many within it, and joined it in her later years. Among her titles are *The Healing Power of the Bible*, *The Healing Gifts of the Spirit*, and many others including a novel, *The Lost Shepherd*. Sanford emphasized the willingness of God to heal and the need for emotional as well as physical healing. She invited the person to visualize the healing taking place, and to visualize the person wrapped in the love of God. She coined the term 'healing of memories' for an emotional release from past wounds through the re-imaging of the event in the presence of Jesus. Her loving approach seemed quite different from the bombastic scenes of Oral Roberts healing people on television in mid-century.

Agnes Sanford influenced Morton Kelsey and helped introduce Francis MacNutt (1925–) to healing ministry. MacNutt was a Dominican professor of preaching before he began a worldwide healing ministry. His first and best-selling book was called simply *Healing* (1974). In it he distinguishes four types of healing: spiritual, physical, emotional and deliverance from evil

spirits. He emphasizes that love is just as important as faith in the healing process. Like other charismatics, he encourages people to touch the person prayed for, surrounding them in a group. MacNutt, speaking in Nigeria, asserted that he had not come to show off his healing powers, but to encourage ordinary Christians to pray for one another in confidence.

After several years of team ministry, MacNutt resigned from the order and married an Episcopalian psychotherapist. Now Frank and Judith MacNutt lead their own organization, Christian Healing Ministries. Others who were influential in this movement include Ruth Carter Stapleton, sister of President Jimmy Carter, and the Linn family.

In the UK there has been considerable interest in healing services in the Anglican Church, not always related to a charismatic approach. Bishop Morris Maddocks first led a commission to study the issues involved, and has encouraged the spread of a healing ministry through such books as *The Healing Ministry of the Church*. Episcopalians in the United States founded the Order of St Luke and welcome members of all denominations for training in praying for the sick.

Women's, men's, gay/lesbian and ecological spiritualities

Feminist spirituality

By the middle of the century women gained the vote in most Western democracies. Betty Friedan published *The Feminine Mystique* in 1963. Late in the century, several United Nations events were devoted to the status of women worldwide.

For Christians the feminist movement has often created division and controversy, as did the struggle over slavery. Radical proponents of the movement have no interest in reforming Christianity, but would like to see it destroyed, for they see it as patriarchal and misogynist to the

Rosemary Radford Ruether (1936–)

Many women scholars have remained within the Christian church and sought reform within it along feminist lines. Perhaps none of these is better known or more prolific than Rosemary Radford Ruether. She is a Roman Catholic lay theologian and mother of three. Although she does not commonly write under the heading of 'spirituality', she assured this writer that, for her, theology includes spirituality, and ought not to be separated from it.

Ruether brings to her feminist position an ethical perspective that is common among Christian feminists, a concern for all people, especially people of colour, gays and lesbians, and economically disadvantaged groups. She applies the liberation theology of Latin America to all peoples in North America. She has also been an outspoken critic of Israeli oppression of Palestinians, and taught for ten years at the Howard School of Religion, one of the leading African-American seminaries in the United States.

The breadth of her vision is seen in the following statement from her widely known book, *Sexism and God-Talk*:

> In reflecting androcentrism (males as norms for humanity), women must also criticize all other forms of chauvinism: making white Westerners the norm of humanity, making Christians the norm of humanity, making privileged classes the norm of humanity. Women must also criticize humanocentrism, that is, making humans the norm and crown of creation in a way that diminishes other beings in the community of creation.[97]

Ruether's method

Ruether values two elements very highly in her theology: the Hebrew prophets and the experience of women:

> Feminism appropriates the prophetic principles in ways the biblical writers for the most part do not appropriate them, namely, to criticize this unexamined patriarchal framework. Feminist theology that draws on biblical principles is possible only if the prophetic principles, more fully understood, imply a rejection of every elevation of one social group against others as image and agent of God, every use of God to justify social domination and subjugation. Patriarchy itself must fall under the biblical denunciations of idolatry and blasphemy, the idolizing of the male as representative of divinity. It is idolatrous to make males more 'like God' than females.[98]

Thus Ruether sets aside those parts of the Bible which do not meet this principle. She uses the same logic by which the ritual law was set aside by early Christians, and biblical teaching about slavery by nineteenth-century Christians. This controversial step sets her apart from those theologians who regard the whole Bible as authoritative. As she is agnostic about personal life after death, it is clear that her theology is focused on societal issues in this world:

core. This leads conservative Christians to decry feminism as a foreign element which has no place in the church, where the Bible or church tradition has already decided these issues, and no change is needed. But a considerable number of Christians have come to see the path of reform as the most appropriate. Christian women's voices have

persuaded many people that the whole tradition needs to be rethought on gender issues. The Bible itself describes patriarchal societies, yet there is evidence that Jesus and Paul, among others, treated women differently than their contemporary societies dictated.

Amid this flurry of change, some women have

Prophetic faith denounces religious ideologies and systems that function to justify and sanctify the dominant, unjust social order. These traditions are central to the Prophets and to the mission of Jesus.

Feminist theology makes explicit what was overlooked in male advocacy of the poor and oppressed: the liberation must start with the oppressed of the oppressed, namely, *women* of the oppressed. This means that the critique of hierarchy must become explicitly a critique of patriarchy. All the liberating prophetic visions must be deepened and transformed to include what was not included: women.[99]

Ruether represents the social-prophetic side of Christian feminism. She is unafraid to criticize the oppressive powers of our time, and in this way conforms her practice to the prophets, except that she focuses on gender oppression, which they did not. Other feminist writers take different perspectives. Among the influential Christian writers at the close of the twentieth century were Anne Carr, Elizabeth Johnson, Denise Lardner Carmody, Sally McFague and Mercy Amba Oduyoye.

◆ **Women's Liberation march at the Statue of Liberty, New York, in August 1970.**

American Protestant, has moved into a serious advocacy of Hellenistic religion, in such books as *Why Women Need the Goddess*. In Britain, Daphne Hampson, denied ordination as an Anglican, has written several books as a post-Christian.

Feminism within and outside the church is a global phenomenon. Women of colour have sometimes dissociated themselves from the term feminism, using womanist or *muhajarista* theologies, to express the distinctive character of their struggle for liberation as non-white women. African and Asian women have joined women of the Americas and Europe in calling for a new status for women in spirituality, theology and church life.

left the Christian faith because of its patriarchal sins, the best known of these on different trajectories. One of the earliest and most well known is Mary Daly, a former Roman Catholic, whose early *Beyond God the Father* (1968) was followed by increasingly radical visions of women's religious life. More recently, Carol Christ, an

Masculine spirituality

A number of men have responded to the women's movement with neither full rejection of their stance nor full acceptance. Some have modelled a men's movement on the women's movement. The 'liberation' of men, as with women, has included consciousness-raising, group meetings, criticism of societal stereotypes, and an attempt to rediscover the essential masculine. The movement is not satisfied with the common images of masculinity in our culture. The damaging things which men do are sometimes related to the psychological training of boys and to the 'Father Wound', the absence of the father from the life of the boy. A new word in the lexicon, to parallel 'misogyny' is 'misandry', the hatred of the masculine.

Sam Keen is able to articulate a man's need for liberation from domination of female power, symbolized by his word WOMAN. He also introduces a criterion which acts as a critique of various feminist positions. One section of his book is called, 'Ideological Feminism – No! Prophetic Feminism – Yes!' He goes on to explain:

> Prophetic feminism is a model for the changes men are beginning to experience. / Ideological feminism is a continuation of a pattern of general enmity and scapegoating that men have traditionally practised against women.[100]

What do these perspectives mean for Christian spirituality? A number of writers have taken up the task of exploring the questions involved, and a major movement among evangelicals has emerged. One of the issues, as for feminist spirituality, is the image of God. Should we abandon the traditional liturgical and spiritual language for addressing God (or even the very word 'God') in light of the critique of patriarchy? One of the most thoughtful responses was given in Brian Wren's *What Language Shall I Borrow? God-Talk in Worship: A Male Response to Feminist Theology*.[101]

David James, building on Wren and others, asks and answers,

Is a masculine God necessary for masculine spirituality? The answer is 'yes'... The conclusion of the authors represented in these pages is that masculine images of God are a rich source of reflection for men. To eradicate them from the religious consciousness would be as great an act of gender-violence as any ever perpetrated by patriarchy.[102]

An alternative view is offered by conservative writers and by the movement called Promise Keepers. Founded by football coach Bill McCartney of the University of Colorado, the idea of the Promise Keepers first emerged on 20 March 1990. Its early form featured large sports stadium rallies to call men to faith in Jesus Christ and to responsibility within their families. Later it focused on local churches.

The Promise Keepers' rallies have been criticized by feminists, who see them as an assertion of male power; by liberal Protestants, who don't approve of their ideals; and by men from liturgical backgrounds, who find the freewheeling and highly expressive style of worship off-putting. The relation of Promise Keepers to feminism is not officially hostile, but some spokespersons have gone beyond Promise Keepers' policy in their statements, which seem to put women in second place.

Gay/lesbian spirituality

One of the distinctive developments of the twentieth century has been the expression of gay and lesbian Christian spirituality in print.[103] Gay, lesbian, bisexual and transgender Christians found a new confidence in their ability to define their own experience in a Christian context (to 'come out', so to speak) and to work towards inclusive ministries in their communities of faith. Thus, celebration of the diversity in the human family and the demand for freedom, justice and dignity for all have been emphasized throughout the literature. Agape love must be enfleshed, not just articulated, in order for healthy spiritual communities to flourish.

Many of the early spiritual expressions of gay and lesbian people focused on the difficulty of living with secrets that suffocated one's faith and the journey of working through the pain of honesty into a new life of freedom and integrity in naming the truth, which shall 'set you free'. This personal authenticity with God, self and others forms the basis for the development of spiritual qualities (love, compassion, truth, generosity, forgiveness, tolerance, peace and courage) necessary to live in right relationship with God, self and others. Unhealthy spirituality fosters the opposites of the above qualities: lies, hatred, intolerance, fear, envy, jealousy, social injustice, discrimination and war.

Much of the literature of gay and lesbian spirituality rejects an anti-body dualism which claims that the body and all earthly matter are evil and must be suppressed. This spirituality has a positive view of the physical nature of earthly reality. Gay and lesbian spirituality concurs with feminist spirituality in that it helps individuals to find a voice, and it reclaims sensual embodiment in the world. This appreciation of physical reality carries over into an appreciation of nature and of our ecological responsibility in the cosmos.

Ecological spirituality

Another distinctive development in twentieth-century spirituality has been a new appreciation for the natural world and the role of human beings in enhancing or destroying it. Threats of nuclear winter and global warming, awareness of the extinction of species and of pollution of land, sea and air, have focused urgent attention on ecology in ways not seen in previous history. Christianity has been blamed for this situation by those who see it as exploitative. The text from Genesis 1:28, 'Be fruitful and multiply, and fill the earth and subdue it; and have dominion over the fish of the sea and over the birds of the air and over every living thing that moves upon the earth,' has come in for a great deal of criticism and re-examination. Does it give moral justification for the exploitation of the earth, the consumerist lifestyle so typical of

◆ **Trees in Ontario, Canada, dying from acid rain. An increasing number of Christians now believe it is their responsibility to take an active interest in protecting the environment.**

developed economies? Or have science, technology and commerce worked together to bring us to the present impasse? What spiritualities of ecology have to contribute is that ecology is a spiritual matter, not just a technological one: people will need conversion to a different way of perceiving the world if they are going to act differently.

At this point, remember Teilhard de Chardin whose theology saw an evolving universe as its framework. Recall Albert Schweitzer who taught reverence for life. Recall John Paul II who named Francis of Assisi as the patron saint of ecology. Note Joseph Sitler (1904–87), the Lutheran theologian who began to write about this problem even in the 1950s. These writers are among those who began to call for a change in the attitudes of affluent Christians towards the world they live in.

Rosemary Radford Ruether comments on the spiritual roots of our problems and what can be done about them:

A healed relation to each other and to the earth... calls for a new consciousness, a new symbolic culture and spirituality. We need to transform our inner psyches and the way we symbolize the interrelations of men and women, humans and earth, humans and the divine, the divine and the earth… Rather we must see the work of eco-justice and the work of spirituality as interrelated, the inner and outer aspects of one process of conversion and transformation.[104]

Matthew Fox (1940–) champions 'creation-centred spirituality', or simply 'creation spirituality'. His concerns are wider than ecology alone, but there is a strong emphasis on the ecological in his writing. Fox is a controversial figure, having been expelled from the Dominican Order and the Catholic priesthood in 1993. He became an Episcopal priest in San Francisco in 1994. Fox wrote an account of these events in his *Confessions: The Making of a Post-Denominational Priest*.[105] In his view the expulsion was unjust, and he received support from Bede Griffiths and Leonardo Boff, among others.

Why were Fox's critics so adamant that he was no longer teaching the orthodox Christian faith? Because he seemed to set aside the major theme of Christian salvation, what he calls fall/redemption-centred spirituality. That is, in spite of his calls to reject dualisms and to work as a both/and theologian, Fox cut the Christian faith into two opposing sides and called for the victory of one over the other. He seemed to set the first article of the creeds (on creation) over against the second article (on redemption).

Let us get a taste of the passion of this spiritual reformer from his early book, *On Becoming A Musical Mystical Bear: Spirituality American Style*:

For we have numerous instances in Western spiritualities of a life-denying rather than a life-affirming spirituality. And the fact is that these, more than the Jewish spirituality of life-affirmation (which we should recall Jesus came out of), have held dominance in Western civilization. Repression, not expression; guilt, not pleasure; heaven, not this life;

sentimentality, not justice; mortification, not developing of talents: these are the earmarks of what Western spirituality has for the most part done… The spiritualities of Plato, Augustine, and Denis [Pseudo-Dionysius] can lead to life-denial and deep human pessimism. Yet they have invariably been the more popular and influential spirituality in Christianity.[106]

Finally we note an ecological writer who is not as well known as Ruether or Fox, but who wants to stay much closer to the traditional posture of Christian spirituality. Charles Cummins in *Eco-Spirituality: Toward a Reverent Life* proposes a new paradigm which is neither the fall/redemption tradition of Catholic tradition nor Fox's creation spirituality, but a synthesis of both.[107] Christians who share some of Fox's criticisms of the tradition but who disagree with his rejection of the centrality of the cross will find Cummins approach more acceptable. Cummins offers a helpful survey of the developments, both scientific and spiritual, which led us to our present crises, and offers suggestions for spiritual practice. Among many others, he calls for Christians to simplify their lives. This includes consuming fewer of the world's resources through eating lower on the food chain, using public transport instead of private cars, and resisting the tendency to throw away what can be reused into our vast and growing landfills. Cummins' concerns are widely shared among thoughtful Christians in the developed world, but the practice of them is far behind their moral support.

The media of spirituality

The book is not the only medium!

At the end of the twentieth century the book is still dominant, and may remain so for a long time, because of its portability and the personal attachment one may develop with a physical book. But more and more we are seeking information from other resources. In addition, if spirituality is indeed holistic, it is shared not only in print, but by all the experiences of human life and all the means of human expression.

The primary medium of conveying spirituality is the human being. Sometimes called mentoring, discipling, or directing, the process by which people learn the spiritual life is primarily contact with another person. Evelyn Underhill wrote, 'We most easily recognize spiritual reality when it is perceived transfiguring human character, and most easily attain it by sympathetic contagion.'[108] When we think of Jesus and the first followers, it is surely the most important means by which they learned the spiritual life.

To round out this chapter, the discussion will point to some of the areas other than books of devotion, sermons, biographies of saints, and other traditional spirituality books. Our discussion must be very limited in scope, and the reader will find more information in works devoted especially to these fields: communities (see box, p. 362), literary and visual arts, music, radio and television and the internet.

Literary arts

Poetry and fiction can challenge or nourish the spiritual life, even if they are not written by Christians. Therefore the whole of twentieth-century literature is potentially fruitful for spirituality. In this section, however, the discussion will be limited to a very few writers who are well known and write from an explicitly Christian standpoint.

One of the best-selling novels at the start of the century was Charles Sheldon's *In His Steps*, which made famous the question, 'What would Jesus do?' It demonstrates the changes which occur in a church and a city when people commit themselves to ask this question before making any decision of consequence. The novel showed changes in the newspaper, the saloons and the city government. It is remarkable to see at the end of the century a youth movement in the United States, in which WWJD? is written on bracelets, to raise the same question as Sheldon. Of course there are problems

with this approach, but it demonstrates both the attraction of Jesus as a moral force and the need for guidance in a pluralistic and relativistic society.

At mid-century a group of literary persons gathered in an Oxford pub to read one another's fiction. They called themselves the 'Inklings'.[109] Among them were C.S. Lewis (1898–1963), J.R.R. Tolkien (1892–1973), Dorothy L. Sayers (1893–1957) and Charles Williams (1886–1945). G.K. Chesterton (1874–1936) had been a strong influence on Lewis. This group produced works which took the spiritual realm seriously, but each in a different way. Lewis has perhaps become the best known of them, because of his seven children's stories about Narnia, his space trilogy,

◆ **C.S. Lewis outside an Oxfordshire church in 1938.**

Communities

The twentieth century has seen a burst of imagination in the formation of new Christian communities of all kinds. See the accounts of the Iona community and the Taizé community above. Without attempting to survey all of these communities, this account will give some representative examples.[110]

The Brüderhof (Society of Brothers)

In 1920 a group of Germans under the leadership of Eberhard Arnold (1883–1935), who had been influenced by the Lutheran Pietist Christoph Blumhardt (1805–80), formed a new community.[111] It was forced out of Germany during the time of Hitler, resettled in Paraguay, and finally moved to New York State. This is a community of goods, a residential community which supports itself by making toys and printing books. It is very conservative on gender roles and sexual matters, rather like the Mennonite tradition with regard to the holy supper and pacifism. In the late twentieth century the community affiliated with the Hutterites. This is one of the longest-lasting non-monastic communities, and it is held together by a strict but humane spirituality very much in contrast to the society around it.

Corrymeela

The Corrymeela community was founded to serve the needs of reconciling Catholics and Protestants in Northern Ireland. It was founded by the Reverend Ray Davey, who with others first visited Iona, Taizé and Agape communities to gain an understanding of what was involved. They purchased a former holiday house with the name Corrymeela. After much volunteer work, they celebrated the official opening in 1965.

From October 1968 the 'Troubles' really started and the British Army became directly involved in 1969.

Corrymeela took teenagers out of the battle zones for a while. Later the community formed groups on the ground in Belfast and other trouble spots.

In 1971 Corrymeela joined the Cross of Nails network of communities and formed a special relationship with Coventry cathedral. The London Corrymeela Venture and Dublin Glencree Centre began in 1974.

Koinonia partners

Clarence Jordan (1912–69), a southern Baptist preacher with a doctorate in New Testament Greek and author of the distinctively translated Cottonpatch Gospels, founded a new interracial community in Georgia in 1942:

'Never did Paul or Peter or Stephen point to an empty tomb as evidence of the resurrection,' he said. 'The evidence was the spirit-filled fellowship.' His mind locked in on the channel of thought: 'If that closeness of sharing a common life exhibited the spirit of Jesus alive in those men, why not now…'[112]

The Ku Klux Klan came calling often, but through much tribulation, the community worked to reconcile black and white. Koinonia became the birthplace of a great Christian movement for decent housing: Habitat for Humanity (1976).

the movie and play *Shadowlands* and his many essays about Christian themes. He described his conversion to Christian faith in *Surprised by Joy*, and the demonic realm perhaps better than any theological treatise in *The Screwtape Letters*, a fictional correspondence between a chief demon and his underling. Lewis's imagination has made the Christian message credible for many in the twentieth century.

Also in Britain, another adult convert to Christianity, Susan Howatch (1940–), a successful novelist, took up the subject of developments in the Anglican church. She wrote a series of six novels, one about each decade from the 1920s onwards, about the cathedral at 'Starbridge' (Salisbury) where she took up residence in the cathedral close.[113] Her novels deal very directly with Anglican religious orders and spiritual direction. She has been called the Anthony Trollope of the twentieth century.

In America, the short stories of Flannery O'Connor (1925–64) startle with insights about the human character from a distinctive Roman Catholic perspective. John Updike (1932–) occasionally shows his Lutheran background and convictions in his novels.

Frederick Buechner (1926–), a Presbyterian minister who is now a full-time writer, has published more than twenty books – novels, journals and non-fiction. Among his titles are *Godric*, *The Sacred Journey*, *Telling Secrets* and *Telling the Truth: The Gospel as Tragedy, Comedy and Fairy Tale*. His writing is crisp and insightful, whether discussing the Bible or contemporary life.

Visual arts

All of the visual arts – painting, sculpture and architecture – have expressed and influenced the spirituality of the twentieth century. Again, the materials are far too numerous to describe here. Georges Rouault's (1871–1958) work gave a fresh interpretation of the face of Christ. Jacques Maritain makes a connection between Rouault's painting and the experience of the mystics:

◆ *Christ on the Cross*, by Georges Rouault (1871–1958).

This unity of creative emotion and the working reason… comes to perfection only as the final victory of a steady struggle inside the artist's soul, which has to pass through trials and 'dark nights' comparable, in the line of the creativity of the spirit, to those suffered by the mystics in their striving towards union with God. Such was the case with Rouault.[114]

Music and dance

One thinks immediately of hymnody as most directly related to spirituality, as Christians praise God and arouse community feeling by singing together. But in addition to hymns, music contributes in liturgical chant, choir anthems and short choruses. Taizé has contributed to the universal church through its short, repetitive calls to God.

Dancing is also an expressive form of praise and reflection. Many African churches now feel free to praise God in dance, at least during the offering. Liturgical dances are now well known in Anglican and Episcopal circles, as small groups of dancers lead the congregation in a bodily meditation.

Spirituality on radio and television

Commercial radio and television have become a significant part of twentieth-century culture, for some seemingly the most important part. It is not just religious programming that deals with spirituality, but any programming is potentially helpful or destructive. A great deal of concern has been raised about the Hollywood fascination for violence and sex. In most countries there is a considerable time spent on commercials, increasingly clever advertisements which seek to convince the viewer that she or he is inadequate without the product displayed. Consumerism is perhaps the most important obstacle to growth in spirit and television is a major instrument of consumerist views.

The problem with the 'electronic church' is that it removes people from the need to interact with others in a congregation. The spirituality of someone who relies entirely on television will be limited by the lack of interpersonal contact and physical community.

Spirituality on the internet

The latest electronic development affecting large numbers of people is the use of the internet to communicate on a global scale. One may use this network in a wide variety of ways: for personal communication, conveying large amounts of business or academic data, or for entertainment. It is also a tool for those interested in Christian spirituality, and functions in different ways in that connection.

One of these is the development of Christian websites, locations which contain text, pictures or music. The 'surfer' who is exploring the medium can respond in different ways. What may happen is transfer of information. For example, someone may learn for the first time about Julian of Norwich, or learn where the nearest Cursillo is taking place, or read a text of a papal encyclical. Or the surfer may become engaged on a deeper level and experience the website as meditation, praise or worship.

In addition to websites, the internet includes chat rooms devoted to specific subjects. One may find conversation partners about specific spiritual subjects, such as Thomas Merton or charismatic renewal. Here people can react in much more personal ways, and be transformed by dialogue, just as this can happen in face-to-face dialogue. Such participation is often anonymous, by using a pseudonym on the web, but for some it leads to meeting others in person.

Jeff Zaleski suggests in *The Soul of Cyberspace* that the development of the web is bigger than merely another means of communication and that the web leads humanity into a new level of consciousness, by potentially connecting all the persons around the globe. Zaleski discusses the influence of Teilhard de Chardin on philosophers of cyberspace:

> Teilhard's influence on thinking about cyberspace is incalculable. Nearly every formulation about the arising of a global brain – the global network of computers with human beings at the terminals – finds its roots in interpretations of his thought, as does the ancillary idea that this arising will lead to some sort of transformation of humanity, and hence of Gaia... But Teilhard's specific formulation is Christian, indeed Roman Catholic, as he was a Jesuit... By *a distinct Centre* Teilhard means precisely the 'personal God' of Christianity... Teilhard was a Christian, and the Omega he

describes is... not digital but mystical.[115] (original italics)

Zaleski's survey of websites shows that all world religions have significant numbers of sites. This young, rapidly developing medium is becoming a factor for more and more of the world's population. It is potentially very helpful for those growing in spirit, but its capability is still unknown.

Conclusion

This chapter has focused on selected themes that make the twentieth century distinctive in the history of Christian spirituality. The century witnessed a proliferation of spiritualities. Pentecostal/charismatic spiritualities appeared, and the growth of Christianity in non-European settings sparked efforts to indigenize or contextualize Christian spirituality in various cultural environments.

It was a century of appalling genocide, war and starvation. Christians lost an easy optimism about the course of the world and revived a commitment to spiritualities of social justice for the oppressed. The role of Christians in the suppression of native peoples and in the Holocaust led Pope John Paul II to confess and ask forgiveness in a formal document and during a dramatic visit to Israel in 2000.

As peoples came to see themselves as a global village, symbolized by the photo of the earth taken from the moon, the importance of inter-religious relations became evident. Christians wrestled with their identity as new immigrants in Europe and America brought other religions and spiritual practices. In addition, Western non-religious spiritualities, such as twelve step and New Age, challenged Christian identity. Christians sought to employ the insights of the new disciplines of psychology and sociology in their teaching and practice while retaining their integrity.

As in previous centuries, the arts, travel and communities were important expressions of Christian spirituality, but what was new was a global network of electronic communication, whose full effects will not be seen until the twenty-first century reveals its perils and potential.

EPILOGUE

A Spirituality for
a New Millennium

Christianity enters its third millennium in the context of a world changing more rapidly and unpredictably than ever before. That makes generalizations about the past, or predictions about the future, so uncertain as to be scarcely worth attempting. Even so, it is fairly clear that the new millennium will see a steady shift of gravity within Christianity from northern to southern hemispheres. Churches are, in general, growing far more vigorously in the latter than they are in the former. International headquarters, at present located in northern centres like Rome, Geneva and Canterbury, may in the next century be relocated in Africa, Asia or South America.

Such relocations can only increase the importance of the relationship between Christianity and other historic world faiths. Spirituality may have a vital part to play here, not least in insisting that such a relationship must be based on far more than doctrinal formulations, and needs to acknowledge the growing recognition of how much the great spiritual traditions of humanity have in common. This is not at all to argue for some bland synthesis between them, or even for a postmodern consumerist temptation to fashion one's own designer spirituality by drawing small amounts from all of them. But it is to emphasize that the search for shared moral and spiritual values, and the longing for a deeper mutual respect and understanding between different religious traditions, must continue and grow. At the academic and leadership levels it is in many respects far advanced. At the grass roots, it has hardly begun. And interreligious clashes in the Balkans, Indonesia and Nigeria (to name only a few flashpoints) remind us of why it matters.

At the dawn of the new millennium, it is not only the human societies of the world that face an unpredictable and rapidly changing future. The earth itself does too. The enormous increase in human population, and the threat to the earth's delicate ecological balance as a result of global warming, are only the two most prominent threats on the horizon: there are many more. A Christian spirituality whose primary concern is with the inner processes of the psyche, or the search for self-fulfilment on the part of the leisured, may find itself doing little more than rearranging deckchairs on the *Titanic*.

Yet these very challenges may serve to send us all back to our roots, and to rediscover, in the inexhaustible riches of the Bible, resources which can sustain and direct us as we look towards so uncertain a future. The Bible reminds us constantly of the chaos from which all that exists emerged, and which remains an ever-present source of destruction if it is not subjected to God's continuing work of creation and redemption. It reminds us of the delicate interrelationship that holds together human beings and all other creatures – and of the terrible cost of failing to maintain that relationship. But above all it reminds us of the nature of the God who is revealed to us in Jesus Christ – a God whose love has no limits and whose willingness to bear the terrible consequences of human evil opens up for us and our descendants the way to the heavenly Jerusalem that is both the transfiguration of this world and the life of the world to come.

In scripture, life is a journey, frequently (indeed usually) undertaken without any certain knowledge of where we are going, a journey during which we are only briefly and intermittently in control. The experience of exile and restoration, the collision between past blessings and present sorrows, the tension between the greatness of our vocation and the frailty of our natures – all these are explored in the Bible in ways that are enduringly relevant, and never more so than they are now. But something else is even more relevant still: the extraordinary persistence of the God whom Christians believe in, the stubborn refusal of that God to abandon us, irrespective of the number of times we abandon God. The story of Christian spirituality bears witness to the countless ways in which individuals and communities have felt the presence and heard the call of that God, have been disturbed by the divine anger or delighted by the divine beauty, and have felt impelled to give all they had to give in response. The sheer attractiveness of the God who is revealed in Jesus Christ is in itself the strongest cause for hope as we set out, like Abraham, not knowing where we are going.

If we were to single out just one of the innumerable resources offered to us by the Bible and the Christian spiritual tradition as we face the new millennium, it might be the sabbath. For this is at once the crown and the conundrum of the divine creation. The day on which God paused for breath is an enduring reminder to us that we are made for more than work. We are made for worship, for play, for childlike wonder, for a constant experience of renewal and re-creation, for a right balance between activity and rest. We are made for one another, and for God, and only when we remember all this will we be able to cooperate with God in furthering the divine purposes, and experience for ourselves the firstfruits of all that God longs to share with us. When that happens, all of us, with unveiled faces, seeing the glory of the Lord as though reflected in a mirror, are being transformed into the same image from one degree of glory to another; for this comes from the Lord, the Spirit.

In these words from his second letter to the Corinthians, Paul passionately articulates the vision of what lies ahead, the goal and potential of physical life, the eternal sabbath for which we were made. That vision has stretched, summoned and sanctified millions of people during the past two millennia of Christian history. There is every reason to hope it will do the same in the third.

Gordon Mursell

FURTHER READING

Please see the Endnotes for further sources.

INTRODUCTION
Jesus and the Origins of Christian Spirituality
Paul F. Bradshaw, *The Search for the Origins of Christian Worship*, London: SPCK, 1992.

Richard A. Burridge, *Four Gospels, One Jesus?* London: SPCK, 1994.

Donald Coggan, *The Prayers of the New Testament*, London: Hodder & Stoughton, 1967.

C.F.D. Moule, *Worship in the New Testament*, London: Lutterworth, 1961.

H.H. Rowley, *Worship in Ancient Israel*, London: SPCK, 1967.

E.P. Sanders, *Judaism: Practice and Belief, 63* BCE–66 CE, London: SCM Press, 1992.

CHAPTER 1
The Early Church Fathers
Timothy Barnes, *Early Christianity and the Roman Empire*, London: Variorum, 1984.

Peter Brown, *The World of Late Antiquity*, London: Thames & Hudson, 1971.

Henry Chadwick, *The Early Church*, London: Hodder & Stoughton, 1968.

Derwas Chitty, *The Desert a City*, Crestwood, New York: St Vladimir's Seminary Press, 1977.

William Frend, *The Rise of Christianity*, London: Darton, Longman & Todd, 1984.

John McGuckin, *At the Lighting of the Lamps: Hymns from the Ancient Church*, Oxford: SLG Press, 1995.

Frances Young, *From Nicaea to Chalcedon*, Philadelphia: Fortress Press, 1983.

CHAPTER 2
Celtic and Anglo-Saxon Spirituality
Oliver Davies, *Celtic Christianity in Early Medieval Wales*, Cardiff: University of Wales Press, 1996.

Douglas Dales, *Called to Be Angels*, Norwich: Canterbury Press, 1998.

Douglas Dales, *Dunstan: Saint and Statesman*, Cambridge: Lutterworth Press, 1988.

Douglas Dales, *Light to the Isles*, Cambridge: Lutterworth Press, 1997.

Kathleen Hughes, *The Church in Early Irish Society*, London, 1966.

James Mackey, *Introduction to Celtic Christianity*, Edinburgh, 1989.

Henry Mayr-Harting, *The Coming of Christianity to Anglo-Saxon England*, London: Batsford, 1991.

Benedicta Ward, *High King of Heaven*, London: Mowbrays, 1999.

Benedicta Ward, *The Venerable Bede*, London: Geoffrey Chapman, 1990.

CHAPTER 3
Saints and Mystics of the Medieval West
The Atlas of the Crusades, ed. Jonathan Riley Smith, London: Times Books, 1991.

The Cistercian World: Monastic Writings of the Twelfth Century, ed. Pauline Matarasso, Harmondsworth: Penguin Classics, 1993.

Eamon Duffy, *The Stripping of the Altars: Traditional Religion in England, c. 1400–c. 1580*, Yale University Press, 1992.

David Farmer, *The Oxford Dictionary of Saints*, Oxford: Oxford University Press, 1997.

Bruno Scott James, *Letters of St Bernard*, London: Burns and Oates, 1953.

David Knowles, *The English Mystical Tradition*, London: Sheed & Ward, 1961.

Vladimir J. Koudelka, *Dominic*, ed. Simon Tugwell, London: Darton, Longman & Todd, 1997.

L'Histoire des Saints et de la Sainteté Chretienne, ed. F. Chiovaro and others, Paris: Hachette, 1986–88, vols 6 and 7.

John R.H. Moorman, *A History of the Franciscan Order from its Origins to the Year 1517*, Oxford: Clarendon Press, 1968.

Oxford Dictionary of the Christian Church, ed. F.L. Cross, (3rd edition, E.A. Livingstone), Oxford: Oxford University Press, 1997.

Richard W. Southern, *Saint Anselm: A Portrait in a Landscape*, Cambridge: Cambridge University Press, 1990.

André Vauchez, *Sainthood in the Later Middle Ages*, Cambridge: Cambridge University Press, 1997.

CHAPTER 4
The Eastern Christian Tradition
Cheslyn Jones, Geoffrey Wainwright and Edward Yarnold, *The Study of Spirituality*, Oxford/New York: Oxford University Press, 1986.

Vladimir Lossky, *The Mystical Theology of the Eastern Church*, Cambridge: James Clarke, 1997.

Andrew Louth, *The Origins of the Christian Mystical Tradition*, Oxford: Clarendon Press, 1983.

Bernard McGinn, John Meyendorff and Jean Leclercq, *Christian Spirituality: Origins to the Twelfth Century*, New York: Cross Road Publishing, 1993.

John Meyendorff, *Byzantine Theology*, New York: Fordham University Press, 1974.

The Philokalia, tr. and ed. George Palmer, Philip Sherrard and Kallistos Ware, vols 1–3, London: Faber & Faber, 1979–84.

Tomas Spidlik, *The Spirituality of the Christian East*, Kalamazoo: Cistercian Publications, 1986.

Kallistos Ware, *The Orthodox Church*, London: Penguin, 1993.

Kallistos Ware, *The Orthodox Way*, London/Oxford: Mowbrays, 1979.

CHAPTER 5
The Russian Spirit
Nicholas Arseniev, *Russian Piety*, Crestwood, New York: St Vladimir's Seminary Press, 1997.

The Art of Prayer: An Orthodox Anthology, ed. Chariton of Valamo, London: Faber & Faber, 1997.

George Fedotov, *A Treasury of Russian Spirituality*, London: Sheed & Ward, 1989.

Pierre Kovalevsky, *Saint Sergius and Russian Spirituality*, Crestwood, New York: St Vladimir's Seminary Press, 1976.

Valentine Zander, *St Seraphim of Sarov*, Crestwood, New York: St Vladimir's Seminary Press, 1997.

CHAPTER 6
The Protestant Tradition in Europe
John Bunyan, *The Pilgrim's Progress*, ed. Roger Sharrock (Penguin Classics), Harmondsworth: Penguin, 1965.

John Calvin, *Institutes of the Christian Religion*, tr. F.L. Battles, Library of Christian Classics, vols 20–21, Philadelphia/London, 1975.

Timothy George, *Theology of the Reformers*, Nashville, 1999.

Christopher Hill, *A Turbulent, Seditious and Factious People: John Bunyan and His Church*, Oxford: Clarendon Press, 1988.

Martin Luther's Basic Theological Writings, ed. Timothy F. Lull, Minneapolis: Fortress Press, 1989.

Alister McGrath, *Reformation Thought: An Introduction* (2nd edition), Oxford: Blackwell, 1993.

J.I. Packer, *A Quest for Godliness: The Puritan Vision of the Christian Life*, Wheaton, 1994.

Reformed Reader: A Sourcebook in Christian Theology, vols 1 and 2, Louisville, 1993.

The works of Jeremy Taylor, William Law and the Wesleys are available in the 'Classics of Western Spirituality' series, London: SPCK.

CHAPTER 7
Catholic Saints and Reformers

Tessa Bielecki, *Teresa of Avila: An Introduction to Her Life and Writings*, London: Burns and Oates, 1994.

Norbert Cummins, OCD, *Freedom to Rejoice: Understanding St John of the Cross*, London: HarperCollins, 1991.

François Fénelon, *Christian Perfection: Extracts from His Letters*, ed. H. Backhouse, London: Hodder & Stoughton, 1990.

Francis de Sales and Jane de Chantal, Letters of Spiritual Direction, tr. P.M. Thibert, intro. by W.M. Wright and J.P. Power, Classics of Western Spirituality, New York: Paulist Press, 1988.

Margaret Hebblethwaite, *Finding God in All Things: Praying with St Ignatius*, London: Collins Fount Paperbacks, 1987.

Michael Hollings, *Thérèse of Lisieux*, London: Collins, 1981.

Susan Muto, *John of the Cross for Today: The Ascent*, Notre Dame: Ave Maria Press, 1991; and *John of the Cross for Today: The Dark Night*, Notre Dame: Ave Maria Press, 1994.

André Ravier, *Bernadette*, London: Collins, 1979.

The most important and interesting books to read are the actual texts written by people such as Teresa of Avila or Francis de Sales, and by looking in the endnotes to this chapter you can find details of some good modern translations with helpful introductions.

CHAPTER 8
The Anglican Spirit

Patrick Collinson, *The Religion of Protestants: The Church in English Society (1559–1625)*, Oxford: Clarendon Press, 1982.

Frances Knight, *The Nineteenth-Century Church and English Society*, Cambridge: Cambridge University Press, 1995.

Diarmaid MacCulloch, *Thomas Cranmer: A Life*, New Haven and London: Yale University Press, 1996.

The English Religious Tradition and the Genius of Anglicanism, ed. Geoffrey Rowell, Wantage: Ikon, 1992.

Gordon Rupp, *Religion in England 1688–1791*, Oxford History of the Christian Church, Oxford: Clarendon Press, 1986.

CHAPTER 9
The Protestant Tradition in America

Early New England Meditative Poetry: Anne Bradstreet and Edward Taylor, ed. Charles E. Hambrick-Stowe, Sources of American Spirituality Series, New York: Paulist Press, 1988.

Henry Alline: Selected Writings, ed. George A. Rawlyk, Sources of American Spirituality Series, New York: Paulist Press, 1987.

Charles Hodge, *The Way of Life*, ed. Mark A. Noll, Sources of American Spirituality Series, New York: Paulist Press, 1987.

Horace Bushnell: Sermons, ed. Conrad Cherry, Sources of American Spirituality Series, New York: Paulist Press, 1985.

Roger Lundin, *Emily Dickinson and the Art of Belief*, Grand Rapids, Michigan: Eerdmans, 1998.

Phoebe Palmer: Selected Writings, ed. Thomas C. Oden, Sources of American Spirituality Series, New York: Paulist Press, 1988.

Quaker Spirituality: Selected Writings, ed. Douglas V. Steere, Classics of Western Spirituality Series, New York: Paulist Press, 1984.

Albert J. Raboteau, *Slave Religion: The 'Invisible Institution' in the Antebellum South*, New York: Oxford University Press, 1978.

Voices from the Heart: Four Centuries of American Piety, ed. Roger Lundin and Mark A. Noll, Grand Rapids, Michigan: Eerdmans, 1987.

Walter Rauschenbusch: Selected Writings, ed. Winthrop S. Hudson, Sources of American Spirituality Series, New York: Paulist Press, 1984.

CHAPTER 10
Spiritualities of the Twentieth Century

Alcoholics Anonymous, New York: Alcoholics Anonymous World Services, 1976.

Anthony Bloom, *School for Prayer*, London: Darton, Longman & Todd, 1970 (also issued as *Beginning to Pray*, New York: Paulist Press, 1970).

Richard Foster, *Celebration of Discipline*, San Francisco: Harper, 1978.

C.S. Lewis, *The Chronicles of Narnia*, HarperCollins.

Thomas Merton, *Thomas Merton: Spiritual Master*, ed. Lawrence S. Cunningham, New York: Paulist Press, 1992.

M. Scott Peck, *The Road Less Travelled: A New Psychology of Love, Traditional Values and Spiritual Growth*, New York: Simon & Schuster, 1978.

Rosemary Radford Ruether, *Gaia and God: An Equal Feminist Theology of Earth Healing*, San Francisco: Harper, 1992.

Spirituality of the Third World, eds K.C. Abraham, Bernadette Mbuy-Beya, New York: Maryknoll, 1994.

The Study of Spirituality, eds Chelyn Jones, Geoffrey Wainwright, Edward Yarnold, Oxford: Oxford University Press, 1986.

Jeff Zaleski, *The Soul of Cyberspace: How New Technology is Changing Our Spiritual Lives*, San Francisco: Harper, 1997.

This list is intended to give a sample of the breadth of spiritual writing in the century. It is not a choice of those of the highest quality as judged by the author.

ENDNOTES

CHAPTER 1
The Early Church Fathers
1. *First Letter of Clement* 54.
2. *First Letter of Clement* 60.
3. *Second Letter of Clement* 16.
4. *The Shepherd of Hermas*, Vision 2.3.
5. Ignatius of Antioch, *Letter to the Romans* 4.
6. Polycarp of Smyrna, *Letter to the Philippians* 7–8.
7. Polycarp of Smyrna, *Letter to the Philippians* 4.
8. *The Epistle to Diognetus* 5–6.
9. Justin Martyr, *Dialogue with Trypho the Jew* 8.1.
10. Justin Martyr, *Second Apology* 2.1.
11. Justin Martyr, *Dialogue with Trypho the Jew* 96.2.
12. *Sayings* 16.13.
13. *Sayings* 18.1.
14. *Sayings* 8.19.
15. John Chrysostom, *Sermons on the Gospel of St John*, 77.
16. Proskomide ritual of the Romanian Orthodox Church tradition.
17. 'O Blessed Light', attributed to Ambrose, in John McGuckin, *At the Lighting of the Lamps: Hymns from the Ancient Church*, Oxford: SLG Press, 1995.
18. Augustine of Hippo, *On the Spirit and the Letter* 5.
19. Augustine of Hippo, *The City of God* 10.30.
20. Augustine of Hippo, *Confessions* 7.8.

CHAPTER 2
Celtic and Anglo-Saxon Spirituality
1. Adapted from T.O. Clancy and G. Markus, *Iona – The Earliest Poetry of a Celtic Monastery*, Edinburgh: Edinburgh University Press, 1995.
2. Adapted from N.K. Chadwick, *The Age of the Saints in the Early Celtic Church*, Oxford: Oxford University Press, 1961.

CHAPTER 3
Saints and Mystics of the Medieval West
1. Quoted from Benedicta Ward, *The Prayers and Meditations of Saint Anselm*, tr. Benedicta Ward, London: Penguin, 1973, pp. 93, 94, 95, 99.
2. Brian P. Maguire, *The Difficult Saint: Bernard of Clairvaux and His Tradition*, Kalamazoo: Cistercian Publications, 1991.
3. Quoted from Paul Diemer, *Love Without Measure*, London: Darton, Longman & Todd, 1990, pp. 16–17.
4. Paul Diemer, *Love Without Measure*, p. 80.
5. Paul Diemer, *Love Without Measure*, p. 90.
6. Paul Diemer, *Love Without Measure*, p. 25.
7. Paul Diemer, *Love Without Measure*, pp. 29, 27.
8. Bonaventure, *Life of St Francis*, c. 13, quoted from Hugh Mackay, *The Little Flowers of St Francis*, London: J.M. Dent (Everyman), 1975, pp. 384–85.
9. See Xavier Schnieper, *St Francis of Assisi*, London: Frederick Muller, 1981, pp. 13–15.
10. Quoted with slight alterations from *The Mirror of Perfection*, c. 120, in Hugh Mackay, *The Little Flowers of St Francis*, pp. 294–95.
11. Citations from Mary Ann Fatula, *Catherine of Siena's Way*, Darton, Longman & Todd, 1987, p. 189.
12. Mary Ann Fatula, *Catherine of Siena's Way*, pp. 191, 194.
13. Mary Ann Fatula, *Catherine of Siena's Way*, pp. 193–94.
14. Mary Ann Fatula, *Catherine of Siena's Way*, p. 203.
15. See David Knowles, *The Religious Orders in England*, ii, Cambridge: Cambridge University Press, 1979, pp. 122–23.
16. Quoted in Roland P. Bainton, *Erasmus of Christendom*, New York: Scribners, 1969; London: Collins, 1970, pp. 258–59.
17. Quoted from *Counsels on the Spiritual Life*, tr. Leo Sherley-Price, London: Penguin Books, 1995, pp. 70, 71.

CHAPTER 4
The Eastern Christian Tradition
1. Athanasius, *On the Incarnation of the Divine Word*.
2. Cyril of Alexandria, *That the Christ is One*.
3. Gregory of Nazianzus, 'Immortal Monarch', Hymn 1.1.30.
4. Basil of Caesarea, *On the Holy Spirit* 9.23.
5. *Lausiac History* 26.18–20.
6. Evagrius of Pontus, *Chapters on Prayer* 3.
7. Evagrius of Pontus, *Chapters on Prayer* 4.
8. Evagrius of Pontus, *Chapters on Prayer* 11.
9. Evagrius of Pontus, *Praktikos* 48–49.
10. Diadochus of Photike, *On Spiritual Knowledge* 85.
11. Diadochus of Photike, *On Spiritual Knowledge* 56–57.
12. Diadochus of Photike, *On Spiritual Knowledge* 78.
13. Diadochus of Photike, *On Spiritual Knowledge* 59.
14. Shenoute of Atribe, *Enchoria* (fragments), ed. T. Orlandi, quoted in A. Grillmeier, *Christ in Christian Tradition*, 1996, vol. 2, pt 4, p. 186ff.
15. Shenoute of Atribe, *Enchoria*, p. 186ff.
16. Barsanuphius and John, *Questions and Answers* 175.
17. Barsanuphius and John, *Questions and Answers* 711.
18. Dorotheus of Gaza, *Discourses* 5.
19. Dorotheus of Gaza, *Discourses* 5.
20. Ephrem the Syrian, *Hymns on Faith* 31.
21. Isaac of Nineveh, *Ascetical Homilies* 62.
22. Isaac of Nineveh, *Ascetical Homilies* 68.
23. Dionysius the Areopagite, *Divine Names* 7.3.
24. Isaac of Nineveh, *Ascetical Homilies* 35.
25. Maximus the Confessor, *Centuries on Charity* 2.52.
26. See, for example, John 1:1–18; Philippians 2:5–11; Colossians 1:15–20; 1 Timothy 3:16 and Revelation 15:3–4.
27. Romanus the Melodist, 'Akathist Hymn', John McGuckin, *At the Lighting of the Lamps: Hymns from the Ancient Church*, Oxford: SLG Press, 1995.
28. Symeon the New Theologian, adapted from the original, *Hymns of Divine Love*, tr. G. Maloney, New Jersey, 1975, 2.13–29.
29. Symeon the New Theologian, adapted from the original, *Hymns of Divine Love* 27.125–132.

CHAPTER 5
The Russian Spirit
1. Muriel Heppell, *The Paterik of the Kievan Caves Monastery*, tr. Muriel Heppell, Harvard, 1989, pp. 47–48.

CHAPTER 6
The Protestant Tradition in Europe
1. Philipp Melanchthon, *Loci Communes*, 1521, 6.22.
2. Heidelberg Catechism, Lord's Day 1.
3. Martin Luther, *Commentary on Galatians* 3:6.
4. Martin Luther, *Commentary on Galatians* 3:10.
5. Martin Luther, *Commentary on Galatians* 2:16.
6. Martin Luther, *The Freedom of a Christian*, 1520.
7. Martin Luther, *Comments on Romans*.
8. John Calvin, *Institutes of the Christian Religion*, 1.1.1.
9. John Calvin, *Institutes of the Christian Religion*, 1.2.1.
10. John Calvin, *Institutes of the Christian Religion*, 3.1.3.
11. John Calvin, *Institutes of the Christian Religion*, 1.13.14.
12. Ulrich Zwingli, *The Sixty-Seven Articles*, 1523.
13. William Tyndale, *Writings of the Rev. William Tyndale*, London, p. 276.

14. Philip Jakob Spener, *Pia Desideria*, 1675.
15. Count Zinzendorf, address in 1727 to the Herrnhutters.
16. William Perkins, *Exposition Upon Zephaniah*, 1606.
17. William Perkins, *Works* 2:13.
18. Richard Baxter, *The Saint's Everlasting Rest*, 1650.
19. Jakob Boehme, *The Supersensual Life*, 1622.
20. Friedrich Daniel Schleiermacher, *On Religion*, 1799, introduction.
21. John Calvin, *Institutes of the Christian Religion* 3.20.4–11.
22. Charles Haddon Spurgeon, *Till He Come*, 1896.
23. Abraham Kuyper, quoted in R.H. Bremmer, *For a Thistle a Myrtle*, 1892.

CHAPTER 7
Catholic Saints and Reformers
1. 'The Life of Father Ignatius' (para. 96), *St Ignatius's Own Story, as Told to Luis Gonzalez de Camara*, tr. W.J. Young, Chicago: Loyola University Press, 1980, p. 67.
2. Slightly adapted from *The Spiritual Exercises of St Ignatius*, ed. Louis J. Puhl, SJ, Chicago: Loyola University Press, 1951, pp. 52–53.
3. Teresa of Avila, 'Life', Ch. VII, *The Complete Works of Saint Teresa of Jesus*, tr. E.A. Peers, London: Sheed & Ward, 1946, vol. I, p. 50.
4. *The Collected Works of St John of the Cross*, tr. Kieran Kavanaugh and Otilio Rodriguez, Washington: Institute of Carmelite Studies, 1991, pp. 639–40. Copyright © 1979 by Washington Province of Discalced Carmelites. ICS Publications, 2131 Lincoln Rd, NE, Washington, DC, 20002–1199, USA.
5. Lorenzo Scupoli, *The Spiritual Combat*, tr. E.B. Pusey, London, 1846, p. 11.
6. *Oxford Book of Prayer*, ed. George Appleton, Oxford: Oxford University Press, 1985, p. 111.
7. Augustine Baker, *Holy Wisdom or Directions for the Prayer of Contemplation*, ed. Abbot Sweeney, OSB, London, 1890.
8. From letters, etc., *The Heart and Mind of Mary Ward*, Wheathampstead: Institute of the Blessed Virgin Mary, 1985, p. 50.
9. Richard Challoner, *Considerations Upon Christian Truths and Christian Duties Digested into Meditations for Every Day of the Year*, London, 1754, vol. I, pp. 2–4.
10. *Meditations and Devotions by John Henry Newman*, ed. and intro. Meriol Trevor, London: Burns & Oates, 1964, p. 261.
11. Friedrich von Hügel, *The Life of Prayer*, London, 1927, pp. 8–9. Two talks on prayer given to Anglicans at Beaconsfield in 1921.
12. Francis de Sales, *An Introduction to the Devout Life* (III.23), ed. Peter Toon, London: Hodder & Stoughton, 1988.
13. Francis de Sales, *An Introduction to the Devout Life* (II.2–7).
14. Francis de Sales, *The Love of God, A Treatise* (VI.3), tr. V. Kerns, London, 1962, pp. 225–26.
15. Letter of Jeanne de Chantal to Noël Brulart, *Francis de Sales and Jane de Chantal, Letters of Spiritual Direction*, tr. P.M. Thibert, intro. W.M. Wright and J.P. Power, Classics of Western Spirituality, New York: Paulist Press, 1988.
16. Brother Lawrence, *The Practice of the Presence of God*, tr. E.M. Blaiklock, London: Hodder & Stoughton, 1981, p. 85.
17. Middle German Strasburg ms. quoted in Karl Richstätter, *Medieval Devotions to the Sacred Heart*, London, 1925, p. 2.

18. Margaret Mary Alacoque quoted in J.V. Bainvel, *La Dévotion au Sacré Coeur de Jésus*, Paris, 1921, p. 53, n. 3 (author's translation).
19. Brother Lawrence, *The Practice of the Presence of God*, p. 77.
20. Evelyn Underhill, *Mystics of the Church*, Cambridge: James Clarke & Co., 1925, p. 207.
21. Blaise Pascal, *Pensées*, tr. A.J. Krailsheimer (revised edition), London: Penguin, 1995, p. 285.
22. François Fénelon, *Christian Perfection*, tr. M.W. Stillman, New York/London: Harper, 1947, p. 137.
23. François Fénelon, *Christian Perfection*, p. 20.
24. François Fénelon, *Christian Perfection*, p. 64.
25. Pierre de Caussade, *The Sacrament of the Present Moment*, tr. K. Muggeridge (translation of *Self-Abandonment to Divine Providence*), Glasgow, 1996 (first published in 1981), p. 84.
26. Pierre de Caussade, *The Sacrament of the Present Moment*, p. 20.
27. Sister Elizabeth of the Trinity (Elizabeth Catez), *Spiritual Writings*, ed. M.-M. Philipon, London: Geoffrey Chapman, 1962, p. 61.
28. Sister Elizabeth of the Trinity, *Spiritual Writings*, p. 45.
29. Sister Elizabeth of the Trinity, *Spiritual Writings*, p. 106; cf. Ephesians 1:2.
30. Sister Elizabeth of the Trinity, *Spiritual Writings*, p. 122.
31. *Eucharistic Meditations, Extracts from the Writings and Instructions of the Blessed J.M. Vianney*, ed. H. Convert, tr. Sister Mary Benvenuta, OP, London, 1923.
32. *The Autobiography of St Thérèse of Lisieux, entitled by herself: 'The Story of the Springtime of a Little Flower'*, tr. T.N.C. Taylor, Glasgow: Burns, 1973, ch. 9 and epilogue.
33. *St Thérèse of Lisieux: Her Life, Times and Teaching*, ed. C. de Meester, Washington: Institute of Carmelite Studies, 1997, p. 154.

CHAPTER 8
The Anglican Spirit
1. Hugh Latimer, Sermon for the First Sunday after the Epiphany, in *Sermons and Remains*, ed. G.E. Corrie, Cambridge: Cambridge University Press, 1845, pp. 150–51.
2. Adrian Hastings, *A History of English Christianity 1920–1985*, London: Collins, 1986, p. 32.
3. *Of the Right Use of the Church or Temple of God*, 1547.
4. *An Homily for Repairing and Keeping Clean, and Comely Adorning of Churches*, 1547.
5. Richard Hooker, *Laws of Ecclesiastical Polity*, 1597, 5:56:10.
6. Richard Hooker, *Laws of Ecclesiastical Polity* 5:67:6.
7. Lancelot Andrewes, Sermon 9 on the Nativity, in *Ninety-Six Sermons by Lancelot Andrewes*, ed. J.P. Wilson, Oxford: Parker, 1841–43, vol. 1, pp. 139–40.
8. Lancelot Andrewes, Sermon 1 on Prayer, vol. 5, p. 306.
9. Lancelot Andrewes, Sermon 7 on Prayer, vol. 5, p. 369.
10. Lancelot Andrewes, Sermon 19 on Prayer, vol. 5, p. 472.
11. Lancelot Andrewes, Sermon 3 on Prayer, vol. 5, p. 325.
12. Lancelot Andrewes, Sermon 8 on Prayer, vol. 5, p. 380.
13. Lancelot Andrewes, Sermon 11 for Whitsun, vol. 4, pp. 318–19.
14. Lancelot Andrewes, Sermon 4 on Prayer, vol. 5, p. 339.
15. Lancelot Andrewes, 'Prayers for the Evening', from *Preces privatae*, published posthumously, 1675.
16. 'Visitation Articles of Bishop Henry Cotton of Salisbury' (1614), in *Visitation Articles and Injunctions of the Early Stuart Church*, ed. K. Fincham, Woodbridge: Boydell and Brewer, 1994, vol. 1, p. 17.

17. Ralph Josselin, *Diary*, Entry for 22 August 1680, p. 629.
18. John Donne, *The Sermons of John Donne*, eds G.R. Potter, E.M. Simpson, Berkeley: California University Press, 1953–62, vol. 8, no. 9.
19. John Donne, *Devotions upon Emergent Occasions* (1624), ed. A. Raspa, London and Montreal: McGill–Queens University Press, 1975, s. 9.
20. John Donne, *The Sermons of John Donne*, vol. 3, no. 4.
21. John Donne, *The Sermons of John Donne*, vol. 1, no. 9.
22. John Donne, *The Sermons of John Donne*, vol. 2, no. 1.
23. John Donne, *The Sermons of John Donne*, vol. 5, no. 8.
24. John Donne, *The Sermons of John Donne*, vol. 6, no. 13.
25. John Donne, *The Sermons of John Donne*, vol. 2, no. 3.
26. John Donne, *The Sermons of John Donne*, vol. 4, no. 3.
27. John Donne, *The Sermons of John Donne*, vol. 3, no. 16.
28. John Donne, *The Sermons of John Donne*, vol. 3, no. 16.
29. John Donne, *Devotions Upon Emergent Occasions*, s. 17.
30. John Donne, *The Sermons of John Donne*, vol. 4, no. 2.
31. John Donne, *The Sermons of John Donne*, vol. 4, no. 12.
32. John Donne, *The Sermons of John Donne*, vol. 5, no. 17.
33. John Donne, *The Sermons of John Donne*, vol. 3, no. 5.
34. John Donne, *The Sermons of John Donne*, vol. 3, no. 3.
35. Robert Leighton, *Works*, ed. W. West, London: Longmans, Green, 1869, vol. 2, p. 201.
36. Jeremy Taylor, *A Course of Sermons* 1:17, in *The Whole Works of Jeremy Taylor*, ed. R. Heber and revised by C.P. Eden, London: Brown, Green and Longmans, 1856, vol. 4.
37. Jeremy Taylor, *A Course of Sermons* 1:19.
38. Jeremy Taylor, *A Course of Sermons* 1:15.
39. Jeremy Taylor, *A Course of Sermons* 2:2.
40. Jeremy Taylor, *Holy Living* 1:1, in *The Whole Works of Jeremy Taylor*, vol. 3; cf. *Holy Dying* 1:3, in *The Whole Works of Jeremy Taylor*, vol. 3.
41. Jeremy Taylor, *Holy Living* 1:1.
42. Jeremy Taylor, *Holy Living* 1:1.
43. Jeremy Taylor, *Holy Living* 1:1.
44. Jeremy Taylor, *Holy Living* 1:1.
45. Jeremy Taylor, *The Golden Grove*, in *The Whole Works of Jeremy Taylor*, vol. 7, p. 611.
46. Jeremy Taylor, *The Worthy Communicant* 2:2, in *The Whole Works of Jeremy Taylor*, vol. 8; cf. *A Course of Sermons* 1:5; *Miscellaneous Sermons* 1, in *The Whole Works of Jeremy Taylor*, vol. 8.
47. Jeremy Taylor, *Holy Living* 1:2.
48. Jeremy Taylor, *Holy Living* 1:2.
49. Jeremy Taylor, *Holy Living* 1:3.
50. Jeremy Taylor, *A Course of Sermons* 1:13.
51. Jeremy Taylor, *A Course of Sermons* 1:6.
52. Jeremy Taylor, *A Course of Sermons* 1:13.
53. Jeremy Taylor, *Holy Dying* 2:4.
54. William Law, *The Absolute Unlawfulness of the Stage-Entertainment* (1726), in *The Works of the Revd William Law*, ed. G.B. Moreton, London: Richardson, 1762, reprinted 1892–93, vol. 2.
55. William Law, *Christian Perfection 2*, in *The Works of the Revd William Law*, vol. 3.
56. William Law, *Christian Perfection 2*.
57. William Law, *A Serious Call 20*, in *The Works of the Revd William Law*, vol. 4.
58. H.D. Best, *Personal and Literary Memorials*, quoted in G.B. Hill, *Johnsonian Miscellanies*, Oxford, 1897, vol. 2, pp. 390–91.
59. Samuel Johnson, *Diaries, Prayers, and Annals*, ed. E.L. McAdam, Jr, New Haven: Yale University Press, 1958, vol. 1, p. 46.
60. Samuel Johnson, Letter to Bennet Langton,

21 September 1758, *The Letters of Samuel Johnson*, ed. B. Redford, Oxford: Clarendon Press, 1992–94, vol. 1, p. 167.
61. Samuel Johnson, quoted in W.J. Bate, *Samuel Johnson*, London: Chatto & Windus, 1978, p. 458.
62. Sarah Trimmer, *The Oeconomy of Charity*, vol. 2, pp. 50–51.
63. Sarah Trimmer, *The Oeconomy of Charity*, vol. 2, p. 33.
64. Sarah Trimmer, *The Oeconomy of Charity*, vol. 2, p. 17; cf. vol. 2, p. 25.
65. Hannah More, *Practical Piety*, London: Cadell and Davies, 1812, vol. 1, pp. 5–6, 23.
66. Hannah More, *Practical Piety*, vol. 1, p. 41.
67. Hannah More, *Practical Piety*, vol. 1, p. 43.
68. Hannah More, *Stories for Persons in the Middle Ranks*, in *The Works of Hannah More*, London: Fisher, Fisher and Jackson, 1834, vol. 1, p. 14.
69. Hannah More, *Thoughts on the Manners of the Great*, in *The Works of Hannah More*, vol. 2, p. 276.
70. Hannah More, *Practical Piety*, vol. 1, p. 102.
71. John Newton, *Cardiphonia*, in *The Works of John Newton*, Edinburgh: Brown and Nelson, 1834, p. 181.
72. John Newton, *Cardiphonia*, p. 138.
73. John Newton, *Cardiphonia*, p. 186.
74. John Newton, *Letters on Religious Subjects*, in *The Works of John Newton*, no. 24, p. 90.
75. John Newton, *Cardiphonia*, p. 140.
76. John Newton, *Cardiphonia*, p. 259.
77. Charles Simeon, *Horae Homileticae*, London: Holdsworth, 1840, vol. 1, pp. 3–4.
78. Charles Simeon, *Evangelic and Pharisaic Righteousness Compared*, quoted in A. Pollard, *Let Wisdom Judge*, London: Inter-Varsity Press, 1959, p. 82.
79. Charles Simeon, *Horae Homileticae*, vol. 1, p. 673.
80. Charles Simeon, *Horae Homileticae*, vol. 2, p. 330.
81. Charles Simeon, *Appeal to Men of Wisdom and Candour*, quoted in A. Pollard, *Let Wisdom Judge*, p. 58.
82. Charles Simeon, *Horae Homileticae*, vol. 3, p. 247.
83. Edward Bouverie Pusey, *The Holy Eucharist a Comfort to the Penitent*, Oxford, 1843.
84. John Keble, *Sermons for the Christian Year*, Oxford: James Parker/London: Walter Smith, 1880, vol. 1, no. 3.
85. John Keble, *Sermons for the Christian Year*, vol. 1, no. 15.
86. Edward Bouverie Pusey, *Parochial Sermons*, 1833, vol. 2, no. 15.
87. Edward Bouverie Pusey, *Parochial and Cathedral Sermons*, 1887, no. 19.
88. Henry Liddon, *Some Elements of Religion*, London: Longmans, Green, 1898, p. 178.
89. Edward Bouverie Pusey, *Parochial Sermons*, vol. 2, no. 17.

CHAPTER 9
The Protestant Tradition in America

1. Philip Schaff, *The Principle of Protestantism*, tr. John W. Nevin, Philadelphia: United Church Press, 1964, p. 149.
2. H. Richard Niebuhr, *Christ and Culture*, New York: Harper and Row, 1951.
3. Geoffrey Wainwright, 'Types of Spirituality', in *The Study of Spirituality*, eds Cheslyn Jones, Geoffrey Wainwright and Edward Yarnold, SJ, New York: Oxford University Press, 1986, p. 602.
4. Quoted in *Voices from the Heart: Four Centuries of American Piety*, ed. Roger Lundin and Mark A. Noll, Grand Rapids, Michigan: Eerdmans, 1987, p. 5.

5. Roger Williams, 'Helps to Preserve Spiritual Health and Cheerfulness', *Experiments of Spiritual Life and Health and Their Preservatives* (1652), ed. Winthrop S. Hudson, Philadelphia: Westminster Press, 1951.

6. *Early New England Meditative Poetry: Anne Bradstreet and Edward Taylor*, ed. Charles E. Hambrick-Stowe, Sources of American Spirituality Series, New York: Paulist Press, 1988, pp. 92–94.

7. *Voices from the Heart*, pp. 31–37.

8. *Early New England Meditative Poetry*, pp. 172–73.

9. *The Journal of John Woolman, and A Plea for the Poor*, intro. Frederick B. Tolles, The John Greenleaf Whittier Edition Text, New York: Corinth Books, 1961, p. 5.

10. *The Journal of John Woolman*, pp. 14–15.

11. Thomas Jefferson, 'The Philosophy of Jesus' and 'The Life and Morals of Jesus', in *Extracts from the Gospels*, ed. Dickinson W. Adams, Princeton: Princeton University Press, 1983, p. 19.

12. Quoted in Richard G. Hutcheson, Jr., *God in the White House: How Religion Has Changed the Modern Presidency*, New York: Macmillan, 1988, p. 39.

13. *Voices from the Heart*, p. 119.

14. *Henry Alline: Selected Writings*, ed. George A. Rawlyk, New York: Paulist Press, 1987, p. 24.

15. *Henry Alline: Selected Writings*, pp. 61, 79, 87.

16. Bernard A. Weisberger, *They Gathered at the River: The Story of the Great Revivals and Their Impact Upon Religion in America*, Chicago: Quadrangle Books, 1966, p. 29.

17. *Autobiography of Peter Cartwright*, ed. Charles L. Wallis, New York: Abingdon Press, 1956, p. 64.

18. *The Biography of Eld. Barton Warren Stone: Written by Himself: With Additions and Reflections by Elder John Rogers* (1847), Cane Ridge: Hoke Smith Dickinson, 1972, pp. 39–42.

19. *The Memoirs of Charles G. Finney: The Complete Restored Text*, eds Garth M. Rosell and Richard A.G. Dupuis, Grand Rapids, Michigan: Zondervan, 1989, pp. 23, 27.

20. *Fanny J. Crosby: Memories of Eighty Years: Her Own Story of Her Life and Hymns*, London: Hodder & Stoughton, 1908, p. 33.

21. Charles G. Finney, *Lectures to Professing Christians*, London: Milner and Company, 1837, pp. 214–29; reprinted in Charles G. Finney, *Principles of Holiness*, ed., Louis G. Parkhurst, Jr, Minneapolis, Minnesota: Bethany House Publishers, 1984, p. 19.

22. Keith J. Hardman, *Charles Grandison Finney, 1792–1875*, Grand Rapids, Michigan: Baker Book House, 1990, p. 99.

23. Quoted in Albert J. Raboteau, *Slave Religion: The 'Invisible Institution' in the Antebellum South*, New York/Oxford: Oxford University Press, 1978, p. 214.

24. Albert J. Raboteau, 'Down at the Cross: Afro-American Spirituality', *U.S. Catholic Historian*, vol. 8, 1989, p. 38.

25. Albert J. Raboteau, *Slave Religion*, p. 234.

26. James H. Cone, *The Spirituals and the Blues: An Interpretation*, New York: Seabury Press, 1972, p. 35.

27. *Dictionary of Christianity in America*, ed. Daniel G. Reid, Downers Grove, Illinois: Inter-Varsity Press, 1990, p. 1189.

28. Quoted in Stanley N. Gundry, *Love Them In: The Life and Theology of D.L. Moody*, Grand Rapids, Michigan: Baker Book House, 1976, p. 92.

29. Dwight Lyman Moody, *Moody's Latest Sermons*, Chicago: Rhodes and McClure, 1899, pp. 459, 465.

30. Roger Lundin, *Emily Dickinson and the Art of Belief*, Grand Rapids, Michigan: Eerdmans, 1998, p. 3.

31. Quoted in Roger Lundin, *Emily Dickinson and the Art of Belief*, p. 149.

32. Roger Lundin, *Emily Dickinson and the Art of Belief*, p. 174.

33. *Lincoln: Speeches and Writings, 1859–1865*, New York: Library Classics of the United States, 1989, pp. 686–87.

34. Harriet Beecher Stowe, *Uncle Tom's Cabin, or Life Among the Lowly*, Boston: Houghton Mifflin, 1929, pp. 460–62.

35. Quoted in Elisha Hunt Rhodes, *All for the Union*, New York: Orion Books, 1985, p. 123.

36. Sam R. Watkins, *Co. Aytch*, Wilmington, North Carolina: Broadfoot Publications, 1990, p. 200.

37. *Phoebe Palmer: Selected Writings*, ed. Thomas C. Oden, New York: Paulist Press, 1988, p. 8

38. *Phoebe Palmer: Selected Writings*, p. 19.

39. The Publishers, 'Foreword', in Hannah Whitall Smith, *The Christian's Secret of a Happy Life*, Westwood, New Jersey: Fleming H. Revell, 1952, p. 8.

40. Hannah Whitall Smith, *The Christian's Secret of a Happy Life*, p. 15.

41. Charles Hodge, *The Way of Life*, Philadelphia: American Sunday School Union, p. 3, reprinted in *Charles Hodge: The Way of Life*, ed. Mark A. Noll, New York: Paulist Press, 1987, pp. 45–46.

42. David L. Smith, *Symbolism and Growth: The Religious Thought of Horace Bushnell*, Chico, California: Scholars Press, 1981, p. x.

43. *Horace Bushnell: Sermons*, ed. Conrad Cherry, New York: Paulist Press, 1985, p. 2.

44. *Horace Bushnell: Sermons*, p. 16, from Mary Bushnell Cheny, *Life and Letters of Horace Bushnell*, New York: Harper and Brothers, 1880, p. 192.

45. *Horace Bushnell: Sermons*, p. 17, from Horace Bushnell, *The Spirit in Man: Sermons and Selections*, New York: Charles Scribner's Sons, 1903, p. 41.

46. Philip Schaff, 'The New Liturgy', *Mercersburg Review*, 1858, pp. 208–209.

47. *Walter Rauschenbusch: Selected Writings*, ed. Winthrop S. Hudson, New York: Paulist Press, 1984, p. 4.

48. *Walter Rauschenbusch: Selected Writings*, p. 32.

49. *Walter Rauschenbusch: Selected Writings*, pp. 228–29.

CHAPTER 10
Spiritualities of the Twentieth Century

1. See Philip Sheldrake, *Spirituality and History: Questions of Interpretation and Method*, New York: Crossroad, 1992.

2. Norman F. Cantor, *The American Century: Varieties of Culture in Modern Times*, New York: HarperCollins, 1997, p. 497.

3. *World Christian Encyclopedia*, ed. David B. Barrett, New York: Oxford, 1982.

4. Dave Roberts, *The 'Toronto' Blessing*, Eastbourne: Kingsway Publications, 1994; Guy Chevreau, *Pray with Fire: Interceding in the Spirit*, Toronto: HarperCollins, 1995; James A. Beverley, *Holy Laughter and the Toronto Blessing: An Investigative Report*, Grand Rapids, Michigan: Zondervan, 1995.

5. Jaroslav Pelikan, *Mary Through the Centuries: Her Place in the History of Culture*, New Haven: Yale, 1996.

6. Jeanette Rodriguez, 'Contemporary Encounters with Guadalupe', *Journal of Hispanic/Latino Theology*, vol. 5:1, August 1997, pp. 48–60.

7. *Spirituality of the Third World: A Cry for Life*, eds K.C. Abraham and Bernadette Mbuy-Beya, Maryknoll, New York: Orbis, 1994; William A. Dyrness, *Learning About Theology from the Third World*, Grand Rapids, Michigan: Zondervan, 1990; and Susan Rakoczy, HHM, *Common Journey, Different*

Paths: Spiritual Direction in Cross-Cultural Perspective, Maryknoll, New York: Orbis, 1992.

8. Vincent J. Donovan, *Christianity Rediscovered: An Epistle from the Masai,* Notre Dame, Indiana: Fides/Claretian, 1978.

9. See *African Christian Spirituality,* ed. Aylward Shorter, London: Geoffrey Chapman, 1978; Harry Sawyerr, *The Practice of Presence: Shorter Writings of Harry Sawyerr,* ed. John Parratt, Grand Rapids, Michigan: Eerdmans, 1996; and John Parratt, *Reinventing Christianity: African Theology Today,* Grand Rapids, Michigan: Eerdmans, 1995.

10. Desmond Tutu, *The Words of Desmond Tutu,* selected by Naomi Tutu, New York: Newmarket Press, 1989, p. 26.

11. *The Words of Desmond Tutu,* p. 28.

12. *The Words of Desmond Tutu,* p. 29.

13. Alan Paton, *Instrument of Thy Peace,* New York: Seabury Press, 1968, pp. 58–59.

14. Kosuke Koyama, *Waterbuffalo Theology,* Maryknoll, New York: Orbis, 1974.

15. Kosuke Koyama, *Three Mile an Hour God,* Maryknoll, New York: Orbis, 1979.

16. Kosuke Koyama, *Mount Fuji and Mount Sinai: A Critique of Idols,* Maryknoll, New York: Orbis, 1984.

17. Toyohiko Kagawa, *Song from the Slums,* London: SCM Press, 1935, pp. 21f.

18. Bede Griffiths, *A Human Search: Bede Griffiths Reflects on His Life: An Oral History,* ed. John Swindells, Liguori, Missouri: Triumph Books, 1997, p. 22.

19. Bede Griffiths, *A Human Search,* p. 30.

20. Bede Griffiths, *The Golden String,* New York: P.J. Kennedy, 1954.

21. Bede Griffiths, *The Golden String,* pp. 84–85.

22. Bede Griffiths, *The Golden String,* p. 558.

23. Anthony de Mello, SJ, *The Prayer of the Frog: A Book of Story Meditations,* Anand, India: Gujarat Sahitya Prakash, 1988, vol. 1, p. xviii.

24. Carlos G. Valles, SJ, *Unencumbered by Baggage: Father Anthony de Mello: A Prophet for Our Times,* Anand, India: Gujarat Sahitya Prakash, 1987, p. 27.

25. *The Way of a Pilgrim* is an anonymous work first published in 1884 that drew heavily upon the *Philokalia.*

26. Mother Teresa, *A Simple Path,* comp. Lucinda Vardey, New York: Ballantine, 1995, quoted from Eileen Egan, *Such a Vision of the Street: Mother Teresa – The Spirit and the Work,* Garden City, New York: Doubleday, 1985, p. 357.

27. Mother Teresa, *A Simple Path,* p. 25.

28. Mother Teresa, *A Simple Path,* p. 79.

29. Carlos G. Valles, SJ, *Unencumbered by Baggage,* p. 43.

30. E. Stanley Jones, *A Song of Ascents: A Spiritual Autobiography,* Nashville: Abingdon, 1968, pp. 52–53.

31. E. Stanley Jones, *A Song of Ascents,* pp. 91, 92, 94.

32. Jon Sobrino, *Spirituality of Liberation: Toward Political Holiness,* Maryknoll, New York: Orbis, 1988.

33. Ernesto Cardenal, *The Gospel in Solentiname,* tr. Donald D. Walsh, Maryknoll, New York: Orbis, 1976, pp. 46–49.

34. Michael Ramsey, 'Foreword', in C. Armstrong, *Evelyn Underhill,* Grand Rapids, Michigan: Eerdmans, 1975, p. x.

35. Evelyn Underhill, *Concerning the Inner Life,* Minneapolis: Seabury Press, 1984, pp. 93–94.

36. Karl Barth, *Prayer,* ed. Don E. Saliers, Philadelphia: Westminster, 1985, pp. 35–36.

37. Pierre Teilhard de Chardin, *Hymn of the Universe,* London: Collins Fontana Books, 1970, pp. 64f.

38. Pierre Teilhard de Chardin, *The Divine Milieu: An Essay for the Interior Life,* New York: Harper & Row, 1960, p. 15.

39. Teilhard de Chardin, *The Heart of Matter,* New York: Harcourt Brace Jovanovich, 1978, pp. 57–58.

40. Dietrich Bonhoeffer, *Life Together/Prayerbook of the Bible, Dietrich Bonhoeffer Works,* vol. 5, ed. Geoffrey B. Kelly. Minneapolis: Fortress Press, 1996, p. 35.

41. Karl Rahner, *The Content of Faith: The Best of Karl Rahner's Theological Writings,* New York: Crossroad, 1992; and Harvey D. Egan, *What Are They Saying About Mysticism?* New York: Paulist, 1982, p. 98.

42. Karl Rahner, *The Content of Faith,* p. 149.

43. Karl Rahner, *The Content of Faith,* p. 507.

44. John Main, *Moment of Christ: The Path of Meditation,* London: DLT, 1984.

45. Jean Vanier, *Community and Growth* (1979), New York: Paulist Press, 1989, p. 11.

46. A.M. Ramsay, *Sacred and Secular: A Study in the Otherworldly and This-worldly Aspects of Christianity,* London: Longmans, 1965, p. 42.

47. A.M. Ramsay, *Sacred and Secular,* p. 45

48. A.M. Ramsay, *An Era in Anglican Theology: From Gore to Temple: The Development of Anglican Theology Between Lux Mundi and the Second World War 1889–1939,* New York: Charles Scribner's Sons, 1960, pp. 164–65.

49. *Wit and Wisdom of Good Pope John,* ed. Henri Fesquet, tr. Salvator Attanasio, New York: P.J. Kennedy & Sons, 1964, p. 110.

50. *Wit and Wisdom of Good Pope John,* p. 157.

51. *Wit and Wisdom of Good Pope John,* pp. 161–62.

52. Pope John XXIII, *Journal of a Soul,* tr. Dorothy White, New York: McGraw-Hill, 1965, p. 343.

53. John Paul II, *Crossing the Threshold of Hope,* ed. Vittorio Messori, New York: Knopf, 1994, p. 142.

54. John Paul II, *Crossing the Threshold of Hope,* pp. 89–90.

55. John Paul II, *Crossing the Threshold of Hope,* pp. 212–13.

56. Karol Wojtyla (Pope John Paul II), *The Way to Christ: Spiritual Exercises,* tr. Leslie Wearne, San Francisco: Harper & Row, 1984, p. 88.

57. Anthony Bloom, *Beginning to Pray,* New York: Paulist, 1970, p. xii. [*School for Prayer,* London: DLT, 1970.]

58. Anthony Bloom, *Beginning to Pray,* p. xvii.

59. Anthony Bloom, *Beginning to Pray,* pp. 18–19.

60. Lauren Artress, *Walking a Sacred Path: Rediscovering the Labyrinth as a Spiritual Tool,* New York: Riverhead, 1995.

61. Kathleen Norris, *Dakota: A Spiritual Geography,* Boston: Houghton Mifflin, 1993.

62. Kathleen Norris, *Amazing Grace: A Vocabulary of Faith,* Oxford: Lion Publishing, 2000, p. 251.

63. M. Basil Pennington wrote *Call to the Centre: The Gospel's Invitation to Deeper Prayer, Centred Living: The Way of Centring Prayer, Lectio Divina: Renewing the Ancient Practice of Praying* and *A Place Apart: Monastic Prayer and Practice for Everyone.* Thomas Keating has published *Open Mind, Open Heart: The Contemplative Dimension of the Gospel, The Mystery of Christ* and *Invitation to Love: The Way of Christian Contemplation.*

64. Thomas Merton, *Conjectures of a Guilty Bystander,* Garden City, New York: Doubleday, 1966, pp. 140–41.

65. Thomas Merton, *Life and Holiness* (1963), Garden City, New York: Doubleday Image, 1964, pp. 9–10.

66. Dorothy Day, *The Long Loneliness: An Autobiography* (1952), San Francisco: Harper, 1981, p. xxii.

67. Dorothy Day, *The Long Loneliness,* pp. 285–86.

68. D. Elton Trueblood, *The People Called Quakers,* New York: Harper and Row, 1966, p. 221.

69. *Quaker Spirituality: Selected Writings,* ed. Douglas V. Steere, The Classics of Western Spirituality, New York: Paulist Press, 1984, p. 29.

70. Richard J. Foster, *Celebration of Discipline: The Path*

to Spiritual Growth, San Francisco: Harper, 1988.

71. Richard J. Foster, *Celebration of Discipline*, p. 8.

72. Richard J. Foster, *Streams of Living Water: Celebrating the Great Traditions of Christian Faith*, San Francisco: Harper, 1998.

73. John Pollock, *Billy Graham: Evangelist to the World: An Authorized Biography of the Decisive Years*, San Francisco: Harper & Row, 1979, p. 120

74. John Pollock, *Billy Graham*, p. 148.

75. Howard Thurman, *With Head and Heart*, New York and London: Harcourt Brace Jovanovitch, 1979, p. 128.

76. Martin Marty and Micah Marty, *The Promise of Winter: Quickening the Spirit on Ordinary Days and in Fallow Seasons*, Grand Rapids, Michigan: Eerdmans, 1997.

77. Eugene H. Peterson, *Subversive Spirituality*, Grand Rapids, Michigan: Eerdmans, 1997, p. 15.

78. Eugene H. Peterson, *Take and Read: Spiritual Reading: An Annotated List*, Grand Rapids, Michigan: Eerdmans, 1996, p. 109.

79. *Black Elk Speaks: Being the Life Story of a Holy Man of the Oglala Sioux* (1932), as told through John G. Neihardt, Lincoln, Nebraska: University of Nebraska, 1988.

80. Chester P. Michael and Marie C. Norrisey, *Prayer and Temperament: Different Prayer Forms for Different Personality Types*, Charlottesville, Virginia: The Open Door, 1991.

81. Karl G. Jung, *The Portable Jung*, ed. Joseph Campbell, New York: The Viking Press, 1971, pp. 20–21.

82. Karl G. Jung, *The Portable Jung*, pp. 38–39.

83. Morton Kelsey, *The Other Side of Silence: Meditation for the Twenty-First Century*, New York: Paulist Press, 1997, pp. 13–14.

84. M. Scott Peck, *In Search of Stones: A Pilgrimage of Faith, Reason, and Discovery*, New York: Hyperion, 1995, pp. 389–90.

85. M. Scott Peck, *The Road Less Travelled: A New Psychology of Love, Traditional Values and Spiritual Growth*, New York: Simon & Schuster, 1978, p. 81.

86. M. Scott Peck, *The Road Less Travelled*, p. 97.

87. M. Scott Peck, *The Different Drum: Community-making and Peace*, New York: Simon and Schuster, 1987, p. 17.

88. *Mornings with Henri J.M. Nouwen: Readings and Reflections*, Ann Arbor, Michigan: Servant, 1997.

89. Kenneth Leech, *Experiencing God: Theology as Spirituality*, San Francisco: Harper, 1989, pp. 7, 23–24.

90. John Ackerman, *Spiritual Awakening: A Guide to the Spiritual Life in Congregations*, Bethesda, Maryland: Alban Institute, 1994.

91. Robert H. Schuller, *Self-Esteem: The New Reformation*, Waco, Texas: Word, 1982, p. 19.

92. Robert H. Schuller, *Self-Esteem*, pp. 12, 21.

93. Dennis C. Morreim, *Changed Lives: The Story of Alcoholics Anonymous*, Minneapolis: Augsburg, 1992.

94. Ernest Kurtz, *Not-God: A History of Alcoholics Anonymous*, Center City, Minnesota: Hazeldon, 1979.

95. Reinhold Niebuhr, 'Written for a service in the Congregational Church of Heath, Massachusetts, where Dr Niebuhr spent many summers, the prayer was first published in a monthly bulletin of the Federal Council of Churches': John Bartlett, *Familiar Quotations*, Boston: Little, Brown, 1980, p. 823.

96. Gerald May, *Addiction and Grace*, San Francisco: Harper, 1988.

97. Rosemary Radford Ruether, *Sexism and God-Talk: Toward a Feminist Theology*, Boston: Beacon, 1983, p. 20.

98. Rosemary Radford Ruether, *Sexism and God-Talk*, p. 23.

99. Rosemary Radford Reuther, *Sexism and God-Talk*, pp. 24, 32.

100. Sam Keen, *Fire in the Belly: On Being a Man*, New York: Bantam, 1991, pp. 195–96.

101. Brian Wren, *What Language Shall I Borrow? God-Talk in Worship: A Male Response to Feminist Theology*, New York: Crossroad, 1989.

102. David C. James, *What Are They Saying About Masculine Spirituality?* New York: Paulist, 1996, pp. 51–52.

103. Richard Cleaver, *Know My Name: A Gay Liberation Theology*, Westminster John Knox Press, 1995; Chris Glaser, *Coming Out To God: Prayers for Lesbians and Gay Men, Their Families and Friends*, Kentucky: Westminster John Knox Press, 1991; Anita C. Hill and Leo Treadway, 'Rituals of Healing: Ministry with and on Behalf of Gay and Lesbian People', *Lift Every Voice: Constructing Christian Theologies from the Underside*, Harper and Row, 1990; John J. McNeill, *Taking a Chance on God: Liberating Theology for Gays, Lesbians, and Their Lovers, Families, and Friends*, Boston: Beacon, 1988; Melanie Morrison, *The Grace of Coming Home: Spirituality, Sexualilty, and the Struggle for Justice*, Pilgrim Press, 1995; Mel White, *Stranger at the Gate: To Be Gay and Christian in America*, New York: Simon and Schuster, 1994. The author would like to thank Janelle Bussert for her contribution of this section.

104. Rosemary Radford Ruether, *Gaia & God: An Ecofeminist Theology of Earth Healing*, San Francisco: Harper, 1992, p. 4.

105. Matthew Fox, *Confessions: The Making of a Post-Denominational Priest*, San Francisco: Harper, 1996.

106. Matthew Fox, *On Becoming A Musical Mystical Bear: Spirituality American Style*, New York: Paulist, 1976, p. xv.

107. Charles Cummins, *Eco-Spirituality: Toward a Reverent Life*, New York: Paulist Press, 1991.

108. Evelyn Underhill, 'Sources of Power in Human Life', *The Hibbert Journal*, vol. 19, no. 3, April 1921, p. 397.

109. Humphrey Carpenter, *The Inklings: C.S. Lewis, J.R.R. Tolkien, Charles Williams, and their Friends*, Boston: Houghton Mifflin, 1979.

110. A fuller acount is given in Olive Wyon, *Living Springs: New Religious Movements in Western Europe*, Philadelphia: Westminster Press, 1962.

111. Eberhard Arnold, *Why We Live in Community* (1925, German), Farmington, Pennsylvania: Plough Publishing, 1995.

112. Dallas Lee, *The Cotton Patch Evidence: The Story of Clarence Jordan and the Koinonia Farm Experiment*, New York: Harper, 1971, p. 25.

113. See, for example, Susan Howatch, *Glamorous Powers*, New York: Fawcett, 1990.

114. Jacques Maritain, *Georges Rouault*, New York: Harry N. Abrams, 1952, p. 8.

115. Jeff Zaleski, *The Soul of Cyberspace: How New Technology is Changing Our Spiritual Lives*, San Francisco: Harper, 1997, pp. 270–71.

INDEX